...AS ONE MAD WITH WINE

AND OTHER SIMILES

...As One Mad With Wine

AND OTHER SIMILES

E L Y S E   S O M M E R
M I K E   S O M M E R

VISIBLE
INK
PRESS

NEW YORK   CHICAGO   DETROIT   LONDON

...As One Mad With Wine and Other Similes

Published by Visible Ink Press,
a division of Gale Research Inc.
835 Penobscot Building
Detroit, MI 48226–4094

Visible Ink Press is a trademark of Gale Research Inc.

ISBN 0–8103–9401–4

Cover Design: Cynthia Baldwin
Interior Design: Arthur Chartow, Mary Krzewinski
Illustrations: Terry Colon

Printed in the United States of America

10 9 8 7 6 5 4 3 2 1

First Edition

Contents

Introduction

**The English language is like
an enormous bank account
—Robert Claiborne**

Baseball great George Brett once observed that "If a tie is like kissing your sister, losing is like kissing your grandmother with her teeth out," employing a simile that vividly conveys his distaste for defeat. Industrialist Henry Ford explained his fiscal philosophy by coining a simile that sounds surprisingly modern for having been uttered fifty years ago: "Money is like an arm or a leg, use it or lose it." Teddy Roosevelt once noted that President McKinley had "no more backbone than a chocolate eclair," using a simile to prove that public figures knew the value of a "soundbite" long before it took a snappy snippet to make the evening news.

The simile is, of course, much more than an attention-getter. It colors and clarifies ideas by comparing two dissimilar things and does so in a straightforward way by introducing the comparison with the word **like** or **as**—or sometimes with the phrases **as if, as though, is comparable to, can be likened to, akin to, similar to.** This directness makes the simile the most accessible of all figures of speech, a favorite device for both literary and ordinary self-expression.

What Is a Simile?

Its popularity notwithstanding, until now the simile has not had an up-to-date book of its own available in bookstores for wordsmiths and booklovers to purchase, peruse, and treasure. This book's title is taken from the simile "babble as one mad with wine," which you'll find under the heading *Talkativeness.* Its author, the poet Algernon Swinburne, was one of the most prolific simile coiners during the nineteenth century and he generally aimed for a more pronounced dissimilarity between the comparison and what was being compared—to wit, his **ageless as the sun** and **bent like a broken flower.** ... *As One Mad With Wine* suggests that, when drunk on the richness of the text, you may discover the simile's power to loosen tongues and overcome writer's block.

... *As One Mad With Wine* spans two millennia and illustrates the simile in all its permutations—literary and colloquial, humorous and serious, original and derivative. The similes are arranged by thematic categories with extensive **See** and **See Also** cross-references. Other features include:

Inside This Book

Table of Thematic Categories. It's designed to help those who use this book as a thesaurus, to quickly locate an apt simile on a specific subject. In keeping with the thematic principle, the entries within each category are arranged in alphabetical order. Alphabetizing is letter-by-letter, except for the articles **a, an,** and **the.**

Editorial comments. To enhance the browser's enjoyment and increase the book's utility, many entries include brief comments. These might shed light on the source or give examples of variations and cross-references specific to that simile.

Additional clarifying text. When the descriptive reference frame for a simile is not crucial to its meaning but would enhance reading, or illustrate its use, additional source text is included. This is enclosed in parentheses. Text that I have added for clarification is set off by square brackets instead of parentheses.

Author attribution. It's much harder to pinpoint authorship for a phrase than for a quotation. Therefore, while much research went into providing attributions, they are not one hundred percent error-proof. In the interest of uncluttered browsing and a maximum number of entries, text sources are not included. Whenever information about the source promises to add an extra dimension to an entry, however, an explanatory comment is included.

Author Index. This enables readers to quickly check out the "similistic" output of a favorite author and includes a number of catchall headings for finding similes of unknown authorship. These include The Bible, colloquialisms of unknown authorship, proverbs, and slogans.

As you browse through ...*As One Mad With Wine* you'll find amusing illustrations as well as loads of inspiration for your own simile creation. To add spark, color, and precision to your conversations, writing, and speeches, follow these twelve tips:

Twelve Tips for Creating Similes

1. **Suit the simile to the subject.** There's a stronger connection between your topic and what you're comparing it to if there is a subtle link between the two. *New York Times* drama critic Frank Rich forged just such a link when he summed up a play about a black-listed actor as **one long evening of evasions, as if the playwright were taking the Fifth Amendment on advice of counsel.** (See: *Criticism, Dramatic*).

2. **Match your style to the occasion.** A successful simile must fit its stylistic landscape as a hollow fits a circle. Robert Burns's beautiful **my luv is like a red, red rose,** while perfect for a love poem, would be misplaced in a business article or a spy novel. In the same vein, the piquant and often ironic comparison that ideally suits many fictional sleuths' brusque manners and keenly developed powers of perception could misfire in a romance novel or a business brochure.

3. **Surprise readers or listeners with comparisons that go beyond the obvious.** As you browse through these pages you'll understand the eighteenth-century wit Sydney Smith's counsel to choose comparisons "remote from all the common tracks and sheep-walks made in the mind." On the other hand, don't sacrifice uniqueness for common sense.

4. **Test your simile for its visual value.** Visual imagery is integral to a good simile, but it's also crucial that your word picture really does portray your meaning explicitly. **Busy as a frisbee** would be a nice twist to the overworked **busy as a bee,** except for the fact that an inanimate object doesn't evoke the same clear-cut picture as the bee comparison. If at this testing stage, you expand the image to show the frisbee in action, as in **busy as a frisbee being tossed back and forth at the shore,** the simile begins to make sense (even though you've lost some of the snap and crackle).

5. **Appeal to all the senses.** Draw comparisons readers or listeners will not only see in their mind's eye but hear or taste or feel. When a character in a short story tries to contain her laughter at a situation but finally **comes apart like a slow ripping seam** (See: *Burst),* the reader not only sees control giving way but hears the escaping laughter.

6. **Try irony for a different flavor.** One of the most effective ways to lend piquancy and wit to your similes is to express the comparison in words that are the opposite of what you mean. The thematic headings *Absurdity, Necessity* and *Usefulness/Uselessness* are good starting points for examples.

7. **Don't hesitate to combine similes with other figures of speech.** An obvious choice here is the metaphor. After all, it also draws a comparison, but with this difference: it does so implicitly, by substituting or attributing one thing for another. Thus, to compare a woman to a tiger, you can use the simile **she's fierce as a tiger** or the metaphor **she's a tigress.** T. Coraghessan Boyle, a contemporary writer whose work is notable for its unique and always appropriate imagery, often marries similes and metaphors, like this description of a face: **a**

grid of scratches, thin as cut hair.

8. **Extend or expand your comparisons to give extra emphasis to your point.** When you extend a simile you use two or more comparisons; for example: **Dwight Gooden pitching without his fastball was like Nureyev dancing on a broken leg or Pavarotti singing with a sore throat** (See: *Baseball*). The trick here is for each comparison to tie into the same basic theme. An expanded simile takes several individual similes that—when grouped together—establish a common theme. Check out Beverly Mansfield's use of this technique for drawing a word picture of author Judith Krantz under the heading *Skin*.

9. **Consider cliches as sources of inspiration and adaptation.** Because good similes draw such vivid, instantly comprehended word pictures, many become language fixtures. A closer look at these once **bright as a new penny** and now **familiar as an old shoe** cliches will help you to understand why so many continue to be used as communication shortcuts. What's more, with a twist here and there, you can often breathe new life into an overused phrase.

10. **Practice moderation.** Don't get carried away. For business writers and speakers, a single simile is often all that's needed. In creative writing, a good story without a single simile can still be a good story. But a bunch of great similes in a bad story is **like a jeweled handle on a broken knife.**

11. **Don't expect to use every simile you jot down.** Writing down ideas for similes is an excellent creative exercise, but don't be surprised if you never use even the best ones, for as W. Somerset Maugham once explained, "Trying to fit a phrase from a notebook into a manuscript tends to interrupt the flow."

12. Above all, make sure it works. This tip really sums up all the others, but it's so important that it's worth restating: The simile's primary purpose is to cause the reader or listener to feel, "Yes, that's what it's like!" To have this effect, the image must be correct, appropriate to the frame of reference and visually sound.

Elyse Sommer
Forest Hills, New York/Lee, Massachusetts

Table of Thematic Categories

In the following table, categories used throughout the text and synonyms that are cross-references to categories are combined in one alphabetic order.

Abandonment
See: Aloneness, Bearing, Friendship

Ability

Absurdity
See Also: Difficulty, Impossibility, Inappropriateness

Abundance
See: Closeness

Accomplishment
See: Ability, Cleverness, Success/Failure

Actions
See: Jumping

Activeness/Inactiveness
See Also: Enthusiasm, Excitement, Personality Profiles

Actors
See: Stage and Screen

Admiration
See: Words of Praise

Advancing

Adversity
See: Fortune/Misfortune

Advertising
See: Business

Advice
See: Friendship

Affection
See: Friendship

Affliction
See: Health, Pain

Affluence
See: Riches

Age
See Also: Life, Youth

Aggression
See: Personal Traits

Agitation
See: Excitement

Agreement/Disagreement
See: Compatibility, Fighting

Ailments
See: Health, Illness

Aimlessness
See: Emptiness

Air

Airplanes
See: Vehicles

Alertness
See: Attention, Cleverness, Scrutiny

Alienation
See Also: Aloneness, Remoteness

Allure
See: Attraction

Aloneness

Aloofness
See: Personal Traits, Remoteness

Ambition

Anger
See Also: Irritableness

Animals
See Also: Birds

Animation
  See: Activeness/Inactiveness, Enthusiasm

Annoyance
  See: Irritableness

Anxiety
  See Also: Tension

Apartness
  See: Aloneness

Apathy
  See: Remoteness

Apparel
  See: Clothing

Appearance
  See: Physical Appearance

Appetite
  See: Hunger

Applause
  See: Enthusiasm, Noise

Approval
  See: Words of Praise

Argument
  See: Fighting

Arm(s)
  See Also: Hand(s)

Art and Literature

Atmosphere
  See: Air

Attention
  See Also: Scrutiny

Attire
  See: Clothing

Attraction

Attractiveness
  See: Beauty, Physical Appearance

Authenticity
  See: Realness

Authority
  See: Power

Automobiles
  See: Vehicles

Bachelor
  See: Men And Women

Bad Luck
  See: Fortune/Misfortune

Badness
  See: Evil

Baldness
  See: Hair, Physical Appearance

Bareness

Barrenness
  See: Emptiness

Baseball
  See Also: Sports

Basketball
  See: Sports

Beards
  See: Hair, Physical Appearance

Bearing
  See Also: Personality Profiles; Physical Appearance

Beauty
  See Also: Face; Physical Appearance

• **Beginnings/Endings**
  See Also: Sex

Behavior
  See: Action, Life

Belief
  See: Politics/Politicians

Belonging
  See: Compatibility/Incompatibility

Bending/Bent

Bereavement
  See: Grief

Bewilderment
  See: Strangeness

Bicycling
  See: Sports

Bigness
  See: Physical Appearance

Bigotry
  See: Intolerance

Birds
  See Also: Animals, Insects

Birth
   See: Beginnings/Endings, Death, Life
Bitterness
   See: Anger, Friendship
Black
   See: Colors, Dejection
Blankness
   See: Emptiness
Blessedness
   See: Fortune/Misfortune
Blindness
   See: Eye(s)
Blue
   See: Colors
Blushes
   See: Shame
Boats
   See: Seascapes
Body
   See Also: Physical Appearance, Shoulders, Strength, Thinness
Body Organs
   See: Sex
Boisterousness
   See: Noise
Boldness
   See: Courage
Books
   See: Readers/Reading
Boredom/Boring
   See Also: Life
Bouncing
   See: Rocking and Rolling
Boxing and Wrestling
   See: Sports
Brain
   See: Intelligence, Mind
Bravery
   See: Courage
Breasts
   See: Body
Brevity
   See: Time

Brightness
   See: Shining
Brown
   See: Colors
Buildings
   See: Houses
Burst
Business
   See Also: Success/Failure
Busyness
   See Also: Activeness, Work
Calumny
   See: Slander
Calmness
Candor
   See Also: Secrecy
Capability
   See: Ability
Carefulness
   See: Attention
Celebrity
   See: Fame
Certainty
Change
   See Also: Permanence
Chaos
   See: Order/Disorder
Character
   See Also: Personal Traits
Charitableness
   See: Kindness
Chastity
   See: Virtue
Cheapness
   See: Thrift
Cheeks
   See: Face(s), Skin
Cheerfulness
   See: Happiness, Smiles
Childishness
   See: Youth
Children
   See: Clinging
Chin
   See: Face(s), Mouth

Churches
    See: Houses
Cities
    See: Places
City/Streetscapes
    See: Places
Cleanliness/Uncleanliness
    See: Order/Disorder
Cleverness
    See Also: Intelligence
Clinging
    See Also: Persistence; People, Interaction
Closeness
    See Also: Compatibility, Friendship
Clothing
Clothing Accessories
    See: Jewelry
Clothing, Its Fit
    See: Clothing
Cloud(s)
    See Also: Sky
Coldness
    See Also: Remoteness
Colors
Comfort
Compassion
    See: Kindness
Compatibility/Incompatibility
Competence
    See: Ability
Competition
    See: Business, Sports
Complaints
    See: Anger
Completeness/Incompleteness
Complexion
    See: Skin
Complexity
    See: Difficulty
Compliments
    See: Words of Praise
Conceit
    See: Vanity

Concentration
    See: Attention, Scrutiny
Confidence
    See: Self-Confidence
Confidentiality
    See: Secrecy
Connections
    See: Clinging
Consideration
    See: Thought
Contemplation
    See: Scrutiny, Thought
Contentment
    See: Happiness, Joy
Continuity
    See: Permanence
Conversation
Coolness
    See: Calmness
Cooperation
    See: Agreement
Corporations
    See: Business
Correctness
    See: Manners
Cost
    See: Thrift
Countenances
    See: Face(s)
Courage
Courtesy
    See: Manners
Courtship
    See: Men and Women
Covertness
    See: Secrecy
Cowardice
    See: Fear
Coziness
    See: Comfort
Craftiness
    See: Cleverness
Craving
    See: Desire

Crime
See: Dishonesty, Evil

Crispness
See: Sharpness

Criticism, Dramatic/Literary

Crookedness
See: Bending/Bent

Crowdedness
See: Closeness

Crowds
See: Closeness

Cruelty
See: Coldness, Evil

Cunning
See: Cleverness

Curses
See: Word(s)

Dancing
See: Insults, Words of Praise

Daring
See: Courage

Darkness

Day
See: Time

Deafness
See: Attention

Death
See Also: Advancing;
Beginnings/Endings

Dedication
See: Attention

Dejection

Delight
See: Joy

Democracy
See: Freedom

Density
See: Thickness

Dependability
See: Reliability/Unreliability

Depression
See: Dejection

Desire
See Also: Sex

Destruction/Destructiveness

Detachment
See: Remoteness

Dew
See: Nature

Diets
See: Eating and Drinking

Difficulty
See Also: Impossibility

Dignity
See: Pride

Directness
See: Candor

Disappearance
See Also: Beginnings/Endings

Disappointment
See: Facial Expressions

Disaster
See: Fortune/Misfortune

Discomfort
See: Pain

Discontent
See: Dejection

Discouragement
See: Dejection

Dishonesty

Disintegration
See: Destruction

Disorder
See: Order/Disorder

Dissension
See: Fighting

Distance
See: Remoteness

Diverseness
See: Personal Traits

Docility
See: Meekness

Dogs
See: Animals

Domination
See: Power

Dreams
See Also: Ambition, Sleep

5

Drinking
   See: Eating and Drinking
Drivers/Driving
   See: Vehicles
Dullness
   See: Boredom/Boring
Dumbness
   See: Stupidity
Duty
   See: Reliability/Unreliability
Eagerness
   See: Enthusiasm
Earth
   See: Nature
Ease
Ease (Opposite Meaning)
   See: Difficulty
Eating and Drinking
Education
Eeriness
   See: Strangeness
Effectiveness
   See: Ability, Success/Failure,
   Usefulness/Uselessness
Effortlessness
   See: Ease
Ego
   See: Vanity
Elation
   See: Excitement, Joy
Elegance
   See: Clothing
Eloquence
   See: Persuasiveness
Elusiveness
   See: Difficulty
Embarrassment
   See: Shame
Embraces
   See: Men and Women,
   People Interactions
Eminence
   See: Fame
Emotions
   See: Anxiety, Dejection,

Emptiness, Envy, Fear, Grief,
   Happiness, Hate, Joy,
   Loneliness, Tension,
   Weariness
Empathy
   See: Kindness
Emptiness
   See Also: Aloneness
Endurance
   See: Permanence
Energy
   See: Activeness/Inactiveness,
   Busyness, Enthusiasm
Enthusiasm
   See Also: Excitement
Entrances/Exits
   See: Beginnings/Endings,
   Death
Entrapment
   See: Advancing; People,
   Interaction
Envy
Epitaphs
   See: Death, Pride
Epithets
   See: Word(s)
Evil
   See Also: Actions
Examination
   See: Scrutiny
Excitement
   See Also: Enthusiasm,
   Idleness
Exercise
   See: Sports
Exhaustion
   See: Weariness
Exits
   See: Beginnings/Endings,
   Disappearance
Explosion
   See: Burst
Eye(s)
Eye Color
   See: Eye(s)

Face(s)
See Also: Blushes, Eye(s), Mouth, Physical Appearance, Skin

Facial Color
See: Colors

Facts
See: Truth

Failure
See: Success/Failure

Fall
See: Seasons

Fame

Family
See: People, Interaction

Farewells
See: Beginnings/Endings

Fashion
See: Clothing

Fate
See: Life

Fatigue
See: Weariness

Fatness
See: Body, Insults, Physical Appearance

Fear
See Also: Anxiety

Fervor
See: Enthusiasm

Fighting

Figure
See: Body

Fingers
See: Hand(s)

Finish
See: Beginnings/Endings

Fire and Smoke

Fishing
See: Sports

Fists
See: Hand(s)

Fitness
See: Health

Flatness
See: Shape

Flattery
See: Friendship, Words of Praise

Flavor
See: Taste

Flight
See: Disappearance

Flowers
See Also: Nature

Fog
See: Mist

Food and Drink
See: Eating and Drinking

Foolishness
See: Absurdity, Stupidity

Football
See: Sports

Forcefulness
See: Power

Foreboding
See: Anxiety, Fear

Forehead
See: Face(s)

Forgetfulness
See: Memory, Mind

Forlornness
See: Aloneness

Formality/Informality
See: Order/Disorder

Fortitude
See: Courage, Persistence

Fortune/Misfortune
See Also: Riches

Fragility
See: Weakness

Frankness
See: Candor

Fraud
See: Dishonesty

Freckles
See: Skin

Freedom

Friendship

Frowns
See Also: Looks

Frustration
See: Dejection

Furniture and Furnishings
See Also: Houses

Furtiveness
See: Secrecy

Fury
See: Anger

Futility
See: Absurdity, Difficulty, Impossibility, Usefulness/Uselessness

Future
See: Advancing, Destruction/Destructiveness, Success/Failure, Time

Garden Scenes
See: Landscapes, Flowers, Nature

Generosity
See: Kindness

Gentleness
See: Kindness

Giddiness
See: Lightness

Gifts
See: Kindness

Glance
See: Looks

Glitter and Gloss
See: Shining

Gloom
See: Dejection

Glory
See: Fame, Success/Failure

Gluttony
See: Eating and Drinking

Gold
See: Colors, Money

Golf
See: Sports

Good Health
See: Health

Goodness
See: Kindness

Gossip

Government
See: Law, Politics

Gracefulness
See: Beauty

Graciousness
See: Manners

Grass
See: Nature

Graveness
See: Seriousness

Gray
See: Colors, Sky

Greatness
See: Fame, Intelligence, Mind

Greed
See: Eating and Drinking, Envy

Green
See: Colors, Envy

Grief

Grins
See: Smiles

Guilt

Hair

Hand(s)
See Also: Arm(s)

Happiness
See Also: Joy

Hardship
See: Fortune/Misfortune

Hard Work
See: Ambition, Work

Harmlessness
See: Innocence, Kindness

Harmony
See: Agreement, Compatibility, Peace

Head(s)

Health
See Also: Pain

Heart(s)
Heat
Helpfulness
See: Kindness
Hesitancy
See: Uncertainty
Hills
See: Mountains
History
See: Memory
Hockey
See: Sports
Hollowness
See: Emptiness
Home
See: Furniture and
Furnishings, Houses
Honesty
See: Reliability/Unreliability
Hope
See: Dreams
Horror
See: Fear
Hostility
See: Anger
Houses
See Also: Furniture and
Furnishings
Humility
See: Meekness
Humor
See Also: Cleverness
Hunger
See Also: Eating and
Drinking
Ideas
Idleness
See Also: Activeness/
Inactiveness
Ignorance
See Also: Stupidity
Illness
See Also: Compatibility/
Incompatibility, Health

Ill Temper
See: Anger
Illustriousness
See: Fame
Imagination
See: Ideas
Immobility
See Also: Death
Impartiality
Impassiveness
See: Coldness, Remoteness
Impermanence
See: Change, Life
Impertinence
See: Manners
Impoliteness
See: Manners
Importance/Unimportance
See Also: Memory, Necessity
Impossibility
See Also: Absurdity,
Difficulty
Improbability
See: Impossibility
Inactivity
See: Activeness/Inactiveness,
Idleness, Immobility
Inappropriateness
See Also: Compatibility/
Incompatibility
Inattentiveness
See: Attention
Incisiveness
See: Sharpness
Incompatibility
See: Compatibility/
Incompatibility
Incompleteness
See: Completeness/
Incompleteness
Incongruity
See: Absurdity
Independence
See: Freedom

Indifference
See: Remoteness

Indignation
See: Anger

Indolence
See: Idleness

Industriousness
See: Ambition, Work

Ineffectiveness
See: Usefulness/Uselessness

Inevitability
See: Certainty

Influence
See: Power

Infrequency
See: Rarity

Ingratitude
See: Sharpness

Injustice
See: Justice

Innocence

Inquisitiveness
See: Questions/Answers

Insects
See Also: Animals

Inseparability
See: Closeness, Friendship

Insignificance
See: Memory,
Importance/Unimportance,
Necessity

Insults

Intelligence
See Also: Cleverness, Mind

Intensity
See Also: Sharpness

Intimacy
See: Closeness

Intolerance

Irony
See: Humor

Irritableness
See Also: Anger, Tension

Isolation
See: Aloneness

Jealousy
See: Envy

Jewelry
See Also: Clothing

Jobs
See: Work

Jokes
See: Humor

Joy
See Also: Happiness

Jumping
See Also: Rocking and
Rolling

Justice

Kindness

Kisses
See: Insults

Knowledge
See: Education, Intelligence,
Mind

Landscapes
See Also: Mountains, Nature,
Trees

Language
See: Word(s)

Laughter
See: Humor, Smiles

Law

Lawyers
See: Law

Laziness
See: Idleness

Leaping
See: Jumping, Rocking and
Rolling

Learning
See: Education

Leaves
See: Flowers, Nature, Trees

Legs
See: Pain, Physical Feeling

Liberty
See: Freedom

Lies/Liars
See: Dishonesty

Life
    See Also: Age
Lighting
    See: Shining
Lightness
    See Also: Softness
Lightning
    See: Thunder and Lightning
Likelihood
    See: Impossibility
Limbs
    See: Arm(s)
Limpness
    See: Softness, Weakness
Lips
    See: Mouth
Literature
    See: Art and Literature
Liveliness
    See: Activeness/Inactiveness,
    Enthusiasm
Localities
    See: Places
Logic
    See: Sense
Loneliness
    See: Aloneness
Longing
    See: Desire
Long-Windedness
    See: Talkativeness
Looks
    See Also: Frowns, Physical
    Appearance, Scrutiny
Loudness
    See: Noise
Love
    See: Friendship; Love,
    Defined; Men and Women
Love, Defined
Loyalty/Disloyalty
    See: Friendship
Luck
    See: Fortune/Misfortune

Lust
    See: Desire, Sex
Lying
    See: Bearing, Bending/Bent,
    Immobility, Sleep
Malice
    See: Evil, Slander
Manipulation
    See: Power
Mankind
    See: Life
Manners
Marriage
    See: Men and Women
Meaningfulness/Meaninglessness
    See: Memory,
    Importance/Unimportance,
    Necessity
Meekness
Meetings
    See: Beginnings/Endings;
    People, Interaction
Melancholy
    See: Dejection
Memory
Men and Women
Mercy
    See: Kindness
Merit
    See: Virtue
Merriment
    See: Joy
Middle Age
    See: Age
Mind
    See Also: Attention; Insults;
    Thought
Miserliness
    See: Thrift
Misery
    See: Dejection
Misfortune
    See: Fortune/Misfortune

Mist

Mistress
See: Men and Women

Modesty
See: Meekness, Personal Traits

Money
See Also: Riches

Months
See: Seasons

Mood Changes
See: Change

Moon

Morality
See: Virtue

Mortality
See: Death

Motionlessness
See: Immobility

Motivation
See: Ambition

Mountains
See Also: Landscapes, Nature

Mourning
See: Grief

Mouth

Movement
See: Advancing, Jumping, Rocking and Rolling

Movies
See: Stage and Screen

Muscles
See: Strength

Mustaches
See: Hair

Mysteriousness
See: Strangeness

Nakedness
See: Bareness

Names
See: Memory

Narrowness
See: Thinness

Nature
See Also: Flowers, Moon, Seascapes, Sky, Sun, Thunder and Lightning, Trees

Nearness
See: Closeness

Neatness
See: Order/Disorder

Necessity
See: Importance/ Unimportance

Neck
See: Physical Appearance

Need
See: Desire

Nerve
See: Courage

Nervousness
See: Anxiety, Tension

Neutrality
See: Impartiality

News
See: Gossip

Night
See: Darkness

Nightmares
See: Dreams

Noise
See Also: Irritableness

Nonsense
See: Absurdity, Impossibility

Nostalgia
See: Memory, Sentiment

Obedience
See: Meekness

Oblivion
See: Memory

Observation
See: Scrutiny

Obstinacy
See: Persistence

Ocean/Oceanfront
See: Seascapes

Odor
See: Smell

Old
   See: Age
Openness
   See: Candor
Opinion
   See: Ideas
Opportunity
   See: Fortune/Misfortune,
   Impossibility
Orange
   See: Colors
Order/Disorder
Outburst
   See: Burst
Pain
   See Also: Health
Paintings
   See: Art and Literature
Parting
   See: Beginnings/Endings
Passion
   See: Desire, Sex
Past, The
   See: Memory
Patience
Paunchiness
   See: Body
Peacefulness
   See: Calmness
Peculiarity
   See: Strangeness
Penetration
   See: Pervasiveness
Pensiveness
   See: Thought
People, Interaction
   See Also: Friendship, Men
   and Women
Perceptiveness
   See: Sensitiveness
Permanence
Persistance
   See Also: Clinging
Personality Profiles
   See Also: Personal Traits

Personal Traits
Pervasiveness
   See Also: Clinging
Physical Appearance
   See Also: Arm(s), Beauty,
   Body, Eye(s), Face(s), Hair,
   Hand(s), Thinness
Physical Feelings
   See: Health, Pain
Pictures
   See: Art and Literature
Pink
   See: Colors
Pity
   See: Kindness
Places
   See Also: Insults
Plays
   See: Stage and Screen
Pleasure
   See: Happiness, Joy
Poise
   See: Bearing
Politeness
   See: Manners
Politics/Politicians
Ponds and Streams
   See: Nature, Seascapes
Posture
   See: Bearing, Bending/Bent
Power
Praise
   See: Words of Praise
Praiseworthiness
   See: Virtue
Predictability
   See: Certainty
Prejudice
   See: Intolerance
Prettiness
   See: Beauty
Pride
Probability
   See: Certainty

Proficiency
    See: Ability
Promise
    See: Reliability/Unreliability
Propriety/Impropriety
    See: Manners
Prosperity
    See: Riches, Success/Failure
Proximity
    See: Closeness
Public, The
    See: Politics
Purity
    See: Virtue
Purple
    See: Colors
Questions/Answers
Quiet
    See: Silence
Rage
    See: Anger
Ranting
    See: Anger
Rarity
Readers/Reading
Realization
    See: Truth
Reason
    See: Sense
Recollection
    See: Memory
Red
    See: Colors, Hair, Mouth
Reduction
    See: Disappearance
Reflection
    See: Thought
Reform
    See: Change
Relationships
    See: Men and Women;
    People, Interaction
Relentlessness
    See: Persistence

Reliability/Unreliability
Remembrance
    See: Memory
Remoteness
Renown
    See: Fame
Resentment
    See: Anger
Reserve
    See: Personality Traits,
    Remoteness
Resignation
    See: Meekness
Resourcefulness
    See: Ability
Response
    See: Questions/Answers,
    Word(s)
Responsibility
    See: Reliability/Unreliability
Retreat
    See: Disappearance
Revenge
Revolutions
    See: Politics
Rhetoric
    See: Word(s)
Riches
    See Also:
    Fortune/Misfortune, Money,
    Success/Failure
Ridicule
    See: Insults
Ridiculousness
    See: Absurdity, Impossibility
Righteousness
    See: Justice, Virtue
Rising
    See: Bearing
Road Scenes
    See: Noise, Vehicles
Roars
    See: Noise
Robbery
    See: Dishonesty

Rocking and Rolling

Romance
See: Men and Women

Rooms
See: Furniture and
Furnishings, Houses

Roundness
See: Shape

Rowdiness
See: Noise

Rudeness
See: Manners

Rumor
See: Gossip

Sadness
See: Dejection, Grief

Sales
See: Success/Failure

Sarcasm
See: Humor

Scandal
See: Shame

Scarcity
See: Rarity

Scowls
See: Frowns

Screams
See: Noise

Scrutiny
See Also: Intensity

Seascapes
See Also: Nature

Seasons

Secrecy

Sedateness
See: Seriousness

Self-Confidence
See Also: Pride, Vanity

Selfishness

Selling
See: Business

Sense
See Also: Intelligence

Senselessness
See: Absurdity

Sensitiveness
See Also: Kindness

Sentiment

Separation
See: Beginnings/Endings

Seriousness

Servility
See: Meekness

Sex
See Also: Men and Women,

Sexual Interaction
See: Insults

Shadow

Shallowness
See: Importance/
Unimportance

Shame

Shape

Sharpness
See Also: Pain

Shining

Shock

Shoulders
See Also: Body

Shrewdness
See: Cleverness

Shyness
See: Meekness, Personal
Traits

Sickness
See: Illness

Significance
See: Importance/
Unimportance

Silence
See Also: Secrecy

Silliness
See: Absurdity, Impossibility,
Stupidity

Similarity
See: Dissimilarities

Simplicity
See: Ease

Sin
See: Evil

Sincerity
 See: Candor
Sitting
 See: Bearing, Immobility
Skills
 See: Ability
Skin
Sky
 See Also: Cloud(s), Moon
Slander
Sleep
 See Also: Dreams
Slightness
 See: Weakness
Slimness
 See: Thinness
Sloppiness
 See: Order/Disorder
Smallness
Smell
 See Also: Air
Smiles
Smoke
 See: Fire and Smoke
Snores
 See: Sleep
Snow
 See: Nature
Soap Opera
 See: Stage and Screen
Softness
Solidity
 See: Strength
Solitude
 See: Aloneness
Sorrow
 See: Grief
Soundness
 See: Health
Sounds
 See: Noise
Speaking
 See: Conversation,
 Talkativeness

Speechlessness
 See: Silence
Spirit
 See: Courage
Spite
 See: Meaness
Sports
 See Also: Baseball
Spreading
 See: Pervasiveness
Sprightliness
 See: Activeness
Spring
 See: Seasons
Stage and Screen
Standing
 See: Bearing, Immobility,
 Personal Profiles
Stares
 See: Frowns, Looks
Starting and Stopping
 See: Beginnings/Endings
Stateliness
 See: Bearing
Stealth
 See: Secrecy
Sterility
 See: Emptiness
Stickiness
 See: Clinging
Stiffness
 See: Pain
Stillness
 See: Immobility, Silence
Stinginess
 See: Thrift
Stomach
 See: Body, Shape, Thinness
Strangeness
Strength
 See Also: Body, Courage
Struggle
 See: Life
Stubbornness
 See: Persistence

Students
See: Education

Stupidity
See Also: Absurdity, Insults, Mind

Sturdiness
See: Strength

Style
See: Clothing

Subservience
See: Meekness

Success/Failure
See Also: Business

Suddenness
See: Shock

Summer
See: Seasons

Sun
See Also: Moon, Sky

Superfluousness
See: Necessity

Surprise
See: Shock

Survival
See: Impossibility, Success/Failure

Suspense
See: Excitement

Swearing
See: Word(s)

Sweat
See: Smell

Sweetness
See: Taste

Swimming
See: Sports

Sympathy
See: Kindness

Tact
See: Insults

Talent
See: Ability

Talkativeness
See Also: Conversation

Taste

Teaching/Teachers
See: Education

Tedium
See: Boredom

Teeth

Temper
See: Anger

Temperament
See: Personal Traits

Temptation
See: Attraction

Tenacity
See: Persistence

Tenderness
See: Kindness

Tennis
See: Sports

Tension
See Also: Anxiety, Candor

Tentativeness
See: Uncertainty

Terror
See: Fear

Theater
See: Stage and Screen

Theories
See: Ideas

Thickness

Thinness
See Also: Body

Thoughts
See Also: Ideas, Intelligence

Thrift

Thunder and Lightning
See Also: Nature

Tidiness
See: Order/Disorder

Tightness
See: Tension, Thrift

Time
See Also: Death, Life,

Tiredness
See: Weariness

17

Tobacco
See: Smells

Tongue
See: Mouth, Sharpness

Trading
See: Success/Failure

Traffic
See: Vehicles

Transience
See: Death, Life

Transportation
See: Vehicles

Trees
See Also: Nature

Trembling
See: Rocking and Rolling

Triumph
See: Success/Failure

Troublesomeness
See: Difficulty

Trust/Mistrust
See: Uncertainty

Truth
See Also: Candor

Tyranny
See: Power

Uncertainty

Undemonstrativeness
See: Coldness, Remoteness

Unemployment
See: Work

Unfairness
See: Intolerance

Ungraciousness
See: Manners

Unhappiness
See: Dejection

Unhelpfulness
See: Usefulness/Uselessness

Unlikelihood
See: Impossibility

Unpleasantness
See: Undesirableness

Unpredictability
See: Uncertainty

Unreliability
See: Reliability/Unreliability

Unresponsiveness
See: Coldness, Remoteness

Untidiness
See: Order/Disorder

Untrustworthiness
See: Trust/Mistrust

Urgency
See: Importance/
Unimportance

Usefulness/Uselessness
See Also: Necessity

Valor
See: Courage

Value
See: Importance/
Unimportance

Vanity
See Also: Pride

Vehicles

Verboseness
See: Talkativeness

Vexation
See: Anger, Irritableness

Vice
See: Evil

Victory
See: Success/Failure

Vigor
See: Enthusiasm, Strength

Violence
See: Advancing

Virtue

Voice(s)

Voters
See: Politics

Vulgarity
See: Taste

Vulnerability
See: Sensitiveness

Warmth
See: Comfort, Heat

Watchfulness
See: Attention, Scrutiny

Water
See: Seascapes

Weakness
See Also: Insults, Personality Traits, Softness

Wealth
See: Riches

Weariness

Weather
See: Cloud(s), Coldness, Heat, Mist, Sun, Thunder and Lightning, Wind

Weight
See: Lightness

Well-Being
See: Health

White
See: Colors

Wickedness
See: Evil

Wind

Winning
See: Sports, Success/Failure

Winter
See: Seasons

Wisdom
See: Education

Wish
See: Desire

Wit
See: Cleverness, Humor

Women
See: Heart(s), Men and Women

Word(s)
See Also: Words of Praise

Wordiness
See: Talkativeness

Words of Praise

Work
See Also: Attention, Boredom

World
See: Life

Worry
See: Anxiety

Worthiness
See: Virtue

Worthlessness
See: Importance/ Unimportance

Wound
See: Pain

Wrath
See: Anger

Wrinkles
See: Skin

Wrists
See: Arms

Yawn
See: Mouth, Open/Shut

Yearning
See: Desire

Yellow
See: Colors, Hair

Youth
See Also: Age

Zeal
See: Ambition, Enthusiasm

SHOULDERS LIKE THE PARTHENON

The Similes

ABANDONMENT
SEE: ALONENESS, BEARING, FRIENDSHIP

ABILITY

Able to absorb punishment as open buds absorb the dew
—Grantland Rice

The abilities of man must fall short on one side or other, like too
scanty a blanket —Sir William Temple

The ability to make a great individual fortune ... is a sort of
sublimated instinct in a way like the instinct of a rat-terrier for
smelling out hidden rats —Irvin S. Cobb

Being creative without talent is a bit like being a perfectionist and
not being able to do anything right —Jane Wagner

Chose [people] with swift skill, like fruit tested for ripeness with a
pinch —Paul Theroux

(My wife ...) cooks like Escoffier on wheels —Moss Hart

Cuts like a saw through soft pine through the chatter of freeloaders,
time-wasting delegations —Stephen Longstreet
> In Longstreet's novel, *Ambassador*, from which this is
> extracted, the efficiency tactics are diplomatic.

Efficient as a good deer rifle —Bruce DeSilva

Functioned as smoothly as a hospital kitchen —Laurie Colwin

Resourceful and energetic as a street dog —James Mills

Having communists draft the law for the most capitalist society on
earth is like having a blind man guide you through the Louvre
museum —Mark Faber, *Wall Street Journal*, June 19, 1986
> Faber's simile pertained to the basic law that will govern
> Hong Kong in future.

21

Ability

His [Brendan Sullivan's] management (of Oliver North) is like one of those pictures that museum directors settle for labeling "Workshop of Veronese" because the hand of the master is not there for certain but his touch and teaching inarguably are —Murray Kempton, *New York Post*, December 12, 1986
> Kempton's simile describes the legal abilities of a member in the Edward Bennett Williams law firm, representing Colonel North during the Iran weapons scandal.

I can walk like an ox, run like a fox, swim like an eel ... make love like a mad bull —David Crockett, speech to Congress

• Instinct as sure as sight —Edgar Lee Masters

Native ability without education is like a tree without fruit —Aristippus

Natural abilities are like natural plants, that need pruning by study —Francis Bacon

Played bridge like an inspired card sharp —Marjory Stoneman Douglas

To see him [Chief Justice Hughes] preside was like witnessing Toscanini lead an orchestra —Justice Felix Frankfurter

Skilled ... like a mischievous and thieving animal —Émile Zola

Skillful as jugglers —Daphne du Maurier

Talent is like a faucet. While it is open, one must write (paint, etc.) —Jean Anouilh, *New York Times*, October 2, 1960

Talent, like beauty, to be pardoned, must be obscure and unostentatious —Marguerite, Countess Blessington

You must work at the talent as a sculptor works at stone, chiselling, plotting, rounding, edging and making perfect —Dylan Thomas

Absurdity

ABSURDITY
SEE ALSO: IMPOSSIBILITY, INAPPROPRIATENESS, USEFULNESS/USELESSNESS

Absurd as a monkey in a dinner jacket —Anon

Absurd as an excuse —Anon

Absurd ... as expecting a drowning man to laugh —German proverb

Time and use often transform proverbs into similes. In this case, the original proverb was "A fool will laugh when he is drowning."

Absurd as hiring a street vendor to run a major corporation —Anon

Absurd as looking for hot water under the ice —Latin proverb

Absurd as mathematics without numbers —Anon

Absurd as to expect a harvest in the dead of winter —Robert South

Absurd as to instruct a rooster in the laying of eggs —H. L. Mencken

Absurd as ... to put bread in a cold oven —Latin proverb

Absurd as ... to put water in a basket —Danish proverb

Absurd as trying to drink from a colander —Latin proverb

Absurd ... like baking snow in the oven —German proverb
   The simile has evolved from "He baked snow in the oven."

Absurd ... like jumping into the water for fear of the rain —French proverb

Absurd, like using a guillotine to cure dandruff —Clare Booth Luce

Absurd ... like vowing never to be sick again —Lynne Sharon Schwartz

As logical as trying to put out a fire with applications of kerosene —Tallulah Bankhead

Attending the Gerald R. Ford Symposium on Humor and the Presidency is sort of like attending the Ayatollah Khomeini Symposium on the sexual revolution —Pat Paulsen, at September 19, 1986 symposium in Grand Rapids, Michigan.

Bizarre and a little disconcerting, like finding out that the Mona Lisa was a WAC —Jonathan Valin

(His ...) body so sleek with health, that his talk of death seemed ludicrous, like the description of a funeral by a painted clown —Christopher Isherwood

Comparing [Ronald] Reagan with [Franklin D.] Roosevelt is like comparing Charles Schulz ["Peanuts" cartoonist] to Rembrandt —Mike Sommer

Absurdity

Incongruous as a mouse dancing with an elephant —Anon

Incongruous as a priest going out with a prostitute —Anon

Looks as well as a diamond necklace about a sow's neck
—H. G. Bohn's *Handbook of Proverbs*

Makes about as much sense ... as it would to put army shoes on
a ... French poodle —William Diehl

Ridiculous as monkeys reading books —Delmore Schwartz

Stupid and awkward, like chimpanzees dressed up in formal gowns
—Scott Spencer

That's absurd, like Castro calling Tito a dictator —John Wainwright

You just can't go around thinking that McDonald's food is going to
be steaming hot. It's like expecting the hamburger to be served
on a French roll —Ann Beattie

ABUNDANCE
SEE: CLOSENESS

ACCOMPLISHMENT
SEE: ABILITY, CLEVERNESS, SUCCESS/FAILURE

ACTIONS
SEE: JUMPING

Activeness / Inactiveness

ACTIVENESS/INACTIVENESS
SEE ALSO: ENTHUSIASM, EXCITEMENT, PERSONALITY PROFILES

About as active as a left-over fly in January —Anon

About as animated as a suit on a hanger —Elyse Sommer

(This region was as) active as a compost heap —Julia O'Faolain

Active as the sun —Isaac Watts

Alive as a vision of life to be —Algernon Charles Swinburne

(He looks) dead as a stump —Pat Conroy
   In Conroy's novel, *The Prince of Tides*, a character hearing
   someone described as above disagrees with another simile:
   "On the contrary, I think he looks as though he could rise
   up and whistle a John Philip Sousa march."

Frisky as a frisbee —Helen Hudson

Frisky as a colt —Geoffrey Chaucer

He was behaving as though the party were his: like an energetic octopus, he was shaking martinis, making introductions, manipulating the phonograph —Truman Capote

He is like a moving light, never still. He has the temperature and metabolism of a bird —Joy Williams

He [James Cagney] was like fireworks going off —Television obituary, 1986

Lively as a boy, kind like a fairy godfather —Robert Louis Stevenson

Lively as a weasel —Wallace Stegner

Lusty as June —Wallace Stevens

Mechanically animated, like the masterwork of some fiendishly inventive undertaker —Sharon Sheehe Stark

Pert as a sparrow —Walker Percy

(She had) rolled up her sleeves with all the vigor of a first-class cook confronting a brand-new kitchen —Mary McCarthy

She is active and strong as little lionesses —William James
    From a letter describing the energy of women in Dresden, July 24, 1867.

She was like a strong head wind —Marguerite Young

Simmering ... like a coal fire in the Welsh mines —Marvin Kittman
    About British actor Roy Marsden whose popularity thus simmers "in the collective unconscious of the American public" and bursts into flame whenever he makes an appearance in a new British import, Newsday, March 27, 1987.

Small and sprightly, like a bantam hen —Truman Capote

Sprightly as a Walt Disney cricket —Jean Thompson

Tireless as a spider —Eudora Welty

Vibrant as an E string —Carl Van Vechten

ACTORS
SEE: STAGE AND SCREEN

ADMIRATION
SEE: WORDS OF PRAISE

ADVANCING

Advanced like armies —Anon
> This is used to describe forward sweeps in a figurative as well as literal sense. For example, book critic Anatole Broyard used it about William Faulkner's sentences in a *New York Times Book Review*, May 17, 1987.

(The terrible old miser) advanced, like the hour of death to a criminal —Honoré de Balzac

Advance like the shadow of death —John Ruskin

Approached ... as stealthily as a poacher stalking a hind —Donald Seaman

Bearing down like a squad of tactical police —Marge Piercy

Bearing down like a tugboat busily dragging a fleet of barges —Frank Swinnerton

Came on like a last reel of a John Wayne movie —Line from "L. A. Law," television drama segment, 1987
> The simile describes a sexually aggressive woman.

Came [toward another person] ... like a tidal wave running toward the coast —Isak Dinesen

Came with slow steps like a dog who exhibits his fidelity —Honoré de Balzac

Come down, like a flock of hungry corbies, upon them —George Garrett
> Garret is comparing the corbies to a group of beggars.

Come like a rolling storm —Beryl Markham

Coming after me ... like a wave —Calder Willingham

Coming at him like a fullback —Wallace Stegner

(She'd seen it) coming like a red caboose at the end of a train —Denis Johnson

(Cancer) coming like a train —William H. Gass

Coming like a truck —James Crumley
> Here the strong advance describes an aggressive woman.

(People) converged upon them, like a stream of ants —Hortense Calisher

(Faith's father) descended ... like a storm —Charles Johnson

Descend on me like age —Margaret Atwood

Forges ahead, lashing over the wet earth like a whipcrack
        —T. Coraghessan Boyle

Glide toward them, as softly and slyly as a fly on a windowpane
        —Donald Seaman

He was upon them like a sun-flushed avalanche —Frank Swinnerton

• Invade like weeds, everywhere, but slowly —Margaret Atwood

Leaned forward like a magnificent bird of prey about to swallow its
        victim whole —Mike Fredman

Like a figurehead on the prow of a foundering ship his head and
        torso pressed forward —John Updike

Like fowls in a farm-yard when barley is scattering, out came the
        children running —Robert Browning

Moved forward [towards an attractive woman] like so many iron
        filings to a magnet —J. B. Priestley

(He was) moving toward me like a carnivorous dinosaur advancing
        on a vegetarian sibling —Joan Hess

Pressing forward like the wind —Sir Walter Scott

Pushed forward like the nervous antennae of a large insect
        —Rita Mae Brown

[An odor] roll up ... like fog in a valley —C.D.B. Bryan

Slid forward slowly as an alligator —Rudyard Kipling

(He could hear the roar of darkness) sweeping toward him like a fist
        —Jay McInerney

Swooped like chickens scrambling for a grain of corn
        —Aharon Megged

Went firmly on as if propelled —Stephen Crane

ADVERSITY
SEE: FORTUNE/MISFORTUNE

ADVERTISING
SEE: BUSINESS

ADVICE
SEE: FRIENDSHIP

AFFECTION
SEE: FRIENDSHIP

AFFLICTION
SEE: HEALTH, PAIN

AFFLUENCE
SEE: RICHES

Age

AGE
SEE ALSO: LIFE, YOUTH

Age covered her like a shawl to keep her warm —Rose Tremain

Age ... indeterminate as a nun —Sharon Sheehe Stark

Age is a sickness, and youth is an ambush —John Donne

Age is like love, it cannot be hid —Thomas Dekker

Age, like a cage, will enclose him —Alastair Reid

Age, like distance, lends a double charm
    —Oliver Wendell Holmes, Sr.

Age like winter weather ... age like winter bare
    —William Shakespeare
        These comparisons of age to the weather, from the poem
        The Passionate Pilgrim, are alternated with youth and the
        weather similes.

Age, like woman, requires fit surroundings —Ralph Waldo Emerson

Ageless as the sun —Algernon Charles Swinburne

The age of man resembles a book: infancy and old age are the blank
    leaves; youth, the preface; and man, the body or most important
    portion of life's volume —Edward Parsons Day

(Each year in me) ages as quickly as lilac in May —F. D. Reeve
        The simile marks the opening of a poem entitled
        Curriculum Vitae.

Antique as the statues of the Greeks —Edward Bulwer-Lytton

As a white candle in a holy place, so is the beauty of an aged face
    —Joseph Campbell

28

At middle age the soul should be opening up like a rose, not closing up like a cabbage —John Andrew Holmes

At thirty-nine, the days grow shorter, and night kneels like a rapist on the edge of your bed —Richard Selzer

At twenty man is like a peacock, at thirty a lion, at forty a camel, at fifty a serpent, at sixty a dog, at seventy an ape, at eighty nothing at all —Valtasar Gracian

Awareness [of one's own age] comes ... like a slap in the eye —Ingrid Bergman, on seeing a friend no longer young

Being seventy-five means you sometimes get up in the morning and feel like a bent hairpin —Hume Cronyn, "Sixty Minutes" interview with Mike Wallace, April 12, 1987

He could account for his age as a man might account for an extraordinary amount of money he finds has slipped through his fingers —John Yount
> In his novel, *Hardcastle*, Yount expands on the simile as follows: "Sure, he could think back and satisfy himself that nothing was lost, but merely spent. Yet the odd notion persists that, if he knew just how to do it, he might shake himself awake and discover that he is young after all."

Grow old before my eyes ... as if time beat down on her like rain in a thunderstorm, every second a year —Erich Maria Remarque

He had reached the time of life when Alps and cathedrals become as transient as flowers —Edith Wharton

He who lives to see two or three generations is like a man who sits some time in the conjurer's booth —Arthur Schopenhauer

How earthy old people become ... moldy as the gravel —Henry David Thoreau

Old women and old men ... huddle like misers over their bag of life —Randall Jarrell

Some men mellow with age, like wine; but others get still more stringent, like vinegar —Henry C. Rowland

The span of his seventy-five years had acted as a magic bellows—the first quarter century had blown him full with life, and the last had sucked it all back —F. Scott Fitzgerald

To be seventy years old is like climbing the Alps
—William Wadsworth Longfellow

Years steal fire from the mind as vigour from the limb —Lord Byron

You know you're getting older when every day seems like Monday
—Kitty Carlisle quoting her mother, 1985 television interview

Youth is like a dream; middle age, a forlorn hope; and old age a
nostalgia with a pervasive flavor of newly turned earth
—Gerald Kersh

AGGRESSION
SEE: PERSONAL TRAITS

AGITATION
SEE: EXCITEMENT

AGREEMENT/DISAGREEMENT
SEE: COMPATIBILITY, FIGHTING

AILMENTS
SEE: HEALTH, ILLNESS

AIMLESSNESS
SEE: EMPTINESS

AIR

Air as clear as water —Maya Angelou

Air ... as cool as water —Ethan Canin

The air, as in a lion's den, is close and hot —William Wordsworth

The air brightens as though ashes of lightning bolts had been
scattered through it —Galway Kinnell

The air flowed like a liquid —Dan Jacobson

The air had a sweet, keen taste like the first bite of an apple
—Phyllis Bottome

Air ... hot like the air of a greenhouse —Rose Tremain

The air hovered over the city like a fine golden fog —Isak Dinesen

Air had lain about us like a scarf —Irving Feldman

The air ... lay stifling upon the city, like a cat indifferently sprawled
upon a dying mouse —Brian W. Aldiss

The air in the room was jumpy and stiff like it is before a big storm outside —Lee Smith

The air is calm as a pencil —Frank O'Hara

The air is pure and fresh like the kiss of a child —Mihail Lermontov

Air light and pleasant as children's laughter —James Crumley

Air like a furnace —Benjamin Disraeli, about Spain

Air like bad breath —T. Coraghessan Boyle

Air like honey —John Updike

The [hazy] air muffles your head and shoulders like a sweater you've got caught in —William H. Gass

Air pure as a theorem —Lawrence Durrell

The air smelled like wet clothes —Andrew Kaplan

The air softly began a low sibilance that covered everything, like the night expiring —Richard Ford

Air so thick and slow it's like swimming —Jayne Anne Phillips

Air streams into me like cold water —Erich Maria Remarque

Air sweet and fresh like milk —George Garrett

Air thicker than chowder —Peter Meinke

The air was like soup —Derek Lambert

The air was like the silk dress Sharai wore, clean and complex and sensual —A. E. Maxwell
>Sharai is the name of a character in a novel entitled *The Frog and the Scorpion.*

The air was mild and fresh, and shone with a faint unsteadiness that was exactly like the unsteadiness of colors inside a seashell —Maeve Brennan

The air was smoky and mellow as if the whole earth were being burned for its fragrance like a cigar —John Braine

The air was so heavy that we could feel it pressing down on us like mattresses —Jean Stafford

The air was so rich and balmy it seemed that it could be scooped up with the hand —Rosine Weisbrod

Air

The air was still as if it were knotted to the zenith —Saul Bellow

The cold air was like a quick shower —Paul M. Fitzsimmons

The crystal air cut her like glass —Sharon Sheehe Stark

(The air was moist, odorous and black; one) felt it [the air] like a soft weight —Saul Bellow

The gray air in summer burned your eyes and throat like tractor exhaust trapped in a machine shed —Will Weaver

There was a slow pulsation, like the quiver of invisible wings in the air —Ellen Glasgow
> In Glasgow's novel, *Barren Ground,* this simile sets the scene for an approaching storm.

The warm air and moisture ... close in around her like a pot —Susan Neville

AIRPLANES
SEE: VEHICLES

ALERTNESS
SEE: ATTENTION, CLEVERNESS, SCRUTINY

ALIENATION
SEE: ALONENESS, REMOTENESS

ALLURE
SEE: ATTRACTION

Aloneness

ALONENESS

Alone as a nomad —Richard Ford

Alone as a scarecrow —Truman Capote

Alone as a wanderer in the desert —Anon

Alone ... like a lost bit of driftwood —Harvey Swados

Alone, like a planet —Richard Lourie

Alone ... like bobbing corks —Jean Anouilh
> Playwright Anouilh's simile from *Thieves' Carnival* describes two characters who thus bob about because their adventures are over.

Alone like some deserted world —Bayard Taylor

Like the moon am I, that cannot shine alone —Michelangelo

[Building] as isolated as an offshore lighthouse —Nicholas Proffitt

By himself he felt cold and lifeless, like a match unlighted in a box
        —Stefan Zweig
                The simile, from a short story entitled *The Burning Secret*,
                describes a man content only in the company of others.

Feel lonely as a comet —Anton Chekhov, letter to his wife

Felt like an island —Derek Lambert

In your absence it is like rising every day to a sunless sky
        —Benjamin Disraeli

Isolated as if it were a fort in the sea or a log-hut in the forest
        —Israel Zangwill

Isolated like a tomb —Ian Kennedy Martin

Left him standing like a stump —Willa Cather

Loneliness became as visible as breath that turned to vapor
        —Tennessee Williams

Loneliness fell over me and covered my face like a sheet
        —Susan Fromberg Schaeffer

Loneliness overcame him like a suffocating guilt —Irving Stone

Loneliness ... rises like an exhalation from the American landscape
        —Van Wyck Brooks

Loneliness surrounded Katherine like a high black fence
        —Tess Slesinger

(I wandered) lonely as a cloud —William Wordsworth
                One of the poet's most famous lines.

Lonely as a Hopper landscape —Brian Moore

Lonely as a lighthouse —Raymond Chandler

Lonely as a wave of the sea —Katherine Anne Porter

Lonely as priests —Anon

Lonely as Sunday —Mark Twain

The lonely, like the lame, are often drawn to one another
        —Harvey Swados

33

Aloneness

Lonesome as a walnut rolling in a barrel —Edna Ferber

Lonesome ... like the A sharp way down at the left-hand end of the keyboard —O. Henry

Lone women, like empty houses, perish —Christopher Marlowe

(And I) sit by myself like a cobweb on a shelf —Oscar Hammerstein II, from lyric for *Oklahoma*

Solitary as a lonely eel —Richard Ford

Solitary as a tomb —Victor Hugo

Solitary as an explorer —Donald Hall

Solitary as an oyster —Charles Dickens

A solitary figure, like the king on a playing card —Marcel Proust

Solitary ... like a swallow left behind at the migrating season of his tribe —Joseph Conrad

Solitude affects some people like wine; they must not take too much of it, for it flies to the head —Mary Coleridge

Solitude is as needful to the imagination as society is wholesome for the character —James Russell Lowell

Solitude ... is like Spanish moss which finally suffocates the tree it hangs on —Anaïs Nin

Solitude swells the inner space like a balloon —May Sarton

Solitude wrapped him like a cloak —Francine du Plessix Gray

Stand ... alone, like a small figure in a barren landscape in an old book —John D. MacDonald

Stand alone on an empty page like a period put down in a snowfall —William H. Gass

Survive like a lonely dinosaur —Mary McCarthy

(Celibate and) unattached,like a pathetic old aunt —Alice McDermott

Undisturbed as some old tomb —Edgar Allen Poe

Walk alone like one that had the pestilence —William Shakespeare
In common usage, most generally "Like one who has the plague," or whatever contagious disease might be afoot.

We whirl along like leaves, and nobody knows, nobody cares where we fall —Katherine Mansfield

When I am alone, I feel like a day-old glass of water
—Diane Wakoski

ALOOFNESS
SEE: PERSONAL TRAITS, REMOTENESS

AMBITION

Ambition ... coursed like blood through her —Vita Sackville-West

[One woman's] ambition expanded like yeast —Rita Mae Brown

Ambition is as hollow as the soul of an echo —Anon

Ambition is a sort of work —Kahlil Gibran

Ambition is like a treadmill ... you no sooner get to the end of it than you begin again —Josh Billings

Ambition is like hunger; it obeys no law but its appetite
—Josh Billings

Ambition is like love, impatient both of delays and rivals
—Sir John Denham

Ambition is like the sea wave, which the more you drink the more you thirst —Alfred, Lord Tennyson

Ambition, like a torrent, never looks back —Ben Jonson

Ambitious as the devil —Francis Beaumont

As ambitious as Lady MacBeth —James Huneker

Aspirations prancing like an elephant in a skirmish —Frank O'Hara

Good intentions ... like very mellow and choice fruit, they are difficult to keep —G. Simmons

How like a mounting devil in the heart rules the unrestrained ambition! —N. P. Willis
> The word 'unrestrained' has been substituted for 'unrein'd.'

A man without ambition is like a woman without beauty
—Frank Harris

35

Ambition

Overambitious ... like a musician trying to play every instrument in the band —Anon

(I think of) that ambition of his like some sort of little engine tick, tick, ticking away, and never stopping —Gore Vidal about Abraham Lincoln

To reach the height of ambition is like trying to reach the rainbow; as we advance it recedes —William Talbot Burke

Zeal without knowledge is like an expedition to a man in the dark —John Newton

Anger

ANGER
SEE ALSO: IRRITABLENESS

Anger ... flowing out of me like lava —Diane Wakoski

Anger ... hard, like varnished wood —Lynne Sharon Schwartz

Anger ... hot as sparks —Wallace Stegner

Anger is a short madness —Horace

Anger is as useless as the waves of the ocean without wind —Chinese proverb

Anger like wind is like a stone cast into a wasp's nest —Malabar proverb

Anger like a scar disfiguring his face —William Gass

Anger like grief, is a mark of weakness; both mean being wounded and wincing —Marcus Aurelius

Anger ... like Mississippi thunderstorms, full of noise and lightning, but once it passed, the air was cleared —Gloria Norris

The anger of a meek man is like fire struck out of steel, hard to be got out, and when got out, soon gone —Matthew Henry

Anger spreading through me like a malignant tumor —Isabel Allende

Angers ... crippling, like a fit —May Sarton

The anger [of a crowd of people] shot up like an explosion —H. E. Bates

Anger ... smoldered within her like an unwholesome fire —Charles Dickens

AMBITION IS LIKE A TREADMILL ... YOU NO SOONER GET
TO THE END OF IT THAN YOU BEGIN AGAIN

Anger ... spreading like a fever along my shoulders and back
—Philip Levine

Anger standing there gleaming like a four-hundred-horsepower car you have lost your license to drive —Marge Piercy

Anger surged suddenly through his body like a quick pain —Beryl Markham

(His) anger was quick as a flame —Phyllis Bottome

Anger welled up in him like lava —Frank Ross

Rage ... as infectious as fear —Christopher Isherwood

Rage, as painful as a deep cut —Jean Stafford

Rage ... burst in the center of my mind like a black bubble of fury —Lawrence Durrell

Rage sang like a coloratura doing trills —Marge Piercy

Rages like a chafed bull —William Shakespeare

Rage swells in me like gas —Marge Piercy

Rage whistling through him like night wind on the desert —Paige Mitchell

Raging back at her [an angry woman] like a typhoon —T. Coraghessan Boyle

Raging like some crazed Othello —Suzi Gablik describing Marc Chagall's behavior in review of *My Life With Chagall* by Virginia Haggard, *New York Times Book Review*, August 17, 1986

(Enemy chase me) sore as a bird —*The Holy Bible/Lamentations*

Sore as a boil —American colloquialism

Sore as a crab —John Dos Passos

Stammering with anger like the clucking of a hen —Émile Zola

Stewing hostility and mordant self-pity ... pooled like poison almost daily in his soul —Joseph Heller

Tempers boil over like unwatched spaghetti —Tonita S. Gardner

When he is angry he is like those creatures that lurk in hollow trees. His glare ... causes brave men to run like scalded cats —George F. Will

The angry man described by Will is football coach Woody Hayes.

Words heat up the room like an oven with the door open —Anon

The young man's wrath is like straw of fire, but like red hot steel is the old man's ire —Lord Byron

ANIMALS
SEE ALSO: BIRDS, INSECTS

The cat ... carried his tail like a raised sword —Helen Hudson

The cat was sleeping on the floor like a tipped-over roller skate —Paul Theroux

Crows ... circle in the sky like a flight of blackened leaves —Stephen Vincent Benét

Dogs ... all snarls and teeth like knives —George Garrett

Dog ... with a marking down his breast like a flowing polka-dot tie. He was like a tiny shepherd —Eudora Welty

Dour as a wet cat —Warren Beck

Fins [on fish] like scimitars —Richard Maynard

Frogs sparkling like wet suns —Margaret Atwood

He [a dog] dragged her around the block like a horse pulling a wheelless carriage —Margaret Millar

A herd of black and white cows moved slowly across a distant field, like pieces of torn paper adrift on a dark pond —Hilary Masters

His tail [a cat's] waved like a pine tree —Sheila Kaye-Smith

The Llama is a wooly sort of fleecy hairy goat with an indolent expression and an undulating throat. Like an unsuccessful literary man —Hilaire Belloc

[A cow] lying on her back like a fat old party in a bathtub —Edward Hoagland

[A cat] purring like a Packard engine. It worked like a lullaby —Harold Adams

Sheep huddled like fallen clouds —George Garrett

39

Animals

Silver whiskers ... like rice-threads —D. H. Lawrence
> The silver whiskers described by Lawrence belong to a fox, from which his story takes its title.

Squirrels ... fat as housecats —Doris Lessing

Swarms of bees like a buzzing cloud flew from flower to flower —Erich Maria Remarque

A white poodle ... like an animated powder puff —Penelope Gilliatt

Wings of the swans are folded now like the sheets of a long letter —Donald Justice

ANIMATION
SEE: ACTIVENESS/INACTIVENESS, ENTHUSIASM

ANNOYANCE
SEE: IRRITABLENESS

Anxiety

ANXIETY
SEE ALSO: TENSION

Anxiety flowed through the core of his bones like lava —Calder Willingham

(It is in those marriages and love affairs which are neither good or bad ... that) anxiety flows like a muddy river —Norman Mailer

Anxiety ... is somewhat like a blow on the head —Delmore Schwartz

Anxiety moved like a current through his belly —Bernard Malamud

Anxiety receives them like a grand hotel —W. H. Auden

Anxious as a law associate during his sixth year with a major law firm —Elyse Sommer

Anxious as an aspiring Miss Universe contestant sequestered in a soundproof booth and brought out moments later to tell what she loves most about America —Susan Barron, New York Times

Anxious as a mid-level manager in a corporate takeover —Mike Sommer

Anxious as an investor watching his stock go down —Anon

Anxious as a taxpayer with an audit notice from the IRA —Anon

40

As worried as she would have been over a lover she had cared for passionately —Sumner Locke Elliott

A case of the dreads so thick they seemed to whistle out the heating ducts and swarm the room like a dark mistral —Richard Ford

Desperation rising from him like a musk —Paule Marshall

A feeling of foreboding ... like a wind stirring the tapestry, an ominous chill —Evelyn Waugh

A feeling of vague anxiety ... snuffling about me like cold-nosed rodents, like reading of a favorite baseball player whose star has descended to the point where he parks cars at a restaurant or sits in a room above a delicatessen in Indianapolis, drinking vodka and waiting for his pension —W. P. Kinsella

Felt as if a serpent had begun to coil round his limbs —George Eliot

Felt as if her nerves were being stretched more tightly, like strings on violin pegs —Leo Tolstoy

Felt chilled as by the breath of death's head —Victor Hugo

Felt like a switchboard with all my nerves on Emergency Alert —Dorothy B. Francis

Frantic as a mouse in a trap —Anon

Had a chill and heavy feeling in his stomach like a lump of lead —Vicki Baum

Her mild, constant worries had engraved no lines in her bisque china face but had gradually cracked it like a very old plate —Lael Tucker Wertenbaker

His heart seemed to slide like the hook on a released pulley —Frank Swinnerton

I'm 'bout as worried as a pregnant fox in a forest fire —Peter Benchley

Over it [a face that had looked hopeful] now lay like a foreign substance a film of anxiety —Thomas Hardy

Second-hand cares, like second-hand clothes, come easily off and on —Charles Dickens

Stress is like an iceberg. We can see one-eighth of it above, but what about what's below —Patrice O'Connor

41

Anxiety

Suspended in his own anxiety as if in a cloudy solution of some acid —Lawrence Durrell

There is the same pain and panic (when your computer locks up) as when you have an attack of appendicitis —Brendan Gill quoted *New York Times*, August 2, 1986 in article by William E. Geist about a man (computer tutor Bruce Stark), who helps people with their computer problems.

> This is typical of similes that are borrowed and modified to fit a personal sphere of interest.

Unease ... it slipped out without his being able to control it, like sweat from his pores —Clive Barker

Worry is like a rocking chair. It gives you something to do, but it doesn't get you anywhere —Anon

APARTNESS
SEE: ALONENESS

APATHY
SEE: REMOTENESS

APPAREL
SEE: CLOTHING

APPEARANCE
SEE: PHYSICAL APPEARANCE

APPETITE
SEE: HUNGER

APPLAUSE
SEE: ENTHUSIASM, NOISE

APPROVAL
SEE: WORDS OF PRAISE

ARGUMENT
SEE: FIGHTING

Arm(s)

ARM(S)
SEE ALSO: HAND(S)

Arm ... like a fat bread roll —James Lee Burke

Arms and legs like tendrils —Jonathan Kellerman

(Her bare) arms and legs were like white vines —James Robison

Arms delicate as daisy stems —Sharon Sheehe Stark

Arms folded across his chest as primly as two blades in a Swiss Army knife —Pat Conroy

(An old man with) arms like driftwood scoured by salt and wind —Marge Piercy

Arms like gateposts —Leslie Thomas

Arms like logs —James Crumley

Arms like pythons —Nicholas Proffitt

Arms loose ... like ropes dangling toward the floor —Cornell Woolrich

Arms ... pink and thick as country hams —Robert B. Parker

Arms ... rounded and graceful and covered with soft down, like a breath of gold —Wilbur Daniel Steele

Arms, soft and smooth; they must be like peeled peaches to the touch —Stefan Zweig

Arms spread like a crucifix —Carolyn Chute

Arms swinging wildly, like a great gull flapping toward the sea —Kay Boyle

Arms thick as firs —Paige Mitchell

Arms ... thick as hickory logs —Elinor Wylie

Arms thick like a butcher's —Richard Maynard

Arms ... very thin and pale, as though they'd been tucked away in some dark place, unused —Margaret Millar

Bent arms like pothooks —Erich Maria Remarque

Delicate wrists that moved bonelessly as snakes —Margaret Millar

Elbows ... pointy, like a hard lemon —Ann Beattie

Forearms so hard and well-defined that the skin looked as if it had been flayed away, like drawings in an anatomy book —Jonathan Valin

Held their arms like bundles to their chest —William H. Gass

Arm(s)

It [arm] was so thin ... its covering didn't look like flesh but like paper wrapped around a bone to take home to a dog —Margaret Millar

Let her arms drop like folded wings —Julie Hayden

My arms fit you like a sleeve —Anne Sexton
The descriptive frame of reference in Sexton's poem, *Unknown Girl,* is a baby.

My arms lie upon the desk like logs sogged with rain —David Ignatow

One of her arms hung down to the floor like an overfed white snake —Ross Macdonald

Skinny, muscular arms ... like the twisted branches of an old apple tree —Arthur Miller

Swarthy arms like rolls of copper —Aharon Megged

Thin arms ... ridged like braided leather —R. Wright Campbell

Upper arms big as legs —Will Weaver

Wrists like twigs —Eleanor Clark

Wrists ... like two by fours —Charles Bukowski

Wrists ... looked thin as a dog's foreleg —John Updike

Wrist ... small like the throat of a young hen —Philip Levine

Wrist that looked like a lean ham —William Faulkner

Art and Literature

ART AND LITERATURE

Aesthetics is for the artist like ornithology is for the birds —Barnett Newman, *New York Times Book Review,* February 18, 1968

Art is a jealous mistress —Ralph Waldo Emerson

Art is an absolute mistress —Charlotte Cushman

Art is like a border of flowers along the course of civilization —Lincoln Steffens

Art is like baby shoes. When you coat them with gold they can no longer be worn —John Updike

Art is like religion. As long as you do your best to stamp it out of existence, it flourishes in spite of you, like weeds in a garden. But if you try and cultivate it, and it becomes a popular success, it goes to the dogs at once —Jane Wardle

Art is science in the flesh —Jean Cocteau

Art is wild as a cat and quite separate from civilization —Stevie Smith

The artist, like the neurotic, has withdrawn from an unsatisfying reality into this world of imagination; but, unlike the neurotic, he knew how to find a way back from it and once more to get a firm foothold in reality —Sigmund Freud

Artists ... like bees, they must put their lives into the sting they give —Ralph Waldo Emerson

Art, like eros, stirs senses to full life, demands devotion —Steven Millhauser

Art like life is an open secret —Lawrence Durrell

Art, like life, should be free, since both are experimental —George Santayana

Art, like morality, consists of drawing the line somewhere —G. K. Chesterton

Art, like the microscope, reveals many things that the naked eye does not see —George Moore

As the sun colors flowers, so does art color life —Sir John Lubbock

Great art is as irrational as great music. It is mad with its own loveliness —George Jean Nathan

I have seen the beauty evaporate from poems and pictures, exquisite not so long ago, like hoar frost before the morning sun —W. Somerset Maugham

In art, as in diet, as in spiritual life, the same rules of elimination apply: the more one can do without the better —Anne Freemantle

In art, as in love, instinct is enough —Anatole France

In art, as in politics, there is no such thing as gratitude —George Bernard Shaw

In literature, as in love, we are astonished at what is chosen by others —André Maurois, *New York Times,* April 14, 1963

(Nine times out of ten,) in the arts as in life, there is actually no truth to be discovered; there is only error to be exposed —H. L. Mencken

Literature, like a gypsy, to be picturesque, should be a little ragged —Douglas Jerrold

Literature, like virtue, is its own reward —Lord Chesterfield

Literature's like a big railway station ... there's a train starting every minute —Edith Wharton
> In her short story, *The Angel at the Grave,* Wharton continues the simile as follows: "People are not going to hang around the waiting room. If they can't get to a place when they want to, they go somewhere else."

It [empty white canvas] looks like an anemic nun in a snow storm —James Rosenquist, quoted in television documentary about his work, 1987

Modern paintings are like women. You'll never enjoy them if you try to understand them —Harold Coffin

Most works of art, like most wines, ought to be consumed in the district of their fabrication —Rebecca West

Naïveté in art is like zero in a number; its importance depends on the figure it is united with —Henry James

One must act in painting as in life, directly —Pablo Picasso, *Time* interview

Two modern paintings ... like Rorschach inkblots gone to seed —Pat Conroy

A picture is a poem without words —Latin proverb

(Some of the canvases had no pictures at all, just colors,) swirls and patches and planes of color, thickened and lumped, like hunks of emotion —Dan Wakefield

Without favor art is like a windmill without wind —John Ray's *Proverbs*

The youth of an art is, like the youth of anything else, its most interesting period —Samuel Butler

ATMOSPHERE
SEE: AIR

ATTENTION
SEE ALSO: SCRUTINY

Attention

(When listening he is) as focused and as still as a chipmunk spying something unknown from atop a stone wall —Philip Roth about Primo Levi, *New York Times Book Review*, October 12, 1986

The attention [of listeners] is like a narrow mouthed vessel; pour into it what you have to say cautiously, and, as it were, drop by drop —Joseph Joubert

Attention rolled down like a window shade —Sharon Sheehe Stark

Attention [of students] sinking ... like sluggish iron from the cooling crust —John Updike

Attentive and indifferent as a croupier —George Garrett

Attracted about as much attention as a flea in a dog pound —Ross Thomas

Attracted about as much attention (in the artistic world) as the advent of another fly in a slaughter house —James L. Ford

Attracted as little attention as a dirty fingernail in the third grade —Ring Lardner

Attracted attention like the principal heads in a picture —Honoré de Balzac

Collected attention like twists of silver paper or small white pebbles —Elizabeth Bowen

Concentrates ... like a cancer victim scanning a medical dictionary in hopes that the standard definitions have been repealed overnight in favor of good news —James Morrow

Curiosity, keen and cold as a steel knife —Maxim Gorky

Deaf as a door nail —Thomas Wilson
> This is the best known of many "Deaf as" similes. It's used in its literal sense as well as to describe inattentiveness. Popular variants include "Deaf as a post," "Deaf as a door," and "Deaf as a stone."

Deaf as a piecrust —Lawrence Durrell

47

(Had honed her ability to turn) deaf as a snail —Joseph Wambaugh

Drinking it [information] like a bomber pilot getting ready for a mission —Harvey Swados

(The hoot of laughter that always made Mary) flick him off like television —Sumner Locke Elliott

Had taken in her every anecdote as completely as a recording machine —Louis Auchincloss

Heads are turning like windmills —Arthur Miller

Heedless as the dead —Lord Byron

His eyes wandered, like a mind —Penelope Gilliatt

His mind keeps slipping away like a fly —John Rechy

Inattentive, like the ear of a confessor —Mary McCarthy

Intent as a surgeon —Jean Stafford

Interest spread like a net —Nadine Gordimer

(She could not keep her mind on anything); it [her mind] kept darting around like a darning needle —Jean Stafford

Leaned forward ... like hounds just before they get the fox —Stephen Vincent Benét

Leapt from theme to theme like a water-bug —Eleanor Clark

Listened as intently as a blind woman —Rita Mae Brown

Listened, very still, like a child who is being told a fascinating and gruesome fairy tale —Isak Dinesen

Listen like an uncle —Herbert Gold

Listen ... like snakes to a charmer's flute —Jan de Hartog

Mind jumps from one thing to another like drops of water bouncing off a larded pan when you test whether the griddle is hot enough to pour the pancake batter in —John Hagge

My mind wanders like smoke —Clifford Odets

Pricked up his ears like two railroad signals —Lewis Carroll

[Poets] receive the same care as xylophones and equestrian statues —Delmore Schwartz

Seems not to listen to her words, but rather watches her forming them ... like some fervent anthropologist —William Boyd

Snaps to attention like a thumb —Irving Feldman

(He tried to apply his mind to the work he was doing but his) thoughts fluttered desperately, like moths in a trap —W. Somerset Maugham

The words bounced off Harry, like pebbles skipped on water —Paul Kuttner

(So scatter-brained that) words went by him like the wind —Louisa May Alcott

ATTIRE
SEE: CLOTHING

ATTRACTION

Absorbing as a love affair —Elyse Sommer

(A charismatic man) attracting young men to himself like filings to a magnet —Linda West Eckhardt

Come at him [girls to a boy] like ducks to popcorn —Max Apple

Drawn to as children to amusement parks —Anon

Drawn to as bathers to seashore —Anon

Drawn to as readers to a library —Anon

Drawn to us warily but helplessly, like a starved deer —Louise Erdrich

Drew ... like pipers charming rats —Lynne Sharon Schwartz
> In her novel, *Disturbances in the Field,* Schwartz alludes to ideas that are attractive to the heroine and her college friends.

Drew (many confidences ...) as unintentionally as a magnet draws steel filings —Vita Sackville-West

Enchanted ... like a meadow full of four-leaf clovers —Mary McCarthy

Fascinated like sick people are fascinated by anything ... any scrap of news about their own case —James Thurber

Attraction

Fascinating and fantastic as toys in a shop window to a little poor boy in the street —Isak Dinesen

Fascinating as a burning fuse —William McGivern, about fellow writer Michael Gilbert's espionage novel, *Overdrive*.
> Whenever a simile is used to praise a book, it is invariably highlighted on the book jacket or in ads, as this one was.

(The salesgirls) fell on me like pigeons on breadcrumbs —Judith Rascoe

Had drawn her to him like a flower to the sun —John Le Carré

(The warm sweet center of her) had taken hold of him like a hand —John Yount

Held her mesmerized like a snake —Julia O'Faolain

He moves to you like a stable hand to a new horse —Allan Miller
> This comes from Miller's dramatization of D. H. Lawrence's short novel, *The Fox*. It did not appear in the Lawrence text.

Irresistible [thoughts] as intruders who force their way into your house —Dan Wakefield

Like children taking peeps at pantry shelves, we think we're tempted when we tempt ourselves —Arthur Guiterman

Men just love to buzz around me like there was a sweet smell coming from me —Pat Conroy

Mesmerizing as a flickering neon sign —Anon

(Kept watching because) something about her stayed with me. Like a cold matzo ball —Nat Hentoff

Take to the way a hypochondriac takes to a bed —Lorrie Moore

Temptation leapt on him like the stab of a knife —Edith Wharton

Temptations, like misfortunes, are sent to test our moral strength —Marguerite de Valois

Took to as an ant to a picnic —Harry Prince

Took to it ... like a retriever to water-ducks —Ouida

Was drawn to ... as if by strong cords —Aharon Appelfeld

ATTRACTIVENESS
SEE: BEAUTY, PHYSICAL APPEARANCE

AUTHENTICITY
SEE: REALNESS

AUTHORITY
SEE: POWER

AUTOMOBILES
SEE: VEHICLES

BACHELOR
SEE: MEN AND WOMEN

BAD LUCK
SEE: FORTUNE/MISFORTUNE

BADNESS
SEE: EVIL

BALDNESS
SEE: HAIR, PHYSICAL APPEARANCE

BARENESS

Bare as the back of my hand —John Ray's *Proverbs*

As naked as the last leftover clap in a theatre —Joe Coomer

Bare as a birch at Christmas —Sir Walter Scott
      Scott used this in both *The Fortunes of Nigel* and *Quentin Durward.*

Bare as a bird's tail —Edward Ward

Bare as a newly shorn sheep —John Lydgate
      The simile has been modernized from "Bare as a sheep that is but newe shorn."

(There she was, on the bed beside me, as) bare-assed as Eve in Eden —George Garrett

Bare as shame —Algernon Charles Swinburne

Bare as winter trees —William Wordsworth

Bare like a carcass picked by crows —Jonathan Swift

More desolate than the wilderness —*The Holy Bible/Ezekiel*

Bareness

Naked as an egg —F. van Wyck Mason

Naked as a peach pit —Helen Dudar, *Wall Street Journal*, November 26, 1986
> Even writers not given to using similes often use them as attention-grabbers at the beginning of an article, as Helen Dudar did to introduce her subject, novelist Paget Powell.

Naked as a stone —Angela Carter

Naked as a table cloth —Frank O'Hara

Naked as a weather report —Robert Traver

Naked as rain —Wallace Stevens

Nude as fruit on limb —George Garrett

(Voice wearing) raw as a rubbed heel —Sharon Sheehe Stark

(I'm simply against) showing girls as if they were pork chops —Germaine Greer on Playmate features in *Playboy Magazine*, January, 1972

Standing naked as a dead man's shadow —A. D. Winans

BARRENNESS
SEE: EMPTINESS

Baseball

BASEBALL
SEE ALSO: SPORTS

The ball ... came floating up to the plate like a generous scoop of vanilla ice cream bobbing to the top of a drugstore soda —Howard Frank Mosher

A ballpark at night is more like a church than a church —W. P. Kinsella
> Kinsella's novels are small treasure troves of baseball-related similes.

The ball ... sailed through the light and up into the dark, like a white star seeking an old constellation —Bernard Malamud

The ball was coming in like a Lear jet —T. Glen Coughlin

Baseball games are like snowflakes and fingerprints, no two are ever alike —W. P. Kinsella

Baseball is like writing. You can never tell with either how it will go —Marianne Moore
    Baseball, like writing, was a Marianne Moore passion.

Boston hit Dwight Gooden like they were his wicked stepparents —Vin Scully, commenting on the second game of the 1986 World Series

The catcher is padded like an armchair —*London Times,* 1918

Defeat stains a pitcher's record as cabernet stains a white carpet —Marty Noble, *Newsday,* August 25, 1986

The dirt flew as if some great storm had descended and would have ripped up the entire [baseball] field —Craig Wolff, *New York Times,* August 3, 1986

Dwight Gooden [of New York Mets] pitching without his fastball was like Nureyev dancing on a broken leg or Pavarotti singing with a sore throat —Anon item, *Newsday,* October 25, 1986

The earth around the base is ... soft as piecrust. Ground balls will die on the second bounce, as if they've been hit into an anthill —W. P. Kinsella

[Baseball] field ... cool as a mine, soft as moss, lying there like a cashmere blanket —W. P. Kinsella

He bats like a lightning rod —W. P. Kinsella

He gets power from his bat speed ... it's like he has cork in his arms —Pete Rose about Eric Davis, David Anderson column *New York Times,* May 7, 1987

He ran the bases as if he was hauling William H. Taft in a rickshaw —Heywood Broun

[Dwight Gooden] his fastball crackling, his curveball dropping as suddenly as a duck shot in the air, has begun his charge for a third straight award-winning season —Ira Berkow, *New York Times*/Sports of the Times, August 3, 1986

Homers are like orgasms. You run out of them after a time —Norman Keifetz

It [the patched-up Shea Stadium field] was dangerous underfoot as the Mets and the Cubs tiptoed their way though a 5-0 Met victory the way soldiers would patrol a mine field —George Vecsey, *New York Times*/Sports of the Times, September 19, 1986

Baseball

The ball players had to navigate their way through the field like soldiers because their fans had behaved so destructively the day before.

Knowing all about baseball is just about as profitable as being a good whittler —Frank McKinney

Outfielders ran together as if directed by poltergeists —George Vecsey, *New York Times*/Sports of the Times column on dreadful things that happen to the Mets when they play against the Houston outfielders, October 8, 1986

Someone once described the pitching of a no-hit game as like catching lightning in a bottle (How about catching lightning in a bottle on two consecutive starts?) —W. P. Kinsella

Sometimes I hit him like I used to hit Koufax, and that's like drinking coffee with a fork. Did you ever try that? —Willie Stargell on Steve Carlton, *Baseball Illustrated*, 1975

Stepping up to the plate now like the Iron Man himself. The wind-up, the delivery, the ball hanging there like a piñata, like a birthday gift, and then the stick flashes in your hands like an archangel's sword —T. Coraghessan Boyle

To be an American and unable to play baseball is comparable to being a Polynesian and unable to swim —John Cheever

Trying to sneak a pitch past him is like trying to sneak the sunrise past a rooster —Amos Otis, baseball outfielder, about Rod Carew, former first baseman

Twenty years ago rooting for the Yankees was like rooting for IBM —George F. Will, on the Chicago Cubs, *Washington Post*, March 20, 1974

BASKETBALL
SEE: SPORTS

BEARDS
SEE: HAIR, PHYSICAL APPEARANCE

Bearing

BEARING
SEE ALSO: PERSONALITY PROFILES, PHYSICAL APPEARANCE

Carried it [a bright, haggard look] ... like a mask or a flag —William Faulkner

Exuded an air, almost an aroma, of justification, like a mother who
   has lived to see her maligned boy vindicated at last
   —Harvey Swados

Sitting up against the pillow, head back like a boxer between rounds
   —John Le Carré

Head lifted as though she carried life as lightly there as if it were a
   hat made of tulle —Paule Marshall

Held her body with a kind of awkward pride mixed with shame, like
   a young girl suddenly conscious of her flesh —Ross Macdonald

Held herself like a daughter of the Caesars —W. Somerset Maugham

Held his shoulders like a man conscious of responsibility
   —Willa Cather

He leaned back and crossed his legs, as if we were settling in front
   of the television set to watch "Masterpiece Theater" —Joan Hess

Her head ... carried well back on a short neck, like a general or a
   statesman sitting for his portrait —Willa Cather

He seemed enduringly fixed on the sofa, the one firm object in a
   turbulent world ... like a lighthouse ... the firm, majestic
   lighthouse that sends out its kindly light —Isak Dinesen

He seemed to have collapsed into himself, like a scarecrow in the
   rain —Christopher Isherwood

His chin hung on his hand like dead weight on delicate scales
   —Reynolds Price

His erect figure carrying his white hair like a flag —John Updike

His shoulders slumped like a man ready to take a beating
   —James Crumley

His straight black hair and craggy face gave off a presence as
   formidable as an Indian in a gray flannel suit —Norman Mailer

Holding herself forward [as she walks] like a present —Alice Adams

I felt that if he [man with threatening presence] were to rise violently
   to his feet, the whole room would collapse like paper
   —Margaret Drabble

Lay piled in her armchair like a heap of small rubber tires
   —Patricia Ferguson

Bearing

Leaned forward eagerly ... looking like a bird that hears a worm in the ground —Robert Lowry

A lofty bearing ... like a man who had never cringed and never had a creditor —Herman Melville

Looked like a prisoner in the dock, hangdog and tentative —T. Coraghessan Boyle

Looking regal as a king —Gloria Norris

Perched on her armchair like a granite image on the edge of a cliff —Edith Wharton

(Sat) prim and watchful as a schoolgirl on her first field trip —Robert Traver

Relaxed and regal as a Siamese cat —Harold Adams

(They were mute, immobile, pale—as) resigned as prisoners of war —Ignazio Silone

Sat like a bronze statue of despair —Louisa May Alcott

Sat like a Greek in a tragedy, waiting for the gods to punish her for her way of life —Jonathan Valin

Sat helpless and miserable, like a man lashed by some elemental force of nature —Flannery O'Connor

Sat like a man dulled by morphine —Albert Maltz

(The leading members of the Ministry) sat like a range of exhausted volcanoes —Benjamin Disraeli

Sat on the arm of the sofa with a kind of awkward arrogance, like a workman in a large strange house —Paul Theroux

(Professor Tomlinson) sat up in the witness chair like a battleship raising its most powerful gun turret into position to fire —Henry Denker

She drew herself up with a jerk like a soldier standing easy called to stand-at-attention position —Kingsley Amis

She holds up her head like a hen drinking —Scottish proverb

She walked like a woman at her lover's funeral —Derek Lambert

She was still and soft in her corner [of the room] like a passive creature in its cave —D. H. Lawrence

HIS ERECT FIGURE CARRYING HIS WHITE HAIR
LIKE A FLAG

She wore defeat like a piece of cheap jewelry —Pat Conroy

Slumped into her seat like a Pentecostal exhausted from speaking in tongues —Sarah Bird

Spread his arms and went springy like a tennis player —Graham Swift

Slumps in his chair like a badly hurt man, half life-size —Ted Hughes

Standing like a lost child in a nightmare country in which there was no familiar landmark to guide her —Margaret Mitchell

Standing ... poised and taut as a diver —George Garrett

Standing still alone, she seemed almost somber, like a statue to some important but unpopular virtue in a formal garden —Douglas Adams

Stands there like a big shepherd dog —Clifford Odets

Stands there like a prizefighter, like somebody who knows the score —Raymond Carver

Stands there vacantly, like a scared cat —Bobbie Ann Mason

Stately [movement] like a sailing ship —William H. Gass

Stood around casual as tourists —James Crumley

Stood before them, like a prisoner at the bar, or rather like a sick man before the physicians who were to heal him —Edith Wharton

Stood in one place, staring back into space and grinding fist into palm, like a bomb looking for someplace to go off —William Diehl

Stood looking at us like a figure of doom —Edith Wharton

Stood morosely apart, like a man absorbed in adding millions of pennies together, one by one —Frank Swinnerton

Stood stiffly as a hanged man —Leigh Allison Wilson

Stood ... stiffly, like a page in some ancient court, or like a young prince expecting attention —Mary Hedin

Stood there like an angry bull that can't decide who to drive his horns in next —Danny Santiago

Walked like a man through ashes, silent and miserable
—Robert Culff

Went about looking as though she had had a major operation that had not proved a success —Josephine Tey

Wore abuse like widow's weeds —Lael Tucker Wertenbaker

Wore their beauty and affability like expensive clothes put on for the occasion —Edith Wharton

BEAUTY
SEE ALSO: FACE; PHYSICAL APPEARANCE

(He was) all beauty, as the sun is all light —Phyllis Bottome

As fair as day —William Shakespeare

Beautiful and faded like an old opera tune played upon a harpsichord —Amy Lowell

Beautiful and freckled as a tiger lily —O. Henry

Beautiful as a feather in one's cap —Thomas Carlyle

(He is) beautiful as a law of chemistry —Robert Penn Warren

Beautiful as a motherless fawn —Bruce De Silva

Beautiful as an angel —William Paterson

Beautiful as an icon —Rachel Ingalls

Beautiful as an illusion —Angela Carter

Beautiful as a prince in a fairy story —Mary Lee Settle

Beautiful as a rainbow —John Dryden

Beautiful as a well-handled tool —Stephen Vincent Benét

Beautiful as a woman's blush and as evanescent too —Letitia Landon

(For he was) beautiful as day —Lord Byron

Beautiful as fire —Ambrose Bierce

Beautiful as honey poured from a jar —*People* book review

(There was a woman) beautiful as morning —Percy Bysshe Shelley

Beautiful as nature in the spring —O. S. Wondersford

Beautiful as sky and earth —John Greenleaf Whittier

(She was as) beautiful as the devil, and twice as dangerous
 —Dashiell Hammett

Beautiful as youth —Dollie Radford

Beautiful ... like a dream of youth —Oliver Wendell Holmes, Sr.

Beauty as definite as that of a symphony by Beethoven or a picture
 by Titian —W. Somerset Maugham

Beauty ... extraordinary, as if it were painted —Anita Brookner

Beauty in a woman's face, like sweetness in a woman's lips, is a
 matter of taste —M. W. Little

Beauty is as good as ready money —German proverb

Beauty is striking as deformity is striking —Edmund Burke

Beauty, like a lantern's light, will shine outward from within him
 —George Garrett

Beauty ... like fine cutlery —John Gardner

Beauty, like supreme dominion, is best supported by opinion
 —Jonathan Swift

Beauty, like wit, to judges should be shown —Lord Lyttleton

Beauty passes like a breath —Alfred, Lord Tennyson

Beauty without grace is the hook without the bait
 —Ralph Waldo Emerson

Donned beauty like a robe —Iris Murdoch

Exquisite as the jam of the gods —Tennessee Williams

Fair as a lily —Diaphenia
  One of the most popular and enduring flower/beauty
  comparisons.

Fair as any rose —Christina Rossetti

Fair as a star —William Wordsworth

Fair as heaven or freedom won —Algernon Charles Swinburne

Fair as is the rose in May —Geoffrey Chaucer

Fair as marble —Percy Bysshe Shelley

Fairer than the morning star —Oscar Wilde

A fair face without a fair soul is like a glass eye that shines and
   sees nothing —John Stuart Blackie

Gorgeous as Aladdin's cave —Eleanor Mercein Kelly

(In the dingy park) her beauty fled as swiftly as the marmalade
   kitten had leapt from her grasp —William Trevor

Her beauty was as cool as this damp breeze, as the moist softness of
   her own lips —F. Scott Fitzgerald

He's as pretty as those long-defunct lover-gods —Charles Simic

(A novel that would be as) lovely as a Persian carpet, and as unreal
   —Oscar Wilde

Lovely as Spring's first rose —William Wordsworth

Lovely as the evening moon —Amy Lowell

Outstanding beauty, like outstanding gifts of any kind, tends to get
   in the way of normal emotional development, and thus of that
   particular success in life which we call happiness
   —Milton R. Sapirstein

Pretty as a diamond flush —Alfred Henry Lewis

(Face ...) pretty as a greeting card —Donald E. Westlake

Pretty as a new-laid egg
   —American colloquialism, attributed to Midwest

(There sat Mary) pretty as a rose —Jump Rope Rhyme

Pretty as a spotted pony
   —American colloquialism, attributed to Southeast

Pretty as a spotted pup —Mary Hood

Pretty as a wax doll —Katherine Mansfield

Pretty as the carved face on a ... cameo —Davis Grubb

Pretty like children on their birthdays —Truman Capote

Shed beauty like winter trees —George Garrett

She walks in beauty like the night —Lord Byron

Beauty

A timeless and much quoted Byron line. It continues with "Of cloudless nights and starry skies."

She was lovely as a flower, and, like a flower, she passed away
—Richard Le Gallienne

There is in true beauty, as in courage, something which narrow souls cannot dare to admire —William Congreve
In the original manuscript of *The Old Bachelor* the word 'something' was 'somewhat.'

A thing of beauty is a joy forever —John Keats
A Keats classic that embodies the rule that when it comes to including or implying 'like' or 'as,' discretion is best.

Women's beauty, like men's wit, is generally fatal to the owners —Lord Chesterfield
Had Chesterfield lived to become attuned to nonsexist language he might have eliminated the gender references as follows: "Beauty, like wit, is generally fatal to the owners."

Beginnings/Endings

BEGINNINGS/ENDINGS
SEE ALSO: SEX

Breaking off with a hard dry finality, like a human relationship
—Lawrence Durrell

[A distressing event] came like a door banging on to a silent room
—Hugh Walpole

Comes and goes like a cyclone —Marianne Hauser

Comes and goes like a fever —George Garrett

(My urge to gamble) comes and goes like hot flashes
—Tallulah Bankhead

Come to a final end like a step climbed or a text memorized
—John Cheever

[The ecstacies and tears of youth] die like the winds that blew the clouds from overhead —Noël Coward, lyrics for *Light Is the Heart*

Ebbing then flowing in again, like mud tides around a mollusc
—Julia O'Faolain

62

Finished, like the flipped page of a book (this day was finished ...)
—Isaac Bashevis Singer

- The first springs of great events, like those of great rivers, are often mean and little —Jonathan Swift

- It was over, gone like a furious gust of black wind
—William Faulkner

Leaving [a place to which one has become accustomed] is like tearing off skin —Larry McMurtry

- Like a horse breaking from the gate, my life had begun
—Scott Spencer

- Like some low and mournful spell, we whisper that sad word, "farewell" —Park Benjamin

Parted [husband and wife] as an arrow from the bowstring
—Amy Lowell

Parting is inevitably painful ... like an amputation
—Anne Morrow Lindbergh

(You and that money are going to be) separated like yolks and whites —Saul Bellow

Spent is my passion like a river dried up by the sun's fierce rays
—W. Somerset Maugham

Things [like, popularity] come and go, like the business cycle
—William Brammer

BEHAVIOR
SEE: ACTION, LIFE

BELIEF
SEE: POLITICS

BELONGING
SEE: COMPATIBILITY/INCOMPATIBILITY

BENDING/BENT

As crooked as a corkscrew —George Kaufman and Moss Hart

As crooked as a dog's elbow —F. T. Elworthy

As crooked as a ram's horn —Charles Caleb Colton

Bending from the waist as if he was going to close up like a jackknife —John Dos Passos

Bend like a finger joint —Charles Wright

Bend like sheets of tin —Palmer Cox

Bends with her laugh ... like a rubber stick being shaken —Alice McDermott

Bent as a country lane —John Wainwright

Bent double like a tree in a high wind —Caryl Phillips

Bent down like violets after rain —Thomas Bailey Aldrich

Bent like a birch ice-laden —James Agee

Bent like a bow —Aharon Megged
> A variation on the bent bow image from William McIlvanney's novel, *Laidlow:* "Arching his body like a bow."

Bent like a broken flower —Algernon Charles Swinburne

Bent like a rainbow —Robert Southey
> Another way to express this image is to be "Bent like a rainbow arch."

Bent ... like a soldier at the approach of an assault —Victor Hugo

Bent like a wishbone —William Kennedy

Bent slightly like a man who has been shot but continues to stand —Flannery O'Connor

(The headwaiter) bowed like a poppy in the breeze —Ogden Nash

Bows down like a willow tree in a storm —Erich Maria Remarque

Coiled like a fetus —William H. Gass
> A variation by Derek Lambert: "Curled up like a bulky fetus."

Coiled up like the letter 'S' —Damon Runyon

Crooked like a comma —Sharon Sheehe Stark

Curled himself like a comma into the waiting cab —William H. Hallhan

Curled like a ball —Sterling Hayden

Curled up in a ball like a wet puppy —Amos Oz

Curled up [in sleeping position] like a fist around an egg
    —Leonard Michaels

Curled up like a gun-dog —Colette

(Bent over your books) curled up like a porcupine with a bellyache
    —Marge Piercy

Curled up like fried bacon —Anon

Curling up like a small animal —Nina Bawden

Curling up like burning cardboard —Lawrence Durrell

[A cat] curls up like a dormer mouse —Jayne Anne Phillips

Drooped like a flower in the frost —John Greenleaf Whittier

Folded over like a ruler from the waist —William H. Gass

Folded up, like a marionette with cheap wooden hinges, and sat
    down —Graham Masterton

(Never will I be) gibbous like the moon —Diane Ackerman

Lean forward like firemen pulling a hose —Miller Williams

Tilting like a paper cutout —Susan Minot

Twisted as an old paint tube —Fannie Hurst

A very old lady, her back curved over like a snail's
    —Daphne Merkin

BEREAVEMENT
SEE: GRIEF

BEWILDERMENT
SEE: STRANGENESS

BICYCLING
SEE: SPORTS

BIGNESS
SEE: PHYSICAL APPEARANCE

BIGOTRY
SEE: INTOLERANCE

Birds

Bird, its little black feet tucked under its belly like miniature bombs
—Peter Meinke

Birds afloat, like a scarf —Babette Deutsch

Birds ... bobbed like clothespins on the telephone line
—Elizabeth Savage

Birds ... circling like black leaves —Hugh Walpole

Birds flew up like black gloves jerked from a line —Paul Theroux

Birds ... gliding like pieces of dark paper abandoned suddenly by an
erratic wind —John Rechy

Bird, shaped like the insides of a yawning mouth —Charles Simic

Birds in flight, fluid as music on a page —Anne Morrow Lindbergh

Birds ... like planes stacked up over the airport, circling until they get
a permission-to-land signal —Italo Calvino

Bird songs rang in the air like dropped coins —George Garrett

Birds rose into the air like blown leaves (at his approach)
—Margaret Millar

The birds sang as if every sparkling drop were a fountain of
inspiration to them —Charles Dickens

Birds ... they roll like a drunken fingerprint across the sky
—Richard Wilbur

A solid line of pelicans flew ... in graceful unison like a crew of
oarsman in a racing shell —George Garrett

Sparrows scatter like handfuls of gravel —William H. Gass

Storks and pelicans flew in a line like waving ribbons
—Hans Christian Andersen

Swans floated about like white lanterns —Lawrence Durrell

Swans go by like a snowy procession of Popes —George Garrett

Terns rise like seafoam from the breaking surf —Robert Hass

White gulls ... in such close formation they were like a cloud
—Phyllis Roberts

BIRTH
SEE: BEGINNINGS/ENDINGS, DEATH, LIFE

BITTERNESS
SEE: ANGER, FRIENDSHIP

BLACK
SEE: COLORS; DEJECTION

BLANKNESS
SEE: EMPTINESS

BLESSEDNESS
SEE: FORTUNE/MISFORTUNE

BLINDNESS
SEE: EYE(S)

BLUE
SEE: COLORS

BLUSHES
SEE: SHAME

BOATS
SEE: SEASCAPES

BODY
SEE ALSO: PHYSICAL APPEARANCE, SHOULDERS, STRENGTH, THINNESS

(A big soft) ass as wide as an axhandle —George Garrett

Body and mind, like man and wife, do not always agree to die together —Charles Caleb Colton

Body grown light as a shell, empty as a shell —Joyce Carol Oates

The body is like a piano. It is needful to have the instrument in good order —Henry Ward Beecher

The body, lady, is like a house: it don't go anywhere; but the spirit, lady, is like an automobile: always on the move
—Flannery O'Connor

Body ... light as milk —Philip Levine

Body like a block of granite —Brian Glanville

Body like a spring —Marguerite Duras

Body

Her body seemed somehow to hang on her, like somebody else's clothing —William McIlvanney

Her broad sexless body made her resemble a dilapidated Buddha —Ross Macdonald

Her firm protruding ass looked like a split peach —Steve Shagan

Hips like hills of sand —*Arabian Nights*

Hips like jugs —Eugene McNamara

His ancient, emaciated body looked as though it were already attacked by the corruption of the grave —W. Somerset Maugham

His body was covered with a dense mat of black hair. He looked like an overfed chimpanzee —Andrew Kaplan

His body waved like a flame in the breeze —Television obituary describing James Cagney's physical grace, 1986

His pectorals hung flabbily, like the breasts of an old woman —Gerald Kersh

It [worn body] was as if it were charred by a thunderbolt —Honoré de Balzac

Long body, devoid of developed muscles, like a long, limp sash —Yukio Mishima

Look like a hot-air balloon with insufficient ballast —Anna Quindlen, *New York Times*/Hers, March 27, 1986
> The cause for the hot-air balloon appearance is pregnancy.

(A man with) a middle like a flour bag —Sharon Sheehe Stark

(His body looked soft, his) waist puffing out like rising bread dough —Sue Grafton

We are bound to our bodies like an oyster to its shell —Plato

Weight was ... beginning to hang like slightly inferior clothing —William McIlvanney

(Jill Martin was what they call a healthy lady.) Well rounded, like something out of Rubens —Mike Fredman

(He was) wide as a door —Andre Dubus

BODY ORGANS
SEE: SEX

BOISTEROUSNESS
SEE: NOISE

BOLDNESS
SEE: COURAGE

BOOKS
SEE: READERS/READING

BOREDOM/BORING
SEE ALSO: LIFE

Bored as Greta Garbo —Alice McDermott

Boredom enveloped her like heavy bedding —Yukio Mishima

Boredom ... like a cancer in the breast —Evelyn Waugh

Boredom, like hookworm, is endemic —Beryl Markham

Boredom wafted from her like the scent of stale sweat —Anon

Boredom was increasing ... like a silent animal sadly rubbing itself
    against the sultry grass —Yukio Mishima

Bore me the same as watching an industrial training film, or hearing
    a lecture on the physics of the three-point stance —Richard Ford

Boring as airline food —Anon

Boring as going to the toilet —Sylvia Plath

Boring, like reading the *Life Cycle of the Hummingbird*
    —Dan Wakefield

Could feel his boredom like an actual presence, like a big German
    shepherd that must be fed and restrained —Marge Piercy

Life's tedious as a twice-told tale —William Shakespeare
            This famous simile also appeared in Homer's *Odyssey* in
            the format of a question, ''What's so tedious as a twice-
            told tale?.''

Yawns [caused by a dull discussion] inflated in his throat like
    balloons —Derek Lambert

BOUNCING
SEE: ROCKING AND ROLLING

BOXING AND WRESTLING
SEE: SPORTS

BRAIN
SEE: INTELLIGENCE, MIND

BRAVERY
SEE: COURAGE

BREASTS
SEE: BODY

BREVITY
SEE: TIME

BRIGHTNESS
SEE: SHINING

BROWN
SEE: COLORS

BUILDINGS
SEE: HOUSES

Burst

BURST

(Your unexpected letter has just) burst into my existence like a
     meteor into the sphere of a planet —William James letter from
     Dresden to Oliver Wendell Holmes, Jr., May 15, 1868

(My poor head would) burst like a dropped watermelon
     —Maya Angelou

Burst like a raw egg —William Diehl

Burst like a ripe seedpod —Beryl Markham

Burst like a thunderbolt —Alfred, Lord Tennyson

(Seeds) burst like bullets —Anne Sexton

[Details of an event would] burst open like garbage from a bag
     dropped from a height —Thomas Keneally

Burst out like a rash —Nadine Gordimer

Bursting like an overdone potato —Sir Arthur Conan Doyle

Comes apart like a slow-ripping seam —Sharon Sheehe Stark

70

The character coming apart in the author's story, *In the Surprise of Life*, is a girl who has been trying to contain her laughter.

Flashed [a remark] like a sheet of heat lightning —Rita Mae Brown

(The cursing and grumbling) flashed like a storm —Enid Bagnold

Like the buds let us burst —Ogden Nash

(He had a real gift for those flaring exclamations, those raucous) outbursts, like wounds suddenly opened —Romain Gary

Sputtering like a leaky valve —John Peter Toohey

(Our imaginations seem to have been) torn open ... as by a charge of dynamite —Dorothy Canfield Fisher

BUSINESS
SEE ALSO: SUCCESS/FAILURE

As oxygen is the disintegrating principle of life, working night and day to dissolve, separate, pull apart and dissipate, so there is something in business that continually tends to scatter, destroy and shift possession from this man to that. A million mice nibble eternally at every business venture —Elbert Hubbard

Business is like a man rowing a boat upstream. He has no choice; he must go ahead or he will go back —Lewis E. Pierson

Business is like oil. It won't mix with anything but business —J. Grahame

Business ... is very much like religion: it is founded on faith —William McFee

Business policy flows downhill from the mountain, like water —Anon

A business without customers is like a computer without bytes —Anon
    As the entries that follow show, this concept lends itself to many additional twists.

A business without customers is like a stage without light —Anon

A business without orders is like a room without windows —Anon

Buying and selling like a Rockefeller —Arthur A. Cohen

Business

A corporation is just like any natural person, except that it has no pants to kick or soul to damn —Ernst and Lindley
> Playwrights Ernst and Lindley wrote this simile to be spoken by a judge in their 1930's play *Hold Your Tongue*.

Corporate politics is like the days of Andrew Jackson, the spoils system —Rita Mae Brown

Customers drop away like tenpins —Anon

Inventory that just sits there like it's nailed to the floor —Anthony E. Stockanes

Nowadays almost every business is like show business, including politics, which has become more like show business than show business is —Russell Baker

Orders fell like stones —Anon

(Being in the microcomputer business is) risky, like going 55 miles an hour three feet from a cliff. If you make the wrong turn you're bankrupt so fast you don't know what hit you —George Morrow, quoted in *New York Times*, March 11, 1986 when his company went bankrupt

Some businesses are like desert flowers. They bloom overnight, and they're gone —George Morrow, quoted *New York Times*, March 11, 1986
> The first two words are transposed from "Computer companies" to generalize the comparison.

The tide of business, like the running stream, is sometimes high and sometimes low, a quiet ebb, or a tempestuous flow, and always in extreme —John Dryden

Tradespeople are just like gardeners. They take advantage of your not knowing —Agatha Christie

Busyness

BUSYNESS
SEE ALSO: ACTIVENESS, WORK

Busier than a cat covering shit on a marble slab —American colloquialism

Busier than a Gulag gravedigger —Joseph Wambaugh

Bustled about like so many ants roused by the approach of a foe —J. Hampden Porte

Ants rank with bees as a means to describe busyness. In modern day usage and literature the above is usually shortened; for example, "Busy as an ant" used by Ogden Nash in his poem *Children.*

(I've been) busy as a bartender on Saturday night —Irwin Shaw

Busy as a bee —Geoffrey Chaucer
> Chaucer's Old English version of what has become a commonly used expression read "Bisy as bees ben they."

Busy as a dog with fleas —Anon

Busy as a fiddler's elbow —Harry Prince

Busy as a hen with one chicken —John Ray's *Proverbs*
> To strengthen the impact of the simile there's, "Busy as a hen with ten chickens" and "As a hen with fifteen chickens" attributed to James Howell and "Busy as a hen with fifteen chickens in a barnyard."

Busy as an oven at Christmas —Michael Denham

Busy as ants in a breadbox —Anon

(I am) busy as a one-armed paperhanger with the itch
   —American colloquialism
> This is often attributed to Theodore Roosevelt who used it in a letter to his daughter. Some extensions on the one-armed paperhanger image include: "Busy as a one-armed paperhanger with the hives" (one of many common expressions in Carl Sandburg's *The People, Yes*), "Busy as a one-armed paperhanger with the seven-year itch" (H. W. Thompson, *Body, Boots and Britches*) and "Busy as a one-armed paperhanger with the nettle rash" (O. Henry, *The Ethics of a Pig*).

Busy as a one-legged man in an ass-kicking contest all week long
   —Pat Conroy

Busy as a pair of lizards on a warm brick —James Cain

Busy as a ticking clock —Anon

(Birds shrill and musical,) busy as bullets —John Farris

Busy as catbirds —Hilary Masters

Busy as jumper cables at a Mexican funeral —Thomas Zigal

Busyness

Busy as maggots —Marge Piercy

Busy as the day is long —Vincent Stuckey Lean

Busy as the devil in a gale of wind —Walter Scott

Get busy like a bomb —Erich Maria Remarque

Humming like a hive —John Gardner

Hurried ... like one who had always a multiplicity of tasks on hand
—Charlotte Brontë

[Being Secretary of Defense] is like getting a shave and having your
appendix out at the same time —Robert Lovett, *Saturday Evening
Post*, May 28, 1960

Like a squirrel in a cage, always in action —Aphra Behn

Like the bee, we should make our industry our amusement
—Oliver Goldsmith

CALUMNY
SEE: SLANDER

Calmness

CALMNESS

Calm as a bathtub —George Garrett

Calm as a Buddhist —Elizabeth Taylor

Calm as a convent —Anon

Calm as a cud-chewing cow —Harold Adams

Calm as a frozen lake when ruthless winds blow fiercely
—William Wordsworth

Calm as a gliding moon —Samuel Taylor Coleridge

Calm as a marble head —Eudora Welty

(I'm) calm as a Mediterranean sky —Frank Swinnerton

Calm as a mirror —Alexandre Dumas, père

(The sky was) calm as an aquarium —Antoine de Saint-Éxupéry

Calm as an iceberg —Gelett Burgess

Calm as a slumbering babe —Percy Bysshe Shelley

As part of our daily language this has evolved into "Calm as a sleeping baby."

(Said it as) calm as a virgin discussing flower arrangement
   —George MacDonald Fraser

Calm as beauty —Robert Browning

Calm as dewdrops —William Wordsworth

Calm as fate —John Greenleaf Whittier

Calm as glass —Charlotte Brontë

Calm as ice —Nathaniel Hawthorne

Calm as if she were sitting for her portrait —Henry James

Calm as in the days when all was right —Friedrich von Schiller

Calm as night —Victor Hugo

(Voice) calm as the deepest cold —Sharon Sheehe Stark

Calm as the sky after a day of storm —Voltaire

Calm as virtue —William Shakespeare

Calm as water in a glass—standing water in clean cut glass
   —Reynolds Price

Calm descended (on the pool hall) as nerve shattering as if the (long barnlike) room were the ship from which Jonah had been cast into the sea —Flannery O'Connor

Calmed down, like a Corinthian column —John Ashbery

A calm ... like the deep sleep which follows an orgy —Mark Twain

Cold as cucumbers —Beaumont and Fletcher
      In its original meaning this referred to sexual coldness. As currently used it means being calm, collected, or "Cool as a cucumber." Poet Stevie Smith used the simile as a title for a poem which begins with this and two other clichés to describe the subject of the poem, a girl named Mary: "Cool as a cucumber calm as a mill pond sound as a bell was Mary." (Ed: The quote from the Smith poem has no commas!)

Cool and collected as a dean sitting in his deanery —Ogden Nash

75

Cool and ordinary as a gallon of buttermilk —Borden Deal

Cool as a Buddha —Jan Epton Seale
> The simile, from a short story about a new mother entitled *Reluctant Madonna*, reads as follows in full context: "Christie intends to be cool as a Buddha about this baby. Unflappable."

Cool as a cop with a clipboard —Gary Gildner

Cool as a cube of cucumber on ice —Carl Sandburg
> This extension of the familiar "Cool as a cucumber" is particularly apt in Sandburg's epic, *The People, Yes,* which beautifully and cleverly incorporates many familiar similes.

Cool as a frozen daiquiri —Linda Barnes

Cool as an Easter lily —Erich Maria Remarque

Cool as a quarterback —Dan Wakefield

(He was) cool as a refrigerator —R.A.J. Walling

Cool as a veteran horse race jockey —Carl Sandburg

Cool as lettuce —Jay Parini

(He's as) cool as the other side of your pillow
> —Merlin Olsen, NBC-TV broadcaster, about Ken O'Brien, quarterback for the Jets, January, 1987

Expression ... as calm and collected as that of a doctor by a patient's bedside —Stefan Zweig

Felt a certain calm fall over me like a cloak —R. Wright Campbell

Have kept composure, like captives who would not talk under torture —Richard Wilbur

His calmness was like the sureness of money in the bank —Anzia Yezierska

Looked as cool as a yellow diamond —Robert Campbell

Looking calm as an eggshell —Edith Wharton

(The April morning) mellow as milk —Sharon Sheehe Stark

Mellow as moonlight —Slogan, Vogan Candy Co.

Mellow as old brandy —Anon

Mild as cottage cheese —Stephen Vincent Benét

Mild as milk —Dame Edith Sitwell

Nonchalant as a shoplifter in the checkout line —Donald McCaig

The sea was calm like milk and water —Isak Dinesen

The sense of rest, of having arrived at the long-promised calm
centre, filled him like a species of sleep —John Updike

Serene as a man who has just got a promotion and raise
—Geoffrey Wolff

Stayed calm, like a hero before the battle when all the cameras are
on him —Clancy Sigal

(Your opinion at the moment) worries me exactly as much as
dandruff would a chopped-off head —William McIlvanney

CANDOR
SEE ALSO: SECRECY,

About as sincere as the look upon the face of an undertaker
conducting a nine-hundred-dollar funeral —H. L. Mencken

As candid as the C.I.A. —Anon

As devoted to candor as a high school valedictorian —Jonathan Valin

As forthcoming as *Pravda* —Joseph Wambaugh

As frank as a candid camera shot —Anon

As open [about revealing self] as an unsteamed clam —Elyse Sommer

As revealing as a locked diary —Anon

Candid as mirrors —Robert G. Ingersoll

Direct as a bullet —Flannery O'Connor

Phony as a laugh track —Vincent Canby, about the movie *Murphy's
Romance, New York Times*, January 17, 1986

Sincerity is like traveling on a plain beaten road, which commonly
brings a man sooner to his journey's end than by-ways in which
men often lose themselves —John Tillotson

Took off the mask of tranquility she had worn ... like an actress returning weary to her room after a trying fifth act and falling half-dead upon a couch, while the audience retains an image of her to which she bears not the slightest resemblance
—Honoré de Balzac

(You get right) to the point ... like a knife in the heart
—Harvey Fierstein
Fierstein's simile is a line from *La Cage aux Folles*, the musical based on Jean Poiret's play by the same name.

Two-sided, like Janus —L. P. Hartley

CAPABILITY
SEE: ABILITY

CAREFULNESS
SEE: ATTENTION

CELEBRITY
SEE: FAME

CERTAINTY

Absolute as a miser's greed —Anon

An absolute, like the firmness of the earth —Tom Wolfe

Almost as predictable as the arrival of solstice and equinox
—Russell Baker, *New York Times*/Observer, September 17, 1986
Baker's comparison referred to Chief-Justice-to-be William Rehnquist's judicial opinions.

As certain as a gun —Samuel Butler

As certain as beach traffic in July —Anon

As certain as bodies moved with greater impulse, progress more rapidly than those moved with less —Voltaire

As certain as death and taxes —Daniel Defoe
Often attributed to Benjamin Franklin, the simile continues to be popular, with many humorous twists such as "Certain as death and hay-fever," used in Philip Barry's 1923 play, *You and I*.

As certain as dye penetrates cotton —Daniela Gioseffi
The simile, from a poem, continues with "The orange is a part of the living animal."

As certain as end-of-the-season inventories —Anon

As certain as June graduates scanning the want ads —Anon

As certain as leaves falling in September —Anon

As certain as lines at return counters after Christmas —Anon

As certain as rise of taxi meter —Anon

As certain as that a crooked tree will have a crooked shadow
    —Anon

As certain as that bread crumbs will attract a flock of pigeons
    —Anon

As certain as that leaves will fall in autumn —Anon

As certain as that night succeeds the day —George Washington

As certain as that your shadow will follow you —Anon

As certain as the morning —Thomas Wolfe

As certain as the sunrise —Anon

As certain as thunderclap following lightning —Anon

As certain as wrinkles —Anon

As certainly as day follows day —Anon

As certainly as Segovia had been born to finger a fretboard or Willie
    Mays to swing a bat —T. Coraghessan Boyle

As inevitable as a dog at a hydrant —Anon

As inevitable as the turning of the earth on which you stand
    —Harvey Swados

As sure as a club —Mary Hedin

As sure as a goose goes barefoot
    —American colloquialism, attributed to Northeast

As sure as a tested hypothesis —Lorrie Moore

As sure as a wheel is round —American colloquialism

As sure as behave and misbehave —John Ciardi

As sure as day —William Shakespeare

Certainty

As sure as death —William Shakespeare
> Ben Jonson's use of this same simile in *Every Man in His Humor* if not the first, is certainly one of the earliest encountered.

As sure as meat will fry
> —American colloquialism, attributed to Southeast

As sure as rain —Ben Ames Williams
> A more specific variation of this is "Sure as rain in April."

As sure as shooting —Anon
> This common expression probably stems from the no longer used "Sure as a gun," variously attributed to the poet John Dryden and the playwright William Congreve.

As sure as snakes crawl
> —American colloquialism, attributed to Midwest

As surely as that two ends of a seesaw cannot both be elevated at the same time —Alexander Woolcott

As surely as the eye tends to be long-sighted in the sailor and short-sighted in the student —Herbert Spencer

As surely as the harvest comes after the seedtime —John Brown

As surely as the tree becomes bulky when it stands alone and slender if one of a group —Herbert Spencer

As surely as water will wet us, as surely as fire will burn —Rudyard Kipling

As unpreventable as blinking your eyes when a light flashes suddenly —Anon

Certain things will follow inevitably, just like a little trail of horseshit behind a fat old draught horse —George Garrett

Definite as a counter-signed contract —Anon

Inevitable as a comet's return —Marge Piercy

Inevitable as noon —Thomas Wolfe

Inevitable as the snick of a mouse-trap —Carl Sandburg

Inevitable ... like a stone rolling down a mountain —Mary Gordon

Predictable as a physical law —Charles Johnson

80

(The man was as) predictable as rainwater seeking a low spot
    —William Beechcroft

Predictable as the prints left by a three-legged dog
    —Sharon Sheehe Stark

Predictable as the arrival of Monday morning —Harry Prince

Predictable as the menu at charity dinner —Anon

Predictable, like a diplomatic reception —A. Alvarez

Secure as an obituary in the *Times* —Marge Piercy

So predictable ... just like tuning in the same radio station every
    night —Lee Smith
            A character in Smith's novel, *The Last Day the Dogbushes
            Bloomed*, uses this simile to describe a dull suitor.

A sweet and sure annuity; it's like taking a bath at Fort Knox
    —Moss Hart
            This line from *Light Up the Sky* likens a national tour for an
            ice show to sure-fire success.

CHANGE
SEE ALSO: PERMANENCE

Anticipate change as though you had left it behind you
    —Rainer Maria Rilke

Any essential reform must, like charity, begin at home —John Macy

Changeable as a baby's diaper —Anon

Changeable as the weather
    —American colloquialism, attributed to New England
            The variations this has sprouted typify the simple simile's
            extension through more particularization. Some examples:
            "Changeable/unpredictable as April weather or as the sky
            in April" and "Changeable like Midwestern weather—
            violent and highly volatile."

(Her expression would) change as quickly as a sky with clouds racing
    across the moon —Madeleine L'Engle

(Hopes) changed daily like the stock market —Margaret Millar
            In her novel, *The Murder of Miranda Millar*, expands the
            simile as follows: "Gaining a few points here, losing a few
            there."

Change

Changed his mind regularly, like shirts —Anon

Changed ... like the shift of key in a musical score
   —Lawrence Durrell

Changed moods like a strobe of shifting lights —Alvin Boretz

Changeful as a creature of the tropical sea lying under a reef
   —Saul Bellow

A change, like a shift of wind, overcame the judge —Truman Capote

Change of attitude ... like a fish gliding with a flick of its tail, now
   here, now there —Jean Rhys

(Life) changed like fluffy clouds —Rita Mae Brown

Changes ... as breath-taking as a Celtics fast break
   —Larry McCoy, *Wall Street Journal* article about changes at CBS
   network, December 4, 1986

Changes his mood like a wizard —Joan Chase

Ever changing, like a joyless eye that finds no objects worth its
   constancy —Percy Bysshe Shelley

Everything changed ... like the rug, the one that gets pulled
   —Alberto Alvaor Rios

Fickle as the sunlight —William Alfred

Fickle as the wind —Horace

Get used to [changes] ... like listening to your own heart
   —Marguerite Duras

In our changes we should move like a caterpillar, part of which is
   stationary in every advance, not like the toad —James A. Pike
         Reverend Pike's advice was aimed at preventing anxiety.

[Moving from slow to fast-paced life] it was like stepping from a
   gondola to an ocean steamer —Edith Wharton

[Personality of a character] metamorphoses ... like a butterfly bursting
   out of a cocoon —Frank Rich, *New York Times,* January 21, 1986

Mood ... swinging like an erratic pendulum from being hurt to
   hurting —Ross Macdonald

82

Most reformers, like a pair of trousers on a windy clothesline, go
through a vast deal of vehement motion but stay in the same
place —Austin O'Malley

Popped out and disappeared like a heat rash —George Garrett

Sailing through change as effortlessly as gulls —Gail Godwin

(And all the shapes of this grand scenery) shifted like restless clouds
before the steadfast sun —Percy Bysshe Shelley

(Streets) shift like dunes —Lisa Ress

The switch is like going from Star Wars to stagecoaches
—David "Doc" Livingston, commenting on enforced job switch
(from controlling air traffic to controlling commuter trains), as
quoted in *New York Times* article about fired air controllers by N.
R. Kleinfield, September 28, 1986

Up and down like mercury —May Sarton

(Moods may) veer as erratically as the wind —Milton R. Sapirstein

CHAOS
SEE: ORDER/DISORDER

CHARACTER
SEE ALSO: PERSONAL TRAITS

As the sun is best seen at its rising and setting, so men's native
dispositions are clearest seen when they are children and when
they are dying —Robert Boyle

A character is like an acrostic ... read it forward, backward, or
across, it still spells the same thing —Ralph Waldo Emerson

Character is like a tree, and reputation like its shadow. The shadow
is what we think of it; the tree is the real thing
—Abraham Lincoln

Character is like white paper; if once blotted, it can hardly ever be
made to appear white as before —Joel Hawes

A character, like a kettle, once mended always wants mending
—Jean-Jacques Rousseau

Character, like porcelain ware, must be painted before it is glazed.
There can be no change after it is burned in
—Henry Ward Beecher

Character

A man of words and not of deeds is like a garden full of weeds. And when the weeds begin to grow, it's like a garden full of snow —Nursery rhyme
> This dates back to the eighteenth century.

The reputation of a man is like his shadow, gigantic when it precedes him, and pigmy in its proportions when it follows —Alexandre de Talleyrand

Some people, like modern shops, hang everything in their windows and when one goes inside nothing is to be found —Berthold Auerbach

The soundness of his nature was like the pure paste under a fine glaze —Edith Wharton

A vein of iron buried inside her moral frame, like a metal armature inside a clay statue —Carlos Baker

Your moral character must be not only pure, but, like Caesar's wife, unsuspected —Lord Chesterfield

CHARITABLENESS
SEE: KINDNESS

CHASTITY
SEE: VIRTUE

CHEAPNESS
SEE: THRIFT

CHEEKS
SEE: FACE(S), SKIN

CHEERFULNESS
SEE: HAPPINESS, SMILES

CHILDISHNESS
SEE: YOUTH

CHILDREN
SEE: CLINGING

CHIN
SEE: FACE(S), MOUTH

CHURCHES
SEE: HOUSES

CITIES
SEE: PLACES

CITY/STREETSCAPES
SEE: PLACES

CLEANLINESS/UNCLEANLINESS
SEE: ORDER/DISORDER

CLEVERNESS
SEE ALSO: INTELLIGENCE

Adroit as a rhinoceros —Franklin P. Adams

Brains like the frogs, dispersed all over his body —Charles Dickens

Clever as a bird-dog
    —American colloquialism, attributed to New England

Clever as sin —Rudyard Kipling

Crafty as a new religious convert pledged to win over a sinner
    —Gloria Norris

Crafty as an exorcist —Miles Gibson

Crafty as the sea —W. B. Yeats

Cunning as a dead pig, but not half so honest —Jonathan Swift

Cunning is a sort of short-sightedness —Joseph Addison

Has as many tricks as a bear —John Ray's *Proverbs*

Hinted with the delicacy of a lilac bud —Sinclair Lewis

Ingenious as magicians —Delmore Schwartz

Like rats, his wits were beginning to busy themselves again
    —Walter De La Mare

Little clevernesses are like half-ripened plums, only good eating on
    the side that has had a glimpse of the sun —Henry James

Played on his misfortune as on a cello —Marguerite Yourcenar

Sharp and bright as a blade of sunlight —Alice Walker

Sharp as a cut-throat razor —Donald Seaman

Cleverness

Sharp as a knife
—American colloquialism, attributed to New England
An equally popular variation, also attributed to New England folklore: "Sharp as a razor."

Sharp as a needle —Anon
Common usage has made this interchangeable with "Sharp as a pin." A variation of more recent vintage, "Sharp as a tack," has become a cliche in its own right.

Sharp as mustard —Ogden Nash
In Nash's poem, *The Tale of the Custard Dragon,* the descriptive frame of reference is a little dog.

Shrewd as a barrel-load of monkeys —Robin Sheiner

Shrewd as a sparrow —Janet Flanner

Shrewdness is often annoying, like a lamp in the bedroom
—Ludwig Boerne

Sly and slick as a varmint —Robert Penn Warren

(Every move had been as stealthy and as) sly as a hungry coyote
—William Humphrey

Smart as a whip —Anon
Used to the point of abuse since the seventeenth century. A variation in keeping with the phrase's origin in the smarting pain caused by a whip: "Sharp as a whiplash."

Smart as new nails —Sharon Sheehe Stark

Tricky as palmistry —Karl Shapiro

Wily as a fox —John Clarke
The fox continues to be a favorite link to clever, crafty behavior. Often 'cunning' is substituted for 'wiley', and the fox is not just any fox but "An old one."

Clinging

CLINGING
SEE ALSO: PEOPLE, INTERACTION

Adhere like lint —Anon

Adhere like ticks to a sheep's back —Maurice Hewlett

Adhering ... like shipwrecked mariners on a rock —J. M. Barrie

Clinging ... like lichen to a rock —Ross Macdonald

LIKE RATS, HIS WITS WERE BEGINNING TO BUSY
THEMSELVES AGAIN

Clinging

Clinging like a limpet in the heaviest sea —William H. Hallhan

Clinging ... like a monkey-on-a-stick —Julia O'Faolain

Clinging ... stupidly, like a mule —Joseph Conrad

Clinging to her like chewing gum to a boot sole —Julian Gloag

Cling ... like a wart —Tony Ardizzone
>The simile, as used in *The Heart of the Order*, describes the way a cowboy clings to the back of a bull.

Cling like chewing gum to a shoe sole —Anon

Cling like ivy —Robert Burton

Clings fiercely to all his titles, like an old soldier to his medals —Robert Traver

Clings to as a baby clings to its pacifier —Anon

Clings to me like a bed-bug —Maxim Gorky

Cling to (as to another person) as an exhausted man does to a rock —Brooks Bakeland

Cling to ... like a drowning person to a piece of timber —Isak Dinesen

Cling to like a leech
—American colloquialism, attributed to New England

Cling to like a vine
—American colloquialism, attributed to New England
>A variation is to "Cling like ivy."

Cling to ... like tenacious barnacles upon rocks —Mary Ellen Chase

Clung like a basket enfolding a tithe offering —Arthur A. Cohen

Clung [to an idea] like a shipwrecked sailor hanging on to the only solid part of his sinking universe —Marguerite Yourcenar

(The baby) clung like a sloth —Louise Erdrich

Clung ... like a tarantula —Terry Southern

(Rancour) clung like curses on them —Percy Bysshe Shelley

Clung ... like magnet to steel —T. Buchanan Read

Clung the way a tree animal clings to a branch —Rachel Ingalls

Clung to each other like double sweet peas —*A Broken-Hearted Gardner*, anonymous 19th century verse

Clung together hand in hand like men overboard —George Garrett

Clung to her like a man on a swaying subway car whose grip on the overhead rail keeps him from tumbling to the floor —Paul Reidinger

Clung to his consciousness like a membrane —John Updike

Clutched [at her blanket] as a faller clutches at the turf on the edge of a cliff —Virginia Woolf

Clutching hold of ... with the grasp of a drowning man —Charles Dickens

Clutching is the surest way to murder love, as if it were a kitten, not to be squeezed so hard, or a flower to fade in a tight hand —May Sarton

(There she sat), glued to the tube like a postage stamp —A. Alvarez

Gummed together like wet leaves —Lawrence Durrell

[A term to describe a problem] had stuck with him like day-old oatmeal —T. Glen Coughlin

Hang on like a summer cold —Anon

Hang on ... like a tick —Rita Mae Brown

Hang on to ... [some small, unimportant point] ... like a dog to a bone —Barbara Greene, on her cousin Graham Greene
Some people like to get more specific; for example, "Hang on to ... like a terrier" found in Iris Murdoch's novel, *The Good Apprentice.*

Hang over like a heavy curtain —Anon

Hang over like a layer of smog —Anon

Hang over like crepe —Anon

Hang over like murder on a guilty soul —Sciller

Hang together like burrs —John Ray's *Proverbs*

Hung like bees on mountain-flowers —Percy Bysshe Shelley

(The thought ...) hung like incense around Francis
    —Dorothy Canfield Fisher

It [something that had been said] stuck up in the girl's consciousness like a fallen meteor —John Cheever

(A scar of horror, if not of guilt), lay consciously on his breast, like the scarlet letter —George Santayana

Clinging ... like starving children to a teat —Margaret Millar

Like swarming bees they clung —Lord Byron

Remained like a black cloud —Frank Swinnerton

She clings to me like a fly to honey —Anton Chekhov

She clung to him like a shadow —Margaret Mitchell

She's coiled around her family and her house like a python
    —Jane Bowles

She was like a sea-anemone—had only to be touched to adhere to what touched her —John Fowles

Sticking to [another person's side] like a melting snowbank
    —Marge Piercy

Stick like a wet leaf —Anton Chekhov

Sticks like a burr to a cow's tail —Edward Noyes Westcott

Sticks like crazy glue —Anon

(My touch) sticks like mud —Marge Piercy

Stick together like overcooked pasta —Elyse Sommer

Stick together like peanut butter and jelly —Ed McBain

Sticky as fire —Terry Bisson

Sticky as rubber cement —Anon

Stuck ... like a barnacle to a ship's keel, or a snail to a door, or a little bunch of toadstools to the stem of a tree —Charles Dickens

Stuck to [him or her] like shit to a blanket —American colloquialism

Stuck to my side like a lung infected with pleurisy —Patrick White

Stuck with ... like gas on water —Will Weaver

Tenacious as a Boston bull —Anon

They [people who cling to outmoded political concepts] are like degenerates who are color blind, except that they see something which is NOT there, instead of failing to see something which is —Janet Flanner

They [narrator's daughters] cling together like Hansel and Gretel —Ogden Nash

Tied to each other back to back [long-married people] ... like dogs unable to disengage after coupling —Lawrence Durrell

CLOSENESS
SEE ALSO: COMPATIBILITY, FRIENDSHIP

Always together ... like Siamese twins —Nina Bawden

[Cid and his wife Juena] are like the nail [fingernail] and the flesh —*The Lay of the Cid*, epic poem
> According to a grad student at SUNY, Stony Brook, NY, this is the only simile in this 3500-verse epic poem dating back to 1140 a.d.

As close to him as sticking plaster —Cornell Woolrich

Close as an uncracked nut —Play: *All Vows Kept*, Anon

Close as a dead heat —Anon

Close as fingers inside a pair of mittens —Anon

Close as flies in a bottle —Shana Alexander

Close as the bark to a tree —Sir Charles Sedley
> This simile is also used to describe stinginess.

Close as the 'cu' in cucumbers —Anon

Close as the gum on a postage stamp —Anon

Close as two peas in a pod —H. I. Phillips
> Common usage has created twists such as "Close as two peas on a plate."

Close like exiles from a remote and forgotten land —A. R. Guerney, Jr.

Close together as the two shells of an oyster —Leonard McNally

Closeness

Get as close as an Eskimo does to a fire in his igloo in the tundra
—Anon, from radio broadcast

His face was so close to hers that it was out of focus, like a cloud
passing in front of the sun —Michael Korda

Inseparable as a baseball fan and a bag of peanuts —Anon

Inseparable as finger and thumb —George Farquhar

Inseparable as a shadow to a body —Robert Burton

Inseparable as Don Quixote and Sancho Panza —Anon

Inseparable like ivy, which grows beautifully so long as it twines
around a tree, but is of no use when it is separated —Molière
The original has been transcribed from "A woman is like
ivy" for a less gender-oriented interpretation.

Intimate as two sardines in a can —Anon

Near as the end of one's nose —Anon

Near as twilight is to darkness —Thomas Paine

Stayed as close to that woman as a pimple —Charles Johnson

They're as thick as three in a bed —Scottish saying

They were all standing around him thick as bees —Cornell Woolrich

(It is proper that families remain) thick like good soup
—J. P. Donleavy

We were like two kernels in one almond —Sadi

Wrapped tight an as eggroll —Donald McCaig

CLOTHING

Clothing

A little-girl-type sundress that was about as sexy as a paper bag
—Dan Wakefield

All dressed up like Christmas trees —Rosamund Pilcher

A baggy blue flowered housedress that looked like old slipcovers
—Louise Erdrich

A bikini is like a barbed-wire fence. It protects the property without
obstructing the view —Joey Adams

A BIKINI IS LIKE A BARBED-WIRE FENCE. IT PROTECTS
THE PROPERTY WITHOUT OBSTRUCTING THE VIEW

Clothing

Blouses thin as the film of tears in your eyes —Bin Ramke

Clothes, pressed stiff as cardboard —Jay Parini

Coat like a discarded doormat —T. Coraghessan Boyle

A dark blue suit so rigidly correct that it looked like a uniform
——Harvey Swados

Draped in a muumuu that covered her like a Christo curtain
shrouding a California mountain —Paul Kuttner

Dressed all in brown, like a rabbit —Anon

Dressed as if she were going to a coronation —Shelby Hearon

Dressed in black jersey, without ornament, like a widow
——Ross Macdonald

Dressed like a bookie —Gavin Lyall

Dressed like a Hollywood bit player hoping to be discovered leaning
on a bar —Robert Campbell
> In his novel, *In La-La Land We Trust*, Campbell expands
> upon this simile for several sentences with details about
> the outfit.

Dressed up like a dog's dinner —American colloquialism
> This means to be overdressed, usually badly so.

Dresses conservatively as a corpse —Harvey Swados

(The Queen) dresses like a whistlestop town librarian
——Stephen Longstreet

Dresses like he's got a charge at Woolworth's —Robert B. Parker
> With names of stores, companies and products constantly
> changing, Woolworth's may not always be synonymous
> with cheap; however, the simile could live on with an
> appropriate substitution.

Dress ... gone limp in the heat, like a wilted plant —Louise Erdrich

A dress like ice-water —F. Scott Fitzgerald

Dress that was as small as scarf —Laurie Colwin

Fancy as a rooster up for the fair —Linda Hogan

Garments as weathered as an old sail —George Eliot

A girl who dressed like an Arabian bazaar —T. Coraghessan Boyle

Her white silk robe flowed over her like a milk shower
    —Harold Adams

He was dressed for this death-watch job [hotel desk clerk] as if for a
    lively party —Christopher Isherwood

In her orange fringed poncho she looked like a large teepee
    —Michael Malone

Ladies wrapped like mummies in shawls with bright flowers on them
    —Virginia Woolf

Like her husband she carried clothes, carried them as a train carries
    passengers —Henry James

Looks like she's wearing her entire wardrobe all at once and all of it
    hand-me-downs from someone bigger than she is
    —Julie Salamon, describing appearance of character played by
    Debra Winger in the movie, *Black Widow, Wall Street Journal,*
    February 6, 1987

A party frock sticking out all around her [a little girl's] legs like a
    lampshade —Joyce Cary

Peeled off his trousers like shucking corn —Rita Mae Brown

Ragged as a scarecrow —Thomas Heywood

Shirt [heavily patched] lays on his body like a ratty dishtowel
    —Carolyn Chute

Skirts swirling like a child's pennant caught in a stiff breeze
    —Tony Ardizzone

Slickers [worn by cops] that shone like gun barrels
    —Raymond Chandler
        Raymond Chandler used this simile in his early days as a
        pulp magazine writer (*Killer in the Rain, Black Mask
        Magazine,* 1935), and later in his novel, *The Big Sleep.*

Starched clothes sat in the grass like white enameled teapots
    —Isaac Babel

[Formal attire] suited them the way an apron suits a grizzly bear
    —William McIlvanney

Sweater as sopped as wet sheep —Susan Minot

Clothing

Tailored and bejeweled like a pampered gigolo —James Mills

Tightly wrapped in a red skirt like a Christmas present
    —Helen Hudson

Trousers pressed as sleek as a show dog's flank —R. V. Cassill

A wedding gown like a silver cloud —Mazo De La Roche

A white robe, flowing, like spilled milk —Paige Mitchell

Wide sleeves fluttering like wings —Marcel Proust

Wore his clothes as if they were an official uniform
    —Vernon Scannell

You wear your clothes as if you want to be helped out of them
    —W. P. Kinsella

Zipped and buttoned into a polyester pantsuit, she was like a
    Christmas stocking half-filled with fruit —Mary Ward Brown

CLOTHING ACCESSORIES
SEE: JEWELRY

CLOTHING, ITS FIT
SEE: CLOTHING

Cloud(s)

CLOUD(S)
SEE ALSO: SKY

A cloud like a torn shirt —Katherine Mansfield

Clouds are like Holy Writ, in which theologians cause the faithful or
    the crazy to see anything they please —Voltaire

Clouds ... as white as leghorn feathers —Saul Bellow

The cloud showed motion within, like an old transport truck piled
    high with crate on crate of sleepy white chickens —Eudora Welty

The clouds hung above the mountains like puffs of white smoke left
    in the wake of a giant old-fashioned choochoo train
    —Sue Grafton

The clouds lie over the chiming sky ... like the dustsheets over a
    piano —Dylan Thomas

Clouds like a marble frieze across the sky —Helen Hudson

Clouds like cruisers in the heaven —Edna O'Brien

Clouds like dark bruises were massing and swelling [on the horizon]
   —George Garrett

Clouds ... like drowsy lambs around a tree —Romain Gary

(The sky turned sooty with) clouds like enormous thumbprints
   —Helen Hudson

Clouds like lights among great tombs —Wallace Stevens

Clouds like tattered fur —Jean Thompson

Clouds piling up like a bubble bath —Sue Grafton

Clouds, plump and heavy as dumplings —Anthony E. Stockanes

The clouds were asses' ears —Dylan Thomas

The clouds were huddled on the horizon like dirty sheep from the
   steppes —Joyce Renwick

The clouds were like an alabaster palace —Johnny Mercer, from his
   1954 lyrics for *Midnight Sun*

The clouds were like old fiddles —Joyce Cary

A few clouds were drawn against the light like streaks of lead
   pencils —John Cheever

Fluffy white clouds, like flecks of lather, were floating across the sky
   —Alexander Solzhenitsyn

Clouds ... wild and black and rolling like locomotives
   —W. P. Kinsella

Frail clouds like milkweed floss —John Dos Passos

Gleaming, white fluffy clouds peeped over the hills ... like kittens
   —Stella Benson

High fat clouds like globs of whipped cream —William Faulkner

Like a grave face, lit by some last, sad thought, a cloud, tinged by
   the fading glow of sunset —John Hall Wheelock

Like blurred lenses, winter clouds cast a shade over the sun
   —Truman Capote

(Above the falling sun,) like visible winds the clouds are streaked
   and spun —Roy Fuller

97

Cloud(s)

Little white clouds ... like a row of ballet-girls, dressed in white, waiting at the back of the stage, alert and merry, for the curtain to go up —W. Somerset Maugham

Little white clouds like flags were whipped out in the scented wind —Paul Horgan

Little white puffs of cloud ... like a cat steeped in milk —W. P. Kinsella

A long thin cloud crossed it [the moon] slowly, drawing itself out like a name being called —Eudora Welty

Low clouds, drooping at the edges like felt, sailed over the woods —Boris Pasternak

Low on the horizon hung a fugitive wisp of cloud, spiraled and upthrust like a genie emerging from a bottle —Robert Traver

A massive cloud like dirty cotton —William Faulkner

One cloud intruded [into the blue of the sky] puffy, precise, as if piped from a pastry bag —Margaret Sutherland

Parcels of clouds lying against the mountainside like ghosts of dead mackerel —Paul Theroux

A single puff of cloud so still, it seems as if it had been painted there —Delmore Schwartz

Small thin clouds like puffs of frosty breath —Joyce Cary

Some small clouds, like rosy petals, seemed to his eyes to be dancing, gently and carefully, against the blue —Hugh Walpole

They [the clouds] peel the morning like a fruit —Lawrence Durrell

When clouds appear like rocks and towers, the earth's refreshed by frequent showers —English weather rhyme

White and fluffy clouds ... one looked like a fish and one looked like a movie star, all curvy, and another looked like Santa Claus gone wrong —Lee Smith

Coldness

COLDNESS
SEE ALSO: REMOTENESS

(There was) a certain coldness, like that of a spinster about her —Boris Pasternak

Behave exactly like a block of ice
    —Noël Coward, lyrics for "I'm So In Love"

The chill in the air was like a constant infinitely small shudder
    —M. J. Farrell

(Some laughs are as) cold and meaningless as yesterday's buckwheat
    pancake —Josh Billings
            In Billings' phonetic dialect 'as' was written as 'az.'

Cold as a dead man's nose —William Shakespeare

Cold as a fish —American colloquialism, attributed to New England

Cold as a fish caught through the ice —F. van Wyck Mason

Cold as a hole in the ice —Bertold Brecht

(It grew as) cold as a key —Thomas Heywood

Cold as a lizzard —Walter Savage Landor
            In one of Landor's *Conversation* pieces, he has Fra Filippo
            Lippi commenting to Pope Eugenius IV that while an
            ordinary person could use an expression like "Cold as ice,
            a true poet would reach for more originality." The above is
            one suggestion, "Cold as a lobster" is another.

Cold as a miser's heart —Donald Seaman

[A smile] cold as a moan —Marge Piercy

Cold as a murder's heart —Richard Ford

Cold as an igloo —Reynolds Price

Cold as any stone —William Shakespeare

Cold ... as a pane of glass —Reynolds Price

Cold as a snowman's dick —William H. Gass

(A kiss) cold as bacon —Joyce Cary

Cold as charity —Anon
            An English phrase in use since the seventeenth century.

Cold as coldest hell —Sylvia Berkman
            In a short story entitled *Who Killed Cock Robin*, the simile
            describes a character's personality and continues as
            follows: "Cruel to every fingernail, and invariably polite."

Cold as dew to dropping leaves —Percy Bysshe Shelley

Cold as fears —Algernon Charles Swinburne

(I felt as) cold as Finnegan's feet (the day they buried him)
    —Raymond Chandler

Cold as if I had swallowed snowballs —William Shakespeare
        A variation of this snowball simile from *The Merry Wives of Windsor* is from another Shakespeare play, *Pericles:* "She sent him away as cold as a snowball."

(Your heart would be as heavy and) cold as iron shackles
    —George Garrett

Cold as Monday morning's barrenness —F. D. Reeve

Cold as moonlight —Yvor Winters

(Face) cold as newsprint —Philip Levine

(Eyes) cold as river ice —Davis Grubb

Cold as snakes —American colloquialism, attributed to Northeast

(Men) cold as spring water —Julia O'Faolain

(The wet air was as ...) cold as the ashes of love
    —Raymond Chandler

Cold as the cold between the stars —Terry Bisson

Cold as the north side of a grave stone in winter —Proverb

Cold as the snow —Lewis J. Bates

Cold as the tomb of Christ —Maxwell Anderson

Colder than a banker's heart —William Diehl

Colder than a dead lamb's tail —Anon

Colder than a lawyer's heart —George V. Higgins

Colder than a witch's tits
    —American colloquialism, attributed to the South
        Like many regional expressions that gained national currency during World War II, this one is often referred to as an Army expression.

(It was) colder than ice —Hans Christian Andersen

Whether used as a pure simile "Cold as ice" or as cited above, the linking of snow and ice to cold has become as "Common as snowflakes in winter." A story in the January 23, 1987 edition of the *New York Times* about a planned freedom march in Atlanta was highlighted with a blurb stating "We are going to march if it's cold as ice ... " proving once again that even without a new twist, a simile usually wins the spotlight.

Cold like a sea mist and as ungraspable —Sylvia Townsend Warner

Cold [in manner] like Christmas morning —Grace Paley

The cold was like a sleep —Wallace Stevens

The cold was like a thick vast sleep —Davis Grubb

Cool and smooth, like the breath of an air conditioner
    —T. Coraghessan Boyle

Cool as a snowbank —Louisa May Alcott

(Her bare arms and shoulders felt as) cool as marble —Leo Tolstoy

(Skin) cool as steel —Elizabeth Hardwick

(Voice) cool as water on shaded rocks —Beryl Markham

Could feel the cold climbing up his ankles like ships' rats
    —Penelope Gilliatt

Hardened her heart, like God had hardened Pharaoh's heart against
    the Jews —Daphne Merkin
        The simile was particularly appropriate in *Enchantment,* a
        novel about an orthodox Jewish family.

A heart as cold as English toast —Harry Prince

It [television show] was hard as fiberglass —Norman Mailer

My flesh was frozen for an inch below my skin, it was as if I were
    wearing icy armour —Rebecca West

Unresponding ... like a wall —D. H. Lawrence

COLORS

An amber mixture like autumn leaves —Francois Maspero

Bright gold like a diadem —Angela Carter

(Sky damp and) colorless as a cough —Sharon Sheehe Stark

Colorless as a desert —Alice McDermott

Colorless like the white paper streamer a Chinaman pulls out of his
    mouth —editor, *Dragonfly Magazine*, 1880
        This simile appeared in a rejection letter sent to Anton
        Chekhov when he was still a fledgling writer.

Colors are as soft as a Mediterranean dawn
    —Bryan Miller, *New York Times*, July 3, 1987
        Miller's simile pertained to the colors of a restaurant.

Colors as clear as notes perfectly played —A. E. Maxwell

Colors [of Christmas candy] ... as piercing as the joys and sufferings
    of the poor ... red like the love that was celebrated in
    doorways ... yellow like the flames in a drunk man's brain
    —Heinrich Böll

Colors clear as fresh-cut flowers —Joan Chase

Deep colored as old rugs —Eudora Welty

As full of color as blood —John Logan

Gold as the seeds of a melon —Dame Edith Sitwell

A good soldier, like a good horse, cannot be of a bad color
    —Oliver Wendell Holmes, Sr.

Orange as the sunset —Dashiell Hammett

Orange bright like golden lamps in a green light —Andrew Marvell

[A taxi] painted in an arabesque of colors, like a psychedelic dream
    gone wild —Andrew Kaplan

(His split lip is as) purple as a nightcrawler stuck on a hook
    —Robert Flanagan
        This simile begins Flanagan's short story, *Naked to Naked
        Goes.*

Purple as a grape —Dashiell Hammett

[Cabbage] purply as cheap stained glass —Babette Deutsch

The reds and browns and golds of the trees seem ready to drip from
    their branches like wet dye —Alice McDermott

Silvery as sleighbells —Diane Ackerman

Two-toned like a layer cake —Donald McCaig

COMFORT

(Feel as) comfortable as a Cossack in Kiev —Richard Ford

(Eugene was) comfortable as a saggy armchair —Donald McCaig

Comfortable as matrimony —Nathan Bailey

Comfortable ... like sleeping on a cloud —Slogan, Sealy Inc.

Comforting as a long soak in a hot tub after a short walk in a
    freezing rainstorm —Elyse Sommer

Comforting as the Surgeon-General's statement on a pack of Lucky
    Strikes —Harry Prince

Comfort [memory of a lover] like a rosary —Sumner Locke Elliot

Cozy and dark as a dreary day —Sharon Sheehe Stark

Cozy as a cup of tea —Anon

Cozy as a nest —Émile Zola

Cozy as visiting your grandmother —Mary Lee Settle

Easy as an old shoe —English proverb
        New Englanders brought this from the old country as
        "Comfortable as an old shoe," an expression still very
        much in use. There's also a Ukranian proverb which
        incorporates a somewhat different form of this simile.

Feels comfortable like in a cloud —François Maspero

Reassured ... like a sheltering wing over a motherless bird
    —Louisa May Alcott

Restful as one's favorite armchair —Frank Swinnerton

(Here Skigg lies) snug as a bug in a rug —Benjamin Franklin, letter
    to Georgiana Shipley, September, 1772

Snug as the yolk in an egg —Henrik Ibsen

Soothing as mother's milk —Anon

[Conversation] soothing, like the quiet, washing sound of an ocean
    —Donald Justice

Comfort

Supported [by attentive performance] as a bold swimmer by the waves —Ivan Turgenev

[Prospect of someone's being there] sustained him like a snug life jacket —Lynne Sharon Schwartz

Sustain like a stream does a trout —Andrew Dubus

Warm and cozy and private as a nursery —John Braine

Warm and old-fashioned as a potbellied stove —Anon, capsule movie review, *Newsday*, January, 1986

(Walls look as) warm and sturdy as a fisherman's hand-knitted sweater —Sheila Radley

(The whole room was as equally and agreeably) warm as a bath full of water —Anon

Warm as piss —American colloquialism

Warm as sunshine, light as floating clouds —Slogan, Torfeaco bedding

Warm like love —Sharon Sheehe Stark

COMPASSION
SEE: KINDNESS

Compatibility/ Incompatibility

COMPATIBILITY/INCOMPATIBILITY

Companionable as a cat and a goldfish —Anon

Companionable [a mother and son] as a pair of collusive old whores —David Leitch

Compatible as the stars and stripes on the American flag —Elyse Sommer

Get on like a house on fire —Ngaio Marsh

Get on like salt and iron —Loren D. Estleman

Good taste and humor are a contradiction in terms, like a chaste whore —Malcom Muggeridge quoted in *Time*, September 14, 1953

Got along like Siamese twins —George Garrett

Go together like a computer and an abacus —Anon

Go together like apples and pie crust —Elyse Sommer

These 'go-togethers' provide endless opportunity for additional twists.

Go together like bagels and cream cheese —Anon

Go together like blueberries and cream —Anon

Go together like coffee and danish —Anon

Go together like ice cream and salt —Anon

Go together like meatballs and spaghetti —Anon

Go together like paper and pencil —Anon

Go together like tea and lemon —Anon

Got on like twin souls —Edward Marsh

Irreconcilable as a jazz band and a symphony orchestra —Paul Mourand

No more affinity for each other than a robin for a goldfish —Eleanor Kirk

Struck [Flanner and Mike Wallace] it off together like a pair of lighted pinwheels —Janet Flanner

COMPETENCE
SEE: ABILITY

COMPETITION
SEE: BUSINESS, SPORTS

COMPLAINTS
SEE: ANGER

COMPLETENESS/INCOMPLETENESS

Completely as hydrogen mixes with oxygen to become water ... the orange is part of the living animal —Daniela Gioseffi

Fragmentary, like the text of a corrupt manuscript whose words have been effaced in the wind and rain —Arthur A. Cohen

Incomplete and unfinished like an apple that has begun to shrink before it has reached maturity —Louis Bromfield

Incomplete as a circus without clowns —Elyse Sommer

Incomplete as the world on the fifth day of creation —Anon

Incomplete like a pastrami sandwich without a pickle —Ed Mc Bain

Incomplete ... like cabbage with all the flavor boiled out
—Richard Brookhiser, *Wall Street Journal* book review, April 1, 1987

> The simile refers to an author's effort to serve up election information without politics.

Incomplete ... like a tree without leaves, a building without a foundation, or a shadow without the body that casts it (The knight-errant without a lady is like ...) —Miguel de Cervantes

Playing cards without money is like a meal without salt
—Bertold Brecht

A store without merchandise to sell is like a library without books to read —Anon

(The antismoking zealots never tell you these things ... colds, weight gain can happen to you after kicking the habit.) They [people giving incomplete information] are like Karl Malden, who is always telling you how happy American Express will be to replace your stolen traveler's checks but never bothers to tell you that if their serial numbers are stolen too, you're out of luck —Russell Baker, *New York Times Magazine*, September 21, 1986

Unfinished [sentence] like a plaster half of an ancient sculptured torso
—Penelope Gilliatt

COMPLEXION
SEE: SKIN

COMPLEXITY
SEE: DIFFICULTY

COMPLIMENTS
SEE: WORDS OF PRAISE

CONCEIT
SEE: VANITY

CONCENTRATION
SEE: ATTENTION, SCRUTINY

CONFIDENCE
SEE: SELF-CONFIDENCE

CONFIDENTIALITY
SEE: SECRECY

CONNECTIONS
SEE: CLINGING

CONSIDERATION
SEE: THOUGHT

CONTEMPLATION
See: SCRUTINY, THOUGHT

CONTENTMENT
SEE: HAPPINESS, JOY

CONTINUITY
SEE: PERMANENCE

CONVERSATION

Conversation ... was like trying to communicate with a ship sinking in mid-Atlantic when you're on shore —William McIlvanney

The American's conversation is much like his courtship ... he gives in and watches for a reaction; if the weather looks fair, he inkles a little —Donald Lloyd, *Harper's Magazine,* September 19, 1963

Chattering as foolishly as two slightly mad squirrels —James Crumley

Conversation ... as edifying as listening to a leak dropping in a tin dish-pan at the head of the bed when you want to go to sleep —O. Henry

A conversation between the two of you must be like listening to two pecans in a bowl —Geoffrey Wolff
> The character who utters this simile in Wolff's novel, *Providence,* follows it up with "Why don't you let him shoot 500 cc of thorazine right in your heart and get it over."

Conversation ... crisp and varied as a freshly tossed salad —Anon

Conversation ... it was like talk at a party, leap-frogging, sparring, showing-off —Nina Bawden

Conversation, like lettuce, requires a good deal of oil to avoid friction, and keep the company smooth —Charles Dudley Warner

(He had) practiced his portion of the conversation so many times ... that he felt like an actor in a stock company —Herbert Gold

Conversation

Quips flew back and forth like balls between two long-experienced jugglers in a circus ring —Natascha Wodin

The room seethes with talk. Always a minimum of three conversations, like crosswinds —Rosellen Brown

Small talk is like the air that shatters the stalactites into dust again —Anaïs Nin

The talk came like the spilling of grain from a sack, in bursts of fullness that were shut off in mid-sentence as if someone had closed the sack abruptly and there was more talk inside —Shirley W. Schoonover

Talked ... like old friends in mourning —Nadine Gordimer

Talking to Bill is like opening a new bottle of ketchup; you gotta wait a while before anything comes out —Jonathan Valin
> In his novel, *Life's Work,* Valin expands on this with "Sometimes you wait and nothing happens."

Talking to him was like playing upon an exquisite violin. He answered to every touch and thrill of the bow —Oscar Wilde

Talking to them is like trying to get a zeppelin off the ground —Penelope Gilliatt

Talking to you is like addressing the Berlin Wall —Colin Forbes

Talking to you is like sending out your laundry, you don't know what the hell is coming back —Neil Simon

Talking to you is like talking to my forearm —Geoffrey Wolff

Talking with him [George McGovern] is like eating a Chinese meal. An hour after it's over, you wonder whether you really ate anything —Eugene McCarthy

Talking with you is more like boxing than talking —Larry McMurtry
> The simile from *Somebody's Darling* continues as follows: "You're always hitting me with a jab."

Talk that warms like wine —Babette Deutsch

Their remarks and responses were like a Ping-Pong game with each volley clearing the net and flying back to the opposition —Maya Angelou

Trading talk like blows —Anne Sexton

COOLNESS
SEE: CALMNESS

COOPERATION
SEE: AGREEMENT

CORPORATIONS
SEE: BUSINESS

CORRECTNESS
SEE: MANNERS

COST
SEE: THRIFT

COUNTENANCES
SEE: FACE(S)

COURAGE

Adventurous as a bee —William Wordsworth

As brave as hell —Petronius

As much backbone as an eel —American colloquialism

As much backbone as cooked spaghetti —Harry Prince

(There was) a tragic daring about her, like a moth dancing around a
    flame —Paige Mitchell

(He died) bold as brass —George Parker
        Common usage has seeded modern-day modifications
        such as "Bold as brass balls."

Bold as a dying saint —Elkanah Settle

Bold as a lion —*The Holy Bible/Proverbs*

Bold as an unhunted fawn —Percy Bysshe Shelley

Bold as love —Edmond Gosse

Bold as Paul in the presence of Agrippa —William Cowper

Brave as a barrel full of bears —Ogden Nash

Brave as a tiger in a rage —Ogden Nash

Brave as winds that brave the sea —Algernon Charles Swinburne

Courage

Courage is like a disobedient dog, once it starts running away it flies all the faster for your attempts to recall it —Katherine Mansfield

Courage is like love; it must have hope to nourish it —Napoleon Bonaparte

Courage, like cowardice, is undoubtedly contagious, but some persons are not liable to catch it —Archibald Prentice

Courageous as a poker player with a royal flush —Mike Sommer

Courageous like firemen. The bell rings and they jump into their boots and go down the pole —Anon

Daring as tickling a tiger —Anon

Fend off pressure like a sharkhunter feeds off danger —Anon

Gallant as a warrior —Beryl Markham

Grew bold, like a general who is about to order an assault —Guy de Maupassant

Have the gall of a shoplifter returning an item for a refund —W.I.E. Gates

Indomitable as a lioness —Aharon Appelfeld

A man without courage is like a knife without edge —Anon

More guts than a gladiator —William Diehl

Nothing so bold as a blind horse —Greek proverb

Over-daring is as great a vice as over-fearing —Ben Jonson

Show nerve of a burglar —Anon

Stand my ground brave as a bear —American country ballad "If You Want to Go A-Courting"

Valiant as a lion —William Shakespeare
> This simile from *Henry the Fourth* has made lion comparisons part of our every day language. Another lion simile by the Bard is "Walked like one of the lions" from *The Two Gentlemen of Verona.*

With all the courage of an escaped convict —Honoré de Balzac

Valiant as Hercules —William Shakespeare

(I've seen plenty of great big tough guys that was as) yellow and
   soft as a stick of butter —George Garrett

COURTESY
SEE: MANNERS

COURTSHIP
SEE: MEN AND WOMEN

COVERTNESS
SEE: SECRECY

COWARDICE
SEE: FEAR

COZINESS
SEE: COMFORT

CRAFTINESS
SEE: CLEVERNESS

CRAVING
SEE: DESIRE

CRIME
SEE: DISHONESTY, EVIL

CRISPNESS
SEE: SHARPNESS

CRITICISM, DRAMATIC/LITERARY

Aired their grievances like the wash —Daphne Merkin

[Reading about Frank Sinatra's escapades] as refreshing as inhaling
   carbon monoxide —Barbara Grizzuiti Harrison, reviewing Kitty
   Kelley's unauthorized biography of Frank Sinatra, *New York Times
   Book Review*, November 2, 1986

[For author W. P. Kinsella] a baseball stadium is a window on the
   human heart, and his novel ... stirs it like the refreshing crack of
   a bat against the ball —*Miami Herald* review of *Shoeless Joe*, a
   baseball novel, by W. P. Kinsella
         Like many comparisons, this one was pulled out of the
         review and used as an attention-getting blurb on back of
         the author's next novel.

The book is like a professor's joke. It's nothing if not erudite
  —Vincent Canby, review of movie adaptation of Umberto Eco's
  The Name of the Rose, New York Times, September 24, 1986

Book reviews ... a kind of infant's disease to which newborn books
  are subject —Georg Christoph Lichtenberg

Critics are like brushers of other men's clothes —Benjamin Disraeli

Critics are like eunuchs in a harem. They see how it should be done
  every night. But they can't do it themselves —Brendan Behan

Even when he's not at his best, his books still are appetizing, much
  like a box of popcorn —Tom Herman, book review (*The Panic of
  '89* by Paul Erdman), *Wall Street Journal,* January 16, 1987

His [author of pamphlet] words, like cavalry horses answering the
  bugle, group themselves automatically into the familiar dreary
  pattern —George Orwell

It [*The House of Seven Gables*] is like a great symphony, with no
  touch alterable without injury to the harmony
  —William James, letter to brother, Henry, January 19, 1869

It's [*Praying for Rain,* Jerome Weidman's autobiography] ... like a
  raisin-laced kugel, the noodles crammed with juicy morsels about
  some people, obscure and famous, who have been near and dear
  to him —Helen Dudar, *New York Times* Book Review, September
  21, 1986

Language is as precise as 'hello!' and as simple as "Give me a glass
  of tea" —Vladimir Mayakovsky about Anton Chekhov

Literary criticism is an art, like the writing of tragedies or the making
  of love, and similarly does not pay —Clifton Fadiman

Much of the text reads about as joyfully as a Volkswagon manual
  —George F. Will

The novel [*A Special Destiny* by Seymour Epstein] reads like the
  fictionalized autobiography of a young writer exorcising
  frustrations and resentments —Bethamy Probst, *New York Times
  Book Review,* September 21, 1986

Novels ... like literary knuckleballs
  —George F. Will, about Elmore Leonard's novels

One long evening of evasions, as if the playwright were taking the Fifth Amendment on advice of counsel
—Frank Rich, *New York Times*, December 12, 1986
Drama critic Rich has the gift for perfectly suiting the comparison to what it describes ... in this case a play entitled *Dream of a Blacklisted Actor*.

The prose lays there like a dead corpse on the page —Anon

Prose rushes out like a spring-fed torrent sweeping the reader away —Chuck Morris

Reviewing an autobiography is the literary equivalent of passing judgment on someone's life —Richard Lourie, prefacing his review of Eric Ambler's *Autobiography, New York Times Book Review*, August 17, 1986

Style ... as strong and personal as Van Gogh's brushstrokes —George F. Will, about Elmore Leonard's novels

(The author's) style is as crisp as if it had been quick-frozen —Max Apple, about T. Coraghessan Boyle, *New York Times Book Review*, 1979

They [critics] bite like fish, at anything, especially at bookes [books] —Thomas Dekker

They [Gorky's stories] float through the air like songs —Isaac Babel, lecture, 1934

Thin stuff with no meat in it, like a woman, who has starved herself to get what she thinks is a good figure —Ben Ames Williams
This simile is used by the novelist-hero of *Leave Her to Heaven* to describe his current work.

To many people dramatic criticism must seem like an attempt to tattoo soap bubbles —John Mason Brown

The undisputed fame enjoyed by Shakespeare as a writer ... is, like every other lie, a great evil —Leo Tolstoy

Watching the movie is like being on a cruise to nowhere aboard a ship with decent service and above-par fast food
—Vincent Canby, *New York Times* movie review, October 2, 1983

[Henry James] writes fiction as if it were a painful duty —Oscar Wilde

(Tolstoy) writes like an ocean, in huge rolling waves, and it doesn't look like it was processed through his thinking —Mel Brook, *Playboy*, 1975

Writes like an angel, a fallen, hard-driving angel —A. Alvarez about Robert Stone, *New York Review of Books*, 1986

CROOKEDNESS
SEE: BENDING/BENT

CROWDEDNESS
SEE: CLOSENESS

CROWDS
SEE: CLOSENESS

CRUELTY
SEE: COLDNESS, EVIL

CUNNING
SEE: CLEVERNESS

CURSES
SEE: WORD(S)

DANCING
SEE: INSULTS, WORDS OF PRAISE

DARING
SEE: COURAGE

Darkness

DARKNESS

Dark and cool as a cave —David Huddle

Dark and heavy like a surface stained with ink —John Ashbery

(It was) dark as a closet —Niven Busch

Dark as a dungeon —Anon
     The simile is the title of a ballad from the American South.

Dark as anger —Sylvia Plath

Dark as a pocket —American colloquialism, attributed to Vermont

(All was) dark as a stack of black cats —J. S. Rioss

Dark as a thundercloud —Steven Vincent Benét

Dark as a troll —W. D. Snodgrass

Dark as a wolf's mouth —Miguel de Cervantes
>"Dark as" and "Black as" have been used interchangeably since the simile's appearance in *Don Quixote.*

Dark as a womb —T. Coraghessan Boyle

Dark as blackberries —Marge Piercy

(The room was) dark as dreamless sleep —Harry Prince

(Eyelashes ...) dark as night —Lord Byron

Dark as sin —Mark Twain

Dark as the devil's mouth —Walter Scott

Dark as the inside of a coffin —Gavin Lyall

Dark as the inside of a magician's hat —Robert Campbell

Dark as the inside of a cow —Mark Twain

Dark as the river bottom —Paige Mitchell

Dark like wet coffee grounds —Ella Leffland

The darkness ahead ... looked like Alaska —Richard North

Darkness as deep and cold as Siberian midnight —Gerald Kersh

Darkness [in a rainstorm] came closer ... like a sodden velvet curtain —Frank Swinnerton

Darkness falls like a wet sponge —John Ashbery
>This is the opening line of an Ashbery poem entitled *The Picture of Little J.A. in a Prospect of Flowers.*

Darkness fell like a swift blow —James Crumley

Darkness fills her like a carbohydrate —Daniela Gioseffi

The darkness flew in like an unwelcome bird —Norman Garbo

Darkness had begun to come in like water —Alice McDermott

Darkness hanging over them like a blotter —T. Coraghessan Boyle

Darkness like a black lake —Erich Maria Remarque

Darkness ... like a warm liquid poured from the throat of an enormous bird —John Hawkes

Darkness settling down round them like a soft bird —Rose Tremain

Darkness

Darkness should be a private matter, like thought, like emotion
—William Dieter

Darkness so total it seemed ... like deep water —William Boyd

The darkness was like a rising tide that covered the gardens and the houses, erasing everything as a still sea erased footprints on a beach —John P. Marquand

Darkness was sinking down over the region like a veil
—Thomas Mann

The darkness was thin, like some sleazy dress that has been worn and worn for many winters and always lets the cold through to the bones —Eudora Welty

Dim as a cave of the sea —Richard Wilbur

Dim as a cellar in midafternoon —Joyce Cary

Dim as an ill-lit railroad coach —Natascha Wodin

(My sun has set, I) dwell in darkness as a dead man out of sight
—Christina Rossetti

Light ... drained out of the windows like a sink —William H. Gass

So dark and murky it [a movie, *The Fugitive Kind,*] looked like everyone was drowning in chocolate syrup —Tennessee Williams, quoted in interview with Rex Reed

DAY
SEE: TIME

DEAFNESS
SEE: ATTENTION

Death

DEATH
SEE ALSO: ADVANCING; BEGINNINGS/ENDINGS

As death comes on we are like trees growing in the sandy bank of a widening river —Bhartrihari

The body of Benjamin Franklin, Printer, like the cover of an old book, its contents torn out, and stripped of its lettering and gilding, lies here, food for worms —Benjamin Franklin
> Franklin's epitaph for himself is a fine example of appropriately suiting the comparison to what's being compared.

116

(Kill him) dead as a beef —William Faulkner

[Sexual feelings] dead as a burned-out cinder —Ellen Glasgow

Death arrives ... sudden as a pasteboard box crushed by a foot
    —Marge Piercy

Death falling like snow on any head it chooses —Philip Levine

Death fell round me like a rain of steel —Herbert Read
        A simile from one of Read's many war poems, *Meditation
        of the Waking English Officer.*

Death has many times invited me: it was like the salt invisible in the
    waves —Pablo Neruda

Death lies on her, like an untimely frost —William Shakespeare

Death, like roulette, turning our wish to its will —George Barker

Death lurking up the road like a feral dog abroad in the swirling
    snow —Marge Piercy

Death, you can never tell where else it will crop up —John Hale

Die alone like a dog in a ditch —Aldous Huxley

Died in beauty, like a rose blown from its parent stem —C.D. Sillery

Die like candles in a draft —Sharon Sheehe Stark
        In the short story, *The Johnstown Polka*, the simile has a
        literal frame of reference; specifically, a room in an old age
        home which is overheated because to open the windows
        would kill the people in it.

Died like flies in a sugar bowl —Rita Mae Brown

(I won't) drown like a rat in a trap —George Bernard Shaw

Like a swift-fleeting meteor, a fast flaying cloud, a flash of lightning,
    a break of the wave, man passes from life to his rest in the
    grave —William Knox

Dying is as natural as living —Thomas Fuller

Dying like flies —Anon
        An even more frequently used variation is to "Drop like
        flies."

(I will) encounter darkness as a bride —William Shakespeare

Death

(You couldn't) expect death to come rushing in like a skivvy because
you'd rung the bell —Paul Barker

Feel my death rushing towards me like an express train
—John Updike

Felt death near, like a garment she had left hanging in her closet
and could not see or find, though she knew it was there
—Abraham Rothberg

Go to their graves like flowers or creeping worms
—Percy Bysshe Shelley

The intimations of mortality appear so gradually as to be
imperceptible, like the first graying in of twilight —Richard Selzer

Like a clock worn out with eating time, the wheels of weary life at
last stood still —John Dryden

Like a led victim, to my death I'll go —John Dryden

Like sheep they are laid in the grave —*The Holy Bible/Psalms*

(I now) look at death, the way we look at a house we plan to move
into —William Bronk

Men fear death, as children fear to go in the dark; and as that
natural fear in children is increased with tales, so is the other
—Francis Bacon

Our fear of death is like our fear that summer will be short, but
when we have had our swing of pleasure, our fill of fruit, and
our swelter of heat, we say we have had our day
—Ralph Waldo Emerson

Passed away, as a dry leaf passes into leaf mold —John Updike

[In old age] the shadow of death ... like a sword of Damocles, may
descend at any moment —Samuel Butler

She passed away like morning dew —Hartley Coleridge

Talking over the fact of his approaching death as though it were a
piece of property for agreeable disposition in the family
—Elizabeth Spencer

There are no graves that grow so green as the graves of children
—Oliver Wendell Holmes, Sr.

From a letter of condolence to W. R. Sturtevant, September 17, 1878, in which the simile continues as follows: "Their memory comes back after a time more beautiful than that of those who leave us at any other age."

We are all kept and fed for death, like a herd of swine to be slain without reason —Palladas

We end our years like a sigh ... for it is speedily gone, and we fly away —*The Holy Bible/Psalms*

Wherever you go, death dogs you like a shadow —Anon, probably dating back to before Christ.

DEDICATION
SEE: ATTENTION

DEJECTION

(There was about him) an air of defeat ... as though all the rules he'd learned in life were, one by one, being reversed —Margaret Millar

Dampened my mood (as automatically) as would the news of an earthquake in Cincinnati or the outbreak of the Third World War —T. Coraghessan Boyle

Dejection seemed to transfix him, to reach down out of the sky and crash like a spike through his small rigid body —Niven Busch

Dejection settled over her like a cloud —Louis Bromfield

Depression crept like a fog into her mind —Ellen Glasgow •

Depression ... is like a light turned into a room—only a light of blackness —Rudyard Kipling

Depressions ... like thick cloud covers: not a ray of light gets through —Larry McMurtry

Despair howled round his inside like a wind —Elizabeth Bowen

Despair is like froward children, who, when you take away one of their playthings, throw the rest into the fire for madness —Pierre Charron

Despair, like that of a man carrying through choice a bomb which, at a certain hour each day, may or may not explode —William Faulkner

119

Despair passed over him like cold winds and hot winds coming from places he had never visited —Margaret Millar

Despondency ... lurking like a ghoul —Richard Maynard

Emptied, like a collapsed balloon, all the life gone out of him —Ben Ames Williams

Feeling of desperation ... as if caught by a chain that was slowly winding up —Victor Hugo

Feel like a picnicker who has forgotten his lunch —Frank O'Hara

(I'm not feeling very good right now. I) feel like I've been sucking on a lot of raw eggs —Dexter Manley, of the Washington Redskins after his team lost important game, quoted in the *New York Times*, December 8, 1986

Feels his heart sink as if into a frozen lake —John Rechy

Felt depression settle on his head like a sick crow —Bernard Malamud

(He often) felt [suicidal] like a deep sea diver whose hose got cut on an unexpected rock —Diane Wakoski

Felt like Willie Loman at the end of the road —T. Coraghessan Boyle

Felt the future narrowing before me like a tunnel —Margaret Drabble

Forlorn ... like Autumn waiting for the snow —John Greenleaf Whittier

(Her) heart dropped like a purse of coins falling through a ripped pocket —Joyce Reiser Kornblatt

His despair confronted me like a black beast —Natascha Wodin

His haughty self was like a robber baron fallen into the hands of rebellious slaves, stooped under a filthy load —Sinclair Lewis

His heart has withered in him and he has been left with the five senses, like pieces of broken wineglass —Lawrence Durrell

Hope and confidence ... shattered like the pillars of Gaza —W. Somerset Maugham

Hope removed like a tree —*The Holy Bible/Job*

It was like having a part of me amputated —W. P. Kinsella

In the novel, *Shoeless Joe*, the comparison is a character's response to being suspended from his baseball team.

(I was) like the old lion with a thorn in his paw, surrounded by wolves and jackals and facing his snaggle-toothed death in a political jungle —T. Coraghessan Boyle

Listless and wretched like a condemned man —Erich Maria Remarque

Live under dust covers like furniture —Michael Frayn
> Frayn's simile vividly portrays the despair of the characters in his adaptation of an untitled Checkhov play, first produced under the title *Wild Honey* in 1984.

Looked suddenly disconsolate, like a scarecrow with no crows to scare —Graham Masterton

Looking forlorn, stricken, like a little brother who, tagging along, is being deserted by the big fellows —Edna Ferber

Crawl back [after unanticipated defeat at golf] looking like a toad under a harrow —P. G. Wodehouse

Look like a dog that has lost its tail —John Ray's *Proverbs*

Look like the picture of ill luck —John Ray's *Proverbs*

Miserable, like dead men in a dream —George MacDonald

Miserable, lonesome as a forgotten child —F. Scott Fitzgerald

Misery is manifold ... as the rainbow; its hues are as various as the hues of that arch —Edgar Allen Poe

Misery rose from him like a stench —Marge Piercy

A mood as gypsy-dark as his eyes —Robert Culff

My life is just an empty road and people walk on me —Tony Ardizzone

Must live hideously and miserably the rest of his days, like a man doomed to live forever in a state of retching and abominable nausea of heart, brain, bowels, flesh and spirit —Thomas Wolfe

Put away his hopes as if they were old love letters —Anon

Relapsed into discouragement, like a votary who has watched too long for a sign from the altar —Edith Wharton

Dejection

Saw himself like a sparrow on the bank-top; sitting on the wherewithal for a thousand thousand meals and dropping dead from hunger the first day of winter —Christina Stead

Seemed like a whipped dog on a leash —Ignazio Silone

The sense of desolation and of fear became bitterer than death —William Cullen Bryant

(I have been) so utterly and suicidally morbid that my letters would have read like an excerpt from the *Undertakers' Gazette* —Dylan Thomas
> The simile is excerpted from a November, 1933, letter to Pamela Hansford Johnson apologizing for the delay in replying to her letter.

(Foster's) stomach felt like a load of wet clothes at the bottom of the dryer —Phyllis Naylor

There's a state of peace following despair ... like the aftermath of an accident —C. J. Koch

Waves of black depression engulf one from time to time ... like a rising tide —Gustave Flaubert

DELIGHT
SEE: JOY

DEMOCRACY
SEE: FREEDOM

DENSITY
SEE: THICKNESS

DEPENDABILITY
SEE: RELIABILITY/UNRELIABILITY

DEPRESSION
SEE: DEJECTION

Desire

DESIRE
SEE ALSO: SEX

A brief surge of sexual desire that crested and passed like a wave breaking —Paige Mitchell

Craves love like oxygen —Marge Piercy

122

Craving [for a man] ... like a cigarette smoker's who knows his desire is unhealthy, knows that the next puff may set off a chain reaction of catastrophe, but nevertheless cannot by such logic tame the impulse —Paul Reidinger

Desire had run its course like a long and serious illness —Harvey Swados

Desire ... like the hunger for a definite but hard-to-come-by food —Mary Gordon

Desire overtook us like a hot, breaking wave —A. E. Maxwell

Desires are either natural and necessary, like eating and drinking; or natural and not necessary, like intercourse with females; or neither natural or necessary —Michel de Montaigne

Desires ... hurried like the clouds —Elizabeth Bowen

Desire ... swept over her like a flame —Robin McCorquodale

Dying for ... like God for a repentant sinner —Bertold Brecht

(She is) gasping after love like a carp after water on a kitchen table —Gustave Flaubert

Her needs stick out all over, like a porcupine's needles —Emily Listfield

His need for her was crippling ... like a cruel blow at the back of his knees —John Cheever

How passionate the mating instinct is, like a giant hippo chasing his mate through the underbrush and never stopping till he finally mounts her in the muddy waters of the mighty Amazon —Daniel Asa Rose

Longing ... afflicted her like a toothache —Harold Acton

Miss like sin —Lael Tucker Wertenbaker
        The simile in full context from the novel, *Unbidden Guests:*
        "I woke up missing Alex like sin."

Miss you like breath —Janet Flanner

More giddy in my desires than a monkey —William Shakespeare

My desire for her is so wild I feel as if I'm all liquid —W. P. Kinsella

123

Desire

A passion finer than lust, as if everything living is moist with her —Daniela Gioseffi

Worldly desires are like columns of sunshine radiating through a dusty window, nothing tangible, nothing there —Bratzlav Naham

Yearning radiating from his face like heat from an electric heater —Larry McMurtry

Destruction/ Destructiveness

DESTRUCTION/DESTRUCTIVENESS

As killing as the canker to the rose —John Milton

(Bones) breaking like hearts —Bin Ramke

Break [a person's spirit] like a biscuit —Beaumont and Fletcher

Break like a bursting heart —Percy Bysshe Shelley

Break like dead leaves —Richard Howard

Cracked like parchment —Sin Ai

Cracked like the ice in a frozen daiquiri —Anon

(Her projects of happiness ...) crackled in the wind like dead boughs —Gustave Flaubert

Crack like walnuts —Rita Mae Brown

Crack like wishbones —Diane Ackerman

Cracks ... like a glass in which the contents turned to ice, and shiver it —Herman Melville

[Fender and hood of a car] crumpled like tinfoil —T. Coraghessan Boyle

Crushed like an empty beer can —Anon

Crushed ... like rats in a slate fall —Davis Grubb
In Grubb's novel, *The Barefoot Man*, the simile refers to miners who lost their lives.

Crushed like rotten apples —William Shakespeare

Crushed me like a grape —Carla Lane, British television sitcom, "Solo," broadcast, May 19, 1987

(And I'll be) cut up like a pie —Irish ballad

Destructive as moths in a woolens closet —Anon

[Time's malevolent effect on body] dragging him down like a bursting sack —Gerald Kersh

(The Communists are) eating us away like an old fruit —Janet Flanner

(Men) fade like leaves —Aristophanes

Flattened her pitiful attempt like a locomotive running on a single track full steam ahead —Cornell Woolrich

(Creditors ready to) gnaw him to bits ... like maggots at work on a carcass —George Garrett

The grass (at Shea Stadium) looked as if it had been attacked by animals that had not grazed for ages
—Alex Yannis, *New York Times*, September 18, 1986
        Yannis, in reporting on the Mets' winning the National League Eastern Division title, used the simile to describe the fans' destruction of the playing field.

If I do [give up] ... I'll be like a bullfighter gone horn-shy —Loren D. Estleman

Like a divorce ... goes ripping through our lives —Book jacket copy describing effect of Sharon Sheehe Stark's novel, *A Wrestling Season.*

Marked for annihilation like an orange scored for peeling —Yehuda Amichai

My heroes [Chicago Cubs] had wilted like slugs —George F. Will

Pollutes ... like ratbite —William Alfred

Self-destructing like a third-rate situation comedy
—Warren T. Brookes, on Republican party, *Wall Street Journal*, July 15, 1986

Shattered like a walnut shell —Charles Dickens
        In Dickens' *A Tale of Two Cities*, the comparison refers to a broken wine cask.

Shatter them like so much glass —Robert Louis Stevenson

Shrivel up like some old straw broom —Joyce Carol Oates

Snap like dry chicken bones —David Michael

Destruction/Destructiveness

[Taut nerves] snap like guy wires in a tornado —Nardi Reeder Campion, *New York Times*/Op-Ed, January, 5, 1987

(Then the illusion) snapped like a nest of threads —F. Scott Fitzgerald

Snapped off [due to frailness] like celery —Lawrence Durrell

(Who can accept that spirit can be) snuffed as finally as a flame —Barbara Lazear Ascher, *New York Times*, October 30, 1986

They [free-spending wife and daughter] ate holes in me like Swiss cheese —Clifford Odets

Wear out their lives, like old clothes —John Cheever

Your destruction comes as a whirlwind —*The Holy Bible /Proverbs*

DETACHMENT
SEE: REMOTENESS

DEW
SEE: NATURE

DIETS
SEE: EATING AND DRINKING

Difficulty

DIFFICULTY
SEE ALSO: IMPOSSIBILITY

As easy as buying a pair of solid leather shoes for ten dollars —Anon

As easy as combing your hair with a broom —Anon

As easy as doing one thing at a time and never putting off anything till tomorrow that could be done today —Baron Samuel von Puffendorf

As easy as drawing a picture in water —Anon

As easy as eating soup with a fork —Anon

As easy as finding a two-bedroom apartment on Manhattan's east side for $400 a month —Anon
> This is the sort of topical and location-specific comparison that is adapted to the user's own locale and economic conditions.

126

As easy as getting rid of cockroaches in a New York apartment —Anon

As easy as making an omelet without eggs —Anon
> A simile probably inspired by the proverb "One can't expect to make an omelet without breaking eggs."

As easy as passing a bull in a close —William McIlvanney

As easy as roller skating on a collapsing sidewalk —Anon

As easy as running with a stitch in your side —Anon

As easy as trying to paint the wind —Anon

As easy as shaving with an axe —Anon

As easy as struggling through a waist-high layer of glue —Anon

As easy as taking a hair out of milk —*Babylonian Talmud*

As easy to ignore as a Salvation Army drum —William McIlvanney

As easy to scare Jack Cady [character in novel] as to scare an oak tree —Speer Morgan

As easy as trying to load a thermometer with beads of quicksilver —Bill Pronzini

As easy as trying to nail a glob of mercury —Anon

As easy as trying to open an oyster without a knife —Anon

As easy as trying to participate in your own funeral —Anon

As easy as trying to read a book on the deck of a sinking ship —Anon

As easy as trying to unscramble an egg —Anon

As easy as wading in tar —Anon

As easy as walking on one leg —Anon

Chasing a dream, a dream no one else can see or understand, like running after a butterfly across an endless meadow, is extremely difficult —W. P. Kinsella

Controlling the bureaucracy is like nailing Jell-O to the wall —John F. Kennedy

Dealing with him is like dealing with a porcupine in heat —Anon

The porcupine simile made by an anonymous White House reporter in 1986 referred to deputy chief Richard G. Darmon.

Demanding as a Dickens novel with a cast of hundreds —Ira Wood

Difficult as an elephant trying to pick up a pea —H. G. Wells

Difficult as climbing pinnacles of ice —Elinor Wylie

Difficult as driving a Daimler at top speed on a slick road
—Barry Tuckwell, quoted in article by Barbara Jepson, *Wall Street Journal*, July 1, 1986

(Getting the truth in the *New York Post* has been as) difficult as finding a good hamburger in Albania
—Paul Newman, *New York Post*, October 14, 1986
The actor's simile referred to the paper's efforts to prove that he is only 5 foot 8 inches tall.

Difficult as getting a concession to put a merry-go-round on the front lawn of the White House —Kenneth L. Roberts
As true and timely a simile today as when it originated in the early part of the twentieth century.

Difficult as making a silk purse out of a sow's ear —Anon
This can be traced to the German proverb "You cannot make a silk purse of a sow's ear." A less well-known French version substitutes velvet for the sow's ear.

Difficult as making dreams come true —Anon

Difficult as putting a bandage on an eel —Anon

Difficult as to sell a ham to a kosher caterer —Elyse Sommer

Difficult as sighting a rifle in the dark with rain falling
—Peter Greer, "Christian Science Monitor" radio program, December 31, 1985

Difficult as trying to draw blood from a turnip —French proverb

Difficult as trying to be old and young at the same time —German proverb
Another proverb that has evolved into simile form, in this instance from "You cannot be old and young at the same time."

Difficult as trying to run and sit still at the same time —Scottish proverb

AS EASY AS SHAVING WITH AN AXE

Difficult ... like trying to play the piano with boxing gloves —William H. Hallhan

Difficult ... like swimming upstream in Jell-O —Loren D. Estleman

Difficult ... like trying to grab a hold of Jell-O in quicksand —Philip K. Meyer, Eberstadt Fleming executive quoted in *New York Times*, July 25, 1986, on estimating an oilfield company's earnings

Difficult ... like walking a frisky, 220-pound dog —Henry D. Jacoby, on trying to manage crude oil prices in face of changing market conditions, *New York Times*, January 26, 1986

Difficult to absorb ... like trying to take a sip of water from a fire hose —Anon comment, television news program
> The comment was a response to Uranus probe, January 22, 1987.

Difficult to get as trying to get a pearl out of a lockjawed oyster —Robert Vinez, quoted in *Wall Street Journal* article on consumer campaign to get Ford to put air bags into all cars, July 3, 1986
> The difficulty in this instance involved getting the air bag out of Ford.

(Satiety is as) difficult to stomach as hunger —Stefan Zweig

Finding a decent, affordable apartment in New York is ... like trying to recover a contact lens from a subway platform at rush hour —Michael de Courcy Hinds, *New York Times*, January 16, 1986

Getting information from him was like squeezing a third cup from a tea bag —Christopher Buckley

Hard as building a wall of sand —Marge Piercy

(It was) hard to do, but quick, like a painful inoculation —Judith Rascoe

Hard to lift as a dead elephant —Raymond Chandler

It [to get woman in story to admit feelings for lover] would be rather like breaking rocks —Laurie Colwin

Laborious as idleness —Louis IV

Life is not an easy thing to embrace, like trying to hug an elephant —Diane Wakoski

Lurching up those steep stairs was like climbing through a submarine
    —Scott Spencer

Not like making instant coffee —David Brierley
        In his novel, *Skorpion's Death,* Brierly uses the comparison
        to describe the difficulty of learning how to fly.

A process that could be likened to trying to drain a swimming pool
    with a soda straw —Thomas J. Knudson, on project to reduce
    flooding of lake in Utah, *New York Times,* April 11, 1987

To get a cent out of this woman is like crossing the Red Sea dry-
    shod —Sholom Aleichem

Trying to define yourself is like trying to bite your own teeth
    —Alan Watts

Trying to get information out of Joe was like trying to drag a cat by
    its tail over a rug —F. van Wyck Mason

Trying to jump-start a business venture over breakfast is like working
    hard at going to sleep or devoting a year to falling in love
    —Anon participant at a business networking breakfast, *New York
    Times*/Column One, Michael Winerif, February 17, 1987

Walking [while feeling dizzy] was like a journey up the down
    escalator —Madison Smart Bell

With effort, like rising out of deep water —Elizabeth Spencer

DIGNITY
SEE: PRIDE

DIRECTNESS
SEE: CANDOR

DISAPPEARANCE
SEE ALSO: BEGINNINGS/ENDINGS

Blown away like clouds —Henry Wadsworth Longfellow

Blows away like a deck of cards in a hurricane —George Garrett

Bobbed away like a soap-bubble —Sylvia Plath

(The premonition had) boiled off like a puff of bad air
    —Herbert Lieberman

Borne away like a cork on a stream —Lawrence Durrell

Disappearance

(The old worlds) died away like dew —Dame Edith Sitwell

Disappeared as if into fairyland —Peter Najarian

Disappeared ... effortlessly, like a star into a cloud
    —F. van Wyck Mason

Disappeared like a sigh —Tom Wolfe

Gone like a flushed toilet —Max Apple

Gone like a morning dream, or like a pile of clouds
    —William Wordsworth

Gone like a quick wind —Ursula Le Guin

(Our world was) gone like a scrap in the wind —Beryl Markham

Gone like a wild bird, like a blowing flame —Euripides

[Smile of a loved one] gone like dreams that we forget
    —William Wordsworth

(And all the students) gone, like last week's snow
    —Delmore Schwartz

Gone like our change at the end of the week —Palmer Cox

(Words) gone like sparks burned up in darkness
    —Jayne Anne Phillips

[A funeral procession] gone ... like tears in the eyes —Karl Shapiro

Gone, like tenants that quit without warning
    —Oliver Wendell Holmes, Sr.

Slips away like a snake in a weed-tangle —Robert Penn Warren

Slips out of my life like sand —Diane Wakoski

A slow fade, like a candle or an icicle —Margaret Atwood

(The nights) snapped out of sight like a lizard's eyelid —Sylvia Plath

Suddenly disappeared with a jerk, as if somebody had given her a
    violent pull from behind —Charles Dickens

(Her voice) suddenly disappeared, like a coin in a magic trick
    —Scott Spencer

Vanish ... as easily as an eel into sand —Arthur Conan Doyle

Vanish as raindrops which fall in the sea —Susan Coolidge

Vanish away like the ghost of breath —George Garrett

Vanished, ghost-like, into air —Henry Wadsworth Longfellow

Vanished like a puff of steam —H. G. Wells
    A frequently used alternative is to vanish or leave "Like a
    puff of wind."

(The stray cat) vanished like a swift, invisible shadow
    —D. H. Lawrence

[Food being served, dessert] vanished like a vision —Charlotte Brontë

Vanished like a wisp of vapor —Edith Wharton

Went away like a summer fly —W. B. Yeats

Went gloriously away, like lightning from the sky —Edgar Allen Poe

[Sense of peace] went out like a shooting star —Edna O'Brien

DISAPPOINTMENT
SEE: FACIAL EXPRESSIONS

DISASTER
SEE: FORTUNE/MISFORTUNE

DISCOMFORT
SEE: PAIN

DISCONTENT
SEE: DEJECTION

DISCOURAGEMENT
SEE: DEJECTION

DISHONESTY

All frauds, like the wall daubed with untempered mortar ... always
    tend to the decay of what they are devised to support
    —Richard Whately

As honest a man as any in the cards, when the kings are out
    —Thomas Fuller

At length corruption, like a general flood ... shall deluge all
    —Alexander Pope

Dishonesty

Borrowed thoughts, like borrowed money, only show the poverty of the borrower —Marguerite, Countess Blessington

Corruption is like a ball of snow ... once set a-rolling it must increase —Charles Caleb Colton

Crooked as a worm writhing on a hook —Herman Wouk
> The people who are likened to worms are characters from Wouk's political novel, *Inside, Outside.*

(Pompous and braggadocian, he seemed to the children as flat and) false as his teeth —Ferrol Sams

(She was) false as water —William Shakespeare

Falser than vows made in wine —William Shakespeare

Fraudulent as falsies —Helen Hudson

He that builds his house with other men's money is like one that gathers himself stones for the tomb of his burial
—*The Holy Bible/Apocrypha:Ecclesiasticus*
> The word 'builds' has been modernized from 'buildeth' and 'gathers' from 'gathereth.'

It is as difficult to appropriate the thoughts of others as it is to invent —Ralph Waldo Emerson

Permit memory to paint it [a long-ago life style] falsely, like the face of some old whore who could wish to be taken as young and innocent —George Garrett

Plays you as fair as if he'd picked your pocket —John Ray's *Proverbs*

Robbers are like rane, tha fall on the just and the unjust
—Josh Billings
> In Billings' phonetic dialect the word 'rane' is 'rain' and 'tha' is 'they.'

Sneaky as a rat in a hotel kitchen —William Alfred

There is something in corruption which, like a jaundiced eye, transfers the color of itself to the object it looks upon
—Thomas Paine

To rob a friend even of a penny is like taking his life
—Johann B. Nappaha

DISINTEGRATIION
SEE: DESTRUCTION

134

DISORDER
SEE: ORDER/DISORDER

DISSENSION
SEE: FIGHTING

DISTANCE
SEE: REMOTENESS

DIVERSENESS
SEE: PERSONAL TRAITS

DOCILITY
SEE: MEEKNESS

DOGS
SEE: ANIMALS

DOMINATION
SEE: POWER

DREAMS
SEE ALSO: AMBITION, SLEEP

The arc of dreams is black and streaked with gray as dead hair is
    —John Logan

Dreamed of unearned riches, like Aladdin —Phyllis McGinley

The dream ... hovered about her still like a pleasant, warm fog
    —Lynne Sharon Schwartz

A dream not interpreted is like a letter not read —*Babylonian Talmud*

Dream safely like any child who has said prayers and to whom a
    lullaby has been sung —George Garrett

Dreams are like a microscope through which we look at the hidden
    occurences in our soul —Erich Fromm

Dreams are thoughts waiting to be thought —Jan de Hartog

Dreams descend like cranes on gilded, forgetful wings
    —John Ashbery

Dreams move my countenance as if it were earth being pelted by
    rain —Diane Wakoski

The dreams of idealists are like the sound of footsteps in a tornado
    —Melvin I. Cooperman, June 8, 1987

Dreams

Dreams pop out like old fillings in the teeth —Diane Wakoski

Dreams rising from your eyes like steam —George Bradley

Dreams withered like flowers that are blighted by frost
  —Ellen Glasgow

Dreamy as puberty —Karl Shapiro

Fantasy is like jam; you have to spread it on a solid slice of bread.
  If not, it remains a shapeless thing, like jam, out of which you
  can't make anything —Italo Calvino, television interview aired
  after his death in 1985

Kept it [private dream] locked in his heart and took it out only when
  he was alone, like a miser counting his gold —Margaret Millar

Like a dog, he hunts in dreams —Alfred, Lord Tennyson

Nightmares have seasons like hurricanes —Lorrie Moore

Old dreams still floated ... like puddles of oil on the surface of a
  pail of water —Paige Mitchell

Our dreams like clouds disperse —Alfred Noyes

Toss wishes like a coin —George Garrett

DRINKING
SEE: EATING AND DRINKING

DRIVERS/DRIVING
SEE: VEHICLES

DULLNESS
SEE: BOREDOM/BORING

DUMBNESS
SEE: STUPIDITY

DUTY
SEE: RELIABILITY/UNRELIABILITY

EAGERNESS
SEE: ENTHUSIASM

EARTH
SEE: NATURE

(I meet men in the city) as easily as a finger stuck in water comes
    up wet —Marge Piercy

As easily as a hot knife cuts through butter —Ben Ames Williams
        In Williams' novel, *Leave Her to Heaven,* the simile
        describes the ease with which flood waters penetrate a
        barrier. The simile has also cropped up in everyday
        language to show something slipping by or through
        easily—as a legal decision past a judge.

As hard to get as a haircut —Raymond Chandler

(Returned to normality) as smoothly as a ski jumper landing
    —John Braine

Did so without effort or exertion, like a chess champion playing a
    routine game —Natascha Wodin

Easy as a smile —Anon

Easy as a snake crawling over a stick —Joseph Conrad

Easy as breathing in and breathing out —Louise Erdrich

Easy as climbing a fallen tree —Danish proverb

Easy as drawing a child's first tooth —Johann Wolfgang von Goethe

Easy as falling out of a canoe —Anon

Easy as finding fault in someone else —Anon

Easy as for a cat to have twins —American colloquialism, attributed
    to New England

Easy as opening a letter —Anon

Easy as peeling the skin off a banana —Anon

Easy as pie —Anon

Easy as pointing a finger —Slogan, Colt Patent Fire Arms Mfg. Co.

Easy as pouring a glass of water —Anon

Easy as riding down smoothly paved road —Anon

Easy as rolling off a log —Mark Twain

Easy as running up charge account bills —Anon

Ease

Easy as scrambling an egg —Anon

Easy as shooting down a fish in a barrel —Anon

Easy as spitting —Anton Chekhov

Easy as stealing pennies from a blind man's can —Donald Seaman

Easy as to set dogs on sheep —William Shakespeare

Easy as turning on the TV set —Anon

Easy as turning the page in a book —Anon

Easy ... like sliding into sin —Harry Prince

An easy thing to do, light and easy like falling in a dream
    —George Garrett

Go through ... like so much dishwater —McKinlay Kantor

Stepped into his position as easily as a pair of trousers —Anon

Stepped into manhood, as one steps over a doorsill —Mark Twain

Went in ... as easily as paper into a vacuum cleaner
    —Derek Lambert

Would happen as the turning of a light bulb on or off
    —John McGahern

EASE (OPPOSITE MEANING)
SEE: DIFFICULTY

Eating and Drinking

EATING AND DRINKING

Ate as if there were a hidden thing inside him, a creature of all jaws
    with an infinite trailing ribbon of gut —T. Coraghessan Boyle

Ate like a cart-horse —H. E. Bates

Ate like a famished wolf —Louisa May Alcott

Ate like a trucker —Jonathan Kellerman

Ate silently like two starving peasants —James Crumley

Ate slowly, thoughtfully, as if fixing the taste of each spoonful in
    her mind —Paule Marshall

Bit off an end of it [a candy bar] like a man biting off a chew from
    a plug —Peter De Vries

The bread slices collapsed like movie-set walls beneath her bite
  —Tom Robbins

Chewed ... in odd little spasms, as if seeking a tooth that wouldn't
  hurt —Paul Horgan

Chews his granola like a Clydesdale —Ira Wood

Chomping popcorn [in a movie theatre] like their upper teeth are
  mad at their lower —Tonita S. Gardner, *It's All a Matter of Luck*,
  1986

Diets, like clothes, should be tailored to you —Joan Rivers

Down poured the wine like oil on a blazing fire —Charles Dickens

Eat breakfast like a king, lunch like a prince and dinner like a
  pauper —Anon

Eating [voraciously] ... like a blowfly on a shit pile —Steve Heller

Eating like three men —Louis Adamic

Eating quickly and silently, like a bunch of taxi drivers eager to get
  back to the job —Daphne Merkin

Eating quickly and abstractedly, like a man whose habits of life have
  made food less an indulgence than a necessity —Elizabeth Bowen

Eat like wolves —William Shakespeare

Eats like a well man and drinks like a sick —Benjamin Franklin

Eats ... like stolen fruit —Ralph Waldo Emerson

Gulped the tea and felt it like sleep in her body —Frank Tuohy

He's like a camel as far as serious liquid refreshment is concerned
  —Iris Murdoch

Lap up the gravy just like pigs in a trough —Lewis Carroll

Mouth moving as rapidly as the treadle on Granny's sewing machine
  —William H. Gass

Nibble ... in quick little bites like a squirrel with a nut
  —George Garrett

Sip [a drink] ... as though he tasted martinis for a living
  —Sue Grafton

(He had) stuffed as full as an egg —Anon English ballad, "The Cork"

Swallowed it [a small sandwich] like a communion wafer —T. Coraghessan Boyle

EDUCATION

Alumni are like the wake of a ship; they spread out and ultimately disappear, but not until they have made a few waves —Anon

Colleges are like old-age homes; except for the fact that more people die in colleges —Bob Dylan

Education begins, like charity, at home —Susan Ferraro, *New York Times*, March 26, 1987
> The charity comparison has been effectively linked with other subjects.

Education, like neurosis, begins at home —Milton R. Sapirstein

Education, like politics, is a rough affair, and every instructor has to shut his eyes and hold his tongue as though he were a priest —Henry Adams

Getting educated is like getting measles; you have to go where the measles is —Abraham Flexner

He was like an empty bucket waiting to be filled [with knowledge] —William Diehl

He who teaches a child is like one who writes on paper; but he who teaches old people is like one who writes on blotted paper —*The Talmud*

Human beings, like plants, can be twisted into strange shapes if their training begins early enough and is vigilantly supervised. They will accept their deformation as the natural state of affairs and even take pride in it, as Chinese women once did in their crippled feet —Milton R. Sapirstein
> Sapirstein, a psychologist, used this simile to introduce a discussion about the educational impulse and its relationship to the educational process.

If it [learning] lights upon the mind that is dull and heavy, like a crude and undigested mass it makes it duller and heavier, and chokes it up —Michel De Montaigne

140

Learning in old age is like writing on sand; learning in youth is like engraving on stone —Solomon Ibn Gabirol

Learning is like rowing upstream: not to advance is to drop back —Chinese proverb

Learning, like money, may be of so base a coin as to be utterly void of use —William Shenstone

Learning without thought is labor lost —Confucius

Many a scholar is like a cashier: he has the key to much money, but the money is not his —Ludwig Boerne

Modern education is a contradiction. It's like a three-year-old kid with a computer in his hand who can multiply 10.6 per cent interest of $11,653, but doesn't know if a dime is larger or smaller than a nickel —Erma Bombeck

The need of a teacher to believe now and again that she fosters genius is like the writer's need to believe that he is one —Lael Tucker Wertenbaker

Rolling on like a great growing snowball through the vast field of medical knowledge —William James

A scholar is like a book written in a dead language: it is not everyone that can read in it —William Hazlitt

A scholar should be like a leather bottle, which admits no wind; like a deep garden bed, which retains its moisture; like a pitch-coated vessel, which preserves its wine; and like a sponge, which absorbs everything —*The Talmud*

Soap and education are not as sudden as a massacre, but they are more deadly in the long run —Mark Twain

Students are like acorns and oaks, there's a lot more bark to the oak and a lot more nuttiness in the acorn —Anon

Study is like the heaven's glorious sun —William Shakespeare

Take it in like blotting paper —Mavis Gallant

The teacher is like the candle which lights others in consuming itself —Giovanni Ruffini

Teachers, like actors, must drug themselves to be at their best —Delmore Schwartz

Teaching a class was in a way like making love. Sometimes he did it with great enthusiasm ... sometimes he did it because it was expected of him, and he forced himself to go through the motions —Dan Wakefield

Teaching a fool is like gluing together a potsherd [pottery fragment] —*The Holy Bible/Apocrypha*

Their learning is like bread in a besieged town; every man gets a little, but no man gets a full meal —Samuel Johnson
Johnson's simile referred to his view of Scottish education.

To study and forget is like bearing children and burying them —*The Talmud*

To transmit wisdom to the unworthy is like throwing pearls before swine —Moses Ibn Ezra

Your education, like ... carrots, is not a manufactured article, but just a seed which has grown up largely under nature's friendly influence —William J. Long

EERINESS
SEE: STRANGENESS

EFFECTIVENESS
SEE: ABILITY, SUCCESS/FAILURE, USEFULNESS/USELESSNESS

EFFORTLESSNESS
SEE: EASE

EGO
SEE: VANITY

ELATION
SEE: EXCITEMENT, JOY

ELEGANCE
SEE: CLOTHING

ELOQUENCE
SEE: PERSUASIVENESS

ELUSIVENESS
SEE: DIFFICULTY

EMBARRASSMENT
SEE: SHAME

EMBRACES
SEE: MEN AND WOMEN; PEOPLE, INTERACTIONS

EMINENCE
SEE: FAME

EMOTIONS
SEE: ANXIETY, DEJECTION, EMPTINESS, ENVY, FEAR, GRIEF,
HAPPINESS, HATE, JOY, LONELINESS, TENSION, WEARINESS

EMPATHY
SEE: KINDNESS

EMPTINESS
SEE ALSO: ALONENESS

(I was) as hollow and empty as the spaces between the stars
   —Raymond Chandler

Barren as a fistful of rock —A. E. Maxwell

Barren as an iceberg of vegetation —Anon

Barren as crime —Algernon Charles Swinburne

Barren as death —John Ruskin
      William Blake voiced the same thought, using 'void'
      instead of 'barren.'

Barren as routine —G. K. Chesterton

Blank and bare and still as a polar wasteland —George Garrett

Blank as a sheet —Reynolds Price

Blank as a vandalized clock —Lorrie Moore

Blank as death —Alfred, Lord Tennyson

Blank as the eyeballs of the dead —Henry Wadsworth Longfellow

Blank as the sun after the birth of night —Percy Bysshe Shelley

Deserted as a park bench after a snowstorm —Anon

Desolate as a summer resort in midwinter —Richard Harding Davis

Emptied like a cup of coffee —John Ashbery

The emptiness inside was like an explosion —Eleanor Clark

Emptiness

Emptiness so vast it yawned like the pit of hell —George Garrett

The emptiness was intense, like the stillness in a great factory when the machinery stops running —Willa Cather

Empty-armed, empty-handed as a lone winter tree —George Garrett

Empty as a barn before harvest —Erich Maria Remarque

Empty as a broken bowl —George Garrett

Empty as a canyon —Elizabeth Spencer

Empty as a church on Monday morning —Anon

Empty as a diary without entries —Anon

Empty as a dry shell on the beach —Daphne du Maurier

Empty as an air balloon —Thomas G. Fessendon

Empty as an egg basket —Eudora Welty

Empty as an office building at night —Anon

(He was ...) empty as an old bottle —F. Scott Fitzgerald

Empty as a person without a past, only present —Anon

(Lonely afternoons, days, evenings) empty as a rusty coffee can —Diane Wakoski

Empty as a waiting tomb —Louis Bromfield

Empty as death's head —Daniel Berrigan

(Eyes) empty as knotholes in a fence —Etheridge Knight

(The campus is as) empty as space —Babs H. Deal

Empty as the beach after a snowstorm —Anon

(The shuttle after morning rush hour is near) empty, like a littered beach after tourists have all gone home —Thomas Pynchon

Faceless as a masked bandit —Anon

Feel as dead and empty as a skeleton on a desert —Robert Traver

Feel as empty as a popbottle in the street —Marge Piercy

A feeling of emptiness, as if I had cut an artery in my wrist and all the blood had drained out —Aharon Megged

Flat and empty as the palm of his hand —Helen Hudson
       In Hudson's novel, *Criminal Trespass,* the comparison's frame of reference is a flat and empty field.

(The street below was) hollow as a bone —Peter Matthiessen

Hollow as a politician's head —Charles Johnson

Hollow as skeleton eyes —Lorrie Moore

A hollow feeling inside, big as a watermelon —Jay Parini

I'm empty ... like a sand bag —Tina Howe

It's like stepping into a church in midweek: space abounding and no one to fill it —Helen MacInnes

Look as hollow as a ghost —William Shakespeare

People, like houses, may be taken over by spirits and inhabited by ghosts when they feel they are deserted and empty —Gerald Kersh

So empty you could fire a canon and not hit anybody —Anon

Sterile as a mule —James Morrow

Sterile as a stone —Cynthia Ozick

Void as death —William Blake

The weight of his emptiness dragged like a dead dog chained around his neck —Bernard Malamud

ENDURANCE
SEE: PERMANENCE

ENERGY
SEE: ACTIVENESS/INACTIVENESS, BUSYNESS, ENTHUSIASM

ENTHUSIASM
SEE ALSO: EXCITEMENT

(Parisians) applaud like pugilists —Janet Flanner

As full of spirit as the month of May —William Shakespeare

Drinking in every conceivable impression and experience like wine —George Garrett

Eager as a deb waiting for the grand march —John MacDonald

Enthusiasm

Eager as a horse player waiting for the 6th race —John MacDonald

Eager as a hostess forcing leftovers on departing guests —Ira Wood

Eager as a leashed terrier quivering to meet every challenge
   —Hallie Burnett

(Looked as) eager as a morning hawk —Carlos Baker

Eager as an understudy —Louis Monta Bell

Eager as bears for honey —David R. Slavitt

Eager [to buy] ... like a starving man at a banquet —Aaron Goldberg

Enthusiasm flows from X like light from a bulb —Anon

Enthusiasm is a volcano on whose top never grows the grass of
   hesitation —Kahlil Gibran

(About as) enthusiastic as a guy going to the chair —H. C. Witwer

Enthusiastic as a sommelier rhapsodizing about wine —Amal Kumar
   Naj, *Wall Street Journal*, November 25, 1986
      Naj used the sommelier simile in an article about chili to
      describe the enthusiasm of a man who grows chilis as a
      pastime.

Fervor, whipping around ... like the flags in the stiff breeze
   —Sumner Locke Elliott

Follow [theatre's artistic steps] with the joy of a Mets fan checking
   the morning box scores —Jack Viertel, *New York Times*, June 1,
   1986

Hearty as a friendly handshake —Anon

Hearty ... like a trombone thoroughly impregnated with cheerful
   views of life —Charles Reade

Loved anatomy ... as a mother her child —Dr. David W. Cheever
      The anatomy enthusiast described by Dr. Cheever is Dr.
      Oliver Wendell Holmes.

Stand like greyhounds in the slips straining upon the start
   —William Shakespeare
      Donald McCaig's simile "Eager as a sprinter at the starting
      gate" and Irving Feldman's "Like a racehorse in the gate, I
      was mad to go" illustrate the many variations in use of this
      simile.

146

Talked about it [business prospects] the way a man dying of thirst might talk about a cold beer —Mike Fredman

With the avidity and determination of a housewife at a Macy's white sale —T. Coraghessan Boyle

With the fervor of castaways grasping at a smudge of smoke on the horizon —Ellery Queen

Zeal without humanity is like a ship without a rudder, liable to be stranded at any moment —Owen Feltham

Zeal without judgment is like gunpowder in the hands of a child —Ben Jonson

Zeal without knowledge is a runaway horse —W. G. Benham

Zeal without knowledge is like a fire without light —John Ray's *Proverbs*

Zeal without knowledge is like fire without a grate to contain it; like a sword without a hilt to wield it by; like a high-bred horse without a bridle to guide him —Julius Bate

Zeal without knowledge is like expedition to a man in the dark —John Newton

ENTRANCES/EXITS
SEE: BEGINNINGS/ENDINGS, DEATH

ENTRAPMENT
SEE: ADVANCING; PEOPLE, INTERACTION

ENVY

As a moth gnaws a garment, so does envy consume a man —Saint John Chrysostam

As iron is eaten by rust, so are the envious consumed by envy —Livy

Envy hit him ... like lack of oxygen —William McIlvanney

(Fools may our scorn, not envy raise, for) envy is a kind of praise —John Gay

Envy is like a fly that passes all a body's sounder parts and dwells upon the sores —George Chapman

Envy, like fire, soars upwards —Livy

Envy

Envy, like the worm, never runs but to the fairest fruit; like a cunning bloodhound, it singles out the fattest deer in the flock —Francis Beaumont

Felt a twinge of jealousy, green as a worm, wiggling deep in my center —W. P. Kinsella

Intense jealousy struck him like a missile —Mark Helprin

It [jealousy] was like a taste in his mouth —Joyce Carol Oates

Jealousy ... descended on his spirit like a choking and pestilence-laden cloud —Thomas Wolfe

Jealousy is a kind of civil war in the soul, where judgment and imagination are at perpetual jars —William Penn

Jealousy is cruel as the grave —*The Holy Bible/Song of Solomon*

Jealousy is like a bad toothache. It does not let a person do anything, not even sit still. It can only be walked off —Milan Kundera

Jealousy is like a polished glass held to the lips when life is in doubt; if there be breath, it will catch the damp and show it —John Dryden

Jealousy that surrounds me like a too-warm room —William H. Gass

Jealousy whirled inside her like a racing motor —Milan Kundera

Stir up jealousy like a man of war —*The Holy Bible/Isaiah*

A wave of jealousy floats in my stomach like a cork —Ira Wood

EPITAPHS
SEE: DEATH, PRIDE

EPITHETS
SEE: WORD(S)

Evil

EVIL
SEE ALSO: ACTIONS

All sin is a kind of lying —St. Augustine

At first the evil impulse is as fragile as the thread of a spider, but eventually it becomes as tough as cart ropes —*Babylonian Talmud*

Bad as a rotten potato —Charlotte Brontë

Corruption is like a ball of snow, when once set a roll, it must increase —Charles Caleb Colton

The Devil ... like influenza he walks abroad —W. H. Auden

Evil actions like crushed rotten eggs, stink in the nostrils of all —Bartlett's *Dictionary of Americanisms*

Evil ... a quality some people are born with, like a harelip —Ross Macdonald

Evil as dynamiting trout —Robert Traver

Evil enters like a needle and spreads like an oak tree —Ethiopian proverb

Evil, like parental punishment, is not intended for itself —Josepiz Albo

Evils in the journey of life are like the hills which alarm travelers on the road. Both appear great at a distance, but when we approach them we find they are far less insurmountable than we had conceived —Charles Caleb Colton

Evils, like poisons, have their uses, and there are diseases which no other remedy can reach —Thomas Paine

He's like a fox, grey before he's good —Thomas Fuller

Immorality in a house is like a worm in a plant —*Babylonian Talmud*

Immoral, like plying an alcoholic with liquor —Anon

Obscene as cancer —Wilfred Owens

Our sins, like our shadows when day is in its glory, scarce appear; toward evening, how great and monstrous they are! —Sir John Suckling

(He is a man of splendid abilities, but utterly corrupt. He shines and stinks like rotten mackerel by moonlight —John Randolph

Sin is a sort of bog; the farther you go in the more swampy it gets —Maxim Gorky

Sins black as night —Robert Lowell

So awful [a crime] it was like an atrocity picture or one of Foxe's lives of the martyrs —Jonathan Valin

Evil

(You're) soft and slimy ... like an octopus. Like a quagmire
—Jean-Paul Sartre

Vice is like a skunk that smells awfully rank, when stirred up by the pole of misfortune —Bartlett's *Dictionary of Americanisms*

Vice, like virtue, grows in small steps —Jean Racine

Vice repeated is like the wandering wind, Blows dust in others' eyes, to spread itself —William Shakespeare

Wrong as stealing from the poor box —Anon

EXAMINATION
SEE: SCRUTINY

Excitement

EXCITEMENT
SEE ALSO: ENTHUSIASM, IDLENESS

The blood burning in all his veins, like fire in all the branches and twigs of him —D. H. Lawrence

The blood surged through me like a sea —R. Wright Campbell

Drunk on your own high spirits, like a salesman at a convention
—Dorothea Straus

Excited and happy as a bride-to-be —Gloria Norris

Excited as a cop making his first pinch —H. C. Witwer

Excited as a puppy at a picnic —Nicholas Proffitt

Excited as a starlet, on the arm of an elderly editor —Philip Roth

Excited as schoolchildren on their way to a treat —Frank Tuohy

Excited ... like a kid with his first dish of ice-cream
—Louis Bromfield

Excitement caused his heart to thud all over his breast like some crazy and fateful drum —Frank Swinnerton

Excitement ... had grown to become an exhausting presence within him, like the constant company of a sleepless troop of revelers
—Joseph Whitehill

Excitement rose like a hot dry wind —Marge Piercy

Exhausting and exhilarating ... it's [tracking Woody Allen's career] like mountain climbing
—Vincent Canby, *New York Times,* February 9, 1986

Exhilarating like a swim in a rough ocean —Mary Gordon

Exhilarating as love —Honoré de Balzac

Exhilarating ... very much like the effects of a strong dose of caffeine —Georges Simenon

Felt exhilarated as a young man at a romantic assignation —Louis Auchincloss

(Music that) fired her blood like wine —Katherine Mansfield

(The hate excited her ... she was) fired up like a furnace in a blizzard night —Harold Adams

Flares up like a match —Sholem Aleichem

Flushed and voluble, like football fans on their way back from a match —Aharon Megged

Has about as much suspense as a loaf of bread being spread through a slicer —Scott Simon, reporting on a basketball game, "All Things Considered," WNYC, January 31, 1987

Her excitement strummed like wire —Marge Piercy

Her excitement was deep down like a desert river under the sands —Oliver La Farge

Life at "Nightline" [Ted Koppel television program] is like being in a popper of popcorn news —Marshal Frady, June, 1987

Responding like an overheated spaniel —Clancy Sigal

Stirring as march music —Paige Mitchell

Thrilled his sleepless nerves like liquor or women on a Saturday night —John Dos Passos

Titillated ... like naked flesh —Paul Theroux

Warmed by what he'd read as if it had been draughts of rum —John Cheever

EXERCISE
SEE: SPORTS

EXHAUSTION
SEE: WEARINESS

EXITS
SEE: BEGINNINGS/ENDINGS, DISAPPEARANCE

EXPLOSION
SEE: BURST

EYE(S)

Eye(s)

Behind the glasses his eyes looked look like little bicycle wheels at dizzy speed —William Faulkner

Dull eyes set like pebbles in a puffy, unwholesome-looking face —Eric Ambler
> Eye/pebble comparisons abound, with examples throughout this section.

Eye-sockets deep as those of a death's head —Thomas Hardy

Eye-sockets ... like dark caves —John Wainwright

Eyeballs like shelled hard-boiled eggs —Ivan Bunin

Eyes as big and as soft and as transparent as ripe gooseberries —Edna O'Brien

Eyes ... as cloudy as poisoned oysters —Miles Gibson

Eyes ... big and shiny, black as oil —Shirley Ann Grau

Eyes blackly circled like those of a raccoon —Lael Tucker Wertenbaker

Eyes ... carefully painted like the eyes on Egyptian frescoes —Anaïs Nin, *Chicago Review*, Winter-Spring, 1962

Eyes ... deep and dark like mountain nights —Mary Hedin

Eyes ... deep as a well —Walter Savage Landor

Eyes flat as glass —James Lee Burke

Eyes ... flat gold, like a lemur's —Sue Grafton

Eyes ... like those of a lobster, as if they were on stalks —William James, letter from Germany to sister Alice, January 9, 1868

Eyes ... like tiny stone wedges hammer between the lids —Ross Macdonald

Eyes like tunnels —Arthur Miller

Eyes like twin daisies in a bucket of blood —Leonard Washborn,
    Inter-Ocean, Chicago newspaper, 1880s

Eyes ... like two black seeds —Dashiell Hammett

Eyes ... like two holes burned in a blanket —Borden Deal

Eyes ... like two obeisant satellites —Cynthia Ozick

Eyes ... like two pissholes in the snow —American colloquialism

Eyes ... like violets by a river of pure water —Oscar Wilde

Eyes like washed pebbles stuck in cement (gave him a slightly
    aggressive look) —Donald MacKenzie

Eyes like white clay marbles —Randall Jarrell

Eyes limpid and still like pools of water —Robert Louis Stevenson

Eyes ... like glass marbles —Herman Wouk

Eye sockets ... as flat as saucers —Z. Vance Wilson

Eyes peering between folds of fat like almond kernels in half-split
    shells —Edith Wharton

Eyes pressed so deep in his head that they seemed ... like billiard
    balls sunk in their pockets —William Styron

Eyes, restless, softly brown like a monkey's —F. van Wyck Mason

Eyes ... round and shiny, like the glass-bead eyes of stuffed animals
    —Margaret Atwood

Eyes, round as cherries —Ignazio Silone

Eyes ... round as quarters —Laurie Colwin

Eyes ... round, inane as the blue pebbles of the rain
    —Dame Edith Sitwell

Eyes shaped like peach pits —Bobbie Ann Mason

Our very eyes are sometimes like our judgements, blind
    —William Shakespeare

Protruding eyes that looked like two fish straining to get out of a
    net of red threads —Flannery O'Connor

Eye(s)

The pupils of his eyes were like disks of blue fire —Oscar Wilde

Round eyes like blue polka dots in her crimson face —Helen Hudson

Sharp stains like poor coffee under her eyes —V. S. Pritchett

She was wearing so much eyeliner that her eyes looked as if they had been drawn in ink —Jonathan Valin

Small eyes, set like a pig's in shallow orbits —Francis Brett Young

Their eyes seemed like rings from which the gems had been dropped —Dante Alighieri

Two little eyes like gimlet holes —Émile Zola

The veins in her eyeballs twisted like a map of jungle rivers —Arthur Miller

EYE COLOR
SEE: EYE(S)

Face(s)

FACE(S)
SEE ALSO: EYE(S); HAIR; MOUTH; PHYSICAL APPEARANCE; SKIN

A beautiful face ... cut as clear and sharp as a cameo —Jack London

Angular face, sharp as the face of the knave in a deck —George Garrett

A bulky white face like that of a Mother Superior —Frank Swinnerton

The countenance is the title page which heralds the contents of the human volume, but like other title pages it sometimes puzzles, often misleads, and often says nothing to the purpose —William Matthews

A desolate, cratered face, sooty with care like an abandoned mining town —Joseph Heller

A dry energetic face which seemed to press forward with the spring of his prominent features, as though it were the weapon with which he cleared his way through the world —Edith Wharton

Face ... as broad and plain as a tin pie pan —Jean Thompson

A face as creased and limited as her conversation —Hortense Calisher

FACE...BUNCHED UP LIKE A FIST

Face ... as creased and brown as a walnut —Margaret Millar

Face ... bunched up like a fist —Jonathan Valin

Face ... changeable as an autumn sky —John O'Connor

Face ... clean as a china plate —Dorothy Canfield Fisher

Face clear as a cloud —Arthur A. Cohen

Face crumpled as if it had been left out in the rain
—Lael Tucker Wertenbaker

Face ... doughy, like a fresh baking of bread just put out to rise
—Paul J. Wellman

Face ... dry and immobile, like a mummy's —Ignazio Silone

Face ... has the compressed appearance, as though someone had
squeezed his head in a vise —Woolcott Gibbs, about Thomas
Dewey 1940 campaign

Face ... heavy as a sack —Honoré de Balzac

Face ... heavy, as if little bags of sand had been painlessly sewn into
various parts of it, dragging the features away from the bones
—Kingsley Amis

A face in many planes, as if the carver had whittled and modelled
and indented to see how far he could go —Willa Cather

Face is like the Milky Way in the sky —Sir John Suckling

Face ... its beauty fortuitous like that of a Puritan woman leaning
over the washtub —Walker Percy

Face lean as a hatchet —William Beechcroft

Face like a pie ... out of the oven too soon —William Faulkner

A face like a 16-oz. boxing glove —Harry Prince

Face ... like a badly packed suitcase —Jimmy Sangster

His unkempt face hung like a bad smell over his dirty clothes
—James Crumley

Intense aquiline profile, like the prow of a boat straining forward
from too close a fastening —Ruth Suckow

Looked like a miniature beside a portrait in oils —Honoré de Balzac

Old slightly wizened face, like minor characters in novels of whom one is told that 'they might have been any age from 20 to 50' —Edward Marsh

A profile like a bread knife —Harvey Swados

A profile like a set of keys and a nose like a bicycle seat —Joey Adams

Profile ... like the blade of a knife, cold and sharp —Honoré de Balzac

A round coarse face like a pomegranate —Frank Swinnerton

Round red face shone like freshly washed china —Katherine Mansfield

A sly, pointed face with something vixen in it, the look of a child evacuee who had lost his parents and grown up too fast —Penelope Gilliatt

They had long tired faces. Their yawns, snapping and unsnapping their jaws, made them look like horses —Boris Pasternak

A thin face, pointed as a paper knife —Helen Hudson
> The man thus described in Hudson's story, *The Tenant,* is trying to pry information out of a troubled woman. The author built upon the paper knife comparison by adding "Ready to slit her open."

Weather beaten face, like it was smoked and cured —George Garrett

Wild faces like men hopped up on dope —George Garrett

FACIAL COLOR
SEE: COLORS

FACTS
SEE: TRUTH

FAILURE
SEE: SUCCESS/FAILURE

FALL
SEE: SEASONS

FAME

Celebrities ... get consumed just as fast as new improved soaps, new clothing fashions and new ideas —Russell Baker

Fame

Celebrities used to be found like pearls in oysters and with much the same defensive mechanisms —Barbara Walters

Celebrity is like having an extra lump of sugar in your coffee —Mikhail Baryshnikov

Fame always melts like ice cream in the dish —Delmore Schwartz

Fame grows like a tree with hidden life —Horace

Fame is a colored patch on a ragged garment —Alexander Pushkin

Fame is like a crop of Canada thistles, very easy to sow, but hard to reap —Josh Billings
> In Billings' phonetic dialect this reads: "Fame is like a crop ov kanada thissels, very eazy tew sew, but hard tew reap."

Fame isn't a thing. It's a feeling. Like what you get after a pill —Joyce Cary

Fame ... it's like having a string of pearls given you. It's nice, but after a while, if you think of it at all, it's only to wonder if they're real or cultured —W. Somerset Maugham

Fame, like a river, is narrowest at its source and broadest afar off —Proverb

Fame, like a wayward girl, will still be coy to those who woo her with too slavish knees —John Keats

Fame, like man, will grow white as it grows old —Abraham Cowley

Fame, like water, bears up the lighter things, and lets the weighty sink —Sir Samuel Tuke
> A slight variation by Francis Bacon: "Fame is like a river, that bears (modernized from 'beareth') on things light and swollen, and drowns things weighty and solid."

Fame to the ambitious, is like salt water to the thirsty, the more one gets the more he wants —Emil Ebers

Glories, like glow-worms afar off, shine bright, but looked at near have neither heat nor light —John Webster
> Slightly modernized from "Afar off shine bright, but look'd too near have neither heat nor light."

Glory is like a circle in the water, which never ceases to enlarge itself till by broad spreading it disperse to nought —William Shakespeare
> Shakespeare used the old English 'ceathes.'

Her life had become akin to living inside a drum with the whole world beating on the outside —Barbara Seaman

In her biography of Susann, *Lovely Me,* this is how Seaman describes her subject's life after she becomes a famous author.

Like grass that autumn yellows your fame will wither away —Phyllis McGinley

Like madness is the glory of this life —William Shakespeare

Men's fame is like their hair, which grows after they are dead, and with just as little use to them —George Villiers

Our glories float between the earth and heaven like clouds which seem pavilions of the son —Edward Bulwer-Lytton

Posterity is a switchboard to past, present and future —Karl Shapiro

The public's appetite for famous people is big as a mountain —Robert Motherwell, *New York Times,* January 22, 1986

The way to fame is like the way to heaven, through much tribulation —Lawrence Sterne

FAMILY
SEE: PEOPLE, INTERACTION

FAREWELLS
SEE: BEGINNINGS/ENDINGS

FASHION
SEE: CLOTHING

FATE
SEE: LIFE

FATIGUE
SEE: WEARINESS

FATNESS
SEE: BODY, INSULTS, PHYSICAL APPEARANCE

FEAR
SEE ALSO: ANXIETY

Afraid, as children in the dark —Dante Gabriel Rossetti

An air of terrifying finality, like the clap of doom —Herbert Lieberman

Fear

(A vague, uncatalogued) apprehension, as cold and disquieting as a first snowflake smudging the window of a warm and complacent room —Derek Lambert

As courage imperils life, fear protects it —Leonardo Da Vinci

As easily daunted as an elephant in the presence of a mouse —Ben Ames Williams

Brute terrors, like the scurrying of rats in a deserted attic, filled the more remote chambers of his brain —Robert Louis Stevenson

Cowardice, like alcoholism, is a lifelong condition
 —Susan Walton, *New York Times*/Hers, June 4, 1987
> The cowardice Walton is comparing to alcoholism is that which drives the person who always does what is expected and when.

Cowardly as the hyena —Beryl Markham

His cowardice ... fixed him like an invisible cement, or like a nail —Cynthia Ozick

Dreaded (her) like fire —Alexander Pushkin

The dread in his lungs lay heavy as cold mud —Peter Matthiessen

An eddy of fear swirled around her, like dust rising off the floor in some barren drafty place —Cornell Woolrich

Fear ... a little like the fear of a lover who realizes that he is falling out of love —May Sarton

Fear ... came and went like the throb of a nerve in an open tooth —James Warner Bellah

Fear ... clutching at his heart ... as if tigers were tearing him —Willa Cather

Fear ... compressed me like a vise —Aharon Appelfeld

Fear fell [on crowd] like the shadow of a cloud —John Greenleaf Whittier

Fear ... gnaws like pain —Dame Edith Sitwell

Fearing them as much ... as a nervous child with memory filled with ghost-stories fears a dark room —W. H. Hudson

Fear is like a cloak which old men huddle about their love, as if to keep it warm —William Wordsworth

Fear ... lay on me like a slab of stone —Norman Mailer

(In my body is a) fear like metal —Marilyn Hacker

The fear of failure ... blew like a Siberian wind on our unprotected backs —John Le Carré

Fear oozed out (of the woods), as out of a cracked bottle —Dorothy Canfield Fisher

Fear ran through him like a sickness —Brian Moore

Fears ... fell from him like dreams from a man waking up in bed —G. K. Chesterton

Fear ... sat heavy in the center of his body like a ball of badly digested food —George Garrett

Fears came scurrying out from their hiding places like mice —Paige Mitchell

Fear ... seized all his bones like water —Hugh Walpole

Fear shot through me like a jolt of electricity —Sue Grafton

Fear spread like a common chill —Paige Mitchell

The fear [of death] ... stood silent behind them like an inflexible and cold-eyed taskmaster —Joseph Conrad

Fear stuck in his throat like a cotton hook —Charles Johnson

Fear swelled like some terrible travail —Heinrich Böll

Fear tangled his legs like a barricade —Harris Downey

Fear tastes like a rusty knife —John Cheever

Fear trills like an alarm bell you cannot shut off —John Updike

Fear worked like yeast in my thoughts, and the fermentation brought to the surface, in great gobs of scum, the images of disaster —Evelyn Waugh

Fear wrapped itself around his chest like a wide leather strap tightened by a maniac —François Camoin

Feeling as if an ice pick had been plunged into his liver —Peter Benchley

(I had) a feeling in my knees like a steering wheel with a shimmy —Rex Stout

Fear

Feel like clammy fingers were poking at my very heart
—Borden Deal

Feel like a tight-rope walk high over hell —Kenneth Fearing

Feels fear, like a water bubble in his throat —Jessie Schell

Felt a chill ... like swimming into a cold pocket in a lake
—Tobias Wolff

Felt a driblet of fear ... like a glug of water backing up the
momentarily opened drain and polluting the bath with a dead
spider, three lice, a rat turd, and things he couldn't stand to
name or look at —Bernard Malamud

Felt like a deer stepping out before the rifle of the hunter
—Piers Anthony

Felt like a nightmare that had yet to be dreamt —Stanislaw J. Lem

Felt (the beginning of) panic, like a giant hand squeezing my heart
—Frank Conroy

Felt panicky, like he was in a bad dream where he did and said all
the wrong things and couldn't stop —Dan Wakefield

Felt the chill of mortality ... like a toddler gifted with some scraping
edge of adult comprehension —Penelope Gilliatt

Felt the sick, oppressive crush of dread, like pinpoint ashes
—Sylvia Berkman

A foreboding, dusky and cold like the room, crept to her side
—Hugh Walpole

Frightened as Macbeth before the ghost of Banquo —Louis Veuillot

Frightened as though he had suddenly found himself at the edge of
a precipice —Honoré de Balzac

Frightened ... like a man who is told he has a mortal illness, yet can
cure it by jumping off a fifty-foot cliff into the water. "No," he
says, "I'll stay in bed. I'd rather die." —Norman Mailer

Frightening ... like one of those films where ghostly hands suddenly
reach in and switch off all the lights —Robert E. Sherwood

Fright stabbed his stomach like a sliver of glass —Arthur Miller

Full of dread and timidness as conscripts to a firing squad doing
—Richard Ford

162

Gives me the creeps ... like petting snakes —Raymond Chandler

Glances round him like a lamb at a convocation of wolves
      —T. Coraghessan Boyle

(Mildred's) heart leapt with relief like a bird in her breast
      —Noël Coward

A hiss of terror, like air whistling out of a punctured tire
      —Cornell Woolrich

Horror should rise up like a clot of blood in the throat
      —Dylan Thomas

[A group of children] huddled in a corner ... like so many wide-
      eyed, trembling mice —Gregory McDonald

I carry a scared silence with me like my smell —W. D. Snodgrass

I pretend that my right foot is like a bottle. I pour my fears down
      into the toes and cork the whole thing at the ankle, so none of
      my fears can escape into the rest of me —Dorothy B. Francis

My heart begins to pound like a thief's with the police after him
      —Isaac Bashevis Singer

My heart in my throat like a wad of sour grease —George Garrett

Panic, like a rabbit in front of the dogs —Peter Meinke

Panic rose as thick as honey in my throat —R. Wright Campbell

Panic shook her ... as awful as if she had been tottering on a cliff
      in a roaring wind —Belva Plain

Panic that was like asphyxiation —Penelope Gilliatt

Ran terror-stricken, as if death were pursuing me —Aharon Megged

Scared as a piss ant —Anon

Scared ... like a rabbit that spies a dog —Shelby Hearon

Shivered with fear like a thin dog in the cold
      —Stephen Vincent Benét

Take fear for granted like a drunken uncle —George Garrett

Terrifying, like a Samurai sword in motion —Robert Silverberg

Terrifying ... like fingers clamped upon your throat —Beryl Markham

Fear

Terror ebbed like water from a basin —Julia O'Faolain

Terror ... filled me as the sound of an explosion would fill a room —Scott Spencer

The terror inside him acted like radar —James Mitchell

Terror [of some hard to accomplish task] mocked, like some distant mountain peak —John Fowles

Terrors that brushed her like a curtain windblown against her back —Andre Dubus

(They) trail their fear behind them like a heavy shadow —Heinrich Böll

FERVOR
SEE: ENTHUSIASM

Fighting

FIGHTING

Clashed like stallions —Diane Ackerman

Defend like a dog —Lopez Portillo
> The former Mexican president's simile to describe how he would defend the peso gave his countrymen cause for anger and ridicule, often expressed by barking at him in public places.

(Self-dependent power can time) defy as rocks resist the billowes and the sky —Oliver Goldsmith

Fierce strife ... stirs one's old Saxon fighting blood, like the tales of "knights who fought 'gainst fearful odds" that thrilled us in our school-boy days —Jerome K. Jerome

Fight as one weary of his life —William Shakespeare

Fight [death] ... body and breath, till my life runs out like water —Stephen Vincent Benét

Fighting is like champagne. It goes to the heads of cowards as quickly as heroes —Margaret Mitchell

Fighting like a wounded puma —George F. Will
> Will used the wounded puma simile to describe Richard Nixon's battle during the Watergate scandal.

Fight like devils —William Shakespeare

164

Fight ... like lions wanting food —William Shakespeare

Fights fierce as duels —Anon

Fought like a pagan who defends his religion —Stephen Crane

Fought like one boxer and his punching bag ... like mismatched twins —Erica Jong

Just when the opponents seem ready to slug each other into senselessness, they clinch and go into a clumsy waltz, like boxers in a comic film —Leonard Silk, *New York Times*/Economic Scene, April 22, 1987
> Silk's reference is to combatants in strained financial markets.

Like sailors fighting with a leak we fought mortality —Emily Dickinson

A quarrel between man and wife is like cutting water with a sword —Chinese proverb

FIGURE
SEE: BODY

FINGERS
SEE: HAND(S)

FINISH
SEE: BEGINNINGS/ENDINGS

FIRE AND SMOKE

Blaze like a box of matches —Joseph Conrad

(His house) burned like a candle —Sholom Aleichem

A cloud of black soot stood in it [a room] like a fairy-tale monster in a thick wood —Boris Pasternak

A flame as clear as a streetlight —Cynthia Ozick

The flame reared like the trunk of an animal —Steve Erickson

Flames fluttered like a school of fishes —Saul Bellow

(Suddenly the) flame shot up, leaping like a dancer in the air —Alix Kates Shulman

Oily flames curl like hair —Jean Thompson

Fire and Smoke

Ribbons of flame slithered like orange serpents across the ... floor —Paul Kuttner

The smoke ascended in a straight column, as though from a pagan altar —Isaac Bashevis Singer

Smoke flared through his nostrils like an old painting of a dragon —David Brierly

Smoke in the air like fog on the New Jersey flats —Carlos Baker

Smoke (from his clay pipe) lay on the air like tule fog in a marsh —Bill Pronzini

Smoke puffed from her nostril like a tiny exhaust —Ross Macdonald

Smoke rose ... like a snake —Hugh Walpole

(In June when earth) smokes like slag —James Wright

Smoke ... spread itself out like an infernal sort of cloud —Joseph Conrad

Smouldering embers of a fire blinked like red eyes —Ellen Glasgow

[Earth and night] smoulder like the slow, curing fire of a Javanese head-shrinker —Ted Hughes

Sparks flew against the [fireplace] screen like imprisoned birds —Margaret Millar

FISHING
SEE: SPORTS

FISTS
SEE: HANDS

FITNESS
SEE: HEALTH

FLATNESS
SEE: SHAPE

FLATTERY
SEE: FRIENDSHIP, WORDS OF PRAISE

FLAVOR
SEE: TASTE

FLIGHT
SEE: DISAPPEARANCE

FLOWERS
SEE ALSO: NATURE

Primroses waving gently like lazy yellow gloves —George Garrett

All white scented flowers, like the perfume of love in fresh sheets
    —Janet Flanner

Blossoms covered trees like colored powder puffs —Rita Mae Brown

Blossoms ... fell to the ground like confetti —Shelby Hearon

Bluebells like grey lace —Joan Aiken

Bougainvillae ... large as basketballs —William Faulkner

The bud came apart ... its layers like small velvet shells
    —Eudora Welty

Flowers burst like bombs —Vachel Lindsay

Forsythia ... sprawling like yellow amoebae —A. R. Ammons

A host of crocuses stood up like yellow trumpets —Howard Spring

Irises, rising beautiful and cool on their tall stalks, like blown glass
    —Margaret Atwood

The jonquils glowed like candles —Helen Hudson

Lilies bunched together in a frill of green ... like faded cauliflowers
    —Katherine Mansfield

The little red and yellow flowers were out on the grass, like floating
    lamps —Virginia Woolf

Magnolia flowers ... like rosettes carved in alabaster —Edith Wharton

Oleanders with their pink flowers like something spun out of sugar
    —George Garrett

Open blooms like ballet-skirted ladies —John Steinbeck

Orange and yellow poppies like just-lit matches sputtering in the
    breeze —John Rechy

Out of the earth came whole troops of flowers, like motley stars
    —Felix Salten

The flowers burned on their stalks like yellow tongues of flame
    —Dorothy Canfield Fisher

Flowers

Patches of tiny wildflowers ... like luminous rugs on the grass
—Gina Berriault

Pink roses blooming like flesh —Bin Ramke

The plants sprang up thick as winter grass —Annette Sanford

Roses, big as a man's fist and red as blood —Eudora Welty

Rows of white flowers ... throwing shadows on the azure-colored
ground like trails of shooting stars —Gustave Flaubert

Small blue flowers like points of sky —Philip Levine
The simile launches Levine's poem, *The Voice.*

The tiny yellow flowers danced underfoot, like jewels in the dust
—Mary Stewart

The tulip-beds across the road flamed like throbbing rings of fire
—Oscar Wilde

Tulips ... bright as the showers —Dame Edith Sitwell

Variations of flowers are like variations in music, often beautiful as
such, but almost always inferior to the theme on which they are
founded, the original air —Leigh Hunt

The yellow dandelions rose up like streaks of golden light
—Guy de Maupassant

FOG
SEE: MIST

FOOD AND DRINK
SEE: EATING AND DRINKING

FOOLISHNESS
SEE: ABSURDITY, STUPIDITY

FOOTBALL
SEE: SPORTS

FORCEFULNESS
SEE: POWER

FOREBODING
SEE: ANXIETY, FEAR

FOREHEAD
SEE: FACE(S)

FORGETFULNESS
SEE: MEMORY, MIND

FORLORNNESS
SEE: ALONENESS

FORMALITY/INFORMALITY
SEE: ORDER/DISORDER

FORTITUDE
SEE: COURAGE, PERSISTENCE

FORTUNE/MISFORTUNE
SEE ALSO: RICHES

Adversity was spreading over him like mold —Irvin S. Cobb

Bad moments, like good ones, tend to be grouped together
    —Edna O'Brien

Blessed as the meek who shall inherit the earth —Anon
        This illustrates how a quote can be transposed into a
        simile.

The day of fortune is like a harvest day, we must be busy when the
    corn is ripe —Johann Wolfgang von Goethe

Disasters ... rolling in the brain like pebbles —Denise Levertov

Fortune is as ... brittle as glass —Publilius Syrus

Fortune is like glass: she breaks when she is brightest
    —Latin proverb

Fortune is like the market, where if you will bide your time, the
    price will fall —German proverb
        A variation by Francis Bacon begins like the above and
        finishes as follows: "If you can stay a little, the price will
        fall."

Fortunes made in no time are like shirts made in no time; it's ten to
    one if they hang long together —Douglas Jerrold

Fortune sits on him like a ton of shit —Irving Feldman

Good fortune, like ripe fruit, ought to be enjoyed while it is present
    —Epictetus

Good fortune seemed to be following me like a huge affectionate dog
    —John Braine

It's a nightmare like trying to conquer the Himalayas on roller skates
    or swim the English Channel lashed to a cannon
    —T. Coraghessan Boyle

Luck is like having a rice dumpling fly into your mouth
    —Japanese proverb

A luckless man ... the kind of man who would have gotten two
    complimentary tickets for the Titanic —William McIlvanney
        The actual text in Scotch author McIlvanney's *Papers of
        Tony Veitch* reads: "The kinnaa man woulda got two
        complimentary tickets for the Titanic."

Luck shines in his face like good health —Anon

Misfortunes disappeared, as though swept away by a great flood of
    sunlight —Émile Zola

Misfortunes, like the owl, avoid the light —Charles Churchill

Misfortunes ... passed over her like wild geese —Ellen Glasgow

Mishaps are like knives, that either serve us or cut us, as we grasp
    them by the blade or the handle —James Russell Lowell

The storms of adversity, like those of the ocean, rouse the faculties
    —Captain Frederick Marryatt

Sweet are the uses of adversity which, like the toad, ugly and
    venomous, wears yet a precious jewel in his head
    —William Shakespeare

Tried to conceal his misfortune as if it were a vice
    —Mihail Lermontov

To wait for luck is like waiting for death —Japanese proverb

FRAGILITY
SEE: WEAKNESS

FRANKNESS
SEE: CANDOR

FRAUD
SEE: DISHONESTY

FRECKLES
SEE: SKIN

FREEDOM

Abstract liberty, like other mere abstractions, is not to be found
   —Edmund Burke

(They just) broke free like the water —Boris Pasternak

Broke free like the sun rising out of the sea —Miller Williams

Feels freedom like oxygen everywhere around him —John Updike

Felt like a volatile gas released from a bottle —Olivia Manning

Foot-loose as a ram —Irvin S. Cobb

(I am) free as a breeze, free like a bird in the woodland wild, free
   like a gypsy, free like a child —Oscar Hammerstein, II, from lyric
   for *Oklahoma*
         Hammerstein used the multiple simile to paint a picture of
         an unattached man bemoaning the speed with which his
         situation can change.

Free as a fat bird —John D. MacDonald

Free as air —Alexander Pope
         The simile in full context is as follows: "Love, free as air at
         sight of human ties, spreads his light wings, and in a
         moment flies."

Free as a pig in a pen —Anon, from American song, "The Lane
   County Bachelor"

Free, as happens in the downfall of habit when the mind, like an
   unguarded flame, bows and bends and seems about to blow from
   its holding —Virginia Woolf

Free as is the wind —William Shakespeare
         A popular variation attributed to James Montgomery is,
         "Free as the breeze."

Free as Nature first made man —John Dryden

Free as Nature is —James Thompson

Free as the grace of God and twice as plentiful —Anon

Freed, like colored kites torn loose from their strings
   —Rainer Maria Rilke

Freedom and responsibility are like Siamese twins, they die if they
   are parted —Lillian Smith

Freedom

Freedom is like drink. If you take any at all, you might as well take enough to make you happy for a while —Finley Peter Dunne
> Several words have been changed from Dunne's dialect: 'any' was 'nny,' 'for' was 'f'r.'

Free speech is like garlic. If you are perfectly sure of yourself, you enjoy it and your friends tolerate it —Lynn White, Jr., *Look*, April 17, 1956

Free will and determinism are like a game of cards. The hand that is dealt you represents determinism. The way you play your hand represents free will —Norman Cousins

Independence, like honor, is a rocky island without a beach —Napoleon Bonaparte

Independent as a hog on ice —American colloquialism, attributed to New England

Independent as a wild horse —Anon
> According to Irving Stone, author of *The Passionate Journey*, this simile was used to describe the father of his fictional biography's hero, John Noble.

A laissez-faire policy is like spoiling a child by saying he'll turn out all right in the end. He will, if he's made to —F. Scott Fitzgerald

Liberty, like charity, must begin at home —James Conant
> Yet another twist on that much adopted and adapted charity comparison.

Perfect freedom is as necessary to the health and vigor of commerce, as it is to the health and vigor of citizenship —Patrick Henry

There is no such thing as an achieved liberty; like electricity, there can be no substantial storage and it must be generated as it is enjoyed, or the lights go out —Robert H. Jackson

Unrestricted like the rain —Mark Twain

Friendship

FRIENDSHIP

An acquaintanceship, if all goes well, can linger in the memory like an appealing chord of music, while a friendship, or even a friendship that deteriorates into an enemyship, so to put it, is like a whole symphony, even if the music is frequently unacceptable, broken, loud, and in other ways painful to hear
—William Saroyan

172

Became like old friends, the kind who can't leave each other on
   deathbeds —Thomas McGuane

Comradeship ... burned and flamed like dry straw on fire
   —Stephen Longstreet

Early friends drop out, like milk teeth —Graham Greene

Every man is like the company he won't keep —Euripides
      An ironic twist on, "A man is known by the company he
      keeps" and, "Tell me the company you keep and I'll tell
      you who you are."

Friendship ought to be a gratuitous joy, like the joys recorded by art
   or life —Simone Weil

Friendship ... should, like a well-stocked cellar, be ... continually
   renewed —Samuel Johnson

A friendship that like love is warm; a love like friendship steady
   —Thomas Moore

Friendship with Cape was like climbing a ladder. You had to wait
   awhile on each rung before he invited you to climb the next
   —Robert Campbell

Friends ... slipping from his orbit like bees from a jaded flower
   —Beryl Markham

He who helps a friend in woe is like a fur coat in the snow
   —Russian proverb

I keep my friends as misers do their treasure —Pietro Aretino
      Aretino's simile dating back to the sixteenth century, was
      followed by this explanation: "Because of all the things
      granted us by wisdom, none is greater or better than
      friendship."

Ill company is like a dog who dirts those most whom he loves best
   —Jonathan Swift

In their friendship they were like two of a litter that can never play
   together without leaving traces of tooth and claw, wounding each
   other in the most sensitive places —Colette

It is as foolish to make experiments upon the constancy of a friend,
   as upon the chastity of a wife —Samuel Johnson

Life without a friend is like life without sun —Spanish proverb

Friendship

Life without a friend is death with a vengeance —Thomas Fuller

Life without a friend is death without a witness —John Ray's *Proverbs*

The light of friendship is like the light of phosphorous, seen plainest when all around is dark —Robert Crowell

Like old friends they wear well —Slogan, Meyer gloves

The loss of a friend is like that of a limb; time may heal the anguish of the wound, but the loss cannot be repaired —Robert Southey

My friendship [with Vita Sackwille-West] is over. Not with a quarrel, not with a bang, but as a ripe fruit falls —Virginia Woolf, March 11, 1935 diary entry

A new friend is like new wine; you do not enjoy drinking it until it has matured —Ben Sira

A new friend is a new wine —*The Holy Bible/Apocrypha*

Their association together possessed a curiously unrelenting quality, like the union of partners in a business rather than the intimacy of friends —Anthony Powell

Went through our friendships like epsom salts, draining us, no apologies, no regrets —Rosa Guy

Without a friend the world is a wilderness —John Ray's *Proverbs*

Frowns

FROWNS
SEE ALSO: LOOKS

A dark scowl playing on his face like a spotlight —Jonathan Valin

Face was screwed up as if he had a stomachache —Nina Bawden

Frowning like the Mask of Tragedy —Max Shulman

Frowned like a public character conscious of the interested stares of a large crowd but determined not to take notice of them —Joyce Cary

Frowning, as if at some infernal machine —Elizabeth Taylor

Frowning like a battered old bison who'd spent too many years at the zoo —Jonathan Kellerman

Frowning like a cat at a mouse hole —John Updike

The frown like serpents basking on the brow —Wallace Stevens

Glared at me like a wolf in a trap —Robert Traver

Glared slightly ... like a judge intent upon some terrible evidence
    —Flannery O'Connor

Glares at me like a starving wolf from the forest —Bernard Malamud

Glares at us, his eyes like the barrels of a shotgun
    —T. Coraghessan Boyle

He was frowning, which tensed his small face up and made his deep
    pockmarks look like holes that went clear through his cheeks
    —Larry McMurtry

His lips curled away from his teeth like he was exposing so many
    switchblade knives —Donald McCaig

His scowl crinkled like crushed paper —F. Scott Fitzgerald

Like a ruffled old eagle on a high, bare rock, she scowled at the
    setting sun —Louis Auchincloss

A reddened grimace of hate and fury, like a primitive mask in a
    museum —Iris Murdoch

Scowl like a cap pulled over the brow —Peter De Vries

Scowl like a child about to receive an injection —Laurie Colwin

Scowl, like he'd turn a cold into cancer if you crossed him
    —J. W. Rider
        The scowler is a doctor.

Scowled like a junkyard dog —Jay Parini

Teeth bared like the rats —Eudora Welty

FRUSTRATION
SEE: DEJECTION

FURNITURE AND FURNISHINGS
SEE ALSO: HOUSES

Armchairs angular as choir stalls —Julia O'Faolain

Bed that sagged like a hammock —John D. MacDonald

Furniture and Furnishings

The big oriental rug glowed like a garden of exotic flowers
——George Garrett

(In a mirrored room) carpeted like spring grass ——William Humphrey

The carpet ... felt like fur laid over clouds ——Alice McDermott

Carpeting as soft underfoot as moss ——Sue Grafton

Carpets threadbare like ancient shrouds ——Jaroslav Seifert

The chairs and tables looked like poor relations who had repaid their
keep by a long career of grudging usefulness ——Edith Wharton

Chairs that looked and felt like unbaked bread dough
——Jonathan Kellerman

Chandeliers as big as locomotives ——Mark Helprin

Chandeliers like crystal clouds ——Gavin Lyall

Chinese lanterns ... hanging like fiery fruit ——Babette Deutsch

A clock clucked like some drowsy hen on the wall ——V. S. Pritchett

Coloured plates, like crude carnival wheels ——V. S. Pritchett

Curtain of red velvet drawn apart like lips ——Beverly Farmer

Curtains billow ... as if large birds were caught in them
——Charles Simic

Curtains billowed slightly like loose clothing ——Bin Ramke

The curtains fluttered coyly like ladies' skirts ——Margaret Millar

Curtains, flying out like flags from the opened, seaward window
——Elizabeth Taylor

The curtains over the open window next to them billow suddenly
like an enormous cloud ——Tony Ardizzone
This simile concludes Ardizzone's story, *The Evening News.*

Each time I'm inside [an apartment] all is precisely as it was the time
before, as if riveted in place ——Richard Ford

An electric night lamp that looks like a big firefly that might have
come in through the half-open window ——Marguerite Yourcenar

The furniture around me thick as elephants ——Richard Ford

Furniture like mismatched plates ——Jonathan Valin

TABLE LAMPS WITH SHADES LIKE EXTRAVAGANT HATS

Furniture and Furnishings

Furniture with legs like those of a very fat woman planted firmly and holding her ground —Linda West Eckhardt

A hard bench about as comfortable as a gridiron —Emily Eden

Huge chandeliers, like clusters of grapes —Helen Hudson

Lace curtains from the parlor flying like flags in the summer sky —Sharon Olds

Long gauze curtains flapping out the open window like ghosts waving —Dianne Benedict

One's chairs and tables get to be almost part of one's life, and to seem like quiet friends —Jerome K. Jerome

A polychromatic rug like some brilliant-flowered rectangular, tropical islet —O. Henry

Shadows [of flowers on window-sill] on curtains ... waving like swans dipping their beaks in water —Jean Rhys

Some aura of grief and transient desperation clings to the curtains and the shabby upholstery like a sour breath —Herbert Lieberman

The swinging-to of a shutter was like the nervous and involuntary flicker of an eyelid —Elizabeth Bowen

The table [set for party] bloomed like a miracle of shining damask and silver spoons —Elinor Wylie

(Grandma's old long wooden dining-room) table, kept as bare and shining as an ad for spar varnish —Robert Traver

Table lamps with shades like extravagant hats —John Rechy

A threadbare carpet that looked like frayed paper —Heinrich Böll

The waxed (rectangular) table shone like a black lake —Alice McDermott

A white curtain like a wedding veil —Beverly Farmer

FURTIVENESS
SEE: SECRECY

FURY
SEE: ANGER

178

FUTILITY
SEE: ABSURDITY, DIFFICULTY, IMPOSSIBILITY, USEFULNESS/USELESSNESS

FUTURE
SEE: ADVANCING, DESTRUCTION/DESTRUCTIVENESS, SUCCESS/FAILURE, TIME

GARDEN SCENES
SEE: FLOWERS, LANDSCAPES, NATURE

GENEROSITY
SEE: KINDNESS

GENTLENESS
SEE: KINDNESS

GIDDINESS
SEE: LIGHTNESS

GIFTS
SEE: KINDNESS

GLANCE
SEE: LOOKS

GLITTER AND GLOSS
SEE: SHINING

GLOOM
SEE: DEJECTION

GLORY
SEE: FAME, SUCCESS/FAILURE

GLUTTONY
SEE: EATING AND DRINKING

GOLD
SEE: COLORS, MONEY

GOLF
SEE: SPORTS

GOOD HEALTH
SEE: HEALTH

GOODNESS
SEE: KINDNESS

Gossip

[News in the computer industry] as rife with rumor as the C.I.A. or the National Security Council —Erik Sandberg-Diment, *New York Times*, January 25, 1987

Collected them [rumors] as a child might collect matchbooks —W. P. Kinsella

Confirmed gossips are like connoisseurs of cheese; the stuff they relish must be stout —Holman Day

Delivered more gossip than the *National Enquirer* —Joseph Wambaugh

Far and wide the tale was told, like a snowball growing while it rolled —John Greenleaf Whittier

Fond of gossip as an old woman —Ivan Turgenev

An indiscreet man is like an unsealed letter, everybody can read it —Sebastian Shamfort

Little words of speculation drone like bees in a bottle —Beryl Markham

News as roaring in the air like a flight of bees —Truman Capote

News ... would have run like a pistol shot through Faithful House [the name of publishing business around which Swinnerton's novel, *Faithful Company*, centers] —Frank Swinnerton

Rumor ... it had gone like a fire in dry grass —William Faulkner

Rumors [on Iranian arms scandal's effect on Washington] are spreading like lava from a volcano —Senator Robert Byrd, CBS-TV news program, broadcast December 5th

Rumors began to thicken like a terrible blizzard —Susan Fromberg Schaeffer

Rumors ... flew like birds out of the unknown —Stephen Crane

Rumors swirled around his name like the waters in a riptide —Peter De Vries

Rumors that rush around ... inflating as they go, like giant balloons until somebody comes along to prick them —Vita Sackville-West

Scandal, like a kite, to fly well, depends greatly on the length of the tale it has to carry —*Punch*, 1854

A secret in his [the gossip's] mouth is like a wild bird put into a cage; whose door no sooner opens, but it is out —Ben Jonson

Spits out secrets like hot custard —Thomas Fuller

Stories, like dragons, are hard to kill ... If the snake does not, the tale runs still —John Greenleaf Whittier

Tale-bearers are as bad as the talemakers —Richard Brinsley Sheridan

Tell tales out of school like a child —Honoré de Balzac

They come together like the coroner's inquest, to sit upon the murdered reputations of the week —William Congreve

They [a talkative family] fly around with news in their beaks like blue jays —Susan Fromberg Schaeffer

Traded in gossip the way grown-ups play the stock market —Nora Johnson. This comparison by the teen-aged narrator in *The World of Henry Orient* would be equally apt without the reference to age.

Trumpeting it [a secret] ... like an elephant in heat —William Alfred

The United States government leaks like a rusty tin can —David Brinkley, "This Week With David Brinkley," ABC-TV, November 16, 1986

Word gets around ... it's like jungle drums —George Axelrod

Word of scandal spreads like a spot of oil —Marcel Proust

GOVERNMENT
SEE: LAW, POLITICS

GRACEFULNESS
SEE: BEAUTY

GRACIOUSNESS
SEE: MANNERS

GRASS
SEE: NATURE

GRAVENESS
SEE: SERIOUSNESS

GRAY
SEE: COLORS, SKY

GREATNESS
SEE: FAME, INTELLIGENCE, MIND

GREED
SEE: EATING AND DRINKING, ENVY

GREEN
SEE: COLORS, ENVY

Grief

GRIEF

The eye, like a shattered mirror, multiplies the images of sorrow
—Edgar Allen Poe

Grief as constant as a cloud of black flies —James Crumley

Grief deep as life or thought —Alfred, Lord Tennyson

Grief floats off, spreading out thin like oil —Elizabeth Bishop

Grief had flown away like a sparrow —Jean Stafford

Grief holds him like a corset —Anon

Grief is like a mine shaft, narrow and deep —Kenzaburo Oë

Grief is to man as certain as the grave —George Crabbe

Griefless as a rich man's funeral —Sidney Dobell

Grief ... like a mallard with clipped wings circles me summer and
winter, settled for life in my lie's reedy lake —Denise Levertov
The simile comes from the closing lines of Levertov's
poem, *Visitant*.

Grief rolled across the space between us like a wash of salt water
—Sue Grafton

Grief sat on his chest like a dragon —Norman Garbo

Griefs ... pain me like a lingering disease —John Milton

I felt as if my chest were banded, like a barrel, with iron straps of
sorrow —John Hersey

Man sheds his grief as his skin sheds rain —Ralph Waldo Emerson

Mourning had lain thick in the room, like dust —Belva Plain

Mourn sore like doves —*The Holy Bible/Isaiah*

The news of his death [Byron's] came down upon my heart like a
   mass of lead —Thomas Carlyle

Our sorrows are like thunder clouds, which seem black in the
   distance, but grow lighter as they approach —Jean Paul Richter

Pure and complete sorrow is as impossible as pure and complete joy
   —Leo Tolstoy

She had borne about with her for years like an arrow sticking in her
   heart the grief, the anguish —Virginia Woolf

She wore her grief like a string of pearls —Anon

Sorrow as true as bread —E. E. Cummings

Sorrow is a kind of rust of the soul, which every new idea
   contributes in its passage to scour away —Samuel Johnson, *The
   Rambler*, August 28, 1750

Sorrows are like tall angels with star-crowns in their hair
   —Margery Eldredge Howell

Sorrows blurred around their edges, like a careless woman's lipstick
   —Jean Thompson

Sorrows, like rain, makes roses and mud —Austin O'Malley

Sorrow was like the wind. It came in gusts
   —Marjorie Kinnan Rawlings

The stains of her grief became her as raindrops to the beaten rose
   —Edith Wharton

There are peaks of anguish in life which establish themselves as
   peerless, like sharp ridges above a range —Davis Grubb

Woman's grief is like a summer storm, short as it is violent
   —Joanna Baille

Wore his broken heart like a mourning band
   —Lael Tucker Wertenbaker

GRINS
SEE: SMILES

GUILT

Branded with his guilt as if he were tattooed —Henry Slesar

Guilt

Berating himself, like an orator grading his own speech
—William Diehl

Gather guilt like a young intern his symptoms, his certain evidence
—Anne Sexton

Guilt is like mothers. Everyone in the world has at least one. And
it's passed down like a torch to the next generation
—Erma Bombeck

> This has been changed to the present tense from the
> original, which read: "I figured out long ago that guilt was
> like mothers. Everyone in the world had at least one. And
> it was passed down like a torch to the next generation."

Guilt, thick as ether, seeped into my body —Jonathan Valin

Guilt will descend on you like London fog —Walter Allen

The heat of shame mounted through her legs and body and sounded
in her ears like the sound of sand pouring —Nadine Gordimer

Looked as guilty as if he'd kicked his grandmother
—Raymond Chandler

Looking behind me ... as guilty as a murderer whose knife drips
blood —Ann Beattie

Looks like a hound caught slipping a chop from the table
—T. Coraghessan Boyle

A sense of guilt like a scent —Louis MacNeice

Shame crowding his throat like vomit —Jean Thompson

The thought of the wrong she had done ... aroused in her a feeling
akin to revulsion such as a drowning man might feel who had
shaken off another man who clung to him in the water
—Leo Tolstoy

We are all like mice: one eats the cheese and all are blamed
—Solomon Ibn Vega

Hair

HAIR

The abundance of his hair gives the impression that his head is not
fully developed, or with time has shrunk —Wright Morris

Bangs down over her forehead like a sheepdog's —Margaret Atwood

Bangs jitter across her forehead like magnets —Susan Minot

Bangs ... like overcooked bacon —Ann Beattie

Black hair hung like a river about her shoulders —Helga Sandburg

Braid of hair ... like a thick black snake —Ann Petry

A crest of stiff white hair, like a prophet or a cockatoo
    —Ellen Currie

Golden hair fountaining around her shoulders like spilled beer
    —Paige Mitchell

Hair ... as smooth and shining as a backbird's wing —John Braine

Hair ... auburn and abundant, like a well-nourished orangutan's coat
    —James Morrow

Hair ... bright and garish as brass —Margaret Millar

Hair floated around my face like wet gauze —Sue Grafton

Hair flying like a pennant —Paul Theroux

Hair foamed around her head like a dandelion cloud
    —Julia O'Faolain

Hair [red] ... gleaming like the sand streaked with sunset
    —Marguerite Young

(Gray) hair grows out of my skin like rot on an ancient tree
    —Anon Irish verse

Hair hanging straight as nylon cord —Alfred Gillespie

Hair ... its fine smooth loops, like slabs of snow, hung low on her
    cheeks —Gustave Flaubert

Hair like a field in bloom —T. Coraghessan Boyle

Hair like dry ashes —Maureen Howard

Hair like metal in the sun —Dorothy Parker

Hair ... like ripe wheat —Nelson Algren

Hair like spilled barley —T. Coraghessan Boyle

Hair ... like the rumpled wig of a clown —Hallie Burnett

Hair ... moving under her comb like a muscular skin —Gary Gildner

Hair

(Whitish) hair pointy and close as a burr or a sunflower when the seeds have been picked out of it —Saul Bellow

(The girl's black curly) hair shone like an eclipsed sun —Carol Ascher

[Blonde] hair shone like well-polished old silver —F. van Wyck Mason

(White) hair smooth as a bird's breast —Raymond Chandler

Hair spread out like feathers —Jayne Anne Phillips

Hair ... straight and sleek, and lay like black satin against her forehead —Vita Sackville-West

Hair ... thin and white and very short, laid over her skull like a placemat —Helen Hudson

Hair tumbled about her like a veil —Jean Stafford

Hair which resembled a horse's mane ... was like filaments of the brightest gold of Araby —Miguel de Cervantes

Hair which was long and smooth on either side of her face, like the shut wings of a raven —Mary Austin

Heavy chestnut hair hanging like a cloak about her shoulders —Marge Piercy

Heavy straight hair swinging behind like a rope —Eudora Welty

Her hair fell in bright ripples like a rush of gold from the ladle of a goldsmith —Stephen French Whitman

Her hair burned about her like a molten copper —Maurice Hewlett
    In the original simile the hair was 'aburned.'

Her hair drooped round her pallid cheeks, like seaweed on a clam —Oliver Wendell Holmes, Sr.

Her hair fell across her shoulders like a nun's veil —Sue Grafton

Her hair ... ran smooth like black water through her hands —Ross Macdonald

Her long, dark hair fell across her eyes like stray crayon marks —Joan Hess

Her long hair hung as straight as rain —Jean Stafford

Her wet hair lay flat as a second skin —Helen Hudson

His hair glittered like a skull cap of beads —Miles Gibson

His hair rose in an unruly swirl, like the topknot of some strange
    bird —John Yount

His hair slicks back, like a baby's or a gangster's ... shiny as a
    record album —Lorrie Moore

His hair stood upright like porcupine quills —Boccaccio

His thin gray hair lay on his scalp like moulting feathers
    —John Cheever

A light fringe of hair, almost like frost —Joyce Carol Oates

A lock of black hair lay on his forehead like a leech —Jean Stafford

Nearly as hairy as a dog —John Yount

Pale brushed heads like candles burning in the summer sunlight
    —John Updike

Peroxide hair like rope ravelings —Paul J. Wellman

Pomaded hair slicked back like shiny Naugahyde —Paul Kuttner

The thick black hair of his chest forced its way out of the opening
    [of his shirt] like a jungle growth seeking sunlight
    —Harvey Swados

A thick sprinkling of dandruff, like a fall of flour, on the shoulder of
    her blouse —Ruth Rendell

Thick yellow hair ... like a palm thatch —Jean Stafford

Tumbling loose dark hair like a wet mop —George Garrett

Uncombed hair hung about her face like an old dog's —H. E. Bates

Untidy hair like a lion's mane —Barbara Pym

The wild hair of his head bloomed like fallen snow
    —Z. Vance Wilson

Wisps of hair, like sunburst grass hanging over eyes as clear as pale
    grey crystals —Edith Wharton

With his tangled mane and beard, he looked like some ridiculous lion
    out of a bestiary —Wallace Stegner

Hand(s)

SEE ALSO: ARM(S)

Big hands like the claws of a crab —Guy De Maupassant

The bones in her narrow wrists were small as chicken bones
    —Mary Hedin

Closed they [hands] looked like clusters of unpainted wooden balls as
    large as walnuts —Sherwood Anderson

A craftsman's hands ... hands quick as cats —William H. Gass

Fist like a piece of iron —Raymond Chandler

Fists ... as large as wastebaskets —Dashiell Hammett

Fists like knotty pine —George Garrett

Hand as wide as a stirrup —Richard Ford

Hand ... dry, hard and cold, rather like a chicken's foot
    —F. van Wyck Mason

His hand felt like the tentacles of a sea anemone —Kate Grenville

Hand ... like a fine piece of ivory carving —Rebecca West

A hand like a side of meat —Douglas Adams

Hand ... like a baseball catcher's glove —Frank Ross

Hand like a boxing glove —T. Coraghessan Boyle

Hand like a bundle of taut wire —Oakley Hall

Hand like a ham —Stephen Vincent Benét

Hand ... like a sharp, icy stake —Ariel Dorfman

Hand like a wood rasp —Raymond Chandler

Hand ... limp as a tassel —Frank Swinnerton

Hand, quick as a bird claw —Eudora Welty

Hands ... as soft as cotton-wool —Ivan Turgenev

Hands ... cool, muted and frail with age like the smoothness of old
    yellow linen —Stephen Vincent Benét

Hands ... crude and functional as if whittled out of hard wood
    —George Garrett

Hands folded like flower petals —Clare Boylan

Hands ... gnarled, huge and misshapen, like chunks of wood hewn from a pale tree —James Stern

Hands gnarled, twisted and earth-stained like the vigorous roots of a tree —Ellen Glasgow

Hands, horny as a laborer's —Harvey Swados

Hands hung like clusters of sausages —Louis Bromfield

Hands ... large and too thin, like empty gloves —Margaret Laurence

Hands like asbestos —Mary Hedin

Hands ... like blocks of wood and about as gentle —Leslie Thomas

Hands like bunches of bananas —Frank Swinnerton

Hands like coal shovels —Gerald Kersh

Hands ... like dangling shovels —Jonathan Gash

Hands ... like elephant's ears —Arthur Baer

Hands ... like great paws —Elizabeth Taylor

Hands like hard rubber —Helen Hudson

Hands like hunks of steak —Julia O'Faolain

Hands like lion's feet —Arthur A. Cohen

Hands ... like wings of butterflies —Hart Crane

Hands ... looked like roots in earth —Ram Dass and Paul Gorman

Hand ... soft, like worn silk —Jayne Anne Phillips

Hands ridged like topography maps —Sharon Sheehe Stark

Hands ... slender and smooth as though they had lifted nothing heavier than a knife to cut corners —Helen Hudson

Hands ... soft from the [dish] water, like old gum erasers —Jean Thompson

Hands ... steady as steel —H. E. Bates

Hands that felt ... like a scrubwoman's hands, red-knuckled and practical —Hortense Calisher

Hand(s)

Hands that have thickened and calloused through the years so they look like tough paws —Louise Erdrich

Hands turned out flat, palms up, like a Balinese dancer —Leonard Michaels

Hands ... which projected like strings upon the finger-board of a violin, and armed with claws like those on the terminations of bats' wings —Théophile Gautier

A hand that felt as though it was reaching for you from the grave —Harvey Swados

Hand that rested like a sparrow on the table —Tony Ardizzone

Hand ... warm as a horn —Walker Percy

Hand ... wet and cold as something fished out of a pond —T. Coraghessan Boyle

Her hands were stunning, like a sublime idea —Boris Pasternak

His hands ... seemed large and awkward as if he was wearing invisible mittens —Stephen Crane

His wrists seemed to dangle from his cuffs as if they were sewn to the cloth —Jonathan Valin

Long hands, like pitchforks —*Arabian Nights*

An old man's hand, hooked and grimy with a couple of nailless fingers, like a hand in a horror film —Jonathan Valin

Veins [beneath skin of hands] tessellated like a blue mosaic, shining like an intricate blue design captured beneath glass —William Styron

Wrists like steel whips —H. E. Bates

Happiness

HAPPINESS
SEE ALSO: JOY

All happiness is a chance encounter and at every moment presents itself to you like a beggar by the roadside —André Gide

The best advice on the art of being happy is about as easy to follow as advice to be well when one is sick —Madame Swetchine

Dry happiness is like dry bread. We eat, but we do not dine —Victor Hugo

In *Les Miserables*, the hero, Jean Valjean, continues: "I wish for the superfluous, for the useless, for the extravagant, for the too much, for that which is not good for anything."

Ecstatic as a scientist who had just discovered the key to immortality
—Susan Fromberg Schaeffer

Elated as though he had stumbled on a treasure —Brian Moore

A gay, light happiness, like bubbles in wine held up against the sun
—Ben Ames Williams

Glowed with happiness, like a child with expectations of a birthday party —Frank Swinnerton

The happiest women, like the happiest nations, have no history
—George Eliot

Happiness as wholesome as honey on the comb —John Braine

Happiness choked my throat like an anthem. It flowed through me like a river from the beginning of the column to its end
—Aharon Megged

(In the midst of happiness grows a seed of unhappiness.) Happiness consumes itself like a flame. (It cannot burn forever)
—August Strindberg

Happiness ... descended upon her heart, like a cloud of morning dew in a dell of wild-flowers —Walter De La Mare

Happiness ... filled her brain like wine —William Dean Howells

Happiness flits from branch to twig to branch like a hummingbird
—Delmore Schwartz

Happiness is falling on us out of the sky ... like a blanket of snow
—Jean Giraudoux

Happiness is like a sunbeam, which the least shadow intercepts
—Chinese proverb

Happiness is like manna; it is to be gathered in grains, and enjoyed every day. It will not keep; it cannot be accumulated
—Tryon Edwards

Happiness is like time and space; we make and measure it ourselves
—George Du Maurier

Happiness

Happiness, like air, is not something you can put in a bottle —Anon

Happiness, like the pink and white anemones of my childhood, is a flower that must not be picked —Andre Maurois

The happiness of the wicked passes away like a torrent —Jean Baptiste Racine

Happiness struck her like a shower of rain —Eudora Welty

Happiness ... was there like light seen through moving leaves, like touching a warm stone —Sumner Locke Elliott

Happy and thoughtless as an apple on a tree —George Garrett

Happy as a butterfly in a garden full of sunshine and flowers —Louisa May Alcott

Happy as a clam —American colloquialism, attributed to New England
> A variation of this found in Bartlett's *Dictionary of Americanisms* is, ''Happy as a clam at high water.''

Happy as a couple of linebackers after winning a high school game —Marge Piercy

Happy as a couple of cherrystone clams —George Garrett

Happy as a dog with a bone —Anon

Happy as a lover —William Wordsworth

(I am)happy as a mother whose good baby sleeps —May Sarton

Happy as a pig in clover —American colloquialism
> In the American army this gave way to ''Being happy as a pig in shit.''

Happy as a robin when he trills —Anon American song ''Love Letters''

Happy as a swallow —Richard Ford

Happy as a tick in a dog's ear —Jay Parini

Happy as trees that find a wind to sway them —Sara Teasdale

He loved happiness like I love tea —Eudora Welty

When it [happiness] comes to one, it comes as naturally as sleep —Willa Cather

I was high as taxes —Loren D. Estleman

I was like a river in flood ... drowning in my own happiness, and buoyed up by it at the same time —Eugene Ionesco

Live together ... as happily as two lobsters in a saucepan, two bugs on a muscle —Dylan Thomas

Looked like the sun at the zenith —Carlos Baker

Happy-looking as if he's just heard the foreman say, "Not guilty" —William Slavens McNutt

Looking for happiness is like clutching the shadow or chasing the wind —Japanese proverb

Looks like he is a kid holding his first puppy —John Wainwright

Moments of happiness hang like pearls on the finest silken thread, certain to be snapped, the pearls scattered away —Joan Chase

On the brink of our happiness we stop like someone on a drunk starting to weep —Galway Kinnell

The rays of happiness, like those of light, are colorless when unbroken —Henry Wadsworth Longfellow

There is nothing which has yet been contrived by man, by which so much happiness is produced as by a good tavern or inn —Samuel Johnson, March 21, 1776

The vicissitudes of life touch him [a happy man] lightly, like the wind in the aspen-tree —Anton Chekhov

Wore his new happiness like an advertisement —Nancy Huddleston Packer

HARDSHIP
SEE: FORTUNE/MISFORTUNE

HARD WORK
SEE: AMBITION, WORK

HARMLESSNESS
SEE: INNOCENCE, KINDNESS

HARMONY
SEE: AGREEMENT, COMPATIBILITY, PEACEFULNESS

Head(s)

HEAD(S)

Great head and neck rising up like a howitzer shell from out of his six-button double-breasted, after the manner of the eternal Occupation Zone commandant —Tom Wolfe
> The man being profiled by Wolfe is Otto Preminger.

Head like a hard apple —Hugh Walpole

Head stiff and to the side like the bust of a minor Roman official —Cynthia Ozick

A head too small for the size of his face, like an underinflated balloon —Sue Grafton

Held his torso like a bit of classical rubble —Cynthia Ozick

Her head looks as if it had worn out two bodies —American colloquialism attributed to New England

His skull curved like a helmet above his deep-set blue eyes —Jonathan Valin
> In the novel, *Life's Work*, Valin follows this with a sentence containing another simile: "His lower face fit into that helmet like a hardwood dowel driven in by a hammer."

A sleek, round head like an umbrella's —Arthur Train

Health

HEALTH
SEE ALSO: PAIN

As clean and strong and healthy as a young tree in the sun —Hugh Walpole

(Has a heart) as sound as a bell —William Shakespeare

Drug addiction is like a light that doesn't shine —Cardinal John O'Connor, speaking at New York City ceremony to fight drug addiction, August 8, 1986

Felt like the symptoms on a medicine bottle —George Ade

(Looking) fit and taut as a fiddle —Robert Louis Stevenson

(I feel as) fit as a bull moose —Theodore Roosevelt to newspaper reporters

Fit as a fiddle —John Ray's *Proverbs*
> This is the most famous of the many "Fit as" comparisons. A modernized extension by novelist Geoffrey Wolff: "Fit as an electric fiddle."

(You're looking this morning as) fit as a flea —Henry James

Gobbled pills like a famished chicken pecking up corn —Dale Kramer

[Narrator's father] gradually sank as if he had a slow leak
　　—Oliver Sacks

Healthy as a kayaker —Richard Ford

Healthy as a steer —Thomas Zigal

A healthy body is the guest-chamber of the soul, a sick, its prison
　　—Francis Bacon

Hones himself down [to stay in top physical condition] sharper than
　　a Gillette blade —Norman Keifetz

It is better to lose health like a spendthrift than to waste it like a
　　miser —Robert Louis Stevenson

No neurotic is cured, he merely substitutes one set of neuroses for
　　another. Like a man who stops biting his fingernails only to start
　　scratching his head —Margaret Millar

Pent-up resentment, aggression and hostility are as bad for health as
　　constipation —George Garrett

Radiate health and good will like a red-hot stove —Robertson Davies
See Also: KINDNESS

Sickness fell upon me like an April cloud —Edward Marsh

So far as ailments went, Uncle Horace was like an insatiable
　　gardener confronted by a seedsman's catalogue. He had only to
　　get news of an untried specimen to have a go at it
　　—Howard Spring

Sound as a bell of brass —Anon
　　　　According to Larry Gottlieb, a one-time handicapper for
　　　　the *New York Morning Telegraph*, this expression used to
　　　　assay a thoroughbred up for sale is the most commonly
　　　　used simile in racing circles. It was introduced in England
　　　　during the nineteenth century.

Sound as a nut —Mazo De La Roche

Temperature as high as a tree —Mary Lee Settle

Unhealthy as the liver of a goose intended for pâté —Israel Zangwill

Heart(s)

Hard hearts, and cold, like weights of icy stone
—Percy Bysshe Shelley

The heart errs like the head —Anatole France

The heart (especially the Jewish heart) is a fiddle: you pull the strings, and out come songs, mostly plaintive —Sholom Aleichem

The heart is like the sky, a part of heaven, but changes night and day too, like the sky —Lord Byron

The heart is like a creeping plant, which withers unless it has something around which it can entwine —Charles James Apperley

The heart is like an instrument whose strings steal nobler music from Life's many frets —Gerald Massey

Heart like a child —Mary Hood

The heart of the wise, like a mirror, should reflect all objects, without being sullied by any —Confucius

Hearts isolated behind the bars of ribs and jumping around like monkeys —Yehuda Amichai

Hearts ... mellow as well-tilled soil in which good seed flourishes
—Valdimir G. Korolenko

Hearts opening like jaws —Sharon Olds

Heart trembling a little like the door for Elijah the Prophet
—Yehuda Amichai

A heart without affection is like a purse without money
—Benjamin Mandelstamm

Her heart divided like two wings —Carson McCullers

Her heart sank like a wounded bird —Ellen Glasgow

His heart ached like Niagara Falls —Frank O'Hara

His heart is like a viper, hissing and spitting poison at God
—Jonathan Edwards

His heart ... like the sea, ever open, brave and free
—F. E. Weatherly

His heart sagged in its net of veins like a rock in a sling
—George Garrett

His heart swelled up in his throat like a toad —Oakley Hall

His heart was open as the day —Anon ballad, "Old Grimes"

The human heart is like a ship on a stormy sea driven about by
    winds blowing from all four corners of heaven —Martin Luther

The human heart is like a millstone in a mill: when you put wheat
    under it, it turns and grinds and bruises the wheat to flour; if
    you put no wheat, it still grinds on, but then 'tis itself it grinds
    and wears away —Martin Luther

A man's heart is like a sponge, just soaked with emotion and
    sentiment of which he can squeeze a little bit out for every
    pretty woman —Helen Rowland

A man's heart, like an automobile, is always apt to skid and ditch
    him just at the psychological moment when he thinks he has it
    under perfect control —Helen Rowland

My heart clenched like a fist —Charles Johnson
        The fist comparison is also effective for describing a grim,
        pinched facial expression.

My heart is like an apple-tree whose boughs are bent with thick-set
    fruit —Christina Rossetti
        The first stanza of *A Birthday*, from which this is taken,
        contains yet another heart comparison: "My heart is like a
        rainbow shell that paddles in a halcyon sea."

My heart is like an outbound ship that at its anchor swings
    —John Greenleaf Whittier

My heart is like a singing bird —Christina Rossetti

My little heart pops out, like springs —Diane Wakoski
        This simile is the title of a poem which begins with yet
        another simile: "A little spirit in me that's wound up like a
        clock."

The heart is like a creeping plant, which withers unless it has
    something around which it can entwine —Charles James Apperley

Without a loved one my heart's like a beet root choked with
    chickweed —A Broken-Hearted Gardener, anonymous 19th
    century verse

197

Heat

HEAT

The days were like hot coals —Henry Wadsworth Longfellow

A glaring, summery heat covered everything like a layer of glass —Jean Thompson

The heat came down on you like a leaden mantle, stifling you as it did so —Dominique Lapierre

[Midsummer] heat closed in like a hand over a murder victim's mouth —Truman Capote

Heat fell on her like a blanket —Julia O'Faolain

Heat gathers like fog —Angela Carter

Heat ... heavy as water —Dan Jacobson

The heat ... hung like a hot dust vapor —H. E. Bates

Heat lay on the pavement like a tired dog in the doorway of a house —Aharon Megged

Heat shimmered and bent the fields like the landscape was a reflection in an old mirror —Will Weaver

The heat thick as a swamp —Margaret Atwood

Heat thick as jelly —Elizabeth Enright

The heat was like a tyrant who hated his subjects —William H. Hallhan

The heat was like a wasting disease —T. Coraghessan Boyle

Heat waves ... rising ... like fumes off kerosene —Larry McMurtry

Heat waves rose writhing like fine wavy hair —Wallace Stegner

(Sun) hot as a blast furnace —Raymond Chandler

Hot as a blister —Sir Francis C. Burnand

Hot as a draft from hell —William H. Gass

Hot as a four-alarm fire —H. C. Witwer

Hot as a fox —Elizabeth Spencer

Hot as a jungle —T. Coraghessan Boyle

Hot as a mink in Africa —Reynolds Price

Hot as an oven —*The Holy Bible*

> Writers and speakers have long repeated and enlarged upon this simile, changing the descriptive frame of reference altogether or switching from the oven to what comes out of it. Some of these old-timers include: "Hot as hell-fire" (John Dryden), "Hot as hate" (Hamlin Garland), "Hot as hammered hell/hot as hammered lightning" (American colloquialisms) and "Hot as a basted turkey" (Will Carleton).

(On some nights, New York is as) hot as Bangkok —Saul Bellow

Hot as live ash —Beryl Markham

(I am as) hot as molten lead, and as heavy too
—William Shakespeare

(I'm) hot as shit —Richard Ford

(Even the fog that day was) hot as soup —Marge Piercy

Hot as the business end of a pistol —Delmore Schwartz

Hot as the hinges of hell —Babs H. Deal

The hot days pressed people flat as irons
—Susan Fromberg Schaeffer

Hot, like a furnace room —Frank Conroy

It was like being inside a radiator —David Brierley

It was more than hot: it was like being under a damp blanket in the tropics —Laurie Colwin

Scorches like nettles —Babette Deutsch

Steaming [from hot weather] like crabs in a soup pot
—Margaret Laurence

(The shallow ditches were) steaming like fresh cowflap
—Paul Theroux

[A hot bath] steams like a bowl of soup —Margaret Atwood

(She was) trapped between the heat of the sun and the heat rising from the earth. It was like being struck simultaneously by gusts of fire from above and from below —Margaret Millar

Warm as a newborn child —William Alfred

Warm as summer —Walter Savage Landor

Warm as veins —Ted Hughes

(The water is) warm like my blood —Marge Piercy

(A novel that) warms like a hug —Anon book blurb, quoted in advertisement from *San Francisco Chronicle*

HELPFULNESS
SEE: KINDNESS

HESITANCY
SEE: UNCERTAINTY

HILLS
SEE: MOUNTAINS

HISTORY
SEE: MEMORY

HOCKEY
SEE: SPORTS

HOLLOWNESS
SEE: EMPTINESS

HOME
SEE: FURNITURE AND FURNISHINGS, HOUSES

HONESTY
SEE: RELIABILITY/UNRELIABILITY

HOPE
SEE: DREAMS

HORROR
SEE: FEAR

HOSTILITY
SEE: ANGER

HOUSES
SEE ALSO: FURNITURE AND FURNISHINGS

[A modern building] all glossy undulations and shining declivities, like a razor haircut in concrete and glass —Jonathan Valin

(The place was) as conspicuously unadorned as a Presbyterian church —Jonathan Valin

(Tenement house with mean little) balconies pulled out one by one like drawers —Vladimir Nabokov

Bricks [in path to front door of house] laid close as your hairs —Sharon Olds

A building long and low like a loaf of bread —Marge Piercy

Buildings as badly painted as old whores —Larry McMurtry

Buildings, lined up like ships —Helen Hudson

Buying a new home is like raising children; there's always room for improvement —Arlene Zalesky, *Newsday*/Viewpoints. September 27, 1986

The church has a steeple like the hat of a witch —William H. Gass

(Church) cold, damp and smelly as a tomb —Sean O'Faolain

Cottages looking like something the three little pigs might have built —Sue Grafton

Darkened houses loomed like medieval battlements —J. W. Rider

Decrepit houses lay scattered around the landscape like abandoned machines on a battlefield —Peter Meinke

Door ... shut like an angry face —John Updike

A duplex co-op that made Lenny's [Leonard Bernstein] look like a fourth-floor walkup —Tom Wolfe

An estate without a forest is like a house without a chimney —Sholom Aleichem

A first home, like the person who aroused our initial awakening to sex, holds forever strong sway over our emotions —Dorothea Straus

Frame houses collapsing at their centers like underdone cakes —Jean Thompson

A glass-and-concrete air-conditioned block of a building cantilevered from the hillside like a Swiss sanitorium —Walker Percy

The great glass doors ... swished together behind him like an indrawn breath —A. Alvarez

Her house is like her chiffon cakes, all soft surfaces and pleasant colors —Bobbie Ann Mason

201

A home is like a reservoir equipped with a check valve: the valve permits influx but prevents outflow —E. B. White

A house like this is like some kinds of women, too expensive —James Hilton

House narrow as a coffin —Angela Carter

Apartments ... looking like giant bricks stabbed into the ground —W. P. Kinsella

Houses, like people, have personalities, and like the personalities of people they are partly molded by all that has happened to them —Louis Bromfield

Houses that aged nicely, like a handsome woman —James Crumley

Houses, their doors and windows open, drawing in freshness, were like old drunkards or consumptives taking a cure —Saul Bellow

The house stood like a huge shell, empty and desolate —H. E. Bates

House ... trim and fresh as a birdcake and almost as small —William Faulkner

It [house] sat among ten acres of blackberry brambles, like an abandoned radio —Tom Robbins

[A ranch-style house] just too cute for words ... it looked as if it had been delivered, already equipped, from a store —Christopher Isherwood

Kept it [an old historic house] up like a museum —Ruth Prawer Jhabvala

Long rows of apartment houses stood bald and desolate, like sad old prostitutes —Erich Maria Remarque

It [a big building] looked as bleak as a barracks —Robert Silverberg

Looked as homey and inviting as the House of Usher —Sarah Bird

Houses (seen from belfry) looked like small caskets and boxes jumbled together —Boris Pasternak

A modern building made of ... big cubes of concrete like something built by a child —Edna O'Brien

DOOR...SHUT LIKE AN ANGRY FACE

Houses

Modern buildings tend to look like call girls who came out of it intact except that their faces are a touch blank and the expression in their eyes is as lively as the tip of a filter cigarette —Norman Mailer

Paint peeled from it [an apartment house] in layers, like a bad sunburn —Paige Mitchell

A peculiar, suggestive heaviness, trapping the swooning buildings in a sweet, solid calm, as if preserving them in honey —Angela Carter

The pink stucco apartment house looked like a cake that was inhabited by hookers about to jump out of it any second —Robert Campbell

A pretty country retreat is like a pretty wife: one is always throwing away money decorating it —Washington Irving

Residences ... of brick, whitewashed and looking faintly flushed, like a pretty girl, with the pink of the brick glowing through where the whitewash had worn off —Harvey Swados

Slate roofs ... like the backs of pigeons —Don Robertson

Tents sprang up like strange plants. Camp fires, like red, peculiar blossoms, dotted the night —Stephen Crane

Victorian house ... shaped like a wedding cake —Laurie Colwin

We require from buildings, as from men, two kinds of goodness: first, the doing their practical day well: then that they be graceful and pleasing in doing it —John Ruskin

HUMILITY
SEE: MEEKNESS

Humor

HUMOR
SEE ALSO: CLEVERNESS

Funny as a crutch —American colloquialism
    This typifies the ironic simile that says one thing while it means quite the opposite. A variation that takes the irony an extra step: "Funny as a rubber crutch."

Funny as a dirty joke at a funeral —William McIlvanney

Funny as your own funeral —Anon

Good jests bite like lambs, not like dogs —Thomas Fuller

Humor ... like good cheese, mellowed and ripened by age
—Dorothy Canfield Fisher

Humor, like history ... repeats itself like a Gila monster
—Harold Adams

Jokes that weren't proper and which therefore went through me like
an electric shock, both pleasant and intolerable
—Thomas Keneally

Like clothes for the needy, they [jokes] were worn, shabby and used
—Henry Van Dyke

Sarcasm should not be like a saw, but a sword; it should cut, and
not mangle —Lord Francis Jeffrey

A sarcastic wit is a kind of human pole-cat —Josh Billings
In Billings' phonetic dialect this reads: "a sarkastic wit iz a
kind ov human pole-cat."

They [poorly told jokes] just lie where they fall, plop, like dropped
jellyfish —Herman Wouk

True sacrcasm is like a swordstick; it appears, at first sight, to be
much more innocent than it really is, till, all of a sudden, there
leaps something out of it, sharp and deadly and incisive, which
makes you tremble and recoil —Sydney Smith

Wheezing out great lumps of irony like a cat spitting up fur
—Wilfrid Sheed

HUNGER
SEE ALSO: EATING AND DRINKING

Appetite ... as hot as a fire —Henry Fielding

Appetite ... as insatiable as the sun's —Wallace Stevens

Had an appetite like a chain saw —Harry Prince

Appetite like a sparrow —Jilly Cooper

Ate as heartily as a hungry pike —Howard Spring

Ate like a gang of hungry threshers —Erich Maria Remarque

Belly as empty as a wind instrument —Isaac Babel

Hunger makes beans taste like almonds —Italian proverb

Hunger

Hunger stirred in him like a small animal —Carlos Baker

Hungry as a bear —John Ray's *Proverbs*
> Of all the "Hungry as" similes, the link with bears, lions and wolves is one of the most enduring

(I came home) hungry as a hunter —Charles Lamb

Hungry as a nanny goat —Ben Hecht
> This simple and direct line from a play entitled *Winkleberg* marks a departure from Hecht's bent for far-fetched comparisons.

Hungry as a schoolboy —Raymond Chandler

Hungry as the grave —James Thomson

Nibbled like a minnow —Howard Spring

Passengers clustered around a food stall like ants trying to drag a crumb of cake back to their nest —Derek Lambert

Ravenous as gulls over a fishing boat —Marge Piercy

[A voracious eater] sits down to eat as thin as a grasshopper and gets up as big as a bug in the family way
—Erich Maria Remarque

So hungry, it was as if there was a hand in our stomachs, like purses, rifling through them —Susan Fromberg Schaeffer

Stomach ... as hollow as any trumpet —Henry Fielding

Ideas

IDEAS

As flowers grow in more tropical luxuriance in a hothouse, so do wild and frenzied ideas flourish in the darkness —Stefan Zweig

Every conjecture exploded like a pricked bubble —Stefan Zweig

The flow of ideas is broad, continuous, like a river
—Gustave Flaubert
> In a letter to George Sand, Flaubert thus refers to her easy writing style. About his own style, he said, "It's a tiny trickle."

Get ideas like other men catch cold —Diane Ackerman

Getting an idea should be like sitting down on a pin; it should make you jump up and do something —E.L. Simpson

His fancy ... ran along with him, like the sails of a small boat, from which the ballast is thrown overboard —Isak Dinesen

The history of ideas is a history of mistakes
—Alfred North Whitehead
> Whitehead follows this simile with "But through all mistakes is also the history of the gradual purification of conduct."

The idea came ... like a ray of light —Vladimir G. Korolenko

The idea danced before us as a flag —Edgar Lee Masters

An idea, like a ghost ... must be spoken to a little before it will explain itself —Charles Dickens

The idea remained, roaming in the dark of his mind ... like a rat in the basement, too canny to be poisoned or trapped
—John Gardner

Ideas are free. But while the author confines them to his study, they are like birds in a cage, which none but he can have a right to let fly; for, till he thinks proper to emancipate them, they are under his own dominion —Sir Joseph Yates

Ideas are like beards; men do not have them until they grow up
—Voltaire

Ideas came with explosive immediacy, like an instant birth. Human thought is like a monstrous pendulum; it keeps swinging from one extreme to the other —Eugene Field

Ideas come and go; they appear on the horizon as fleeting as rainbows, they rise and fall again like hemlines
—Lynne Sharon Schwartz

Ideas die, like men —Marguerite Yourcenar

Ideas good as a fat wallet —Richard Ford

Ideas, like women's clothes and rich men's illnesses, change according to fashion —Lawrence Durrell

Ideas of your own are like babies. They are all right if you can keep them quiet —Anon

Ideas rose out of him, streamed through his hair like wildflowers
—Pat Conroy

Ideas

Ideas should be received like guests, in a friendly way, but with the reservation that they are not to tyrannize their host
—Albert Moravia

Ideas that ... in the light of day, may hide but never quite go away. Like mice in old houses, one knows they're there
—David R. Slavitt

Ideas winged their way swiftly like martins round the bell at dawn
—Ivan Turgenev

The imagination is like the drunk man who lost his watch, and must get drunk again to find it. It is as intimate as speech and custom, and to trace its ways we need to reeducate our eyes
—Guy Davenport

Imagination is like a lofty building reared to meet the sky
—Gelett Burgess

Imagination ... must be immediate and direct like the gaze that kindles it —Italo Calvino

Lack ideas ... as if someone had tied a tourniquet around the left side of his brain —Anon

Like good yeast bread, a good idea needs time to proof
—Erik Sandberg-Diment, *New York Times*, August 24, 1986

(Olga's mind was sensuously slow: she) lingered over an idea like someone lingering in a hot tub —Wilfrid Sheed

Old ideas, like old clothes, put carefully away, come out again after a time almost as good as new —*Punch*, 1856

Picking up the idea by its corner like a soiled hanky
—Rosellen Brown

Planted ideas ... as a gardener will plant sticks for climbing sweet pea —Lawrence Durrell

A shortsighted concept ... rather like a bankrupt saying he's invested his capital in debts —Frank Ross

The theory arrived neither full-blown, like an orphan on the doorstep, nor sharply defined, like a spike through a shoe; nor did it develop as would a photographic print, crisp images gradually memerging from a shadowy soup. Rather, it unwound like a turban, like mummy bandage —Tom Robbins

What America needs now are ideas like shafts of light
  —Ellen Gilchrist, National Public Radio, September 22, 1986

IDLENESS
SEE ALSO: ACTIVENESS/INACTIVENESS

As peace is the end of war, so to be idle is the ultimate purpose of
  the busy —Samuel Johnson

Idle as a painted ship upon a painted ocean
  —Samuel Taylor Coleridge

Idle as if in hospital —Sylvia Plath

Idleness is a disease that must be combated —Samuel Johnson

Idleness is like the nightmare; the moment you begin to stir yourself
  you shake it off —*Punch*, 1853

Idleness, like kisses, to be sweet must be stolen —Jerome K. Jerome

An idler is a watch without both hands, as useless if it goes as
  when it stands —William Cowper
      This is modified from the original which reads ''A watch
      that wants both hands.''

Indolent and shifting as men or tides —Kenneth Patchen

A lazy man is like a filthy stone, everyone flees from its stench
  —*The Holy Bible/Apocrypha*

Like lambs, you do nothing but suck, and wag your tails
  —Thomas Fuller

(I've been) lying around like an old cigarette holder
  —Anton Chekhov

A slacker is just like custard pie, yellow all through but without crust
  enough to go over the top —Don Marquis

Sloth, like rust, consumes faster than labor wears, while the used eye
  is always bright —H. G. Bohn's *Handbook of Proverbs*

IGNORANCE
SEE ALSO: STUPIDITY

The fault unknown is as a thought unacted —William Shakespeare

Ignorance is a form of incompetence —Natsume Sōseki

Ignorance

Ignorance is like a delicate exotic fruit; touch it and the bloom is gone —Oscar Wilde

Ignorance like a fire does burn —Bayard Taylor
Modernized from "Like a fire doth burn."

Ignorant as dirt —Karl Shapiro

A man's ignorance is as much his private property, and as precious in his own eyes, as his family Bible
—Oliver Wendell Holmes, Sr.

A man with little learning is like the frog who thinks its puddle a great sea —Burmese proverb

There are a great multitude of individuals who are like blind mules, anxious enough to kick, but can't tell where —Josh Billings
Here are the words as they appear in Billing's phonetic dialect: "a grate multitude ... but kant tell whare."

Illnesss

ILLNESSS
SEE ALSO: HEALTH

Afflictions are like lightning: you cannot tell where they will strike until they have fallen —Jean-Baptiste Lacordaire

A big pulse of sickness beat in him as if it throbbed through the whole earth —D. H. Lawrence

The disease and its medicine are like two factions in a besieged town; they tear one another to pieces but both unite against their common enemy ... Nature —Lord Francis Jeffrey

Diseases ... attenuate our bodies ... shrivel them up like old apples —Robert Burton

His head seemed to be flying about like a pin wheel —Sherwood Anderson

Illness and doctors go together like priests and funerals —Armand Salacrou

Illness and medicines are invariable as costly as champagne and gaiety at a party —Janet Flanner

An illness is like a journey into a far country; it sifts all one's experience and removes it to a point so remote that it appears like a vision —Sholem Asch

210

Nausea lay like poison in his blood —Heinrich Böll

Our bowels were like running faucets —John Farris

Stricken as if an angel had landed on her bedpost —Gloria Norris

ILL TEMPER
SEE: ANGER

ILLUSTRIOUSNESS
SEE: FAME

IMAGINATION
SEE: IDEAS

IMMOBILITY
SEE ALSO: DEATH

(I am) comatose like a mouse in the sun —Janet Flanner
    The simile was prompted by the writer's being heavily
    medicated.

Fixed as the garden in a wallpaper mural —Anon

Frozen like dogs waiting at night for a bitch in heat —Bertold Brecht

Immobile as a heavily sprayed coiffure —Elyse Sommer

Immobile as despair —Yvor Winters

(Lay), immobile, like something caught, an ungainly fish
    —Daphne Merkin

Immobilized like fishes caught in a net —Dominique Lapierre

Immovable, emotionless, a jade Buddha serenely contemplating some
    quintessential episode of a TV police show
    —T. Coraghessan Boyle

(The corpse still) lay like a smashed fly —G. K. Chesterton

Lay motionless, as if felled by an axe —Stefan Zweig

Lifeless as a string of dead fish —G. K. Chesterton

Motionless as a dog thrown into the street —Émile Zola

(Clouds ...) motionless as a ledge of rock —Willa Cather

Motionless as an idol and as grim —John Greenleaf Whittier

Immobility

(Remained standing in the same place), motionless as if he were a prisoner —Bertold Brecht

Motionless, in an agony of inertia, like a machine that is without power —D. H. Lawrence

Motionless, like a man in a nightmare —G. K. Chesterton

(This play has) no more action than a snake has hips —Anon

Remained rooted in place like an oak —Charles Johnson

Sat as still as a tree —Speer Morgan

Sat like a marble man —Margaret Millar

Sat ... motionless as a drowsing man —Beryl Markham

Sat there like a potted plant —Delmore Schwartz

Sat through it all [revolution] like a slug —Rita Mae Brown

Sits impassive, like Rodin's *Penseur* —Frank Swinnerton

(I'd rather) sit still, like the pilot light inside the gas —Saul Bellow

Standing ... like a hydrant —Rosellen Brown

Standing there like a glee-club president in granite
    —Erich Maria Remarque

Standing motionless as if turned to stone —Ivan Turgenev

Standing stock still ... like George Segal plaster figures
    —Paul Kuttner

Standing there rigid as the Venus de Milo —T. Coraghessan Boyle
        In Boyle's story, *The Descent of Man*, the character voicing
        this simile speaks in dialect, using 'de' and 'dere' instead of
        'there' and 'the' as used here.

Stand motionless as a pillar of the colonial portico of a mansion in a Kentucky prohibition town —O.Henry

Stand motionless ... as though trying to make myself blend with the dark wood and become invisible —William Faulkner

Stand perfectly still, like a scarecrow —Walter De La Mare

Stand stone still —William Shakespeare
        The simile from *The Life and Death of King John* completes
        this statement: "I will not struggle; I will ... "

212

IMMOVABLE, EMOTIONLESS, A JADE BUDDHA
SERENELY CONTEMPLATING SOME QUINTESSENTIAL
EPISODE OF A TV POLICE SHOW

Immobility

Statue-like repose —James Aldrich
> The simile from a poem entitled *A Death-Bed* reads as follows in its full context: "Her suffering ended with the day; yet lived she at its close, and breathed the long, long night away in statue-like repose."

Still as a child in its first loneliness —Theodore Roethke

Still as a cocoon on a branch —Marge Piercy

Still as a folded bat —Eudora Welty

(Became) still as a hare caught in the light of a torch —R. Wright Campbell

Still as a little hare in the hollow of a furrow —Colette

(Sitting as) still as a lizard on a stone —Mary Stewart

Still as a picture —John Greenleaf Whittier

Still as a pillar —Reynolds Price

Still as a post —Fannie Stearns Gifford
> Other similes to express the same idea are to "Sit still as a fence post" and "To stand like an iron post."

Still as a snapshot —Anne Sexton

Still as a turtle on a log which is stuck in the mud near some willows —Elizabeth Spencer

Still as bushes —Helen Hudson

(The air was) still as death —MacDonald Harris

(The next morning was cold and clear and) still as held breath —John Yount

(Ray lay) still as ice —Wilbur Daniel Steele

Still as if a block of ice had formed around him —William McIlvanney

Still as a mummy in a case —Henry James

Still as sleeping princesses —Joyce Cary

Still as the wind's center —Theodore Roethke

Stood frozen like some sort of Mexican stone idol —Robert Silverberg

Stood still, petrified like the pillar of salt —Victor Hugo

Stood there rooted like a plant —Ellen Glasgow

They seemed [tired soldiers] as if they were of stone, without the strength to smile, or to swear —Boris Pasternak

IMPARTIALITY

Feel rather like a bridge [at being caught between problems of two friends] attached neither to one side nor the other of a tumultous river, suspended in space —May Sarton

Impartially welcoming as the host of a television show —Nadine Gordimer

Neutral as a page number —John Braine

(A voice) neutral as Switzerland —Anon

(The Yvette who assembled before me was as) objective as a police sketch —Jill Ciment

IMPASSIVENESS
SEE: COLDNESS, REMOTENESS

IMPERMANENCE
SEE: CHANGE, LIFE

IMPERTINENCE
SEE: MANNERS

IMPOLITENESS
SEE: MANNERS

IMPORTANCE/UNIMPORTANCE
SEE ALSO: MEMORY, NECESSITY

Brittle and meaningless as cocktail party patter —William Brammer

His influence ... it is like burning a ... candle at Dover to show light at Calais —Samuel Johnson
> Had Johnson been an American living in America instead of an Englishman living in England, his comment on Thomas Sheridan's influence on English literature might well have illustrated with "A candle in New York to show light in Boston."

Hollow as the (ghastly) amiabilities of a college reunion
—Raymond M. Weaver

Impact [of information] ... as thin as gold —Raymond Chandler

(About as) important as a game of golf to an astronomer —Anon

Important as mathematics to an engineer —Anon

Inconsequential ... like the busy work that grade school teachers
devise to keep children out of mischief —Ann Petry

Insignificant as the canals of Mars —Frank Conroy

Its loss would be incalculable ... like losing the Mona Lisa
—Dr. Paul Parks, *New York Times*, August 23, 1986 on potential
death of Florida's Lake Okeechobee

Meaningful as love —Kenneth Patchen

Meaningless, like publishing a book of your opinions with a vanity
press —Scott Spencer

Of no more importance than a flea or a louse —Boris Pasternak
In the novel, *Doctor Zhivago*, a character uses this simile to
compare a wife to workers.

Seemed scarcely to concern us, like fairy tales or cautionary fables
that are not to be taken literally or to heart —Joan Chase

Shallow as a pie pan —Anon

[A speech] shallow as time —Thomas Carlyle

Uneventful as theory —A. R. Ammons

Worthless as withered weeds —Emily Brontë

IMPOSSIBILITY
SEE ALSO: ABSURDITY, DIFFICULTY

About as much chance as a man with a wooden leg in a forest fire
—George Broadhurst

About as possible as hell freezing over —Clifford Odets

As feasible as capturing the rain in a thimble —Jonathan Kellerman

As likely as a mouse falling in love with a cat —Anon

As likely as a talk by Doctor Ruth [Dr. Ruth Westheimer, sex
     therapist/media personality] in a fundamentalist church
     —Elyse Sommer

As likely as to see a hog fly —H. G. Bohn's *Handbook of Proverbs*

As likely to happen as hair growing on the palm of my hand
     —Anon

(Anything of a sexual sort seemed) as remote as landing on the
     moon or applying for French citizenship —Kingsley Amis

As unlikely as your car metamorphosing into a rocket ship
     —Elyse Sommer

Calling on [emotional] memory for so long a leap was like asking
     power of a machine wrecked by rust —Wilbur Daniel Steele

Getting him to join (the Federal Witness Program) was like getting
     the Ayatollah Khomenei to enroll in a rabbinical school
     —Doug Feiden

Has about as much chance as a cootie on Fifth Avenue
     —Maxwell Anderson/Laurence Stallings

Has about as much chance of making it into the history books as a
     fart in a cyclone [about fictional President] —Peter Benchley

Have about as much chance as a woodpecker making a nest in a
     concrete telephone pole —Anon sports writer, about a bad
     baseball team

Have about as much chance as a dishfaced chimpanzee in a beauty
     contest —Arthur Baer
          Baer's simile was part of a comment about the 1919
          Willard-Dempsey fight.

Impossible ... like pushing a wet noodle up a hill —Anon
     Washington aide, *Wall Street Journal*, July 3, 1987
          The aide made this comparison to illustrate the difficulty
          of trying to attract attention to economic issues and away
          from the Iran-Contra scandal.

Impossible as expecting a hook to hold soft cheese
     —Anon

Impossible as it would be to fire a joke from a cannon
     —Bartlett's Dictionary of Americanisms

Impossibility

Impossible as putting the genie back in the bottle —Peter Jennings, commenting on "World News Tonight" about trying to undo damage to Gary Hart's presidential campaign after release of story about his private life, May 7, 1987

Impossible as scratching your ear with your elbow —American colloquialism, attributed to Southwest

Impossible as setting a hen one morning and having chicken salad for lunch —George Humphrey
> A comment on quick economic changes during Humphrey's tenure as Secretary of the United States Treasury.

Impossible as to imagine a man without a head —Francisque Sarcey

Impossible as to pull hair from a bald man's head —Anon

Impossible as to rivet a nail in a custard pie —Anon

Impossible as to straighten a dog's tail —Anon

Impossible as trying to put on a laughter exhibition in a morgue —J. B. Priestly

Impossible as trying to blow and swallow at the same time —German proverb
> Another example of usage turning a proverbial statement, "You can't blow and swallow at the same time," into a proverbial comparison.

Impossible as undressing a naked man —Anon
> Another simile with proverbial origins, in this case the Greek proverb "A thousand men cannot undress a naked man."

Impossible as voting "maybe" —Maurine Neuberger
> Transposed from "Many times I wished I could vote 'maybe'."

Impossible ... like compressing the waters of a lake into a tight, hard ball —Vita Sackville-West

Impossible ... like denying a champion fighter the right to compete in the ring on the grounds that he might be hurt —Beryl Markham

Impossible ... like eating chalk or trying to suck sweetness out of paving brick, or being drowned in an ocean of dishwater, or forced to gorge oneself on boiled unseasoned spinach —Thomas Wolfe

> Wolfe's writing tended towards excess. Not surprisingly, he tended to string several similes together.

Impossible ... like looking for a grain of rice in a bundle of straw —Dominique Lapierre

Impossible ... like me trying to wash the Empire State building with a bar of soap —Don Rickles

> The impossible situation described by Rickles is singer Eddie Fisher's ill-fated marriage to Elizabeth Taylor.

Impossible ... like playing tennis with the net down —Robert B. Parker

Impossible ... like selling the cow and expecting to have the milk too —Danish proverb

> Transposed from the proverbial form, "You can't expect to sell the cow and get the blood."

Impossible ... like stopping a runaway horse with your pinkie —William McIlvanney

Impossible, like trying to get blood out of a turnip —English proverb

> Efforts to get new blood out of this cliche focus on changing the object from which to extract blood ... anything from a stone to a corpse.

Impossible like trying to make cheesecake out of snow —Anon

Impossible like trying to write on a typewriter while riding a stagecoach —Dr. Ellington Darden

Impossible like trying to knock down the Great Wall with a nail file —Arty Shaw

Impossible [to keep a secret from my wife] like trying to sneak the dawn past the rooster —Fred Allen

Impossible to explain ... like telling a religious household you had decided God was nonsense —Harvey Swados

It [a hard-to-beat record] was like DiMaggio's consecutive-game hitting streak: unapproachable —T. Coraghessan Boyle

It was like talking to a tree and expecting a reply —Clive Cussler

Impossibility

It was like trying to catch an eagle in a butterfly net
—Wallace Turner, *New York Times,* February 4, 1987, reporting on efforts by Washington State game wardens to capture the large sea lions which had been destroying game fish.

It was like trying to write a description of how to tie shoelaces in a bow for a person who has never seen shoes —W. P. Kinsella

It [changing person's mind about another] was like trying to turn a mule —H. E. Bates

It [trying to sift through events from the past] was not unlike hunting for odd-colored stones in tidal flats —Norman Mailer

(Blackmailing Laidlow would be) like trying to catch a bull with a butterfly net —William McIlvanney

No more chance than a one-legged man in a football game —Elbert Hubbard

No more possible than the development of an orchid in the middle of a crowded street —W. H. Mallock

No more chance than a motorist who passed a red light talking a policeman out of giving him a ticket —Anon

The odds were like poison —Tim O'Brien

To translate this situation to reality would be like trying to stuff a cloud in a suitcase —W. P. Kinsella

Trying to make the company [GM] competitive is like trying to teach an elephant to tap dance —Ross Perot, quoted in *Wall Street Journal* article by George Melloan, February 24, 1987

Unlikely as to see a stone statue walking —Anon

IMPROBABILITY
SEE: IMPOSSIBILITY

INACTIVITY
SEE: ACTIVENESS/INACTIVENESS, IDLENESS, IMMOBILITY

Inappropriateness

INAPPROPRIATENESS
SEE ALSO: COMPATIBILITY/INCOMPATIBILITY

(I) belonged ... like a pearl onion on a banana split —Raymond Chandler

Belonged ... like a virgin in a brothel —William McIlvanney

220

MISPLACED...LIKE A DOG IN CHURCH

Belong like a right shoe on a left foot —Elyse Sommer

Belong like a white poodle on a coal barge —Arthur Baer

Feeling like a Boston schoolteacher in Dodge City —Mary Gordon

(I) feel [out of place] like Babe Paley at a bar mitzvah in the Bronx
    —Sue Mengers, talent agent, quoted by Rex Reed

Felt like a gap —D. H. Lawrence

Fits in about as well as a bird-of-paradise among wrens
    —Leslie Bennetts, about character in *The Mystery of Edwin Drood*,
    New York Times, 1985

Had about as much business teaching in college as a duck has riding
    a bicycle —Richard Ford

Inappropriate as a Size 20 Cinderella —Mike Sommer

Inappropriate as running shoes with a cocktail dress —Anon

It's like a thoroughbred horse pulling a milk wagon
    —line from movie, *The Eagle Has Landed*

Looked like a greyhound puppy in a litter of collies
    —Michael Gilbert

A man without a place to be ... that's like being alone at sea
    without a log to hang on —William H. Gass

Misplaced ... like a dog in church —Anon

Misplaced ... like a fish out of water —English phrase
        Borrowed by the English from the Greek, the simile has
        been much used and adapted since the fourteenth century.

Never fit right, like a pair of cheap shoes that sprouts a nail in the
    sole —Marge Piercy

(Looked as) out of place as a chicken in church —James Crumley

Out of place as matzo balls in clam chowder —Elyse Sommer

Out of place as a house boat on the high seas —Anon

Out of place as an atheist in a seminary —Anon

Out of place as a Presbyterian in Hell —Mark Twain

Out of place as some rare tropical bird —Anon

Out of place ... like an old whale stranded on the beach
    —George Garrett

(Harriet always seemed a little) out of things, like somebody's mother
    —Mary McCarthy

She was like something wrecked and cast up on the wrong shore
    —Elizabeth Bowen

Sticking out like a solitary violet in a bed of primroses
    —Tess Slesinger

INATTENTIVENESS
SEE: ATTENTION

INCISIVENESS
SEE: SHARPNESS

INCOMPATIBILITY
SEE: COMPATIBILITY/INCOMPATIBILITY

INCOMPLETENESS
SEE: COMPLETENESS/INCOMPLETENESS

INCONGRUITY
SEE: ABSURDITY

INDEPENDENCE
SEE: FREEDOM

INDIFFERENCE
SEE: REMOTENESS

INDIGNATION
SEE: ANGER

INDOLENCE
SEE: IDLENESS

INDUSTRIOUSNESS
SEE: AMBITION, WORK

INEFFECTIVENESS
SEE: USEFULNESS/USELESSNESS

INEVITABILITY
SEE: CERTAINTY

INFLUENCE
SEE: POWER

INFREQUENCY
SEE: RARITY

INGRATITUDE
SEE: SHARPNESS

INJUSTICE
SEE: JUSTICE

Innocence

INNOCENCE

Green as apples —Sumner Locke Elliott

Guileless as old Huck —Richard Ford

Guiltless forever, like a tree —Robert Browning

Innocence is like an umbrella: when once we've lost it we must
    never hope to see it back again —*Punch*

(Catherine's) innocence shone like an icon —Rita Mae Brown

Innocent and affectionate as a child —W. H. Hudson

Innocent and artless, like the growth of a flower —Isak Dinesen

Innocent as a baby —Anon

Innocent as a child unborn —Anon
        Jonathan Swift who used the phrase in *Directions to
        Servants* is often credited as its author.

(I was a neophyte about as) innocent as a choirboy being asked to
    conduct a solemn mass at the Vatican —Alistair Cooke, *New York
    Times* interview, January 19, 1986

Innocent as a curl —Clarence Major

Innocent as a devil of two years old —Jonathan Swift

Innocent as a game —Frank Tuohy

Innocent as a new-laid egg —W. S. Gilbert

Innocent as a snowflake —Anne Sexton

(Gaze as) innocent as a teddy bear —Babs H. Deal

Innocent as a tourist's Kodak —William McIlvanney

Innocent, like a hornet that has been disarmed —Jean Stafford

(Sat there as) innocently as small boys confiding to each other the names of toy animals —Henry James

Innocuous as flowers afloat in a pond —John Updike

Perennial innocence like a chicken in a pen —William Faulkner

She was like a young tree whose branches had never been touched by the ruthless hand of man —Katherine Mansfield

INQUISITIVENESS
SEE: QUESTIONS/ANSWERS

INSECTS
SEE ALSO: ANIMALS

Beetles and insects with legs like grass stems —Ernest Hemingway

A big black ant, shaped like a dumbbell —John Gunther

Black beetles ... crawled in all directions like animated ink —Harold Adams

Fireflies begin to rise ... exactly like the bubbles in champagne —Elizabeth Bishop

Fireflies dazzle the night like red pepper —W. P. Kinsella

Fireflies glow like planets in the moist, silent darkness —W. P. Kinsella

Fleas are, like the remainder of the universe, a divine mystery —Anatole France

A fly is as untamable as a hyena —Ralph Waldo Emerson

Insects ... crooned like old women —Stephen Crane

Mosquitoes ... as big as mulberries —William Styron

Moths as large and white as our hands —James Crumley

Nothing is so like a soul as a bee. It goes from flower to flower as a soul from star to star, and it gathers honey as a soul gathers light —Victor Hugo

Spiders which floated like cameos in their jars —Pat Conroy

Yellow butterflies flickered along the shade like flecks of sun —William Faulkner

INSEPARABILITY
SEE: CLOSENESS, FRIENDSHIP

INSIGNIFICANCE
SEE: MEMORY, IMPORTANCE/UNIMPORTANCE, NECESSITY

Insults

INSULTS (Insult similes appear in many categories throughout)

(It was) an affront, like a lewd remark —Scott Spencer

A day away from Tallulah [Bankhead] is like a month in the country
—Howard Dietz

Has a head as big as a horse, and brains as much as an ass
—Thomas Fuller
> A more condensed version: "A head like a horse with the brains of an ass."

He's like a bagpipe, you never hear him till his belly is full
—Thomas Fuller

He's like a man who sits on a stove and then complains that his backside is burning —W. S. Gilbert
> Gilbert's comparison was made in response to his partner's complaint that his (Gilbert's) words limited his desire to write "fine" music while the Gilbert and Sullivan work supported his lavish life style, quoted by Stephen Holden, *New York Times*, July 27, 1986

He [Napoleon] spoke like a concierge and said 'armistice' for 'amnesty' and 'section' for 'session' —Anatole France
> France compared Napoleon's speech to that of a concierge to emphasize that what he said unofficially was quite different from the sayings manufactured for him by hirelings.

He thinks like Nixon, talks like Eisenhower, goofs like Goldwater
—Noel Parmentel on John V. Lindsay, *Esquire*, October, 1965

His arms look like a buggy whip with fingers —Fred Allen

If he be an infidel, he is an infidel as a dog is an infidel; that is to say, he has no thought upon the subject —Samuel Johnson on Samuel Foote, October 19, 1769

I missed you like Booth missed Lincoln —Elmer Rice
> This line comes from one of Rice's best known plays, *Counsellor At Law*.

Insults are like bad coins; we cannot help their being offered to us, but we need not take them —C. H. Spurgeon

The king [Prince Albert of England] looks like a retired butcher —Oliver Wendell Holmes, Sr.
> This much quoted remark originated with a letter to Holmes' parents, on June 13, 1834.

Like a sewer rat that wants to scurry into a hole —Kenzaburo Oë

Like so many country people who lead a natural outdoor life, his features had hardly any definition. He gave me the impression of an underdone veal cutlet —Alexander King

Looks as if he had never been born and could not be extinguished —Harriet Martineau

She looked like a street just before they put on the asphalt —George Ade

She looked rather like a malicious Betty Grable —Truman Capote

A slight (of that kind) stimulates a man's fighting power; it is like getting a supply of fresh bile —Henrik Ibsen

Some insults come like a blow on the head the morning after, but a few are balm —Norman Mailer

They're [the Kennedy men] like dogs, they have to pee on every fire hydrant —Truman Capote

Why don't you buy some stuffing? Your bosoms look like fried eggs —Reynolds Price

Why don't you get a haircut; you look like a chrysanthemum —P. G. Wodehouse

You are like a cuckoo, you have but one song —H. G. Bohn's *Handbook of Proverbs*
> A modern variation of this is "He has as many good features as a cuckoo has songs."

You look as if you'd been put through a washing machine —John Dos Passos

You [Harold Ross] look like a dishonest Abe Lincoln —Alexander Woolcott

Woolcott's much quoted comparison of the *New Yorker* editor Harold Ross to a dishonest Abe Lincoln is one of many quotes seeded around the famous Algonquin Round Table, and widely circulated in the media and books ever since.

You look like a million dollars, green and wrinkled —Saul Bellow

You're funny as a boil on the ass —Harold Adams

Your losing one pound is like Bayonne losing one mosquito —line from the television show "The Honeymooners."
    The simile was delivered by Alice/Audrey Meadows to Ralph/Jackie Gleason.

You talk such convoluted crap you must have a tongue like a corkscrew —William McIlvanney

You've got a foot movement like a baby hippopotamus trying to side-step a jab from a humming-bird ... and your knees are about as limber as a couple of Yale pass-keys (addressed to a dancer) —O. Henry

INTELLIGENCE
SEE ALSO: CLEVERNESS, MIND

Brain like Einstein —H. E. Bates

Compared with the short span of time they live, men of great intellect are like huge buildings standing on a small plot of ground —Arthur Schopenhauer

A country without intellectuals is like a body without a head —Ayn Rand

(I have) a head on my shoulders that's like a child's windmill, and I can't prevent its making foolish words —D. H. Lawrence

Intellect is to emotion as our clothes are to our bodies: we could not very well have civilized life without clothes, but we would be in a poor way if we had only clothes without bodies —Alfred North Whitehead

Intelligence is like money ... if you don't let on how little you've got, people will treat you as though you have a lot —Anon

A man of active and resilient mind outwears his friendships just as certainly as he outwears his love affairs, his politics and his epistemology —H. L. Mencken

One good head is as good as a hundred strong hands
—Thomas Fuller

> In Fuller's collection of aphorisms it's "Better than a hundred strong heads" but common usage has made "As good as" and "Like as" popular.

Smart as a whip —Anon

> A simile very much in the mainstream of every day usage.

Smart as forty crickets —American colloquialism, attributed to the South

Smart ... like an idiot savant, smart enough to be dumb when he needed to —Lynne Sharon Schwartz

INTENSITY
SEE ALSO: SHARPNESS

Acute as the badness of no woman out in the world thinking about you —Richard Ford

Acute like the flow of hope —Joseph Turnley

As deep into ... as a sheep is thick in wool —Anon

Burns like hate —George MacDonald

(Worries and obsessions that) come like hot rivets —Wilfrid Sheed

Deep as first love —Alfred, Lord Tennyson

Deep as earth —Madeleine L'Engle

Deep as hell —Beaumont and Fletcher

Digging in deeper and deeper, like rats in a cheese —Henry Miller

(Lonely and) furious as a hunt —George Garrett

Had a startling intensity of gaze that never wavered from its object, like that of a palmist or a seer —Mary McCarthy

(Curiosity) heating up like an iron —Susan Fromberg Schaeffer

Move through life with the intensity of one for whom each day is the last —Anon

Run deep, like old wounds —William Brammer

Sharp as a pincer —Julia O'Faolain

Intensity

With the intensity of a cat following a rolling ball of yarn
—Ira Berkow on Wade Boggs, Red Sox player's watching of a pitch, *New York Times*, October 7,1986

INTIMACY
SEE: CLOSENESS

Intolerance

INTOLERANCE

Bigotry ... it's like putting your elbows on the table. You know you're not supposed to. But there's that instinct —Bonnie Currie, *New York Times*, January 24, 1986

Closed as a bigot's mind —Anon

Intolerance itself is a form of egoism —George Santayana
Santayana elaborates on his comparison of intolerance to egoism as follows: "And to condemn egoism intolerantly is to share it."

Intolerant as a sinner newly turned saint —Anon

The mind of the bigot is like the pupil of the eye; the more light you pour upon it, the more it will contract
—Oliver Wendell Holmes, Jr.

Prejudice is as a mist, which in our journey through the world often dims the brightest and obscures the best of all the good and glorious objects that meet us on our way
—Anthony Ashley Cooper

Prejudices ... are like rats, and men's minds are like traps; prejudices get in easily, but it is doubtful if they ever get out
—Lord Francis Jeffrey

IRONY
SEE: HUMOR

Irritableness

IRRITABLENESS
SEE ALSO: ANGER, TENSION

Annoying as bird droppings on your windowshield —Elyse Sommer

Bitter exasperation tightened like a knot in Mr. Casper's mind
—William Styron

Bristling like a panther —Victor Hugo

Cross as a sitting hen —American Colloquialism, attributed to New England

Cross as nine highways —John Ray's *Proverbs*

Cross as two sticks —Sir Walter Scott

Cross ... like a beautiful face upon which some one has sat down by mistake —Victor Hugo

Disgust like powder clotted my nose —Cynthia Ozick

Disturbing as a gnat trapped and mucking about in the inner chamber of his ear —John Yount

Disturbing as decay in a carcass —Julia O'Faolain

Excitable ... like a stick of dynamite just waiting for somebody to come along and light your fuse —David Huddle

Feel feisty, like a galloping colt on a Mediterranean hillside —Tony Ardizzone

> In the novel from which this is taken, *The Heart of the Order*, the narrator's irritability is caused by having his name shortened.

Feeling ornery as a bunkhouse cook —Richard Ford

Felt irritably ashamed, like a middle-aged man recalling last night's party, and his unseemly capers and his pawing of the host's wife —Wallace Stegner

Gnaws like a silent poison —George Santyana

Gruff as a billy goat —Mary Hedin

Her grumpiness, her irritability, her crotchets are like static that, from time to time, give way to a clear signal, just as you often hit a pure band of music on a car radio after turning the dial through a lot of chaotic squawk —Laurie Colwin

Irritable like a hedgehog rolled up the wrong way, tormenting himself with his own prickles —Thomas Hood

Irritableness

The prickly hedgehog is a favorite image for describing irritability. A shorter variation of the above by Tolstoy is "Bristly ... like a hedgehog." Expanded versions include "The man who rises in the morning with his feelings all bristling like the quills of a hedge-hog, simply needs to be knocked down" (Josiah Gilbert Holland) and "An irritable man is like a hedgehog rolled up the wrong way, tormenting himself with his own prickles" (Thomas Hood).

Irritated as a young stag is irritated by the velvet on his antlers
    —Rumer Godden

(All the mistakes of my misspent little life came down to) irritate me like so many grains of pepper —Gerald Kersh

Irritating as a coughing fit during a play —Anon

Irritating as a fly that keeps buzzing around your head —Anon

Irritating as one sock or an odd glove —Helen Hudson

Irritating, like a dish of 'chulent' to an old man's gut
    —Stephen Longstreet
        'Chulent' is a Jewish dish of meat, beans, onions. Obviously this is the type of comparison that could easily be modified to be more meaningful to other groups; for example, "Irritating, like a dish of hot chili."

Irritating like a gun that hangs fire —Joseph Conrad

A minor nuisance, like having a tooth filled —Richard Connell

Prickly as thistles —Lawrence Durrell

Sizzle and splatter like batter in a pan —line from British television series "Bergerac," broadcast June 1987

Snappish as a junkyard dog —Robert Campbell

Sulk, like an old man whose son had failed to make varsity
    —Clancy Sigal

Tempers snapping like rubber bands
    —Anon, WNYC, Public Radio March 28, 1987

Troublesome as a lawsuit —Colley Cibber

ISOLATION
SEE: ALONENESS

JEALOUSY
SEE: ENVY

JEWELRY
SEE ALSO: CLOTHING

A pear-shaped diamond, as big as your thumb —Paige Mitchell

An assortment of costly [and of questionable taste] stones ... very
    much like something Hansel and Gretel might well have plucked
    from the witch's house to eat —Henry Van Dyke

Bracelets seemed to grow up her arms like creeping plants
    —Nadine Gordimer

Bracelets ... warm and heavy, alive like flesh —Elizabeth Taylor

A diamond as big as an Englishman's monocle —Lael Wertenbaker

A diamond as big as the Ritz —F. Scott Fitzgerald
            This served as the title for a famous Fitzgerald story.

A diamond ... as big as your fourth fingernail —Gerald Kersch

Diamond pinkie rings sputtering like neon on his manicured fingers
    —Jonathan Valin

Diamonds as big as grapes —Louis Adamic

Diamonds as big as potatoes —Henry James

Diamonds flashed ... like drops of frozen light —Paige Mitchell

Earrings tiny as pinheads —Richard Ford

A medallion that could have anchored the Queen Mary
    —William McIlvanney

Necklace ... flashed like summer lightning —Anaïs Nin

Pearl ... shaped like the full moon, and whiter than the morning star
    —Oscar Wilde

(Wedding) ring ... pink gold like the morning light —Anon

Rubies as big as hen's eggs, and sapphires that were like gloves with
    lights inside them —F. Scott Fitzgerald

Rubies like cherries, sapphires like grapes —Isak Dinesen

Rubies like headlights —Philip Levine

Jewelry

She was encrusted with jewels like a Maharini —MacDonald Harris

JOBS
SEE: WORK

JOKES
SEE: HUMOR

Joy

JOY
SEE ALSO: HAPPINESS

Agitated with delight as a waving sea —Arabian Nights

Exhilaration spread through his breast like some pleasurable form of heartburn —Nadine Gordimer

A joyous feeling ... shot up, like the grass in spring —Ivan Turgenev

(Heart is) as full of sunshine as a hay field —Josh Billings

Bliss ... as though you'd suddenly swallowed a bright piece of that late afternoon sun and it burned in your bosom, sending out a little shower of sparks into every particle —Katherine Mansfield
    The simile sets the mood for one of Mansfield's best known stories, *Bliss.*

Ecstacy warm and rich as wine —Harvey Swados

Elated ... like a lion tamer who has at last found the whip crack which will subdue the most ferocious of his big cats —John Mortimer

Enjoy life like a young porpoise —George Santayana

Gorged with joy like a pigeon too fat to fly —Marge Piercy

Great joys, like griefs, are silent —Shackerley Marmion

Gurgle like a meadowlark —W. P. Kinsella

Heart ... soared like a geyser —William Peden

Her heart became as light as a bubble —Antonia White

Joy careens and smashes through them like a speeding car out of control —Irving Feldman

Joy ... felt it rumbling within him like a subterranean river —André Malraux

Joyful as carollers —David Leavitt

234

Joy is like the ague [malaria]; one good day between two bad ones
    —Danish proverb

Joy leaping within me ... like a trout in a brook —George Garrett

Joy rises in me like a summer morn —Samuel Taylor Coleridge

Joys are bubble-like; what makes them bursts them too —P. J. Bailey

Joy, simple as the wildflowers —George Garrett

Joys ... like angel visits, short and bright —John Norris
        The angel visit comparison has been as effectively linked
        to goodness and fame.

Joys met by chance ... flow for us fresh and strong, like new wine
    when it gushes from the press —André Gide

The joys we've missed in youth are like ... lost umbrellas; we musn't
    spend the rest of life wondering where they are —Henry James

(He is) jubilant as a flag unfurled —Dorothy Parker

Men without joy seem like corpses —Kaethe Kolwitz

My heart lifted like a wave —Norman Mailer

Our joys are about me like a net —Iris Murdoch

Rose and fell, like a floating swimmer, on easygoing great waves of
    voluptuous joy —Christina Stead

A strong exhilaration ran through her like the fumes of wine
    —Ben Ames Williams

The sun in my heart comes up like a Javanese orange
    —Dylan Thomas

Their joys ... ran into each other like water paints mingling to form
    delicate new colors —Sumner Locke Elliott

Triumphant as if I'd just hurled a shutout —W. P. Kinsella
        The term shutout was particularly appropriate in Kinsella's
        baseball novel, *Shoeless Joe.* Baseball expressions do,
        however, work well within other contexts.

A wonderful feeling enveloped him, as if light were being shaken
    about him —John Cheever

235

JUMPING

SEE ALSO: ROCKING AND ROLLING

Bouncing from foot to foot like a child in need of a potty
—Joan Hess

Flapping and jumping like a kind of fire —Richard Wilbur

Hop about like mice on tiptoe —Alistair Cooke, *New York Times*,
January 19, 1986

> Cooke's comparison describes how a speaker's eyes move
> back and forth between viewer and teleprompter.

Hopping about like a pea in a saucepan —Robert Graves

Hopping like a shot putter —Pat Conroy

Jogging up and down like a cheerleader —T. Coraghessan Boyle

Jumped about like sailors during a storm —O. Henry

(Mrs. Brady's mind, hopefully calculating the tip,) jumped and
jumped again like a taxi meter —Katherine Bush. In a short story
entitled *The Night Club*, the character with the jumping mind is a
rest room matron.

Jumped as though he'd been shot —Katherine Mansfield

Jumped back as if he'd been struck by a snake
—T. Coraghessan Boyle

Jumped like a buoy —William Goyen

Jumped like she'd seen a vampire —Dan Wakefield

Jumped like small goats —Theodore Roethke

Jumped on him like a wild wolf —Clifford Odets

Jumped out of the way like an infielder avoiding a sliding runner
—Howard Frank Mosher

Jumped sideways like a startled bird —Jay Parini

Jumped up as if stung by a tarantula —Sholem Asch

Jumped up like I was sitting on a spring —W. P. Kinsella

Jumping up and down like Jack-in-the-boxes —Barbara Pym

Jumping like a toad —Ross Macdonald

Jumping like Nijinsky —Saul Bellow

Jumping up like a squirrel from behind the log —Rudyard Kipling

Jump [with shock] like a flea on a frog's back —Walter Duranty

Jump like a chimp with a hot foot —Anon comment on radio show, about people doing Jane Fonda workout routines, December 10, 1986

Skipping (up the stairs) like a young ghost —Frank Swinnerton

JUSTICE

Even, it [justice] is as the sun on a flat plain; uneven, it strikes like the sun on a thicket —Malay proverb

Injustice ... gathers like dust under everything —Rainer Maria Rilke

Just as a sentence meted out by a kangaroo court —Anon

Justice ... inevitable as the law of cause and effect —L. P. Hartley

Justice is like a train that's nearly always late
    —Yevgeny Yevtushenko

Justice is like the kingdom of God; it is not without us as a fact, it is within us as a great yearning —George Eliot

Shed justice like paladins —Jonathan Valin

The tongue of the just is as choice silver —*The Holy Bible/Proverbs*

An unrectified case of injustice has a terrible way of lingering ... like an unfinished equation —Mary McCarthy

We will not be satisfied until justice rolls down like waters and righteousness like a mighty stream —Martin Luther King Jr., speech, June 15, 1963
        This is from King's famous "I Have a Dream" speech.

Your righteousness is like the mighty mountains. Your judgments are like the great deep —*The Holy Bible/Psalms*
        'Your' replaces the biblical 'thy.'

KINDNESS

(You're) as good as an umbrella on a wet day —H. E. Bates

As kind as Santa Claus —Oscar Hammerstein II, from lyric for *South Pacific*

As much compassion as a toreador moving in for the final thrust
    —Marilyn Sharp

As occupied with worthy projects as Eleanor Roosevelt —Lisa Harris

Doing a favor for a bad man is quite as dangerous as doing an
    injury to a good one —Plautus

Exuding good will like a mortician's convention in a plague year
    —Daniel Berrigan

Gifts are as the gold which adorns the temple; grace is like the
    temple that sanctifies the gold —William Burkitt

Gifts are like fish hooks —Epigram, c. 65 b.c.

Gifts are like hooks —Martial

As good as gold —Charles Dickens
            A simile that's become a common expression. In *A
            Christmas Carol,* its most frequently quoted source, it's a
            response to the question "And how was Tiny Tim today?"
            In *The Gondoliers,* W. S. Gilbert gave it a nice twist with
            "In the wonder-working days of old, when hearts were
            twice as good as gold". In Joseph Heller's novel *Good As
            Gold* it serves as a play on the hero's name (Bruce Gold).

(He'll be) good as pie —Ring Lardner

A good heart ... a heart like a house —Irwin Shaw

The good is, like nature, an immense landscape in which man
    advances through centuries of exploration —José Ortega Gassett

Good to the core like bananas —Marge Piercy

Good will ... is like gentle sunshine in early spring. It invigorates
    and awakens all buds —Berthold Auerbach

Great minds, like heaven, are pleased in doing good, though the
    ungrateful subjects of their favors are barren in return
    —Nicholas Rowe

A hand as liberal as the light of day —William Cowper

A heart as big as a bird cage —James B. Hall

A heart as big as a mountain —Anon

Heart ... as great as the world —Ralph Waldo Emerson

EXUDING GOOD WILL LIKE A MORTICIAN'S
CONVENTION IN A PLAGUE YEAR

In Emerson's essay, *Greatness*, the simile continues with "But there was no room in it to hold the memory of a wrong."

A heart as warm as a desert storm —Ogden Nash

A heart like duck soup —Jean Garrigue
In his short story, *The Snowfall*, Garrigue elaborates on the duck soup comparison as follows: "She's the kind to want to stop a car if she hears some animal crying in the woods."

A heart like warm putty —Mary Stewart

Heart ... soft as any melon —Franklin Pierce

He gives up a buck as quickly as he would a tattoo —Anon

A helping word to one in trouble is often like a switch on a railroad track ... an inch between wreck and smooth-rolling prosperity —Henry Ward Beecher

He was like Florence Nightingale —Tennessee Williams, *Playboy*, April, 1973
Williams used the Florence Nightingale simile to descibe his agent's devotion when he was ill.

(My mother is) soft as a grape —Rita Mae Brown

Kindness as large as a prairie wind —Stephen Vincent Benét

Kindness is like a baby; it grows fast —Anon

Kindness is like snow; it beautifies everything it covers —Anon caller on night-time radio talk show

Kindness, like grain, increases by sowing —H. G. Bohn's *Handbook of Proverbs*

A kind word is like a Spring day —Russian proverb

Made the Good Samaritan look like a cheap criminal —George Ade

Mercy among the virtues is like the moon among the stars, not so sparkling and vivid as many, but dispensing a calm radiance that hallows the whole —E. H. Chapin

(My mother was as) mild as any saint —Alfred, Lord Tennyson

My bounty is as boundless as the sea —William Shakespeare

Our bounty, like a drop of water, disappears when diffused too widely —Oliver Goldsmith

The place of charity, like that of God, is everywhere —Jaques Benigne Bossuet

(She was unsparing of herself, she) poured herself out like cream (into the cups of these dull people) —Sumner Locke Elliott

The record of a generous life runs like a vine around the memory of our dead —Robert G. Ingersoll

Shone [with kindness] like the best of good deeds —Frank Swinnerton

Solicitious as St. Peter —Norman Mailer, about David Susskind

A sympathetic heart is like a spring of pure water bursting forth from the mountain side —Anon

To do a kindness to a bad man is like sowing our seed in the sea —Phocylides

Unselfish as the wind —Ken Kesey

We are never like angels till our passion dies —Thomas Dekker
        'Never' is modernized from 'ne'er.'

KISSES
SEE: INSULTS

KNOWLEDGE
SEE: EDUCATION, INTELLIGENCE, MIND

LANDSCAPES
SEE ALSO: MOUNTAINS, NATURE, TREES

The corn is as high as an elephant's eye and it looks like it's climbin' clear up to the sky —Oscar Hammerstein, II, from opening lyric for *Oklahoma.*

The country lay like an abandoned theatrical backdrop, tarnished and yellow —Beryl Markham

The endless fields glowed like a hearth in firelight —Eudora Welty

A farm ... off the road ... glittering like a photo in a picture book with its twin silos pointing to heaven like two fat white fingers —Harvey Swados

Landscapes

Fields like squares of a chessboard and trees and houses like dolls' furniture —Hugh Walpole

The fields shone and seemed to tremble like a veil in the light —Eudora Welty

The fields were like icing sugar —Joyce Cary

The fields [in March] were white as bones and dry as meal —M. J. Farrell

Gardens, crowded with flowers of every rich and beautiful tint, sparkled ... like beds of glittering jewels —Charles Dickens

Great spots of light like white wine splash over the Jardins Publiques —Katherine Mansfield

Green hummocks like ancient cannon-balls sprouting grass —Elizabeth Bishop

The land flowed like white silk ... flat as a bed sheet and empty as the moon —Frank Ross

Landscape as precise and vibrant as fine writing —Sharon Sheehe Stark

The landscape boiled around her like a pan of beans —Dilys Laing

Landscape ... gaunt and bleak like the face of the moon —Donald Seaman

Landscape ... like a gray sink —Paul Theroux

The landscape [when it snows] lumps like flour gravy —Lisa Ress

Landscapes ... like sorrows, they require some distance —Donald Justice

The landscape was bleak and bereft of color ... like a painting in grisaille with its many tints of gray —Barbara Taylor Bradford

The landscape was yellowish and purple, speckled like a leopard skin —Nikos Kazantzakis

The lawn looked as expensive as a velvet carpet woven in one piece —Edith Wharton

The lawns looked artificial, like green excelsior or packing material —Saul Bellow

The lawn, spread out like an immense green towel
    —Ludwig Bemelmans

Light hits that field, like silk being rubbed the wrong way
    —John Gunther

The long slope of the park dipped like a length of green stuff with a
    ceiling cloth of blue and pink smoke high above —Virginia Woolf

Meadows carpeted with buttercups, like slabs of gold in the somber
    forest —John Fowles

Patches of earth showed through the snow, like ink spots spreading
    on a sheet of white blotting paper —Edith Wharton

Petals ... fell on the grass like spilled paint —Laurie Colwin

Populating the field in dark humps, like elephants moving across
    savannah, were scores of great round straw bales —Will Weaver

Pretty cubes and loaves of new houses are strewn among the pines,
    like sugar lumps —Walker Percy

Smooth swelling fields, like waves —Wilbur Daniel Steele

The stony landscape ... is full of craters and frozen lights like a
    moon —Erich Maria Remarque

Swelling smooth fields like pale breasts —Wilbur Daniel Steele

The reeds and willow bushes looked like little islands swaying in the
    wind —Leo Tolstoy

Vast lawns that extend like sheets of vivid green
    —Washington Irving
        Irving's simile was inspired by English park scenery.

The wet countryside glistened and dripped as though it had been
    freshly scrubbed —Robert Traver

Wet furry fields lay like the stomachs of soft animals bared to the
    sky —Julia O'Faolain

Wet pine growth reflects the sunlight like steel knitting needles
    —Walker Percy

When you drive by them [the woods] fast, the crop rows in between
    spin like spokes on a turning wheel —Alec Wilkinson, *New
    Yorker*, August 12, 1985

Landscapes

The whole landscape loomed absolute, as the antique world was once
—Sylvia Plath

The whole [valley] was like a broad counterpane, hued in rust and yellow and golden brown —Beryl Markham

LANGUAGE
SEE: WORD(S)

LAUGHTER
SEE: HUMOR, SMILES

Law

LAW

Corpuses, statutes, rights and equities are passed on like congenital disease —Johann Wolfgang von Goethe

Exact laws, like all the other ultimates and absolutes, are as fabulous as the crock of gold at the rainbow's end —G. N. Lewis

Going to law is like skinning a new milk cow for the hide, and giving the meat to the lawyers —Josh Billings
> The original in Billings' popular dialect form reads as follows: "Going tew law iz like skinning a new milch ... .tew the lawyers."

Great cases like hard cases make bad law
—Oliver Wendell Holmes, Sr.
> Justice Holmes expanded on his simile as follows: "For great cases are called great not by reason of their real importance in shaping the law of the future but because of some accident of immediate overwhelming interest which appeals to the feelings and distorts the judgment."

Law is a bottomless pit —John Arbuthnot
> Arbuthnot continues as follows: "It is a cormorant, a harpy that devours everything!"

Law is a form of order, and good law must necessarily mean good order —Aristotle

The law is a sort of hocus-pocus science, that smiles in your face while it picks your pocket —Charles Macklin

The law is like apparel which alters with the time
—Sir John Doddridge

Law is like pregnancy, a little of either being a dangerous thing
—Robert Traver

The law often dances like an old fishwife in wooden shoes, with little grace and less dispatch —George Garrett

> In Garrett's historical novel, *Death of the Fox*, this simile is voiced by Sir Francis Bacon.

Laws and institutions ... like clocks, they must be occasionally cleansed, and wound up, and set to true time
—Henry Ward Beecher

(Written) laws are like spiders' webs; they hold the weak and delicate who might be caught in their meshes, but are torn in pieces by the rich and powerful —Anarchis

> The spiders' web comparison to the law has been much used and modified. Here are some examples: "Laws, like cobwebs, entangle the weak, but are broken by the strong"; 'Laws are like spiders' webs, so that the great buzzing bees break through, and the little feeble flies hang fast in them" (Henry Smith); "Laws are like cobwebs, which may catch small flies, but let wasps and hornets break through" (Jonathan Swift); "Laws, like cobwebs, catch small flies, great ones break through before your eyes" (Benjamin Franklin); "Laws, like the spider's web, catch the fly and let the hawk go free" (Spanish proverb).

Law should be like death, which spares no one
—Charles de Secondat Montesquieu

Laws, like houses, lean on one another —Edmund Burke

Laws should be like clothes. They should fit the people they are meant to serve —Clarence Darrow

Laws wise as nature, and as fixed as fate —Alexander Pope

Legal as a Supreme Court decision —Anon

Legal studies ... sharpen, indeed, but like a grinding stone narrow whilst they sharpen —Samuel Taylor Coleridge

Liked law because it was a system like a jigsaw puzzle, whose pieces, if you studied them long enough, all fell into place
—Will Weaver

The science of legislation is like that of medicine in one respect, that it is far more easy to point out what will do harm than what will do good —Charles Caleb Colton

Suits at court are like winter nights, long and wearisome
—Thomas Deloney

Law

To try a case twice is like eating yesterday morning's oatmeal
—Lloyd Paul Stryker

Violations of the law, like viruses, are present all the time. Everybody does them. Whether or not they produce a disease, or a prosecution, is a function of the body politic —Anon quote, *New York Times*/Washington Talk, November 28, 1986

LAWYERS
SEE: LAW

LAZINESS
SEE: IDLENESS

LEAPING
SEE: JUMPING, ROCKING AND ROLLING

LEARNING
SEE: EDUCATION

LEAVES
SEE: FLOWERS, NATURE, TREES

LEGS
SEE: PAIN, PHYSICAL FEELINGS

LIBERTY
SEE: FREEDOM

LIES/LIARS
SEE: DISHONESTY

Life

LIFE
SEE ALSO: AGE

(It seemed to him that) all man's life was like a tiny spurt of flame
—Thomas Wolfe

The art of living rightly is like all arts; it must be learned and practiced with incessant care —Johann Wolfgang von Goethe

The eventful life has dates; it swells and pauses like a plot
—Paul Theroux

How ridiculous it [life] all seems ... like a drop of water seen through a microscope, a single drop teeming with infusoria, or a speck of cheese full of mites invisible to the naked eye
—Arthur Schopenhauer

In life as in a football game, the principle to follow is: Hit the line hard —Theodore Roosevelt

Let us play the game of life as sportsmen, pocketing our winnings with a smile, leaving our losings with a shrug
    —Jerome K. Jerome

Life ... empty as statistics are —Babette Deutsch

Life ... flat and stale, like an old glass of beer —Andre Dubus

Life folds like a fan with a click —Herbert Read

Life goes on forever like the gnawing of a mouse
    —Edna St. Vincent Millay

Life had been like a cloud rainbowed by the sun —Barbara Reid

Life imposes by brute energy, like inarticulate thunder; art catches the ear, among the far louder noises of experience, like an air artificially made by a discreet musician —Robert Louis Stevenson

A life indifferent as a star —Randall Jarrell

A life is composed of a thousand frail strands, like the rainbow tangle of telephone cables. Somehow, we make connections
    —Jean Thompson

Life is shapeless as a glove —Kenneth Koch

Life ... it slips through my hands like a fish —James Reiss

Life, like a child, laughs shaking its rattle of death as it runs
    —Rabindranath Tagore

Life, like a good story, pursues its way from beginning to end in a firm and unbroken line —W. Somerset Maugham

Life, like every other blessing, derives its value from its use alone
    —Samuel Johnson

Life, like war, is a series of mistakes —F.W. Robertson

Life often seems like a long shipwreck, of which the debris are friendship, glory and love —Madame de Staël

Life's bare as a bone —Virginia Woolf

Life is so like a little strip of pavement over an abyss
    —Virginia Woolf

247

Life

Life should be embraced like a lover —Rose Tremain

Life's like an inn where travelers stay, some only breakfast and away; others to dinnerstop, and are full fed; the oldest only sup and go to bed —English epitath
> A variation of this, also found on a gravestone, is "Our life is nothing but a winter's day."

Life swings like a pendulum backward and forward between pain and boredom —Arthur Schopenhauer

A life that moved in spirals turned inward like the shell of a sea-snail —Malcolm Cowley

Life was like [motion] pictures only in that it hardly every managed to be as exciting as its preview —Larry McMurtry

Like a morning dream, life becomes more and more bright, the longer we live —Jean Paul Richter

Like following life through creatures you dissect, you lose it in the moment you detect —Alexander Pope

To live is like love, all reason is against it, and all healthy instincts for it —Samuel Butler

Man's journey through life is like that of a bee through blossoms —Yugoslav proverb

A man's life, like a piece of tapestry, is made up of many strands which interwoven make a pattern; to separate a single one and look at it alone, not only destroys the whole, but gives the strand itself a false value —Judge Learned Hand
> Judge Hand compared life to a piece of tapestry at the 1912 proceedings in memory of Mr. Justice Brandeis.

Men deal with life as children with their play, who first misuse, then cast their toys away —William Cowper

Moved ... through her life, like a clumsy visitor in a museum —Susan Fromberg Schaeffer

Much that goes on behind Life's doors is not fixed like the pillars of a building nor preconceived like the structure of a symphony, nor calculable like the orbit of a star —Vicki Baum

My life felt like a fragile silk chemise —Marge Piercy

My life is like a stroll upon the beach, as near the ocean's edge as I can go —Henry David Thoreau

My life is like the autumn leaf that trembles in the moon's pale ray
—Richard Henry Wilde
   This begins the second stanza of the poem, *My Life.*

My life is like the summer rose that opens to the morning sky, but
before the shade of evening closes is scattered on the ground to
die —Richard Henry Wilde
   Another simile from Wilde's *My Life,* this one the opening
   line.

My life loose as a frog's —Maxine Kumin

Our days on earth are as a shadow —*The Holy Bible/Job*

(I worry that) our lives are like soap operas. We can go for months
and not tune in to them, then six months later we look in and
the same stuff is still going on —Jane Wagner

Our lives are united like fruit in a bowl —W. H. Auden

Our lives run like fingers over sandpaper —Jaroslav Seifert

Perhaps like an ancient statue that has no arms our life, without
deeds and heroes, has greater charms —Yehuda Amichai

Sometimes we do not become adults until we suffer a good
whacking loss, and our lives in a sense catch up with us and
wash over us like a wave and everything goes —Richard Ford

The art of life is more like the wrestler's art than the dancer's that it
should stand ready and firm to meet onsets which are sudden
and unexpected —Marcus Aurelius

There was a dimension missing from his life, as though trees were
flat and rooflines painted on the sky —Margaret Sutherland

The vanity of human life is like a rivulet, constantly passing away,
and yet constantly coming on —Alexander Pope

Viewed from the summit of reason, all life looks like a malignant
disease and the world like a madhouse
—Johann Wolfgang von Goethe

Wear life like an old pair of shoes that's easy on my feet
—Ben Ames Williams

Life

When the highest stake in the game of living, life itself, may not be risked ... becomes as flat, as superficial as one of those American flirtations in which it is from the first understood that nothing is to happen, contrasted with a Continental love-affair in which both partners must constantly bear in mind the serious consequences —Sigmund Freud

Would that life were like the shadow cast by a wall or a tree, but it is like the shadow of a bird in flight —*Palestinian Talmud*

LIGHTING
SEE: SHINING

Lightnesss

LIGHTNESSS
SEE ALSO: SOFTNESS

Airy as the holes in Swiss cheese —Anon

As giddy as a drunken man —Charles Dickens
This is the last of a whole string of similes uttered by a reformed Scrooge in *A Christmas Carol:* I'm as light as a feather, I am as happy as an angel, I'm as merry as a schoolboy. I am as giddy as a drunken man. A merry Christmas to everybody! A happy New Year to all the world.

As lightly as a cloud is blown —John Greenleaf Whittier

Flippancy, like comedy, is but a matter of visual first impressions —Joseph Conrad

(A light blue summer dress as) frothy as high tide —Jonathan Kellerman

Hands were light as moths —John MacDonald

Light as a hand among blossoms —Theodore Roethke

(Mountains ...) light and airy like balloons on a string —George Garrett

[Touch] light as a butterfly —Eleanor Farejons
And lighter still, there's a touch that's "Light as a butterfly's kiss" from a John MacDonald novel.

Light as a flight of tumbling birds —C. S. Lewis

Light as a fly —John Ray's *Proverbs*

Light as a leaf —Anon
> An ancient simile which continues in use to describe lightness of heart, mind and body. "Light as" variants include "Light as a feather," "Light as wind," and "Light as air." With them all, "Lighter than" crops up as frequently as "Light as."

Light as a milkweed puff —Richard Wilbur

[A racing jockey] light as a monkey —Ernest Hemingway

Light as an angel —Donald McCaig

Light as a paper toy —Anon

Light as a petal falling upon stone —Theodore Roethke

(She is) light as a phantom —W. P. Kinsella

Light as a seed —Theodore Roethke

Light as breath —Robert Penn Warren

Light as cork —Henry James

Light as dandelion fluff —Mary Hedin

[Snow] light as dust —Amy Lowell

Light as helium —Elizabeth Bishop

[Snowflakes] light as milkweed —T. Coraghessan Boyle

[Feathers on a hat] light as mist in a breeze —Colette

Light as sea-foam, strong as the tide —Slogan for underwear, Paris-Hecker Co.

(Free and) light as the breath that clung to them like clouds —Arthur Gregor

Light as thistledown —John Yount

(We carry her indoor. She is) light as toast —Louise Erdrich

Lightly ... as a child skips rope, the way a mouse waltzes —E.B. White on James Thurber's writing

Lightly as a wisp of air —Harvey Swados

Weightless as an ache —Sharon Sheehe Stark

Lightnesss

In Stark's novel, *A Wrestling Season,* the simile is used to answer the question of what death might be like.

(Her body was ...) weightless as a strip of cane —Eudora Welty

Weightless as the notes rung out of bells at kindling dawn
    —George Garrett

LIGHTNING
SEE: THUNDER AND LIGHTNING

LIKELIHOOD
SEE: IMPOSSIBILITY

LIMBS
SEE: ARM(S)

LIMPNESS
SEE: SOFTNESS, WEAKNESS

LIPS
SEE: MOUTH

LITERATURE
SEE: ART AND LITERATURE

LIVELINESS
SEE: ACTIVENESS/INACTIVENESS, ENTHUSIASM

LOCALITIES
SEE: PLACES

LOGIC
SEE: SENSE

LONELINESS
SEE: ALONENESS

LONGING
SEE: DESIRE

LONG-WINDEDNESS
SEE: TALKATIVENESS

Looks

LOOKS
SEE ALSO: FROWNS, PHYSICAL APPEARANCE, SCRUTINY

Accusing look ... as Cotton Mather might have looked at a Salem woman in the stocks —Mary Gordon

252

Always looked at you as if you had interrupted him in the performance of some slightly tedious but nonetheless necessary task —Louis Auchincloss

Black glance like ice —Jean Garrigue

Contemplate ... with a kind of quiet premeditation, like that of a slow-witted man fondling an unaccustomed thought —Beryl Markham

Disdainful look like that of a coffee drinker sipping a cup of instant —Anon

Exchanged fidgeting looks like a pair of consternated hamsters —Sarah Bird

Exchanged wide-eyed looks that clinked in the air like fine glassware —Sharon Sheehe Stark

Eyeing me ... like a starved hog watching the trough get filled —Harold Adams

Felt his eyes slide over her like a steamy wet cloak —Joseph Wambaugh

Gaze at me like chastened children sitting silent in a school —Thomas Hardy

Gazed at ... with nudging, sympathetic smiles, like grandmothers watching babies in a play-pen —Mary McCarthy

Gaze ... fixed like a snake's —Donald MacKenzie

Glance as vacant as the smoothness of the pond —David Ignatow

Glanced at one another like tigers taking measure of a menacing new rival —Erich Segal

Glance ... like a needle's flash —Frank Swinnerton

Glowered back like a sullen watchdog —Frank Swinnerton

Her flat dark eyes moved down Melinda like a smudge —Jessamyn West

Her gaze moved like a prison searchlight —Michael Dorris

Her gaze was like a magnet that drew towards it my will-less secret —Jean Stafford

His eyes glowed on me like a warm hand —Borden Deal

Looks

His eyes on me as hot as a bare hand —R. Wright Campbell

His eyes set on Linda's open shirtfront like a cat sighting a fat bird
    —Gloria Norris

His eyes slewed round to meet yours and then cannoned off again
    like a pool-ball —Seán Virgo

His glance came back across mine like saw teeth across a nail
    —Wallace Stegner

His look was like a hand in the scruff of Bruce's neck
    —Wallace Stegner

Like swallows darting about a barn her deep blue eyes flickered from
    one to the other —F. van Wyck Mason

(Gave me) a long [forgiving] look like Christ crucified —Clare Boylan

Look at him as if he were a lamppost —Leo Tolstoy

Looked about him like the fallen archangel whose only wish was for
    eternal enmity —Honoré de Balzac

Looked around her at the crowd, with eyes smarting, unseeing, and
    tearful as if an oculist had put caustic eye-drops into them
    —Boris Pasternak

Looked at each other like schoolboys caught masturbating
    —Lawrence Durrell

Looked at each other in a flicker fast as a snake's tongue
    —Rosellen Brown

Looked at her like she was some kind of Italian sports car and he
    was ready to drive her —Dialogue from "Murder She Wrote"
    television drama, broadcast in March 19, 1987,
        The look thus described is attributed to a jealous husband.

Looked at her like a bird that has been shot —D. H. Lawrence

Looked at him as a guinea pig looks at a big dog
    —Frank Swinnerton

Looked at him as a sergeant in the United States Marines would look
    at a recruit who had just called a rifle a gun —Norman MacLean

Looked at me as if I were a mongrel that had suddenly said, "Hi"
    —Harold Adams

254

LOOKED AT HER LIKE SHE WAS SOME KIND OF ITALIAN
SPORTS CAR AND HE WAS READY TO DRIVE HER

Looked at me as though I had suddenly broke out with a filthy disease —M. C. Blackman

Looked at me expectantly as a poodle —Erich Maria Remarque

Looked at me intently, as if trying to recall something —Mihail Lermontov

Looked at me keenly, like a smart boxer stung in the first round and cagily reappraising the character of his opposition —Robert Traver

Looked at me like she was ready to carve my liver —Larry McMurtry

Looked at Whistler [character in novel] as if she'd like to crush him with her thighs or smother him with her tits —Robert Campbell

Looked at ... with an awakened air, as if she were pricking up her ears like a trooper's horse at the sound of a trumpet —Honoré de Balzac

Looked at you without really seeing you, like a TV broadcaster reading the teleprompter —Elyse Sommer

Looked him up and down like a sergeant inspecting the ranks —George Garrett

Looked knowing and quizzical, like someone smiling with a mouthful of salts —George MacDonald Fraser

Looked through us like glass —Alan Williamson

Looked towards me as towards a jury —F. Scott Fitzgerald

Looking about him as if he had a score to settle —Romain Gary

Looking at him with something cold as dislike —Rebecca West

(She was) looking at us ... like she had emptied her eyes, like she had quit using them —William Faulkner

Looking from face to face like he was judge —Jayne Anne Phillips

Looking on one another, sideways and crossways, and with lowered eyes, like guilty criminals —Anzia Yezierska

A look passed between them, like the silent exchange of two doctors who agree on a simple diagnosis without having to put it in words —Marilyn Sharp

Looks black as thunder —J. R. Planche

Looks ... like the lizard watches the fly —Leslie Silko

A look that burned like live coals on our naked bodies
   —Anzia Yezierska

Playing his eyes over the other's face like the feelers of insects
   —Arthur A. Cohen

Regarded her with raised brows like a doctor who is considering how
   fully to answer a layman's question —Saul Bellow

Regarded me somberly but warily, as you might examine a
   particularly ferocious gorilla from the other side of a set of flimsy
   bars —Harvey Swados

She looked at him with that cunning which those who profess
   unworldliness can wield like a club of stone
   —Francine du Plessix Gray

She took him in as if he were frozen in a block of ice or enclosed
   in a cage of wires —Louise Erdrich

That look that seemed to enter him like an enormous jolt of neat
   whiskey —Daniel Curley

The each-for-himself look in the eyes of the people about her were
   like stinging slaps in the face —Anzia Yezierska

Their eyes caromed off each other like the balls on a table
   —Ed McBain

Their eyes rolled like marbles toward one another —Mary Hedin

Their glances crossed like blades —Stephen Crane

Triumphant look, like the fallen angel restored —D. H. Lawrence

A true-felt look ... laden with sweetness, white, mesmerizing, like the
   blossom that hangs from the cherry trees —Edna O'Brien

Turned to me in blank apprehension like a blind woman taken by
   surprise —Ross Macdonald

Uncomprehending gaze ... like an anxious monkey —Mary Stewart

Watching me as though trying to work out a puzzle —C. J. Koch

LOUDNESS
SEE: NOISE

LOVE
SEE: FRIENDSHIP; LOVE, DEFINED; MEN AND WOMEN

Love, Defined

LOVE, DEFINED

Falling in love is like being thrown from a horse; if you let yourself go it doesn't hurt as badly as if you try to save yourself —Edwin L. Blanchard

It's [love] very like a lizard; it winds itself around your heart and penetrates your gizzard —Anon rhyme

A love affair is like a work of art —Laurie Colwin

Love is a hole in the heart —Ben Hecht

Love is a science where great erudition and great application are needed —Anatole France

Love is like a child that longs for everything that he can come by —William Shakespeare

Love is like a cigar, the longer it burns the less it becomes —*Punch*, 1855

Love is ... like a coconut which is good while it's fresh, but you have to spit it out when the juice is gone, what's left tastes bitter —Bertold Brecht

Love is like a cold. Easy to catch but hard to cure —Anon

Love is like a dizziness —James Hogg
     This is the title and first line of a poem.

Love is like a dream that's too good to be true —Langston Hughes

Love is like a friendship caught on fire —Bruce Lee

Love is like a lovely rose —Christina Georgina Rossetti

Love is like a repeating decimal; the figure is the same but the value gets less and less —Anon

Love is like a wind stirring the grass beneath trees on a black night —Sherwood Anderson

Love is like butter, it goes well with bread —Yiddish proverb

Love is like electricity. It flares up for a second and is soon extinguished —Isaac Bashevis Singer

Love is like fire ... wounds of fire are hard to bear; harder still are
those of love —Hjalmar Hjorth Boyesen

Love is like growing pains; something we all have to experience for
ourselves —Anon

Love is like heaven, a brief possession, unsearchable, hard to
reconstruct with two-by-fours and building blocks
—Leonard Casper
In Casper's story, *Sense of Direction*, the simile is in the past
tense and the word building is spelled without the last
letter.

Love is like learning to walk; we all have to go through it —Anon

Love is like linen, the more often changed, the sweeter
—Phineas Fletcher
The word 'changed' was originally 'chang'd.'

Love is like malaria. You never know when you're going to catch it
—Rita Mae Brown

Love is like measles; you can get it only once, and the later in life it
occurs the tougher it goes —Josh Billing
The simile in Billings' dialect: "Love iz like the meazles; we
kant have it bad but onst, and the later in life we have it
the tuffer it goes with us." Medical science has made this
much quoted comparison obsolete, though another illness,
mishap, or a necessary learning experience could easily be
substituted.

Love is like quicksilver in the hand ... leave the fingers open and it
stays in the palm; clutch it, and it darts away —Dorothy Parker

Love is like soup; it cools when the fire dies out —Anon

Love is like the devil; whom it has in its clutches it surrounds with
flames —Honoré de Balzac

Love is like the measles; we all have to go through it
—Jerome K. Jerome
See the comment with Josh Billings love/measles simile
above.

Love is like a well: a good thing to drink out of, but a bad thing to
fall into —Anon

Love is like the wild rose-briar, friendship like the holly tree
—Emily Brontë

Love is like those shabby hotels in which all the luxury is in the lobby —Paul Jean Toulet

Love is trembling happiness —Kahlil Gibran

Love is very much like a tennis match, you'll never win consistently until you learn to serve well —Dan P. Herod

Love is what is called the Milky Way in Heaven, a brilliant mass formed by thousands of little stars of which each perhaps is nebulous —Stendhal
> One wonders what he might have added had he known about black holes in space and their gravity so enormous it sucks up everything surrounding itself.

Love ... it's like an ocean: if you're no good, if you begin to make a bad smell in it, it just spews you up somewhere to die —William Faulkner

Love, like a poker game starts with a pair; with her getting a flush, him showing a diamond and both ending up together with a full house —Anon

Love, like death, a universal leveller of mankind —William Congreve

Lovers are like drunkards; once a drunkard always a drunkard, once a lover always a lover. It is simply a matter of temperament —Guy De Maupassant

Love's like the measles, all the worse when it comes too late —Douglas Jerrold
> See comment following the Josh Billings love/measles simile above.

Love without return is like a question without an answer —Anon

Loving, like prayer, is a power as well a process. It's curative. It is creative —Zona Gale

The moods of love are like the wind —Coventry Patmore

My love is as a fever —William Shakespeare
> Another famous author, Stendhal, also likened love to a fever, adding: "It comes and goes without the will having any part in the process."

My love is like a red red rose —Robert Burns
> This is the first line and title of Burns' famous poem, in which love was spelled 'luv.'

An old man in love is like a flower in winter —Portugese proverb

Romance is the poetry of circumstance —Robert Louis Stevenson

True love is like seeing a ghost. We talk about it; few of us have
      seen one —Francois, Duc de La Rochefoucauld
            Some quote La Rochefoucauld as linking the ghost
            comparison to perfect instead of true love.

A woman's love is like the dew. It falls as easily on the manure
      heap as on the rose —Donald McCaig

Young love is a flame; very pretty, often very hot and fierce, but
      still only light and flickering. The love of the older and
      disciplined heart is as coals, deep-burning, unquenchable
      —Henry Ward Beecher

LOYALTY/DISLOYALTY
SEE: FRIENDSHIP

LUCK
SEE: FORTUNE/MISFORTUNE

LUST
SEE: DESIRE, SEX

LYING
SEE: BEARING, BENDING/BENT, IMMOBILITY, SLEEP,

MALICE
SEE: EVIL, SLANDER

MANIPULATION
SEE: POWER

MANKIND
SEE: LIFE

MANNERS

As chatty and polite as Rotarians —Richard Ford

Decorously polite as patients in a dentist's waiting room
      —Francis King

Evil manners will, like watered grass, grow up very quickly —Plautus
            While bad manners might no longer be looked upon as
            evil, Plautus' simile in relation to how any evil spreads
            remains true.

Manners

Had the manners of a disobliging steamroller ... and he was rather less particular about his dress than a scarecrow
—George Bernard Shaw

His speech sounds like a spoken bread-and-butter note
—W. P. Kinsella

Manners are like spices, you can't make a meal of them but they add a great deal to the meal's enjoyment —Anon

Manners are like the cipher in arithmetic; they may not be of much value in themselves, but they are capable of adding a great deal to the value of everything else —Anon

Manners ... as soft as wool —Lorenz Hart
This is part of the refrain of a song named "Moon of My Delight" written for *Chee-Chee.*

Our manners, like our faces, though ever so beautiful must differ in their beauty —Lord Shaftesbury

The pleasure of courtesy is like the pleasure of good dancing —Alain

Polite as pie —F. van Wyck Mason

Politeness is like an air-cushion; there may be nothing to it, but it eases our jolts wonderfully —Samuel Johnson

Rudeness (to Mrs. Dosely) was like dropping a pat of butter on to a hot plate, it slid and melted away —Elizabeth Bowen

Sedate as a judge in court —Rhys Davies

Sit bolt upright and smile without cease like a well-bred dinner guest
—Ruth Prawer Jhabvala

To be cordial is like roughing a man's head to jolly him up, or kissing a child that doesn't want to be kissed. You are relieved when it's over —George Santayana

Ungracious as a hog —Tobias Smollett

Ungracious ... like a child who opens a birthday gift and barely glances at it before reaching to unwarp the next
—Barbara Lazear Ascher

An ungracious man is like a story told at the wrong time —*The Holy Bible/Apocrypha*

262

MARRIAGE
SEE: MEN AND WOMEN

MEANINGFULNESS/MEANINGLESSNESS
SEE: MEMORY, IMPORTANCE/UNIMPORTANCE, NECESSITY

MEEKNESS

(Quivering and) abject ... like some unfortunate dog abasing itself
    before its master —Jean Rhys
        The quivering is being done by a young woman in the
        embrace of a lover, in Rhys' novel, *Quartet.*

(Why do you sit there) apologizing to him, as if he were a fuehrer
    or something —Leslie A. Fieldler

Bowed to them like a tree in a storm —Edith Wharton

Complied like hostages with a gun trained on them —Louise Erdrich

Exist unthinkingly like a slave, like a working animal —Iris Murdoch

He's like a bell, that will go for everyone that pulls it
    —Thomas Fuller

Humble, friendly eyes looked up timidly, like the yes of a dog that
    is uncertain whether he is about to receive a pat or a blow
    —Ellen Glasgow

Like an ox, his head bent meekly, he waited for the blow of the axe
    which was raised over him —Leo Tolstoy

Like a victim, she waited: meek, like a sacrifice —Margaret Drabble

Looked humbly about him like a dog slipping into a strange kitchen
    and afraid of kicks —Honoré de Balzac

Meek as a hen —Fyodor Dostoevski

Meek as the dew —Dylan Thomas

Meekness takes injuries like pills, not chewing, but swallowing them
    down —Sir Thomas Browne

A meek soul without zeal, is like a ship in a calm, that moves not
    as fast as it ought —John M. Mason

Obedience simulates subordination as fear of the police simulates
    honesty —George Bernard Shaw

263

Meekness

Obedient as a partner in a dance —Lael Tucker Wertenbaker

Obedient as a sheep —Robert Browning

Obediently as a trained seal —Anon
> The trained seal comparison has become a common cliche, with many variations such as "Obediently as a puppet on a string" and "Obediently like a trained elephant," the latter spotted in Aldous Huxley's *After Many a Summer Dies the Swan.*

Servility is like a golden pill which outwardly gives pleasure but inwardly is full of bitterness —Narun Tate
> The word 'gives' has been modernized from 'giveth.'

Waiting upon her whims like a footman —O. Henry

Went meekly off ... like a repentant boy led away to reform school —Harvey Swados

Yield like a foolish mother —Emily Brontë

MEETINGS
SEE: BEGINNINGS/ENDINGS; PEOPLE, INTERACTION

MELANCHOLY
SEE: DEJECTION

Memory

MEMORY

As bare of memories as a grain of sugar —Viña Delmar

As fixed in my memory ... as the flash of light that is followed by the thunder of pain when your shoulder is pulled out of its socket —Norman Mailer

A breeze like the turning of a page brings back your face —John Ashbery

[Memories] came back to run through his mind like a reel of color film —Carlos Baker

Memories lurk like dustballs at the back of drawers —Jay McInerney

Memories ... no two sets exactly the same, like fingerprints —Daphne Merkin

Memories of embarrassing things he had done and said, of mistakes he had made, buzzed and flitted in his mind like annoying little gnats —Dan Wakefield

Memories of the bad covered the good, as snow covers grass in the fall —Ann Jasperson

Memories ... pierced by moments of brightness, like flashes of lightning —Yasunari Kawabata

Memories [when a lot of people one knows die] return to life as grass grows on graves —Lael Tucker Wertenbaker

Memories swept over her like a strong wind on dark waters —Carl Sandburg

Memories turned up like bills you thought you'd never have to pay —Hugh Leonard
> In Leonard's play, *Da*, the memories turning up like bills are evoked as a character sorts through family memorabilia.

Memory ... as good as a bulldog's handshake —Loren D. Estleman
> In Estleman's mystery novel, *Every Brilliant Eye*, the character with the bulldog-like memory is a policeman.

Memory broke, like an old clock —Karl Shapiro

Memory can be like a dream, cause and effect non-existent —Gordon Weaver

Memory returned like fire —Frank Swinnerton

Memory's like an athlete; keep it in training; take it for cross-country runs —James Hilton

The [unpleasant] memory ... stuck like a fish-hook in her brain —Stefan Zweig

Memory transparent as a dream you strain to recall —Harryette Mullen

Memory unwound within me like a roll of film in which I played no part —Heinrich Böll

Slipped out of her mind like a newspaper dropping from the hands of a sleepy woman —Erich Maria Remarque

Some memories are like lucky charms, talismans, one shouldn't tell about them or they'll lose their power —Iris Murdoch

Stung by memories thick as wasps about a nest invaded —Edna St. Vincent Millay

Memory

There are many moments I cannot forget, moments like radiant flowers in all colors and hues —Jaroslav Seifert

Tries to remember like a deaf man remembering an opera he heard eleven years before —Lyn Lifshin

As unremembered as bird shadows on the grass —Henry Bellamann

Unremembered as old rain —Edna St. Vincent Millay

The world, like an accomplished hostess, pays most attention to those whom it will soonest forget —John Churton Collins

Men and Women

MEN AND WOMEN

Arm in arm ... like a pair of loving turtle-doves —William Shakespeare

Court ... as you would court a farm—for the strength of the silo and the perfection of the title —Josh Billings
> Like many Billings witticisms this one was written in phonetic dialect as follows: "As you wud court a farm—for the strength ov the sile and the parfeckshun ov the title."

Dating a grad student was like making hurried-up popcorn: lots of butter, high heat, instant noise —Will Weaver

The distance between them is like a desert, or an unswimmable body of water —Hilma Wolitzer
> In her novel, *In the Palomar Arms,* Wolitzer is describing an estranged husband and wife, lying far apart on a large bed.

Felt my eyes going down across her mouth, her throat like fingers —Julio Cortázar

Finding a man is like finding a job; its easier to find one when you already have one —Paige Mitchell

Girls (on the Cripple Creek 'bout half grown) jump on a boy like a dog on a bone —American folk song, "Cripple Creek"

He was looking at me the way a butcher must size up a carcass of beef, like I was one of those drawings with the parts of the cow on it, all the choice cuts and the waste —Jonathan Valin

He would always feel for her that impersonal admiration which is inspired by anything very large, like the Empire State Building or the Grand Canyon of Arizona —P. G. Wodehouse

266

HE WAS LOOKING AT ME THE WAY A BUTCHER MUST SIZE UP A CARCASS OF BEEF, LIKE I WAS ONE OF THOSE DRAWINGS WITH THE PARTS OF THE COW ON IT, ALL THE CHOICE CUTS AND THE WASTE

Men and Women

Holds her face in his cupped hands as carefully as a thirsty man
would gather water —Hilma Wolitzer

I dropped her like a bad habit —James Crumley
The simile continues with: "Put her under his arm, and all
but ate ever last crust of her."

It's as natural for women to pride themselves in fine clothes as 'tis
for a peacock to spread his tail —John Ray's *Proverbs*
A look at fashion, both past and present, would indicate
that this could well be a unisex simile.

I want to steep myself in you ... as if you were a South wind
—Wallace Stevens, letter to his fiancée

Just us two ... like two roots joined and widening out into a flower
—David Denby

Like an animal, he was aware of me at once —Robertson Davies

Like two mummies, we have been wrapped tight in love
—Yehuda Amichai

Like two open cities in the midst of some vast plain their two minds
lay open to each other —Katherine Mansfield

Like Ulysses tying himself to the mast to resist the song of the
sirens, Jim had to brace himself to withstand the charm of Kate's
voice —Henri-Pierre Roche

The trouble with being a woman is that you are supposed to
enhance men; to add gaiety to their evening, like balloons, even
if you feel heavy as stone —Daphne Merkin

Twenty years of romance make a woman look like a ruin; but
twenty years of marriage make her something like a public
building —Oscar Wilde

Two couples living together and talking openly for a week ... it was
like a week in a bell jar —Joanne Kates, *New York Times*,
October 2, 1986

Very gently, as to a wild animal, I reached out my hand and made
her turn her head —John Fowles

A woman, I always say, should be like a good suspense movie: the
more left to the imagination, the more excitement there is
—Alfred Hitchcock, *Reader's Digest*, July, 1963

Hitchcock topped off his simile with this bit of advice: "This should be her aim; to create suspense, to let a man discover things about her without her having to tell him."

Women are very much like religion; we must take them on faith or go without —F. Marion Crawford

Women as compared to men are like point lace to canvas —Charles H. Hoyt

Women follow him around like flies after garbage —Paige Mitchell

Women's hearts are like old china, none the worse for a break or two —W. Somer

You've [woman being addressed by a man] got an off-on switch like a circuit breaker —Will Weaver

MERCY
SEE: KINDNESS

MERIT
SEE: VIRTUE

MERRIMENT
SEE: JOY

MIDDLE AGE
SEE: AGE

MIND
SEE ALSO: ATTENTION; INSULTS; THOUGHT

(You can't concentrate. You've got) a brain like a hummingbird —Jane Wagner

Brain as heavy as a grandfather clock —Diane Wakoski

A brain tooled like a twenty-jewel Swiss watch —Stephen Longstreet

Emptied her mind, as if emptying a bottle —Mavis Gallant

Her mind flickered like a lizard —Elizabeth Bowen

Her mind was like a one-way thoroughfare, narrow and flat, maintained in repair —Mavis Gallant

Her mind was like a rushing stream, tumbling downhill over rocks and boulders, eddying, bouncing, shifting direction —Ward Just

Her mind was strangely empty ... an empty room through which vague memories stalked like giants —Jean Rhys

His brain feels like a frail but alert invalid packed inside among a lot of deep pillows —John Updike

His brain was like a brightly-lit factory, full of flying wheels and precision —Edith Wharton

His mind [Oliver Wendell Holmes, Jr.'s] resembles a stiff spring, which has to be abducted violently from it, and which every instant it is left to itself flies right back —William James, letter to brother, Harry, November 24, 1872

His mind's like the feet of a pre-civilized Chinese girl —Frank Swinnerton

The human mind should be like a good hotel, open the year round —William Lyon Phelps

It [his brain] felt like an immense dynamo running at top speed in an empty shed in the middle of the woods —Norman Mailer

Little minds, like weak liquors, are soonest soured —H. G. Bohn's *Handbook of Proverbs*

Mind, as clear as mountain water —Richard Wilbur

Mind ... blank and enclosed as a bubble of glass —Jean Thompson

Mind flapping like a rag on a clothesline in cold wind —Saul Bellow

Mind ... fluffy as a baby's crib —Louis Auchincloss

(He stood for a moment outside the room, his) mind jerking spasmodically, like a severed nerve —Storm Jameson

Mind like a bent corkscrew —Roderic Jeffries

A mind like a puddle. Things fall in and float around in it and she fishes them up later when they've gotten soggy —Jean Thompson

A mind like a sieve —Anon

A mind like a sink —Agatha Christie
    Christie was thus quoted by her nephew about Miss Marple's dark view of humankind.

Mind ... like a sun-dial, it records only pleasantness —Anon

A mind like a tattered concordance —Samuel Beckett

A mind like a wedge of iron —Louise Erdrich

Mind like dead ashes —Robert Silverberg

Mind like moths —Anon

Mind ... like some fertile garden —Edith Wharton

The mind, packed away like a satin wedding dress even in blue
   tissue, yellowing, pressing itself into permanent folds
   —Diane Wakoski
         The title of the poem featuring this line is also a simile: *The
         Mind, Like an Old Fish.*

Minds fossilized like lava —Isak Dinesen

Minds [of students] so earnest and helpless that it takes them half an
   hour to get from one idea to its immediately adjacent next
   neighbor. And when they've got the next idea, they lie down on
   it with their whole weight and can get no farther, like a cow on
   a door-mat, so that you can get neither in nor out with them
   —William James, letter to his wife, 1896

Minds stirring like poplars in a storm —Marge Piercy

(Eleanor's) mind went whirling round like a wheel on the hub of
   this moment —Elizabeth Bowen

A mind wide open to absorb all it could teach him as the flowers of
   the date-palm to receive the fertilizing pollen —Honoré de Balzac

My brain is numb as a piece of liver —W. P. Kinsella

(I seem to have read so little of late, that) my mind is like a desert,
   devoid of roses and leaves —Janet Flanner

Our brains are like fruit stands; all the rubbish is in front and the
   good stuff is in the back —Carla Lane
         Dialogue from "Solo," British television sitcom, broadcast
         June 23, 1987

Our unconscious is like a vast subterranean factory with intricate
   machinery that is never ideal, where work goes on all day and
   night from the time we are born until the moment of our death
   —Milton R. Sapirstein

Some minds are like trunks, packed tight with knowledge, no air and
   plenty of moths —*Life,* January 31, 1918

There is no sea as restless as my mind —Derek Walcott

Mind

When you have a creative mind it sometimes backs up on you like a sewer —John Farris

MISERLINESS
SEE: THRIFT

MISERY
SEE: DEJECTION

MISFORTUNE
SEE: FORTUNE/MISFORTUNE

Mist

MIST

The hot mist ... mixed with the sun like cloudy gin —David Denby

A light morning mist like grain on film —Clive Irving

Like a blanket, the mist came down —Jilly Cooper

Mist arose on the plain and stood round about it like a guard of honor —Vladimir G. Korolenko

Mist draped like ragged bits of cloth over a black line of distant hills —Alice McDermott

[Thinning] mist ... drifted away like slow smoke —Howard Spring

The mist, like love, plays upon the heart of the hills and brings out surprise of beauty —Rabindranath Tagore

The mists, like flocks of trooping sheep, cloudily drifted here and there —John Hall Wheelock

Mist so fine it was like cigarette smoke —Paul Theroux

Mists, whirling and winding, like snakes —Mihail Lermontov

A mist that is like blown snow —W. B. Yeats

Mist thick as cotton batting —William Faulkner

A pure white mist crept over the water like breath upon a mirror —A. J. Cronin

A thick gray mist covered the countryside, as if to conceal the mysteries of the changes that were taking place in nature —Leo Tolstoy

MISTRESS
SEE: MEN AND WOMEN

MODESTY
SEE: MEEKNESS, PERSONAL TRAITS

MONEY
SEE ALSO: RICHES

Ate up money like Crackerjacks —Robert Campbell

Bargain like a gipsy, but pay like a gentleman —Hungarian proverb

(There ain't a chance of putting the bee on me ... .I'm) flat [broke] as a ballroom floor —H. C. Witwer

Getting money is like digging with a needle; spending it is like water soaking into sand —Proverb

Gold, like the sun, which melts wax but hardens clay, expands great souls —Antoine Rivarol

An instinct like a water diviner's where money's concerned —John Braine

Loses money the way a ... balloon loses air —Martin Cruz Smith
In Smith's novel, *Stallion Gate*, a character is likening a great club's money loss to a beautiful balloon's air loss.

Making money ... is, in fact, almost as easy as losing it. Almost but not quite —H. L. Mencken

A man without money is like a bird without wings; if he soars he falls to the ground and dies —Roumanian proverb

He that is without money is like a bird without wings —Thomas Fuller

A man without money is like a ship without sails —Dutch proverb

Money is a bottomless sea, in which honor, conscience and truth may be drowned —Ivan Kozloff

Money is a muscle in our society like that of a leg or arm of a man with a shovel, and both muscles must have a wage —Janet Flanner

Money is in some respects like fire; it is a very excellent servant —P. T. Barnum

Money is like an arm or a leg, use it or lose it —Henry Ford, *New York Times*, November 8, 1931

Money is like an eel in the hand —Welsh proverb

Money is like a sixth sense, and you can't make use of the other five without it —W. Somerset Maugham, *New York Times Magazine*, October 18, 1958

Public money is like holy water: every one helps himself to it —Italian proverb

Money is like promises, easier made than kept —Josh Billings
 In Billing's phonetic dialect: "Munny ... easier maid than kept."

Money is like the reputation for ability, more easily made than kept —Samuel Butler

Money, like a boot, when it's tight is extremely trying —*Punch*, 1864

Money is like muck, not good except it be spread —Francis Bacon
 Variations include: "Money is like dung"; "Riches are like muck, which stink in a heap, but spread abroad, make the earth fruitful"; and "Money like manure does no good till it is spread." Two contemporary figures who have been widely quoted for perversions of the above are Clint Murchison, Jr. and J. Paul Getty. The first quoting his father's advice that, "Money is like manure. If you spread it around, it does a lot of good. But if you pile it up in one place, it stinks like hell"; the latter with "Money is like manure. You have to spread it around or it smells."

Money, like vodka, makes a man eccentric —Anton Chekhov

Money's as cold and neutral as the universe —Hortense Calisher

Money slips from his fingers like a watermelon seed, travels without legs, and flies without wings
 —Bartlett's *Dictionary of Americanisms*

Money ... was exactly like sex, you thought of nothing else if you didn't have it and thought of other things if you did
 —James Baldwin

Serious money is like cancer, it breeds itself —A. Alvarez

Spending money like a pusher —M. S. Craig

Spent her money like a spoiled empress —Marjory Stoneman Douglas

They talk about it [money] as if it were something you got pink gums from —Ogden Nash

MONTHS
SEE: SEASONS

MOON

A bright moon ... like glistening silk —Amy Lowell

Curled moon ... like a feather —Dante Gabriel Rossetti

Everything has in fact another side to it, like the moon
  —G. K. Chesterton

A full new-risen moon like a pale medallion —Hayden Carruth

The moon had lost all its brilliance and looked like a little cloud in
  the sky —Leo Tolstoy

A half moon sailing like a moth up the drained blue sky
  —Jilly Cooper

It looked like a ball of paper from the back pocket of jeans that
  have just come out of the washing machine, which only time
  and ironing would tell if it was an old shopping list or a five
  pound note —Douglas Adams

Bright moonlight lay against its [house] wall like a fresh coat of paint
  —Raymond Chandler

A little slice of moon, curved like a canoe —Helen Hudson

The moon as beautiful as a great camellia —Max Beerbohm

A moonbeam ... shimmers bright as a needle —W. P. Kinsella

Moon, bright as a lemon —Tom Robbins

The moon burned like metal —Pat Conroy

The moon, but half disclosed, was cut off as by a shutter
  —Joyce Cary

Moon curved like a rocker —Helen Hudson

The moon floats belly up like a dead goldfish —Marge Piercy

The moon follows the sun like a French translation of a Russian poet
  —Wallace Stevens

The moon hangs like a neon scythe over the countryside
  —W. P. Kinsella

275

Moon

The moon hung above the yard like a cheap earring —Isaac Babel

The moon hung like a pale lamp above the rim of the bay
    —William Styron

The moon is hidden by a silver cloud, fair as a halo
    —Christina Rossetti

The moon ... is like a cake of white soap —John Phillips

The moon leaned low against the sky like a white-faced clown lolling
    against a circus wall —W. Somerset Maugham

Moonlight drilling in through the window like a bit into coal
    —Richard Wertime

Moonlight ... dripped down like oil —Bernard Malamud

The moonlight invaded the courtyard, until it looked like a field of
    untrodden snow —Stefan Zweig

Moonlight so white that it looked like snow —Ruth Prawer Jhabvala

A moon like a fallen fruit reversing gravity was hoisting itself above
    the rooftop —Ross Macdonald

The moon like a flower in heaven's high bower, with silent delight
    sits and smiles on the night —William Blake

Moon like a monstrous crystal —G. K. Chesterton

The moon, like an eye turned up in a trance, filmed over and
    seemed to turn loose from its track and to float sightless
    —Eudora Welty

Moon ... like a red-faced farmer —T. E. Hulme
        The complete line as it appears in a poem entitled *Autumn:*
        'I walked abroad and saw the ruddy moon lean over the
        hedge like a red-faced farmer.''

The moon like a white rose shone —W. B. Yeats

Moon like the moving dot on sing-along lyrics
    —Sharon Sheehe Stark

The moon looked like the head of a golden bollard in a Venice
    lagoon —John Gunther

The moon, narrow and pale like a paring snipped from a snowman's
    toenail —Tom Robbins

The moon overhead tore through fierce cloud-wrack like a battered ship —Phyllis Bottome

Moon ... pale, full-blown as a flower —Elizabeth Spencer

Moon pitted with holes, like an old brass coin
—Erich Maria Remarque

The moon rattles like a fragment of angry candy —E. E. Cummings

The moon rises like a fat white god —Diane Ackerman

The moon ... rode bonily in the sky, looking stark and abandoned like a decoration kids had put up for Halloween and forgotten to take down —William Dieter

The moon sails up out of the ocean dripping like a just washed apple —Marge Piercy

The moon shines like a lost button —Derek Walcott

The moon shone out like day —Nathanial Hawthorne

Moon slightly more than half full, like a tipped bowl
—Patricia Henley

The moon stood like an arc lamp over the roofs of the houses
—Erich Maria Remarque

The moon stuck like a wafer in the evening sky —Anon

The moon swelled like a plum —Philip Levine

Moon ... waning, like silver that is polished so thin that it has begun to wear away —Mary Stewart

The moon ... was like a slender shaving thrown up from a bar of gold —Joseph Conrad

The moon was like a chip of ice —Wallace Stegner

The moon was like a sickle —Edward Hoagland

The moon was out, cold and faraway as an owl's hoot —John Braine

The moon ... was slowly drifting into an immense, dark and transparent hole like a lake with its depth full of stars
—André Malraux

A pale crescent moon shaped like a woman's earring
—Katharine Haake

Moon

A pale moon, like a claw (looked down through the claw-like branches of dead trees) —Jean Rhys

Quiet moonlight lay like the smile upon a dreaming face —John Hall Wheelock

The rising moon ... winding like a silver thread until it was lost in the stars —Bret Harte

Sometimes in the afternoon sky a white moon would creep up like a little cloud, without display, suggesting an actress who does not have to "Come on" for a while and so goes "In front" in her ordinary clothes —Marcel Proust

The sphere hanging in the not yet darkened sky seemed like a lamp they had forgotten to turn off in the morning (a lamp that had burned all day in the room of the dead) —Milan Kundera

A stream of moonlight cut through the mist and hit the black water, like ink —Paige Mitchell

A thin moon ... gray and marbled like a worn shell —Alice McDermott

A yellow moon rose like a flower blooming —Bernard Malamud

MORALITY
SEE: VIRTUE

MORTALITY
SEE: DEATH

MOTIONLESSNESS
SEE: IMMOBILITY

MOTIVATION
SEE: AMBITION

Mountains

MOUNTAINS
SEE ALSO: LANDSCAPES, NATURE

Cropped, long-faced hills that bristled with pine like so many unshaven cheeks —T. Coraghessan Boyle

The hills here are long and blue, like paintings —Bobbie Ann Mason

Hills like breasts —Karl Shapiro

The hillside is dotted with white plum trees like puffs of smoke —Colette

278

Hills ... lay there like a herd of drowsing buffalo —Yitzhak Shenhar

Hills ... like a young girl's breasts —William Boyd

Hills rose up like bubbles —Phyllis Bottome

Like an enormous landscape lay the mountain —Delmore Schwartz

Mountains ... like crouching camels —Milton Raison

Mountains like puffs of smoke —George Garrett

The mountains rolled like whales through the phosphorous stars
     —Derek Walcott

The mountains rose like worn, dark-skinned fists —Carlos Fuentes

Mountains, stretching themselves like great luxurious cats in the
     sunshine —Hugh Walpole

Mountains ... unreal like movie props —John Rechy

The mountains were jagged like a page ripped out of a book
     —Kate Grenville

The mountains were just visible, dusky and black, like waves of
     charcoal —John Fowles

The mountain tops were whitened by moonlight like crests of waves
     —Lee Smith

The mountain was shining like glass in color —Paul Horgan

The scenery is funny little hills shaped like scoops of ice cream
     —Bobbie Ann Mason

The hills are ... ribbed like the remains of antediluvian breasts
     stretched across the horizon —T. Coraghessan Boyle

To live in mountains is like living with someone who always talks at
     the top of his, or it may be her, voice —Leonard Woolf

Tree-covered folds in the mountains ... lying like a gigantic crumpled
     velvet rug —John Fowles

MOURNING
SEE: GRIEF

MOUTH

Bare his teeth like a yawning tiger —Miles Gibson

Mouth

Cruel red mouth like a venomous flower
—Algernon Charles Swinburne

He had his mouth all prissed up when he talked, like a man acting in a play —Iris Murdoch

Her mouth glistened like a wound —Jerry Bumpus

Her mouth hung loose like a bright ribbon —R. V. Cassill

Her mouth is wide and red as strawberry pie —Rex Reed
The mouth thus described belongs to actress Carol Channing.

Her mouth was as little suited for smiling as a frying-pan for musical purposes —Anatole France

Her peevish mouth looked like a slit cut by a knife —Stefan Zweig

His mouth ran like a thin dark crease between them [chin and nose] —Jonathan Valin

His mouth turned down like he could see death —Richard Ford

His open mouth was like a dark hole in his beard —Ross Macdonald

A loose mouth ... slack with usage, like rubber bands
—William Faulkner

The mouth and ear are like a bow and a fiddle; when the ear is shut, the mouth is mute —Hayyim Nahman Bialik

Mouth as sweet as a ripe fig —Edith Wharton

Mouth broad as an airstrip —Loren D. Estleman

Mouth ... framed in iron-gray fluffy hair, that looked like a chin-strap of cotton wool sprinkled with coal-dust —Joseph Conrad

Mouth ... clamped like a spring and right as the mouth of a witch —Borden Deal

(A big, pink) mouth, curled down at one corner as if he habitually smoked a pipe —Lael Tucker Wertenbaker

A mouth drawn in like a miser's purse —Émile Zola

Mouth ... flabby like a toad's —Christopher Isherwood

Mouth ... like a large wet keyhole —Roald Dahl

Mouth like a fireplace —Ogden Nash

Mouth ... like a fold of skin over a skull, without the life
—Paul Horgan

A mouth like an air-raid trench —Jane Wagner

Mouth like an arrowhead wound —Jean Cocteau about Colette

Mouth ... like a scarlet wound —W. Somerset Maugham

Mouth like a seam —Irvin S. Cobb

Mouth like a slit in the sidewalk —Anon

Mouth like the bottom of a parrot cage —David Niven

A mouth like the inside of a jelly doughnut —Peter De Vries

Mouth open like a funnel's —Eudora Welty

Mouth pinched inward like a fist —Joyce Carol Oates

Mouth pursed up tight like a mushroom —Roald Dahl

Mouth ... red and slightly swollen, as if somebody had been chewing on it —Ross Macdonald

Mouth ... so wide-centred and deep-cornered, so cool and so warm, so lusciously crimson, that flaring out of the pallor of her face, it was like a blood-hot signal to the senses —Inez Haynes Irwin

Mouths like donuts —F. D. Reeve

Mouths like wet velvet —Angela Carter

Mouth ... so thin that the lips seemed to hook together, like the catch of a child's purse —Frank Tuohy

Mouths pink as watermelon —May Sarton

A mouth that stretches from ear to ear when he laughs, like a mouth on a cat piggy bank —Francois Maspero

Mouth that was like a salmon's mouth —Roald Dahl

Mouth thin and straight, like a cut in his face —Honoré de Balzac

Mouth tight as a corset string on the preacher's wife
—Harold Adams

Mouth tugged down on one side like a dead man's —John Updike

Mouth twisted like an epileptic's —Isaac Bashevis Singer

Mouth

The old mouth closed like a zip —Julia O'Faolain

A quibbling mouth that would have snapped verbal errors like a lizard catching flies —Edith Wharton

A wide and expressionless mouth like the juncture of a casserole dish with its lid —Thomas McGuane

MOVEMENT
SEE: ADVANCING, JUMPING, ROCKING AND ROLLING

MOVIES
SEE: STAGE AND SCREEN

MUSCLES
SEE: STRENGTH

MUSTACHES
SEE: HAIR

MYSTERIOUSNESS
SEE: STRANGENESS

NAKEDNESS
SEE: BARENESS

NAMES
SEE: MEMORY

NARROWNESS
SEE: THINNESS

Nature

NATURE
SEE ALSO: FLOWERS, MOON, SEASCAPES, SKY, SUN, THUNDER AND LIGHTNING, TREES,

Big heavy drops [of dew] ... lie on the face of the earth like sweat —Shirley Ann Grau

Bushes ... like heads; you could have sworn sometimes you saw them mounting and swaying in manly talk —Elizabeth Bowen

The damp stands on the long green grass as thick as morning's tears —Emily Brontë

The dawn clings to the river like a fog —Yvor Winters

Dew as thick as frost —Paul Theroux

Dew gleamed and sparkled like myriads of tiny mirrors
    —Dorothy Livesay

The dew is beaded like mercury on the coarsened grass
    —Adrienne Rich

Dew ... like trembling silver leaves —Dame Edith Sitwell

Driftwood gnarled and knobby like old human bones
    —Charles Johnson

The earth is like the breast of a woman: useful as well as pleasing
    —Friedrich Nietzsche

Earth was like a jostling festival of seeds grown fat
    —Wallace Stevens

Flecks of ice still clung to his collar, flashing like brilliants
    —William H. Gass

Frost was like stiff icing sugar on all the roofs —H. E. Bates

The garden we planted and nurtured through the spring ... fills out
    like an adolescent at summer camp —Ira Wood

The grass like a prophet's beard, thoughtful and greying
    —Charles Simic

The grass on the roadside moved under the evening wind, sounding
    like many pairs of hands rubbed softly together —H. E. Bates

Grass patches ... like squares on a game board —Mary Hedin

Grass ... thick as wind —David Ignatow

Hedges as solid as walls —Edith Wharton

Here a giant philodendron twined around a sapodilla tree and
    through the branches of a hibiscus bush like a green arm
    drawing two friends together —Dorothy Francis

Ice-crystals, shaped like fern-leaves —Anatole France

Light hung in the trees like cobwebs —Jay Parini

The light is in the dark river of the hot spring evening like a dry
    wine in a decanter —Delmore Schwartz

Like a great poet, Nature knows how to produce the greatest effects
    with the most limited means —Heinrich Heine

Nature

Like a slim reed of crystal, a fountain hung in the dusky air
—Oscar Wilde

The moisture in the air seemed suspended like tiny pearls
—Rita Mae Brown

Moss that looks and feels like felt —Brad Leithauser

Nature is like a beautiful woman that may be as delightfully and as
truly known at a certain distance as upon a closer view
—George Santayana
> Santayana expanded on the simile as follows: "As to
> knowing her through and through, that is nonsense in
> both cases, and might not reward our pains."

Nature is like a revolving door: what goes out in one form comes
back in another —Anon

Nature like life, she strips men of their pretensions and vanities,
exposes the weakness of the weak and the folly of the fool
—W. Macneile Dixon

Nature, like lives while they are being lived, is subject to laws of
motion; it cannot be stopped and thereby comprehended
—Margaret Sutherland

Pebbles [on beach] lit like eggs —Jay Parini

A plant is like a self-willed man, out of whom we can obtain all
which we desire, if we will only treat him his own way
—Johann Wolfgang von Goethe

A rampant twining vine of wisteria, ancient and knotted like muscles
—Marge Piercy

Sea shells as big as melons. Others like peas —John Cheever

The [clam] shells shone like rainbows —Will Weaver

The shrubs burgeon like magic beanstalks —T. Coraghessan Boyle

The soil [being dug with a spade] slices off like fudge
—Sharon Sheehe Stark

Sun-baked tomatoes ... hung like red balloons filled with water
—Anon

The surrounding nature is soundless as if it were under water
—Shohei Ooka

Thistles stood looking like prophets in the Bible in Solomon's house
—Eudora Welty

Tiny, sand-sized bits of green moss hung in slanted drifts in the
water like grain dust in sunlight —Will Weaver

Trees and flowers that crowded to the path's edge like children
—Helen Hudson

The tufts of moss, like piles of house dust, that hang trembling on
the bare winter trees —Elizabeth Hardwick

The twilight seems like a canopy —Erich Maria Remarque

Undergrowth [of a path] spotted with moonlight like a leapord's skin
—Colette

The water rippled like a piece of cloth —William Faulkner

The white of the snow and sky filled my eyes like the sheet pulled
over the head of a dead man —Steve Erickson

A white sky made the bare branches of the elms [in March] seem
like bones —Louis Auchincloss

NEARNESS
SEE: CLOSENESS

NEATNESS
SEE: ORDER/DISORDER

NECESSITY
SEE ALSO: IMPORTANCE/UNIMPORTANCE

Crucial as the last game of the World Series —Anon

Essential as marrow —Curtis White

I need it like I need a hole in the head —Anon
        A Yiddish simile, typical of the colorful irony that has
        caused so many Jewish immigrant expressions to become
        integrated into American English.

Necessary and invisible like drafts of oxygen —Thomas Lux

Necessary as water to a healthy lawn —Anon

Necessary as a gardener to his garden —John Ray's *Proverbs*

Necessary as an anesthesiologist to an operation —Mary Morris

Necessity

Necessary as applause to an actor —Anon

Necessary as a saw to a carpenter —Anon

Necessary as bytes to a computer —Anon

Necessary as Christmas to retailers —Anon

Necessary as eggs in an omelette —Anon

Necessary as gas to a car —Anon

Necessary as good lines to a play —Anon

Necessary as markings on a scale or a thermometer —Anon

Necessary as a paycheck to a worker —Anon

Necessary as practice to a musician —Anon

Necessary as quartz for a digital watch —Anon

Necessary as snow to a ski weekend —Anon

Necessary as sturdy shoes to a runner —Anon

Necessary as sunshine to a garden —Anon

Necessary as wages —John Braine

Necessary as workouts to an athlete —Anon

Necessary as work to a workaholic —Anon

(Men are as) necessary to her survival as water —Patricia Henley

Need as a dog needs a pocket handkerchief —Anon
>"Need as" similes with opposite meanings lend themselves to endless variations.

Needed a ten minute head start like Sinatra needed singing lessons —John Lutz

Need ... like a fish needs a bicycle —Robert B. Parker

Needs as a dog needs two tails —American colloquialism, attributed to New England
>The exact wording of this, as with anything handed down through common usage varies with each user; for example, a popular variation of the same theme is "He don't need it any more than a dog needs two tails."

286

Need ... to simplify, almost like some painfully obese gourmet craving a stay at a health farm —John Fowles

Something she needs like a new navel —Richard Ford

As superfluous as a Gideon's Bible at the Ritz —F. Scott Fitzgerald

Superfluous as to light as a candle to the sun —Robert South

Unnecessary like rubbish —Henia Karmel-Wolfe

NECK
SEE: PHYSICAL APPEARANCE

NEED
SEE: DESIRE

NERVE
SEE: COURAGE

NERVOUSNESS
SEE: ANXIETY, TENSION

NEUTRALITY
SEE: IMPARTIALITY, GOSSIP

NIGHT
SEE: DARKNESS

NIGHTMARES
SEE: DREAMS

NOISE
SEE ALSO: IRRITABLENESS

Applause ... like pebbles being rattled in a tin —Francis King

Blare, like the clearing of a monstrous throat —Richard Wilbur

(The crowd laughing and) boo-boo-booming like frogs in a barbershop quartet —Ken Kesey

Boomed like a split trombone —O. Henry

Boom like a military band —W. H. Auden

A branch creaked ... like someone turning over in bed —Jonathan Valin

Broke into a long roar like the falling of the walls of Jericho —Katherine Anne Porter

(The house-phone ...) buzzed like an angry hornet
  —Cornell Woolrich

Cawing like a rook —Dame Edith Sitwell

[A dog's teeth] chattered like barbers' scissors —Frank Conroy

Clanged like fifty fire-engines —Herman Melville

Clanging [noise of truck backing out of driveway] like a half-dozen
  cowbells —Carolyn Chute

(Brake drums) clapped like cymbals —T. Coraghessan Boyle

Click like the snapping of a picture with an old box camera
  —W. P. Kinsella

A thin plaintive sound, like a starved cat —Raymond Chandler

The thud of her heart in her ears like wet dirt slapped with a spade
  —Reynolds Price

Ticking [of clock] ... sounds like a convict rhythmically pounding a
  rock —W. P. Kinsella

Twitter like bats —Angela Carter

Whirring, like the buzz of a giant wasp —Eddie Cohen

A whoop woke me up ... as if I'd been prodded by a cattle rod
  —W. P. Kinsella

NONSENSE
SEE: ABSURDITY, IMPOSSIBILITY

NOSTALGIA
SEE: MEMORY, SENTIMENT

OBEDIENCE
SEE: MEEKNESS

OBLIVION
SEE: MEMORY

OBSERVATION
SEE: SCRUTINY

OBSTINACY
SEE: PERSISTENCE

OCEAN/OCEANFRONTS
SEE: SEASCAPES

ODOR
SEE: SMELL

OLD
SEE: AGE

OPENNESS
SEE: CANDOR

OPINION
SEE: IDEAS

OPPORTUNITY
SEE: FORTUNE/MISFORTUNE, IMPOSSIBILITY

ORANGE
SEE: COLORS

ORDER/DISORDER

The big house ran like a Swiss clock —Rita Mae Brown

(The market is in absolute) chaos ... like people running out on the
   field after a Mets game
      —Howard Farber, *New York Times*, October 5, 1986
         The chaos described by Farber refers to the x-rated video
         industry.

Chaotic as the floor of the stock exchange at the closing bell
      —William Diehl

(Chaos and) disorder is like a pebble in my shoe or loose hair under
   my shirt collar —Warren Miller

Disorder piles up like a (local California) mountain —Janet Flanner

Household ordered like a monastic establishment —Gustave Flaubert

Housekeeping, like good manners, is usually inconspicuous
      —Peg Bracken

Keeps house like a Dutch housekeeper —Anaïs Nin
         The person whose neatness is likened to that of a Dutch
         housekeeper is novelist Henry Miller.

(The whole lot was) littered like a schoolroom after a paper fight
      —Mary Hood

Neat and bare as a GI's footlocker —George Garrett

(Withered little Filipino men, as) neat and brittle as whiskbrooms —Fletcher Knebel

Neat and dustless as a good museum —George Garrett

Neat and soft as a puff of smoke —George Garrett

Neat as a Coffin —Anon

Neat as a cupcake —Laurie Colwin

(The little one-story house was as ...) neat as a fresh pinafore —Raymond Chandler

Neat as a hoop —Rosellen Brown

Neat as a morgue —Wilfrid Sheed

Neat as an employee prepared to be given a pink slip and told to clear out his desk within half an hour —Elyse Sommer

Neat as a pin —American colloquialism
This has its roots in the English expression "Neat as a ninepence," and serves as continuing inspiration for catchy "Neat as" comparisons.

(House), neat as a stamp collection —Marge Piercy

(He was) neat as a warm stone —Don Robertson

Neat as pie crust —Julia O'Faolain

(You are) rumpled like a sweater —Marge Piercy
Another example of a simile used as an introducer, in this case a poem entitled *Nothing More Will Happen.*

Their rooms were neat as monk's cells —Babs H. Deal

(He said that) the lawn and house should be neat and pass inspection ... like a soldier's bunk and beard —Mary Morris

Untidy ... like a bird of paradise that had been out all night in the rain —Oscar Wilde

OUTBURST
SEE: BURST

PAIN
SEE ALSO: HEALTH

Ached from head to foot, all zones of pain seemingly
    interdependent ... like a Christmas tree whose lights wired in
    series, must all go out if even one bulb is defective
    —J. D. Salinger

Ached like a bad tooth —Lawrence Durrell

The air burning my lungs like a red-hot iron or cutting into them
    like a sharpened razor —Albert Camus

Anguish poured out like blood from a gaping wound
    —Jonathan Kellerman
        In Kellerman's novel, *When the Bough Breaks,* the anguish
        is being poured out by a patient to the psychologist hero.

Bruised like a half-back in a football game
    —Francis W. Crowninshield

[Rash] burned like dots of acid —William Kennedy

Cut like a whiplash —Ruth Chatterton

(Walked out into) the dazzling sun that cut into his eyes like a knife
    —John Dos Passos

A deadly vise of pain that clamped her head like a steel helmet
    —Arthur A. Cohen

Exposed it [pain] like a beggar used to making a show of his sores
    —Julia O'Faolain

Feel like somebody stuck thumbtacks all over my head
    —James Lee Burke

Felt as if I'd been crushed between two runaway wardrobes
    —J. B. Priestly
        This "similistic" comment is made by the hero of *Lost
        Empires* after being beaten up.

Felt as though his body were wrapped in layers of plaster cast
    —Kenzaburo Oë
        The plaster cast comparison was used by the author to
        describe a character who wakes up feeling stiff and achy
        all over.

Felt her head was going to break open like a coconut struck with a
    hammer —Marge Piercy

291

Pain

Felt pain like hot knives —Anon

A flash of pain darted through her, like the ripple of sheet lightning
  —Edith Wharton

For a second he remained in torture, as if some invisible flame were
  playing on him to reduce his bones and fuse him down
  —D.H. Lawrence

A gash ... as wide as an open grave —Jimmy Sangster

Generalized racking misery that makes him feel as if his pores are
  bleeding and his brain is leaking out of his ears
  —T. Coraghessan Boyle

A head like a sore tooth —Anon

Her stomach reacted as though she'd eaten sulfuric pancakes
  —Rita Mae Brown

An hour of pain is as long as a day of pleasure —English proverb

The hurt had gone through her like the split in a carcass
  —Julia O'Faolain

The hurt I felt ... was something like a thumb struck with a hammer
  —MacDonald Harris

Hurt ... like a knot passing through an artery —Donald McCaig

(My brother's laugh is small, sharp, and) hurts like gravel in your
  shoe —Sharon Sheehe Stark

It [the pain of failure] was like a gnawing physical disability, an ugly
  mark she wanted to hide —H. E. Bates

A knot of pain was set like a malignant jewel in the core of his
  head —Truman Capote

(Your letter was) like a bullet straight into my heart
  —Sholom Aleichem

My back ached as if someone were holding a welding torch against
  my spine, turning the flame on and off at will —W. P. Kinsella

My breast was contracted by a pain like screws clamped on my heart
  —Joyce Cary

My insides burned like pipes in a boiler —Governeur Morris

My intestines felt as if they were playing host to a Bears-Raiders game —Penny Ward Moser, *Discover*, February, 1987

My stomach feels as if I have swallowed razor blades —W. P. Kinsella

My stomach feels like the crop of a hen —Katherine Mansfield

My whole body glows with pain as if I were being electrocuted —Iris Murdoch

Nausea coiled like a snake in her stomach —A. E. Maxwell

Pain and pleasure, like light and darkness, succeed each other —Laurence Sterne

The pain between his eyes seemed to be whirling about like a pinwheel —R. Wright Campbell

Pain comes billowing on like a full cloud of thunder —Dante Gabriel Rossetti

Painful ... like cutting the heart out of her body —Phyllis Bottome
The pain described in Bottome's short story, *The Battle Field*, is that of never seeing someone again.

The pain goes ringing through me like alarms —Delmore Schwartz

Pain ... hard as blows —John Berryman

The pain in his chest was like a tight breastplate —Graham Swift

Pain is immune to empathy ... like love —Barbara Lazear Ascher, *New York Times*/Hers, October 16, 1986

Pain is like a love affair. When it's over, it's over —Elyse Sommer

Pain lifted like a fog that gives way to bright sunlight —Maurice Edelman

Pain ... like a metal bar —Graham Swift

Pain (lingering) ... like a stone pit lodged in the stomach —Anon

Pain rising as periodically as high water —William H. Gass

(The sympathy that it arouses is as) painful as charity —Mihail Lermontov

Pains are flinging her about like an old rag, a filthy torn rag doll —Vicki Baum

Pain

The pain seemed to rock inside him like a weight that would overturn him —Graham Swift

Pains ... like streams of pulsating fire heating him to an intolerable temperature —Ambrose Bierce

Pain ... slopped through his head like water into a sand-castle —Kingsley Amis

Pains that shrieked like alarm bells —Jane Rogers

Pain tightens like a strip of hot metal across Martin's chest —Robert Silverberg

Pain ... twisting like currents in a river —Martin Amis

Pain whistled through my body like splintered glass —Ross Macdonald

Pain would advance and recede like waves on a beach —Nathaniel Benchley

People in pain are like the wandering minstrels of the Renaissance. Any occupied space becomes their court. If the story's told often enough, perhaps the demons will become manifest. Made visible and mastered through words —Barbara Lazear Ascher, *New York Times*, October 16, 1986

A persistent jabbing in her chest that tapped back and forth like an admonishing finger —Molly Giles

Pierce ... like misplaced trust —John Drury

(Though we love pleasure, we) play with pain like a tongue toying with a bad tooth —George Garrett

The pounding in his head was like ten thousand hammers —Niven Busch

Press like a blunt thumb —Lawrence Durrell

Prolonged pain is like a fire in the house, it causes you to flee and wander homeless —Barbara Lazear Ascher, *New York Times*, October 16, 1986

Shudder at the thrust of pain like a virgin at the thrust of love —George Garrett

Spine ached as if it had been twisted like a cat's tail —Bernard Malamud

Sting you like scorn —Thomas Hardy

(Irony ...) stung like squirts from a leaky hose —Geoffrey Wolff

Suffering is cheap as grass and free as the rain that falls on saint
    and sinner alike —George Garrett

A sweet bewildering pain, like flowers in the wind and rain
        —Thomas Ashe

[A broken ankle] swelled like a soccer ball —Clive Cussler

Swollen face throbbing as if it has been pumped up with a bellows
        —Elena Poniatowska

Throat ... like sandpaper soaked in salt —H. E. Bates

Throat ... like a thicket of nettles —Arthur Train

[The lack of respect] tormented him like a raging thirst
        —Marge Piercy

Woke up feeling as if someone had tied sandbags to my hair
        —Jonathan Valin

Writhed like a trampled snake —Oscar Wilde

(Sat on a bench) writhing like a woman in labor —Isaac Babel

Writhing ... like the poor shell-fish set to boil alive
        —John Greenleaf Whittier

PAINTINGS
SEE: ART AND LITERATURE

PARTING
SEE: BEGINNINGS/ENDINGS

PASSION
SEE: DESIRE, SEX

PAST, THE
SEE: MEMORY

PATIENCE

Had the patience of a man who worked a step at a time through
    month-long laboratory experiments —Elizabeth Spencer

Mute and patient, like an old sheep waiting to be let out
        —Flannery O'Connor

Patience and diligence, like faith, remove mountains —William Penn

Patience is passion tamed —Lyman Abbott

Patience is so like fortitude that she seems either her sister or her daughter —Aristotle

The patience of someone who finds a wounded animal in the woods and stays with it —Sharon Olds

Patient as a turtle —Mary Hedin

(I'll be as) patient as a gentle stream —William Shakespeare

Patient as the matador —George Garrett

Patient, like an old man who has just dug his grave —Sharon Olds

Patiently as the spider weaves the broken web
—Edward Bulwer-Lytton

Patiently, like a weaver at his loom —Beryl Markham

Stood as patiently as a horse being groomed —John D. MacDonald

Tolerance ... like that of a grandparent for unpredictable and troublesome children —William Faulkner

Waiting patiently, in silence, as a cat does at a mousehole
—Frank Swinnerton

PAUNCHINESS
SEE: BODY

PEACEFULNESS
SEE: CALMNESS

PECULIARITY
SEE: STRANGENESS

PENETRATION
SEE: PERVASIVENESS

PENSIVENESS
SEE: THOUGHT

PEOPLE, INTERACTION
SEE ALSO: FRIENDSHIP, MEN AND WOMEN

All her life she had looked for someone who would ... settle her in the proper place like a cushion on a couch —Helen Hudson

[Different types of people] all mixed up like vegetables in soup
    —Flannery O'Connor

All the hurtful ugly things that happened between us got somehow
    wrapped around the sweetness like a hard rind around a delicate
    rare fruit. Like a flower garden completely surrounded with
    tangles of barbed wire —Harryette Mullen

(Harris) always managed to make him feel ... like the character in
    the commercial who uses the wrong kind of deodorant soap
    —Andrew Kaplan

Avoid them like piranhas —Richard Ford

Bitching patiently at each other like a couple married much too long
    —James Crumley
        The people doing the bitching in Crumley's novel, *The
        Wrong Case*, are two farmers in a bar.

Dealing with Valentine was like dealing with a king —Saul Bellow

Distance between them ... like the Persian Gulf —Robert Anderson

Faced each other like scruffy bookends —Jonathan Gash

Groups gathered a moment like flies —Bin Ramke

Guided him by one elbow [to a seat] like a tugboat turning a tanker
    —Peter Benchley

Hoisted her up like a parcel —Henri-Pierre Roche

It was as if he could read my mind like an old tale he had learned
    by heart —George Garrett

I want to lean into her [a daughter into her mother] the way wheat
    leans into wind —Louise Erdrich

Lay side by side, like some old bronze Crusader and his lady on a
    sarcophagus in the crypt of some ancient church
    —MacDonald Harris

(Take her by the lily white hand and) lead her like a pigeon
    —Anon American dance ballad, "Weevily Heart."
        The ballad dates to the late eighteenth/early nineteenth
        century.

Leaned on [another person] ... like a wounded man —George Garrett

Like the sun, his presence shone on her —Marge Piercy

Live together like brothers and do business like strangers —Arab proverb

Loneliness sifted between us, like falling snow —Judith Rascoe

Our heart-strings were, like warp and woof in some firm fabric, woven in and out —Edna St. Vincent Millay

People, like sheep, tend to follow a leader—occasionally in the right direction —Alexander Chase

We seemed strangers [a group of three people sitting in room] waiting in a station to take a train to another city —Henry Van Dyke

People sat huddled together [on street benches] like dark grapes clustered on a stalk —W. Somerset Maugham

Read him like a label on a beer can —William H. Hallhan

[Two men who don't like each other] recoiling from one another like reversed magnets —Wyatt Blassingame

Responded to each other nervously, like a concord of music —Lawrence Durrell

Sat ... like a pair of carefully-folded kid-gloves, bound up in each other —Charles Dickens

She could feel the distance between them like a patch of fog —Lynne Sharon Schwartz

She reads my silence like a page —Robert Campbell

Sitting like strangers thrown together by accident —Ross Macdonald

Something in her face spilled over me like light through a swinging door —Sue Grafton

Students, their faces like stone walls around him [a college professor] —Helen Hudson

[Many different kinds of people] swarmed around him like startled fish —Derek Lambert

Tangled together like badly cast fish lines —Katherine Anne Porter

They [a man and woman with child between them] lay like two slices of wheat bread with a peanut-butter center —Will Weaver

FACED EACH OTHER LIKE SCRUFFY BOOKENDS

They needed each other's assistance, like a company, who, crossing a mountain stream, are compelled to cling close together, lest the current should be too powerful for any who are not thus supported —Sir Walter Scott

They were ... like two people holding on to the opposite ends of a string, each anxious to let go, or at least soon, without offending the other, yet each reluctant to drop the curling, lapsing bond between them —Hortense Calisher

Took me about like a roast [to make introductions] —Mark Helprin
This spotlights the importance of using a simile within an appropriate context. The character being taken about "like a roast" in Helprin's story, *Tamar*, is the last arrival at a dinner party. If someone were being introduced in a business setting, being passed around "Like a special report or a memo" might better suit the situation.

Touched him on the breast as though his finger were the fine point of a small sword —Charles Dickens

Treated him like crows treat a scarecrow: they ignored him and avoided him —William H. Hallhan

Wanted me to share her pain like an orgasm, like lovers in poems who slit their wrists together —Max Apple

Watching each other like two cats; and then, as cats do, turn away again, indifferently, as if whatever was at stake between them had somehow faded out —L. P. Hartley

(The Heindricks) were making me feel like a specimen in a jar —Jonathan Gash

We sat half-turned toward one another like the arms of a parenthesis —Cornell Woolrich

You play my heart like a concertina —Harvey Fierstein

PERCEPTIVENESS
SEE: SENSITIVENESS

PERMANENCE

As assured of longevity as the statues on Easter Island
—John W. Aldridge, *New York Times Book Review*, October 26, 1986.

The work to which Aldridge ascribes the longevity of the Easter Island statues is Joseph Heller's *Catch-22.*

(She was) as immutable as the hills. But not quite so green
  —Rudyard Kipling

Bonds ... as immutable as a tribal code —Anon

Changeless as heaven —John Greenleaf Whittier

Changeless as truth —John Keats

Constant as the Northern Star —William Shakespeare

Enduring as a family feud —Anon

(A novelistic structure as harsh and) enduring as any tabby wall
  —John D. MacDonald

Enduring as mother love —Anon

Enduring as the Washington Monument —Anon

Enduring as the Constitution —Anon

Fixed as a habit or some darling sin —John Oldham

Fixed as a leopard's spots —Anon

Fixed as a tiger's stripes —Anon

Fixed as the cycle of life —Anon

Fixed as the days in the week —Anon

Fixed as the sun —Erasmus

(In two years he) had altered as little as the landscape
  —Ellen Glasgow

(My love of art seemed as) as indelible as ink —Jill Ciment

Invariable as a formula —Ellen Glasgow

Irrevocable as death —Charlotte Brontë

Lasts like iron —Oliver Wendell Holmes, Sr.

Like love we seldom keep —W. H. Auden

Of no more true substance than a scarecrow in a field
  —George Garrett

Permanence

(The fine carnation of their skin is) perennial as sunlight
 —Herman Melville

Permanent as the bathroom fixture —Nora Johnson
 In Johnson's novel, *The World of Henry Orient,* the comparative frame of reference is a woman whom the narrator of the novel likes and trusts.

Settled ... like an oil stain —Charles Johnson

Unalterable as the little paper flowers permanently visible inside the lumpy glass paperweights —Ezra Pound

Unchanging as the nation's flag —George Jean Nathan

(Ideas, though painfully acquired,) stick like nails in the best oak
 —Joyce Cary

(My bounded brain was as) unalterable as a ball —Jean Stafford

Binding as a wedding ring used to be —Elyse Sommer

Eternal as the sky —John Greenleaf Whittier

Eternity ... like a great ring of pure and endless light
 —Henry Vaughan
 The simile is introduced with "I saw eternity the other night."

[Eyes] imperishable as diamonds —Ellen du Pois Taylor

(Psychology) will live long as the pyramids —Delmore Schwartz

Persistence

PERSISTENCE
SEE ALSO: CLINGING

As headstrong as an allegory on the banks of the Nile
 —Richard Brinsley Sheridan

(Sorrow) as nagging as envy —Karl Shapiro

(The name was becoming) a teasing obsession, like a tune
 —Wilfrid Sheed

Dogged as a turtle crossing a road —Marge Piercy

Hold on with a bulldog grip —Abraham Lincoln
 From a telegram to General Grant, August 1864.

I'm like a terrier pup. Somebody tells me to do something and it gets done —Sue Grafton

Insistent as a baby's cry at feeding time —Anon

Insistent as remorse —Victor Hugo

Jabs like a prizefighter (at their feelings about each other) —Linda Barret Osborne, reviewing a novel in *New York Times*, August 31, 1986

Obstinate as a Hindu woman contemplating suttee —Frank Swinnerton

Obstinate as death —John Dryden

Persistent annoyance, like the rough place on a tooth —David R. Slavitt

Persistent as a bulldog —Oliver Wendell Holmes, Sr.

Persistent as a fly on a hound's nose —Harold Adams

Persistent as a nagging backache —Anon

(Ugly and) persistent as pain —Carlos Baker

Persist ... like a terrier with a rat ... she wouldn't let go, come hell or high water —James Reeve

Prevail like the false pig in Aesop —G. K. Chesterton

Relentless as decay —Joseph Wambaugh

Relentless as a nagging tongue —Anon

Relentless as a windshield wiper —Anon

Skin ... as thick as his wallet —Jane Gross, *New York Times*, August 22, 1986
> The man with the thick skin and wallet is Abraham Hirshfeld, who ran a persistent campaign for the New York State governorship despite many insults and putdowns.

Stick to it, like salmon swimming upstream —Anon

Stubborn and hardy as a rubber mat —Marge Piercy

(Death bugs me) as stubborn as insomnia —Anne Sexton

Tenacious as remorse —Vincente Blasco-Ibáñez

Persistence

The thought ... unable to move [out of his head] as a jellyfish fixed on the sand —Norman Mailer

Tug at ... like a robin with a worm —T. Coraghessan Boyle

You're like a train; nothing will turn you when you get started —Joyce Cary

Personal Traits

PERSONAL TRAITS

Adventurous ... like a tropical fish. His native habitat was hot water —Anon friend about former C.I.A. director William J. Casey, *New York Times*, July 19, 1987

> The original quote began with "Bill was," implying the first word substituted here to provide a more general reference point.

Dignified, like a clean-shaven Zeus: one who used plenty of aftershave —Kingsley Amis

Good temper, like a sunny day, sheds a brightness over everything —Washington Irving

Hears like a rabbit and strikes like an asp —William Diehl

(She would be) intent and bold and willful, like a gambler —Harold Brodkey

> The author used this simile to describe a woman applying makeup.

A man or woman without personality is like a tree without leaves, or a house without pictures on the wall —Anon

Obstinacy and contradiction are like a paper kite; they are only kept up so long as you pull against them —John Casper

Quiet and smiley and polite, like a traveling salesman —George Garrett

She is like a cat, she will play with her own tail —John Ray's *Proverbs*

Shines like a lighthouse over a dull sea of social tedium —Rita Mae Brown

Temperament ... is permanent, like the color of a man's eyes and the shape of his ears —Mark Twain

A temper as explosive as a gun —Rex Beach

This is modernized from the original which read "As explosive as gun cotton."

A temper like a handsaw —Anon

PERSONALITY PROFILES

An ambitious girl ... that looks as though she should be kneeling before a crackling fire, stroking a pussy cat, but behind it all has nerves of iron, a will of iron, and a rigid mind cast only for the search for success —Harvey Swados

As omnipotent and as full of faults as Jove —Wallace Stegner

As with an iceberg, only the craggy tip [of his personality] was revealed to the stranger's casual eye while the submerged seven eighths carried along like an unseen, irresistible force and solidity —Irvin S. Cobb

Barely seemed human at all: more like some Chinese figurine all ivory and silk, that should suddenly have come to life, begun to dance, to quote the poets, and to laugh at everything in this ridiculous real world —George Santayana

Looked like someone whose spare time was devoted to calligraphy or stamp collecting —Jay McInerney

Looked mid-to late thirties and as if she hadn't wasted any time —William McIlvanney

Looked pale, mysterious, like a lily, drowned under water —Virginia Woolf
See Also: STRANGENESS

Looked ... something like a dissipated Robinson Crusoe —Charles Dickens

Looked weak, exhausted, and helpless, like a man who has been discarded by an enemy who has no further use for him —Scott Spencer

Looking strained and intent like a woman descending voluntarily into hell —Ross Macdonald

Look like a drowned mouse —John Ray's *Proverbs*

Look like a funeral —Clifford Odets
    Odets had a flare for pithy comparisons, like this one from *Awake and Sing*.

305

Personality Profiles

[Tennessee Williams] looks innocent-guilty, like a choirboy who has just been caught sneaking a bullfrog into the collection plate —Rex Reed

That man is freckled like a trout with impropriety —Marianne Moore

They looked like the people you see in ticket lines, trying to get tickets for sold-out football games —Larry McMurtry

They looked as if they had been recruited wholesale from a Jewish nightmare —Angela Carter

The three of them [girls sharing an apartment] ... all as lovely and charming and gay as if they had been turned out by some heavenly production line —Mary Ladd Cavell

(She was radiant; she) twinkled and glittered and dazzled like a diamond —Mary Ladd Cavell

The ubiquitous cigarette in its holder makes him look brittle, like a terrible actor trapped in a "Masterpiece Theatre" production —Sharon Sheehe Stark

Was like certain vegetables; transplant them and you stop their ripening —Honoré de Balzac

With her plump torso balanced on spiked heels, she [Bette Midler] teeters ahead faster than most people run, looking like a pheasant on amphetamines —Julie Salamon, *Wall Street Journal*, January 29, 1987

Pervasiveness

PERVASIVENESS
SEE ALSO: CLINGING

As pervasive as a raging fever —Anon

(Democracy and freedom began) bouncing all over (the world) like bad checks —Ishmael Reed

Cover like a cold sweat —Anon

He's everywhere ... like the mist, like some foul fog —William Diehl

He was all over him, like a cheap suit —Mark Shields

Penetrate [as through a barrier of complacency] ... like the slippage of a dentist's drill through novacaine —Clare Nowell

Pervading [a woman's special magic] as a spilled perfume, irresistible and sweet —F. Scott Fitzgerald

(Egotism that seemed to) saturate them as toys are saturated with paint —O. Henry

(Allowed my thoughts to) sink in like a spoon in a pudding [in order to gain insight] —William H. Gass

PHYSICAL APPEARANCE
SEE ALSO: ARM(S), BEAUTY, BODY, EYE(S), FACE(S), HAIR, HAND(S), THINNESS

As innocent of makeup as an apple he might have polished on his sleeve —John Yount

As straight as a stick and looked as brittle —V. S. Pritchett

Awful [looking] ... like an oil filter that should have been changed five thousand miles ago —Saul Bellow

Began to look like the last solitary frost-touched rose on a November bush —Honoré de Balzac

Looked like a sparrow fallen from its nest —Dominique Lapierre

Belly as bright ivory overlaid with sapphires ... legs are as pillars of marble —The Holy Bible/Song of Solomon

(He was) bowed and gnarled like an old tree
—W. Somerset Maugham

Chorus-line figure, but with a face like a racehorse —Richard Ford

Dry and bony, like a handsome tree withered by blight
—Louis Bromfield

Fragile-looking yet surprisingly voluptuous, she resembled a scaled-down ancient love goddess, the gilded plastic replica sold at museum shops —T. Gertler

Gnarled as a cyprus —Mary Lee Settle

Had a face like a barn owl. The heavy rolls of fat were covered with thick white powder and gave the appearance of a snow-covered mountain landscape. Her black eyes were like deep-set holes and she stared at Kern as though she might fly at him any moment with her claws —Erich Maria Remarque
     An example of a colorful portrait created with a string of similes, from Remarque's novel, Flotsam.

Had the aging body of a poet and the eyes of a starving panther
    —Ellery Queen

Had the rough, blowsy and somewhat old-fashioned look of a whore
    of the Renoir period —Thomas Wolfe

Had the threadbare appearance of a worn-out litigant
    —Sir Walter Scott

He'd been put together with care, his brown head and bullfighter's
    figure had an exactness, a perfection like an apple, an orange,
    something nature has made just right —Truman Capote

He had smooth skin and a thin moustache which made him look
    like the toy groom on a wedding cake —Andrew Kaplan

He looked like a goat. He had little raisin eyes and a string beard
    —Flannery O'Connor

(Up till then I'd assumed that "Gross" was the man's name, but it
    was his description.) He looked like something that had finally
    come up out of its cave because it has eaten the last
    phosphorescent little fish in the cold pool at the bottom of the
    cavern. He looked like something that better keep moving
    because if it stood still someone would drag it out back and bury
    it. He looked like a big white sponge with various diseases at
    work on the inside. He looked like something that couldn't get
    you if you held a crucifix up in front of you. He looked like the
    big fat soft white something you might find under a tomato
    plant leaf on a rainy day with a chill in the air
    —Donald E. Westlake
        A nice bit of comparative excess, something to be indulged
        in sparingly, which may account for the fact that
        Westlake's novel, *The Fugitive Pigeon,* contains few other
        similes.

He [Marvin Hamlish] looks at certain angles, like a cheeseburger with
    all the ingredients oozing awkwardly out of the bun —Rex Reed

Her anxious brown eyes and full, slightly drooping cheeks gave her
    the look of a worried hamster —Sheila Radley

Her face and hands were as white as though she had been drowned
    in a barrel of vinegar —O. Henry

Her great buttocks rolled like the swell on a heavy winter sea
    —Miles Gibson

308

He was handsome, in a brooding, archaic way, like a face from early Asiatic temple sculpture —Christopher Isherwood

He was like a piece of cinnamon bark, brown and thin and curled in on himself —David Brierley

He was ruddy as a ranch hand, and dressed like one —Joyce Reiser Kornblatt

His face and body had an evil swollen look as if they had grown stout on rotten meat —Ross Macdonald

His face and head had an unfinished look, like a sculpture an artist might have left under a damp cloth until he had time to work on it again —Dorothy Francis

(The guy didn't seem to have any neck at all.) His head rested on his shoulders like a bowling ball on a shelf —Jonathan Valin

(She is tall), homely as Lincoln —Alice McDermott

A huge ruin of a woman with a face like a broken statue —Edith Wharton

In appearance she was not unlike a sea cow —Larry McMurtry

A little gnarled fellow like the bleached root of a tree —Zane Grey

Look awful, all trembling and green about the gills, like a frog with shell shock —A. Alvarez

Looked and moved like an elderly gentleman with bowel problems —T. Coraghessan Boyle

[Old people] looked dry as a locust shell stuck on a pear tree —Anthony E. Stockanes

Looked like a pale spectre beneath the moon —Émile Zola

Looked like a bat ... had the ears and the snout and the gray pinched mouse-face, the hunched bony shoulders that were like folded wings —Paul Theroux

Looked like a man recuperating from a coronary or just about to have one —Jonathan Kellerman

Looked like a man who has stepped on the business end of a rake and given himself a good one, whack between the eyes —Stephen King

Looked like an animated skeleton —Jimmy Sangster

Looked like a pearl laid against black velvet —O. Henry

Looked like a seedy angel —William McIlvanney

Looking like a drooping and distracted hen —Patrick White

[Paul Newman in *The Color of Money*] looking like an only slightly
worn Greek statue —Julie Salamon, *Wall Street Journal*, October
16, 1986

Look ... like a fine healthy apple —Katherine Anne Porter

Look like someone who's spent the night in a bus station —Anon

Looks as if when you touch her she'd crackle like cellophane
—Harryette Mullen

Looks like a garage sale waiting for a place to happen
—George V. Higgins

Looks like the side of a barn with the doors open
—Ben Ames Williams

Managing with his mussed fair hair and mustache to look like a
shopworn model for a cigarette advertisement —Derek Lambert

A man like a scarecrow, old and stormbeaten, with stiff, square, high
shoulders, as if they were held up by a broomstick stuck through
his sleeves —Vicki Baum

Men deteriorate without razors and clean shirts ... like potted plants
that go to weed unless they are tended daily —Beryl Markham
Markham makes this observation in her autobiography,
West With the Night, when she lands her plane and is met
by two unshaven hunters, adding this simile about one of
them (Baron Von Blixen): "Blix, looking like an unkempt
bear ... "

(Looks worse every time I see her, so) old and dried out, like a
worn shoe —Jan Kubicki

Pink and glazed as a marzipan pig —Truman Capote about Henri
Soule

A pinprick of a scarlet pimple glowed like blood against the very
pale skin on the side of her nose. Her freshly washed gray hair
was slightly askew, and she looked ... like that demented figure
in the painting of Pickett's charge at Gettysburg —Joseph Heller

Plump and sweet as a candied yam —Marge Piercy

LOOKED LIKE A SEEDY ANGEL

Potbellied, and bearded with extra chins like a middle-aged high
school gym coach —Jonathan Valin

A profile and neck like a pharaoh's erotic dream
—Loren D. Estleman

Raindrops sat on his white skin like sweat —Sue Miller

A regular old jelly ... sliding around like aspic on a hot plate
—Joyce Cary

She is chipped like an old bit of china; she is frayed like a garment
of last year's wearing. She is soft, crinkled like a fading rose
—Amy Lowell

She [a woman of sixty] looked like a lovely little winter apple
—Mary Lee Settle

She looked like a tree trunk ... her big gnarled hands seemed to
protrude from her like branches —Marguerite Yourcenar

She looked, with her red-cherry cheeks and wide semicircle of smile,
like something that might have briskly swung out of a weather-
house predicting sunshine —Peter Kemp

She reminded him, in her limp dust-colored garments, of last year's
moth shaken out of the curtains of an empty room
—Edith Wharton

She was gray as a wick and as thin —Patricia Hampl

She was heavy but not unattractive, like a German grandma
—Peter Meinke

She was in her mid-thirties ... faded, but still fruity, like a pear just
beginning to go soft —Derek Lambert

She was like a fat little partridge with a mono-bosom
—Kate Wilhelm

She [mother dancing before narrator] was like a pretty kite that
floated above my head —Maya Angelou

She was tall like a lily, carried herself like a queen ... was dressed
like a rose —Hugh Walpole

A short woman, shaped nearly like a funeral urn
—Flannery O'Connor

Slender and tall as the great Eiffel Tower —W. H. Auden

Small, chinless and like an emasculated Eton boy —Dylan Thomas
    The simile is a self portrait.

A smallish man who always looked dusty, as if he had been born
    and lived all his life in attics and store rooms —William Faulkner

Small, runty and rooty, she looks like a young edition of an old,
    gnarled tree —Laurie Colwin

Tall and flat like a paper doll —Elizabeth Bishop

Tan and wrinkled all over as if had been dipped and stained in
    walnut juice —George Garrett

They [an old couple] were brown and shriveled, and like two little
    walking peanuts —Carson McCullers

Thin and old-looking ... as if the frame she was strung on had
    collapsed and the stuffing had shifted. Like a badly stuffed toy
    after a month in the nursery —Josephine Tey

A thin man with a collarbone like a wire coathanger
    —Penelope Gilliatt

Thin, white-whiskered ... like a consumptive Santa Claus
    —Dashiell Hammett

With his longish head he looked like an Egyptian king
    —Iris Murdoch

With his small dark eyes and jowly cheeks he looked like an
    intelligent bulldog —Andrew Kaplan

PHYSICAL FEELINGS
SEE: HEALTH, PAIN

PICTURES
SEE: ART AND LITERATURE

PINK
SEE: COLORS

PITY
SEE: KINDNESS

PLACES
SEE ALSO: INSULTS

American cities are like badger holes ringed with trash
    —John Steinbeck

The bargain basement [of store] where everything smelled musty and looked dull ... as if a fine rain of dust fell constantly on the discounted merchandise —Joyce Reiser Kornblatt

A boarding area in an airport is a little like a waiting room in a dentist's office. Everyone tries to look unconcerned, but there's really only one thing on their minds —Jonathan Valin

Buckingham Palace ... like an old prima donna facing the audience all in white —Virginia Woolf

The Capitol buildings look like a version of St. Peter's and the Vatican turned out by a modern firm —Shane Leslie

Chicago ... living there is like being married to a woman with a broken nose; there may be lovelier lovelies, but never a lovely so real —Nelson Algren

Places as magical and removed as toy towns under glass —Robert Dunn

A public library, like a railway station, gets all kinds. They come in groups, like packaged tours —Helen Hudson

Puerto Rico ... it is a kind of lost love-child, born to the Spanish Empire and fostered by the United States —Nicholas Wollaston

The Statue of Liberty [as seen from the sky] tiny but distinct, like a Japanese doll of herself —Richard Ford

Sundays [in New York] the long asphalt looks like a dead beach —Edwin Denby

Texas air is so rich you can nourish off it like it was food —Edna Ferber

Thousands of funeral markers rise from the ground like dirty alabaster arms —Sin Ai
> The scene described in Sin Ai's poem *Two Brothers* is Arlington National Cemetery.

To be raised in Philadelphia is like being born with a big nose ... you never get over it —Anon

To walk along Broadway is like being a ticket in a lottery, a ticket in a glass barrel, being tossed about with all the other tickets —Maeve Brennan

Transylvania without me will be like Bucharest on a Monday night —Dialogue in movie *Love At First Bite* by Count von Dracula

The United Nations looked cool and pure, like its charter
—Derek Lambert

Venice ... at once so stately and so materialist, like a proud ghost
that has come back to remind men that he failed for a million
—Rebecca West

Venice is like eating an entire box of chocolate liqueurs in one go
—Truman Capote, November 26, 1961 news item

Washington, D.C. ... at times as cold as its marble facade
—Maureen Dowd, *New York Times*, March 2, 1987

Washington, D.C. ... looks as if some giant had scattered a box of
child's toys at random on the ground —Captain Basil Hall

Washington, D.C. ... looks like a large straggling village reared in a
drained swamp —George Combe

Writing about most American cities is like writing a life of Chester A.
Arthur. It can be done, but why do it? —Clifton Fadiman

PLAYS
SEE: STAGE AND SCREEN

PLEASURE
SEE: HAPPINESS, JOY

POISE
SEE: BEARING

POLITENESS
SEE: MANNERS

POLITICS/POLITICIANS

The body politic, like the human body, begins to die from its birth,
and bears in itself the causes of its destruction
—Jean Jacques Rousseau

A cannibal is a good deal like a Democrat, they are forced to live
off each other
—Will Rogers, weekly newspaper article, April 14, 1929

The Democratic party is like a man riding backward in a railroad car;
it never sees anything until it has got past it —Thomas B. Reed

The Democratic party is like a mule, without pride of ancestry or
hope of posterity —Emory Storrs

Politics/
Politicians

The Democrats are like someone at a funeral who just found out they won the lottery —Eleanor Clift, McLaughlin Group television show, December 28, 1986
> The comparison was made during a discussion of the Iran Contra aid scandal.

Elections ... are like mosquitoes, you can't very well fight 'em off without cussing 'em —Will Rogers, letter to *Los Angeles Times*, November 10, 1932

In politics as in religion, it so happens that we have less charity for those who believe the half of our creed, than for those that deny the whole —Charles Caleb Colton

In politics, as in womanizing, failure is decisive. It sheds its retrospective gloom on earlier endeavor which at the time seemed full of promise —Malcolm Muggeridge

Like American beers, presidential candidates these days are all pretty much the same, heavily watered for blandness, and too much gas —Russell Baker

A man running for public office is like a deceived husband; he is usually the last person to realize the true state of affairs —Robert Traver

A man without a vote is, in this land, like a man without a hand —Henry Ward Beecher

Merchandise candidates for high office like breakfast cereal ... gather votes like box tops —Adlai Stevenson
> In his August 18, 1956 speech accepting the presidential nomination, Stevenson used this double simile to verbally shake his head at the idea that politics is just like product merchanding.

Ministers fall like buttered bread; usually on the good side —Ludwig Boerne

One revolution is just like one cocktail; it just gets you organized for the next —Will Rogers

Patronage personnel are like a broken gun, you can't make them work, and you can't fire them —Peter Dominick, from the monthly newsletter of Senator Dominick, August, 1966

Political elections ... are a good deal like marriages, there's no accounting for anyone's taste —Will Rogers, weekly newspaper article, May 10, 1925

Political rhetoric has become, like advertising, audible wallpaper, always there but rarely noticed —George F. Will

A politician is like quick-silver; if you try to put your finger on him, you find nothing under it —Austin O'Malley

Politicians are like drunks. We're the ones who have to clean up after them —Bryan Forbes

Politicians are like the bones of a horse's foreshoulder, not a straight one in it —Wendell Phillips, 1864 speech

Politics are almost as exciting as war, and quite as dangerous
    —Sir Winston Churchill
        Churchill followed up the simile with, "In war you can
        only be killed once, but in politics many times."

Politics are like a labyrinth, from the inner intricacies of which it is even more difficult to find the way of escape than it was to find the way into them —William E. Gladstone

Politics is like a circus wrestling match —Nikita S. Khrushchev

Politics is like a race horse. A good jockey must know how to fall with the least possible damage —Edouard Herriot

Politics is like being a football coach. You have to be smart enough to understand the game and dumb enough to think it's important
    —Eugene McCarthy

Politics is like waking up in the morning. You never know whose head you will find on the pillow —Winston Churchill

Politics, like religion, hold up the torches of martyrdom to the reformers of error —Thomas Jefferson

Presidential appointments are left to us like bad debts after death
    —Janet Flanner

Professional politicians are like chain smokers, lighting a new campaign on the butt of the old one —Steven V. Roberts, *New York Times*, November 24, 1986
        This was the only simile in Roberts' article. Yet, as is so
        often the case, it was the phrase highlighted as a boxed
        blurb to get reader attention.

The public is like a piano. You just have to know what keys to poke
    —John Dewey

Politics/ Politicians

The pursuit of politics is like chasing women: the expense is damnable, the position ridiculous, the pleasure fleeting —Robert Traver

Running for public office was not unlike suffering a heart attack; overnight one's whole way of life had abruptly to be changed —Robert Traver

So long as we read about revolutions in books, they all look very nice ... like those landscapes which, as artistic engravings on white vellum, look so pure and friendly —Heinrich Heine

(They said) the range of political thinking is round, like the face of a clock —Tony Ardizzone

A voter without a ballot is like a soldier without a bullet —Dwight D. Eisenhower, *New York Times Book Review*, October 27, 1957

Watching foreign affairs is sometimes like watching a magician; the eye is drawn to the hand performing the dramatic flourishes, leaving the other hand, the one doing the important job, unnoticed —David K. Shipler, *New York Times*, March 15, 1987

PONDS AND STREAMS
SEE: NATURE, SEASCAPES

POSTURE
SEE: BEARING, BENDING/BENT

Power

POWER

About as influential as the 'p' in pneumonia and the 'k' in knitting —Anon

Aggressive as an elbow in the side —Henry James

As omnipotent and as full of faults as Jove —Wallace Stegner

Authority shrivelled as muslin in a fire —Vita Sackville-West

Authority without wisdom is like a heavy ax without an edge, fitter to bruise than to polish —Anne Bradstreet

Compelling as a gun at your head —Anon

[Choice to do something] compelling as the sense of vocation which doctors and missionaries are supposed to experience —John Braine

(He is) consuming ... like a candle —Richard Flecknoe

Feel like a lion in a den of Daniels —W. S. Gilbert

Strong [a person's pull on others] as a riptide —Reynolds Price

Glows with power like a successful shaman —Marge Piercy

Had a ring of authority, like monarchy —Barbara Lazear Ascher

Immoderate power, like other intemperance, leaves the progeny
    weaker and weaker, until Nature, as [if] in compassion, covers it
    with her mantle and is seen no more —Walter Savage Landor

Influence is like a savings account. The less you use it, the more
    you've got —Andrew Young

Influential as gnats —Susan Heller Anderson

It's like a Dead Sea fruit. When you achieve it, there is nothing
    there —Harold Macmillan, *Parade*, July 7, 1963

Like wealth and power, prestige tends to be cumulative: the more of
    it you have, the more you can get —C. Wright Mills

Made him fetch and carry just as if he was a great Newfoundland
    dog —William Makepeace Thackeray

(But her looks have) no power over me ... like a tug on a tree on a
    limb that has lost feeling —William Getz

Once a man of power, always a man of power. Like being a Boy
    Scout —Anthony Powell

(Memories ...) powerful as floods —Elizabeth Spencer

Power [in the Middle East] gravitates towards radicals like iron filings
    toward a magnet —Karen Elliott House

Power, like a desolating pestilence, pollutes whatever it touches
    —Percy Bysshe Shelley
        'Whatever' replaces the old English 'whate'er.'

Power, like lightning, injures before its warning
    —Pedro Calderon de la Barca

Power, like the diamond, dazzles the beholder, and also the wearer
    —Charles Caleb Colton

The right of commanding ... like an inheritance, it is the fruit of
    labors, the price of courage —Voltaire

To rule must be a calling, it seems, like surgery or sculpture
—W. H. Auden

Scenting power like blood —Janet Flanner

Seemed the personification of brute strength ... like a gorilla dripped
in peroxide —Donald Seaman

Strode like a colossus over the [White House] staff
—Dean Rusk, *New York Times*, March 1, 1987
Rusk used this image to compare Lyndon Johnson's
control over the White House staff to Ronald Reagan's
delegation of power.

Swept me ahead of her like a leaf —Elizabeth Bishop

There was authority in his attitude ... and its heat threatened to melt
Bird [name of character] like a piece of candy —Kenzaburo Oë

They pass him on from hand to hand, like a baton in a relay race,
and he ultimately becomes a puppet manipulated by others
—Vladmir Solovyou and Elena Klopikova

To add a little weight to his argument he put a hand like a bunch
of bananas flat on my chest —Jimmy Sangster

Tyranny, like hell, is not easily conquered —Thomas Paine

PRAISE
SEE: WORDS OF PRAISE

PRAISEWORTHINESS
SEE: VIRTUE

PREDICTABILITY
SEE: CERTAINTY

PREJUDICE
SEE: INTOLERANCE

PRETTINESS
SEE: BEAUTY

PRIDE

Accepts [a situation] as proudly as the mother of a Bar Mitzvah boy
accepts his cracked-voice singing at the sabbath service
—Ira Wood

Beamed pride ... like a mother whose son has won everything on school prize day —Louis Bromfield

Dignified and beautiful as a Beethoven sonata —Israel Zangwill

Dignified as a state funeral —Anon

Felt as though he had feathers which had puffed up with pride —Pamela Hansford Johnson

> The pride thus described in Johnson's novel, *The Good Husband*, is caused by the admiring glances lavished upon an attractive companion.

Felt pride rising up through his chest like gas —Margaret Millar

Felt so proud, as though he had saved a life —Mary Hood

For a man to say all the excellent things that can be said upon one, and call that his Epitaph, is as if a painter should make the handsomest piece he can possibly make, and say 'twas my picture —John Selden

Like a freshly lit lamp, expanding and bright with triumph —Julia O'Faolain

Looking very proud like he's discovered some sort of rare bird —Hilary Masters

My pride stung like a slapped cheek —John Hersey

Pride is as loud a beggar as want —Benjamin Franklin

Pride is to character, like the attic to the house ... the highest part, and generally the most empty —John Gay

Pride like humility, is destroyed by one's insistence that he possesses it —Kenneth P. Clark

Pride, like the magnet, constantly points to one object, self; but unlike the magnet, it has no attractive pole but at all points repels —Charles Caleb Colton

Pride steams off you like the stink of cancer —William Alfred

Proud as a cock on his own dunghill —Turkish proverb

Proud as a hen that gets a duck for a chicken —Dion Boucciault

(Sat there ...) proud as an idol —Hermann Hesse

Pride

Proud as a peacock; all strut and show
—H. G. Bohn's *Handbook of Proverbs*
> Probably the best known and most used of the many "Proud as" similes. The original used the Old English 'shew' instead of 'show.'

Proud as a stork —John Betjeman

Proud as Satan himself (and as unapproachable) —Ivan Turgenev

(They carefully tend to their garden and show off their vegetables like...) proud new parents —Marian Thurm

Saw his dignity slip away like a blanket —Beryl Markham

Show [as success or dating a beautiful woman] off like a rose in a buttonhole —Milton R. Sapirstein

(The curate) sounded proud, like somebody who brushed his teeth with table salt —J. F. Powers

Swelled like a frog about to croak —Rita Mae Brown

Swelled with pride like a turkey cock —Ben Ames Williams

Swelling up [with pride] like a robin —Stephen Vincent Benét

Wear your pride like a chevron on your sleeve —George Garrett

PROBABILITY
SEE: CERTAINTY

PROFICIENCY
SEE: ABILITY

PROMISE
SEE: RELIABILITY/UNRELIABILITY

PROPRIETY/IMPROPRIETY
SEE: MANNERS

PROSPERITY
SEE: RICHES, SUCCESS/FAILURE

PROXIMITY
SEE: CLOSENESS

PUBLIC, THE
SEE: POLITICS

PURITY
SEE: VIRTUE

PURPLE
SEE: COLORS

QUESTIONS/ANSWERS

Answered me as gravely as if I had asked the meaning of life
—Borden Deal

Answered slow, like men who wouldn't waste anything, not even
language —Carl Sandburg

Answered with the finality of a bank vault door —Dick Francis

The answer was in front of him ... like a gift-wrapped package
waiting to be opened —Andrew Kaplan

Asked, like a man who didn't want to know —James Crumley

Beat back questions like a ball hitting a brick wall —Anon

A correct answer is like an affectionate kiss
—Johann Wolfgang von Goethe

Curiosity ... unrolls its question mark like a new wave on the shore
—John Ashberry

Deflected answers like a freight train cutting through the Mississippi
Delta —Les Payne on William Renquist's responses to questions
about his civil rights background, *Newsday*, August 3, 1986

Her questions sounded unfelt as though she were speaking from a
deep well of hypnosis —Geoffrey Wolff

His answers trickled through my head, like water through a sieve
—Lewis Carroll

It was like the question asked by Tennyson about the flowers in the
crannied wall —Saul Bellow

One by one, neatly, like index cards out of a machine, the little
questions dropped —Roald Dahl

Pursued [a question] like an inquisitor in a torture chamber who was
hungry and eager to get the signed statement before his supper
—Christopher Isherwood

The question falls ... like a bird from the sky —Aharon Megged

Questions/ Answers

The question hangs like music in my thoughts —W. P. Kinsella

The question immediately bursts in the sky like a shower of fireworks —Isaiah Berlin, June, 1980

Question [directly] ... like a gun —Lael Tucker Wertenbaker

Questions bobbed in her mind like corks on a turbulent sea —Paige Mitchell

Questions like ordered bricks —Mary Hedin

Questions like water gushed ceaselessly —Dame Edith Sitwell

Unpleasant and unanswerable questions flopping around in his head like a bat that had mistakenly flown in through the living room window —Laurie Colwin

Was like a psychiatrist, asking questions which really were not those questions at all, but deeper ones —Elizabeth Taylor

Worried her questions like a dog does a bone —Donald MacKenzie

You start a question and it's like starting a stone. You sit quietly on the top of a hill, and away the stone goes, starting others —Robert Louis Stevenson

QUIET
SEE: SILENCE

RAGE
SEE: ANGER

RANTING
SEE: ANGER

Rarity

RARITY

Exclusive as a mail box —Raymond Chandler

He's unusual all right ... like the last of the orange flamingos —Saul Bellow

A miracle as great as art —Charles Bukowski

(And what is so) rare as a day in June —James Russell Lowell
      One of Lowell's most memorable lines!

(To think of nothing benign to memorize is as) rare as feeling no personal blemish —W. H. Auden

324

Rare as a man without self-pity —Stephen Vincent Benét

Rare and wonderful feeling, like the first moments of love
    —George Garrett

Rare as a black swan —Anon
        This probably evolved from "Rare to be found as black
        swans" featured in Daniel Rogers' seventeenth century
        Matrimonial Honors.

Rare as a Cockney accent at Eton —Anon

Rare as a man without self-pity —Stephen Vincent Benét

Rare as an Emperor moth —Lawrence Durrell

Rare as a New York City subway train without graffiti
    —Elyse Sommer

Rare as a nine dollar bill —Anon

Rare as a politician on the stump who doesn't make promises
    —Anon
        A partner to this one: "Rare as a politician who lives up to
        his campaign promises."

Rare as a well-spent life —Anon

(A lucky man is) rare as a white crow —Juvenal

Rare as a winter swallow —Honoré de Balzac

Rare as discretion in a gossip —Anon

Rare as humility in a grizzly bear —Julian Ralph

(Movies like Paul Mayersberg's *Captive* are as) rare as peacocks' teeth
    —Vincent Canby, *New York Times*, April 3, 1987

Rare as rocking horse manure —Anon

Rare as snow in July —Anon
        Another modern simile which can be traced to an earlier
        form: "Like snow at Midsummer, exceeding rare."

Rare in life as black lightning on a blue sky —Fitz-Greene Halleck

(The liberal "effete snobs" that Spiro T. Agnew railed against are as)
    rare today as Republicans on the welfare rolls
    —Barbara Ehrenreich

325

Rarity

Scarce as below par golf scores —Anon

Scarce as fat men in a long-distance marathon —Anon

Scarce as a six figure advance for a first novel by an unknown author —Elyse Sommer

[Money ... was as] scarce as frogs' teeth, crabs' tails or eunuchs' whiskers —Pat Barr
> Barr's colorful multiple simile refers to the scarcity of money in Korea during the late nineteenth century when the heroine of her book, *Curious Life For a Lady,* was there.

Scarce as ice cream vendors on a snowy day in January —Anon
> The comparative twists on this are endless, for example: "Scarce as lemonade stands in the desert," or "Scarce as women in fur coats in ninety degree weather."

Scarce as low-cost, high profit ideas for an untapped market —Anon

Scarce as squirrels at a busy city street crossing —Elyse Sommer

Scarce as the buffalo that once roamed the prairie
> —Enid Nemy, *New York Times,* July 6, 1986
>> Nemy likened the buffalo scarcity to newsy letters.

Scarce as the cardinal virtues —Ross Macdonald

Scarce as two dollar gourmet lunches —Anon

(One of the kindest-natured persons that I ever knew on this earth, where kind people are) as rare as black eagles or red deer —Ouida

Readers/Reading

READERS/READING

Deprive him [the habitual reader] of printed matter and he grows nervous, moody and restless; then, like the alcoholic bereft of brandy who will drink shellac or methylated spirit, he will make do with the advertisements of a paper five years old; he will make do with a telephone directory —W. Somerset Maugham

A person who cannot read is something like a blind man walking through a pleasant meadow, where there are flowers and fruit trees; there are many pleasant things and many wise and good things printed in books, but we cannot get them unless we read —Timothy Dwight

THE READING OF DETECTIVE STORIES IS AN ADDICTION
LIKE TOBACCO OR ALCOHOL

Reading is to the mind what exercise is to the body
—Sir Richard Steele

The reading of detective stories is an addiction like tobacco or alcohol
—W. H. Auden

Reading that is only whimful and desultory amounts to a kind of cultural vagrancy. It neither wets nor fortifies the mind. It merely distracts and tires it like traffic noises on an overcrowded street —John Mason Brown

Reading the same book over and over again is a mechanical exercise like the Tibetan turning of a prayer-wheel —Clifton Fadiman

Reads like some people wrestle; she gets involved —François Camoin

REALIZATION
SEE: TRUTH

REASON
SEE: SENSE

RECOLLECTION
SEE: MEMORY

RED
SEE: COLORS, HAIR, MOUTH

REDUCTION
SEE: DISAPPEARANCE

REFLECTION
SEE: THOUGHT

REFORM
SEE: CHANGE

RELATIONSHIPS
SEE: MEN AND WOMEN; PEOPLE, INTERACTION

RELENTLESSNESS
SEE: PERSISTENCE

RELIABILITY/UNRELIABILITY

(I found the almond trees as) dependable as the swallows of Capistrano, announcing another spring —Wallace Stegner

As reliable as the day following the night —Dorothea Straus

[A collection of art works] as spotty as a Dalmation and not half as beautiful —Manuela Hoelterhoff, on the new Wallace wing at the Metropolitan Museum of Art, *Wall Street Journal,* March 17, 1987

Consistent and productive as machines —Gay Gaer Luce

Dealing with Owen Roe was like walking across a bog. You never knew when the ground might give way under your feet —Julia O'Faolain

Dependable as a floating crap game —Harry Prince

Dependable as clockwork ...   —Anon

Dependable as daylight —Beryl Markham

A duty dodged is like a debt unpaid; it is only deferred, and we must come back and settle the account at last —Joseph Fort

Duty without responsibility is like pomp without power —Edward, Duke of Windsor

Fickle as a changeful dream —Sir Walter Scott

It [buying a house] was like joining a church because it committed me to spending every weekend I could get ... to working on the place —George V. Higgins

(You've got) no more responsibility than a one-eyed jack rabbit —Elmer Kelton

Reliability's like a string we can only see the middle of —William McFee

(About as) reliable as a Pravda editorial —Joseph Wambaugh

Reliable as a salary —Frank R. Stockton

Reliable as crystal balls, goat innards, and prayer —Harold Adams

Reliable as reading tea leaves or the bumps on one's head —Peter J. Bonacich, letter to editor of *Discover,* April, 1986

Responsibility rested upon him as lightly as the freckles on his nose —Alice Caldwell Hegan

Solid as tombstones —Helen Hudson

Wore, like a garment, an air of wholesome reliability —Mazo De La Roche

329

Would always be there ... like some familiar landmark
—Barbara Pym, *The Sweet Dove Died*

REMEMBRANCE
SEE: MEMORY

REMOTENESS

Acting like an absentee landlord who was either unaware of or indifferent to the tenants smashing the windows or breaking up the furniture —Senator William S. Cohen commenting on President Ronald Reagan's leadership during Iran-contra affair, *New York Times*, March 1, 1987

Alienated as Camus —Richard Ford

As far apart as the sound of waves on the shore —John Updike

(Fury) as unpersonal as disease —David Denby

Behaved like a dowager queen at a funeral, acknowledging everyone's politenesses but keeping her own majestic feelings isolated —Judith Martin

Detached [from an excited crowd] as a droplet of oil —Stefan Zweig

Detached [mind from body] ... like a kite whose string snaps on a windy day —Julia O'Faolain

Detached, passive, still as a golden lily in a lily-pond
—Ellen Glasgow

Distant as an ocean —Reynolds Price

Distant as heart-parted lovers are —Babette Deutsch

(She was as silent and) distant as the moon —Kate Wheeler

Feeling impersonal and fragile as a piece of china waiting on a serving table —F. Scott Fitzgerald

He speaks to me as if I were a public monument —Queen Victoria about her prime minister, Gladstone

Impassive as an apple —Laurie Colwin

Impassive as a tank —Seamus Heaney

Impersonal as a cyclone —Anon

Impersonal as the justice of God —Victor Hugo

Incurious as a stone —Robert Hass

(Until that minute she had been as) impersonal to me as a doll in a well-stocked toy department —R. V. Cassill

Indifferent as a blizzard —Anon

Like the hermit crab, he ventured out of his shell only on the rarest occasions —A. J. Cronin

Looked disinterested, like a customs inspector —Julia Whedon

A look of remoteness ... like cathedrals, like long gleaming conference tables, like the crackling, hissing recordings of the voices of famous men long dead —John D. MacDonald
> An example to illustrate that several distinctly different similes can be effectively linked to a single reference base.

Look through 'em all like windows —Edith Wharton

Otherworldly like a monk —F. Scott Fitzgerald

Personal as a letter addressed to 'Occupant' —Anon

(His father had always been) remote ... as a figure in a pageant —Hortense Calisher

Remote as a nightmare —Walter De La Mare

[Sky scrapers] remote as castles in a fairy tale —Bobbie Ann Mason

(Bomb shelters are as) remote as the covered wagon —Edward R. Murrow broadcast from European front during World War II

Remote, unapproachable, like the expression of an animal that man has forced into sullen submission —Ellen Glasgow

Seemed like a perpetual visitor —Henry Van Dyke

(They get together and tell each other what women are like, but they never listen to find out.) Shut up in their heads like clams —Nancy Price

Stiff and remote, rather like a sleep-walker —Alice Munro

Stolid as ledgers —Julia O'Faolain

(He sat there, heavy and massive, suddenly) sunk back into himself and his drunkenness, like a lonely hill of unassailable melancholy —Erich Maria Remarque

Remoteness

To ask Henrietta was like asking the door knob —Sholom Aleichem

As unreachable as all the landscapes beyond the limits of my eye
—John Fowles

(Face), withdrawn as a castle —Nadine Gordimer

RENOWN
SEE: FAME

RESENTMENT
SEE: ANGER

RESERVE
SEE: PERSONALITY TRAITS, REMOTENESS

RESIGNATION
SEE: MEEKNESS

RESOURCEFULNESS
SEE: ABILITY

RESPONSE
SEE: QUESTIONS/ANSWERS, WORD(S)

RESPONSIBILITY
SEE: RELIABILITY/UNRELIABILITY

RETREAT
SEE: DISAPPEARANCE

Revenge

REVENGE

Revenge is a kind of wild justice, which the more a man's nature
runs to, the more ought law to weed it out —Francis Bacon

Revenge is like a boomerang. Although for a time it flies in the
direction in which it is hurled, it takes a sudden curve, and,
returning, hits your own head the heaviest blow of all
—John M. Mason

Revenge is often like biting a dog because the dog bit you
—Austin O'Malley

REVOLUTIONS
SEE: POLITICS

RHETORIC
SEE: WORD(S)

Appearance of wealth will draw wealth to it. As honey draws
hungry flies —George Garrett

Have money like sand —Louis MacNeice

His bank account swelled like a puff ball —Christina Stead

Inherited wealth is as certain death to ambition as cocaine is to
morality —William K. Vanderbilt

Like our other passions, the desire for riches is more sharpened by
their use than by their lack —Michel de Montaigne

A man that keeps riches but doesn't enjoy them is like an ass that
carries gold and eats thistles —Thomas Fuller
"Doesn't enjoy them" has been modernized from "And
enjoys them not."

More money than the telephone company's got wrong numbers
—Sam Hellman

(The auction was attended by collectors with) pockets as deep as
wells —Anon

Property, like liberty, thought immune under the Constitution from
destruction, is not immune from regulation essential for the
common good —Benjamin Cardozo

Prosperity is like a tender mother, but blind, who spoils her children
—English proverb

Prosperity is like perfume, it often makes the head ache
—Duchess of Newcastle

The rich are driven by wealth as beggars by the itch —W. B. Yeats

Rich as a congressman —Carson McCullers

Riches, like insects, when concealed they lie, wait but for wings, and
in their season fly —Alexander Pope
Pope spelled the fifth word "conceal'd."

The way to wealth is as plain as the way to market. It depends
chiefly on two words, industry and frugality —Benjamin Franklin

Wealth is an engine that can be used for power if you are an
engineer; but to be tied to the flywheel of an engine is rather a
misfortune —Elbert Hubbard

Riches

Wealth is like a viper, which is harmless if a man knows how to take hold of it; but if he does not, it will twine round his hand and bite him —Saint Clement

Wealth like rheumatism falls on the weakest parts —John Ray's *Proverbs*

Worldly riches are like nuts; many clothes are torn in getting them, many a tooth broke in cracking them, but never a belly filled with eating them —Ralph Venning

RIDICULE
SEE: INSULTS

RIDICULOUSNESS
SEE: ABSURDITY, IMPOSSIBILITY

RIGHTEOUSNESS
SEE: JUSTICE, VIRTUE

RISING
SEE: BEARING, NOISE, VEHICLES

ROARS
SEE: NOISE

ROBBERY
SEE: DISHONESTY

Rocking and Rolling

ROCKING AND ROLLING

Bobbed like a duck —F. van Wyck Mason

Bobbed like a ten-cent toy —John Updike
> Like the nickel pickle and cigar, the ten-cent toy is an endangered species, but fond remembrances are likely to have comparisons like this show up for a bit longer.

Bobbing like milkweed —W. D. Snodgrass

Bobbing up and down like a barometer on an April morning —Clifford Mills

Bobbing up and down ... like an apple in a bowl of toddy —Edgar Allan Poe

[Stomach from laughing hard] bounced like a cat in a sack —Gerald Kersh

Bounce ... like a basketball —Raymond Chandler

334

Bounces like an india-rubber ball —G. K. Chesterton

(I was) bouncing around (in my seat) like a pellet of quicksilver in a nervous man's palm —Dashiell Hammett

(Testicles) bouncing ... like peas in a colander —Richard Ford

The bus rocked like a cradle —Carson McCullers

Rocking back and forth like Jews praying —Irwin Shaw

(Franklin stood) rocking from side to side like a man on the deck of a ship in an angry sea —Wilbur Daniel Steele

Roll about ... like a pea —Frank Swinnerton

Rolled down the hills like marbles —Boris Pasternak

Rolled like a stone in a riverbed —Muriel Rukeyser

Rolled like tropic storms along —Edgar Allen Poe
         In Poe's poem 'rolled' was spelled 'roll'd.'

Rolled off the bed like a rolling pin off a kitchen table
    —Rita Mae Brown

Rolled over and over like a shot rabbit —P. G. Wodehouse

[A drunk] rolling about like a ball-bearing —Mark Helprin

Rolling around like a cannon ball in a high sea —Hank Searls

[Baby in pregnant woman's body] rolling around like a basketball
    —Lynne Sharon Schwartz

(The words) roll on like bells —Alastair Reid

Rolls over ... like surf —Lawrence Durrell

Swayed like a bird on a twig —Arnold Bennett

(A tipsy fellow), swaying like a wind-rocked palm —Beryl Markham

Swaying like cobras about to strike —Robert Silverberg

Sways as a wafer of light —Carl Sandburg

ROMANCE
SEE: MEN AND WOMEN

ROOMS
SEE: FURNITURE AND FURNISHINGS, HOUSES

ROUNDNESS
SEE: SHAPE

ROWDINESS
SEE: NOISE

RUDENESS
SEE: MANNERS

RUMOR
SEE: GOSSIP

SADNESS
SEE: DEJECTION, GRIEF

SALES
SEE: SUCCESS/FAILURE

SARCASM
SEE: HUMOR

SCANDAL
SEE: SHAME

SCARCITY
SEE: RARITY

SCOWLS
SEE: FROWNS

SCREAMS
SEE: NOISE

Scrutiny

SCRUTINY
SEE ALSO: INTENSITY

Approach [society section of Sunday paper] like a lapidopterist advances on butterflies —Shana Alexander

[A maitre d'] bent over (his guest list) like a conductor studying a score —Jonathan Valin

Carefully surveyed the living room and, like an auctioneer brought in for appraisal, every object it contained —Richard Russo

Examine [a face] as though it were a portrait in a public gallery —Ella Leffland

Examine like a customs inspector —Anon

Examine like a job hunter finecombs the employment ads or a New York apartment hunter finecombs the real estate ads —Anon

Examine like a monkey picking fleas —Mike Sommer

Examine with care, like a horse player eyeing the "Racing Form" —Shana Alexander

Examine with care of diamond dealer examining a rare stone —Anon

Explore [feelings] ... like someone trying to locate a hollow tooth —Lawrence Durrell

His scrutiny was like a well that pulled on you, making you eager to find your own face in the depths down there —Hortense Calisher

Investigate ... like a burglar twirling the dial of a well-constructed safe, listening for the locks to click and reveal the combination —Mary McCarthy

Like a traveller in unfamiliar regions she began to store for future guidance the minutest natural signs —Edith Wharton

Look at as does an experienced fish at a purchased fly —Gregory McDonald

Looking at it [a letter] as if it were a code in need of breaking —Graham Swift

(Should be) noted with care like the names of places passed on an important journey —John McGahern

Peered around [the room] like a hungry toad —Harold Adams

Pore over ... like a Little-Leaguer entranced by a pack of baseball cards —Jill Ciment

Pore over like possessed students of cabalist text —Joseph Weizenbaum
    Weizenbaum's simile referred to the computer enthusiast's intense absorption.

Prodding [in search of something] like a great bird rummaging for seed —Edith Wharton

Read their faces like texts and their gestures like punctuation marks —Helen Hudson

The character thus studying faces in the novel, *Criminal Trespass,* is not surprisingly, a librarian. The description of the gestures the librarian studies includes another simile: "The way they ... yank down the volumes and riffle the contents like the *Yellow Pages.*"

Scrutinize as if he were a new character in a soap opera —Bobbie Ann Mason

Scrutinized ... with the air of an epicure examining a fly in his vichyssoise —T. Coraghessan Boyle

Studied Barksdale's face, openly, like a man taking inventory —Paige Mitchell

Studies me like a teacher trying to decide how to discipline an unruly student —W. P. Kinsella

Study [a trip schedule] as though it were a pack of Tarot cards in some tricky configuration —Sue Grafton

Studying him like a culture —William McIlvanney

Surveyed [books] like a guard with his flashlight making the midnight rounds —Elizabeth Hardwick

Being watched like a rabbit in a laboratory —Willa Cather

Watching people, probing like a dentist into their innermost thoughts —Ivan Turgenev

Went through everything ... like detectives after fingerprints [describing antiques dealers] —Edith Wharton

SEASCAPES
SEE ALSO: NATURE

The boat sails away, like a bird on the wing —Kate Greenaway

Fishing boats sleep by the docks like men beside their wives —Donald Justice

The great ships dipped low down in the water, like floating swans —Hans Christian Andersen

The lights on the canals [of Holland] like gold caterpillars —Jean Rhys

Little masted boats thick on the water, like blown leaves —Donald Justice

READ THEIR FACES LIKE TEXTS AND THEIR GESTURES
LIKE PUNCTUATION MARKS

Sailboats moved gently in the water like large white butterflies that had dipped down to drink —Margaret Millar

The sea crinkled like foil —Derek Walcott

The sea is like a pale green fabric, stretched but not entirely smooth —Richard Maynard

The sea is sparkling like joy itself —Christopher Isherwood

The sea, like a crinkled chart, spread to the horizon —Daphne du Maurier

The sea was as smooth as a duck-pond —Rudyard Kipling

The sea [on a windless day] was like a sheet of steel —Fred Mustard Stewart

The sea was quite calm, like milk-and-water —Isak Dinesen

The sea was silver, wrinkled like a snake's skin —Sir Hugh Walpole

The sea, wrinkling with light, was stretched taut like a piece of silk —Elizabeth Taylor

Smaller vessels bobbing like petals on the glass of the harbor —Francine du Plessix Gray

There was a shimmer on the sea as though a loitering breeze passed playful fingers over its surface —W. Somerset Maugham

The town seems to lean against the cliffs like a rusting ocean liner, thrown to shore by a storm —Miles Gibson

Water like glass —Joseph Conrad

The water looked flat and impervious, as if a dead membrane had been stretched over it —Cynthia Ozick

Water ... pebbly-surfaced by the insistent breeze that kept sweeping it like the strokes of invisible broomstraws, and mottled with gold flecks that were like floating freckles in the nine o'clock September sunshine —Cornell Woolrich

Water ... rippled like stretched grey silk in the wind —Gavin Lyall

The water that shone smoothly like a band of metal —Joseph Conrad

August steamed in like the first slow day of creation
    —Shelby Hearon

The autumnal radiance fluttered like a blown shawl over the changeless structure of the landscape —Ellen Glasgow

Autumn felt as dark with life as spring —M. J. Farrell

The autumn frosts will lie upon the grass like bloom on grapes of purple-brown and gold —Elinor Wylie

In the spring ... life, like the landscape around us, seems bigger and wider and freer, a rainbow road leading to unknown ends
    —Jerome K. Jerome

The long gray winter settles in like a wolf feeding on a carcass
    —Marge Piercy

March ... comes in like a lion and goes out like a lamb —John Ray's Proverbs

Now that it's spring and the blossoms fall like sighs
    —Louis MacNeice

October had come in like a lamb chop, breaded in golden crumbs and gently sautéed in a splash of blue oil —Tom Robbins

October morning ... sallow as a faded suntan —Jessamyn West

One of those honey-warm fall days that brought out summer habits like chilled bees —Hortense Calisher

The seasons shine like new coins —George Garrett

Sleepy winter, like the sleep of death —Elinor Wylie

The specter of winter hovering like a pale-winged bird
    —W. P. Kinsella

Spring, animating and affecting us all ... like a drug, a pleasant poison of annual mortal gaiety —Janet Flanner

Spring arose on the garden fair, like the spirit of love felt everywhere —Percy Bysshe Shelley

Spring comes like a life raft —George Starbuck

Spring sunlight flowed in the streets like good news
    —William H. Hallhan

Seasons

Spring came that year like a triumph and like a prophecy
  —Thomas Wolfe

Summer ... dropping from the sky like a blanket of steam
  —John Rechy

Summer is like a fat beast —Wallace Stevens

Winter came down like a hammer —Lawrence Durrell

Winter [in Madison Square] ... was tamed, like a polar bear led on a leash by a beautiful lady —Willa Cather

Secrecy

SECRECY

About as loose-lipped as a Swiss banker —Harold Adams

Another person's secret is like another person's money: you are not so careful with it as you are with your own
  —Edgar Watson Howe

As secret as the grave —Miguel de Cervantes

Close up like a cabbage —John Andrew Holmes

Close up like a fist —Anon

Covert as a brass band —George F. Will

Fondles his secrets like a case of tools —Karl Shapiro

Furtive as a chipmunk —R. V. Cassill

Hide ... like a disgrace —George Gissing

In the mind and nature of a man a secret is an ugly thing, like a hidden physical defect —Isak Dinesen

Lurking like a pilot fish among sharks —Speer Morgan

Move ... like a rodent, furtively —John Phillips

Peered out (into the corridor) as stealthily as a mouse leaving its subterranean hole —Donald Seaman

(My face is an open secret but in my letters I) perform like a true diplomat, cunning and sly —Delmore Schwartz

Private and tight as a bank vault —Marge Piercy

Secrecy as tight as a bull's ass in fly time —Stephen Longstreet

342

Secret as silence —Babette Deutsch

A secret at home is like rocks under tide —D. M. Mulock

Secret operations [by a government] are like sin; unless you're good at sinning, you shouldn't do it —George Kennan, CBS/TV, March 31, 1987

Secrets are like measles: they take easy and spread easy —Bartlett's *Dictionary of Americanisms*
> Now that measles is controlled by vaccine, a virus or the common cold would probably be a more appropriate point of reference.

She has a mouth like a padlock —Graham Greene

Sneak away [for an acceptable, honorable activity] ... as furtively as if he were stealing to a lover's tryst —Edith Wharton

Stealthy and slow as a hidden sin —Stephen Vincent Benét

SEDATENESS
SEE: SERIOUSNESS

SELF-CONFIDENCE
SEE ALSO: PRIDE, VANITY

The acceptance of oneself ... is like falling heir to the house one was born in and has lived in all one's life but to which, until now, one did not own the title —Jean Stafford

(Sit there with) all the quiet certainty of a marauding chimp —Carla Lane, line from British television sitcom, "Solo"

As cocksure as if he had a fistful of aces —Honoré de Balzac

Confidence leaking like gas all over the room —Wilfrid Sheed

Confidence, like the soul, never returns whence it has once departed —Publius Syrus

Confident as a man dialing his own telephone number —Jack Bell

(He would be as) confident as a married man of how the evening would turn out —Alice McDermott

Confident as a master baker with a cake in the oven —Elizabeth Irvin Ross

Feel his title hang loose about him, like a giant's robe upon a dwarfish thief —William Shakespeare

Feeling power and confidence rise strongly up in her like wine filling a glass —Celia Dale

Felt like the cock of the walk —John Dos Passos

He displayed like an aura the lordly demeanor of a man who not only had dined on success throughout his lifetime but also had been born to it —Joseph Heller

I feel like a dime among pennies —Fiorello H. La Guardia, *Village Voice*, November 21, 1968
> The former New York City mayor responded thus when asked how it felt to be smallest man in a group.

I'm like a cat. Throw me up in the air and I'll always land on my feet —Bette Davis, quoted in Rex Reed interview

Pitching is a rollercoaster ride through the land of confidence —Ron Darling, New York Mets pitcher, *New York Times*/Sports of the Times, August 3, 1986

(The children) roamed through the neighborhood like confident landlords —Alice Mc Dermott

Self-confidence like an iron bar —Stephen Vincent Benét

Self-confidence surrounds him like force field —William Boyd

She was a human duck off whose back even the most seering of words flowed like harmless rain —H. E. Bates
> A twist on the timeworn "Rolled off him/her like water off a duck's back."

Very pleased with herself ... like a boa constrictor that had just enjoyed a rather large lunch —Mike Fredman

Walked the lane between the indifferently rowed cabins like he owned them, striding from shade into half-light as if he could halve the setting sun —Sherley Anne Williams

SELFISHNESS

The force of selfishness is as inevitable and as calculable as the force of gravitation —Anon

A man is a lion in his own cause —Henry G. Bohn's *Handbook of Proverbs*

The private life of the narcissist, like the private parts of the exhibitionist, ought not to be hung out uninvited in the public space —Willard Gaylin

Self-love ... leaped back into her like a perpetually coiled snake —Anaïs Nin

Wound up in his own concerns like thread on a spool —Anon

SELLING
SEE: BUSINESS

SENSE
SEE ALSO: INTELLIGENCE

As reasonable as Latin —Anne Sexton

Beyond rationality ... like stepping out into deep space, or going to the center of the world, or both at once —Susan Engberg

Common sense is as rare as genius —Ralph Waldo Emerson

Human reason is like a drunken man on horseback; set it up on one side, and it tumbles over on the other —Martin Luther

Like precious stones, his sensible remarks derive their value from their scarcity —W. S. Gilbert

Logic, like whisky, loses its beneficial effect when taken in too large quantities —Lord Dunsany

A mind all logic is like a knife all blade. It makes the hand bleed that uses it —Rabindranath Tagore

Reason in man is rather like God in the world
—St. Thomas Aquinas

Reason is a bladder on which you may paddle like a child as you swim in summer waters; but, when the winds rise and the waves roughen, it slips from under you, and you sink
—Walter Savage Landor

Reason is like the sun, of which the light is constant, uniform, and lasting —Samuel Johnson

Sense, like charity, begins at home —Alexander Pope

Sense

Pope's *Moral Essays* can be credited with the first of many "Charity begins at home" comparisons.

Tried to size up the situation reasonably, to tote odds like a paramutual —Jonathan Valin

SENSELESSNESS
SEE: ABSURDITY

Sensitiveness

SENSITIVENESS
SEE ALSO: KINDNESS

Bruise easily like a ripe pear —A. C. Greene

Ego ... as delicate as tissue paper —Christopher Buckley

Exposed as if on a raft —Joseph Conrad

Felt like a shell-fish that had lost its shell —Olivia Manning

Felt like a vegetable without its skin: raw and vulnerable —Laurie Colwin

Felt myself exposed ... as sharply as in a photograph —John Updike

Gentle as milk —Sylvia Berkman

Inherited sensibilities like jewels as red as rubies and blood —Janet Flanner

Interpreted the episode as sensitively as an unleashed bull would —Z. Vance Wilson

My sensibility begins to screech like chalk upon the blackboard scrawled —Delmore Schwartz

A person who is always having her feelings hurt is about as pleasant a companion as a pebble in a shoe —Elbert Hubbard
> A non-gender specific paraphrased from the original which began with "The woman."

Sensitive as a barometer —Thomas Bailey Aldrich

Sensitive as a stick of dynamite or a hand grenade —Mike Sommer

[An alert horse, with ears turning and twitching to catch all sounds] sensitive as radar —Jilly Cooper

Sensitive as the leaves of a silver birch —Joseph Hergesheimer

Sensitive as the money market —Thomas Hardy

346

(Taste buds as) sensitive as the skin on a mailman's feet —Ira Wood

Thick-skinned as a brontosaurus —Francis Goldwin, quoted on his sensitiveness to anything but imitations of his company's toy dinosaurs, *Wall Street Journal*, June 15, 1987

Touchy as a second degree burn —Harry Prince

Vulnerable as one of those primitive creatures between two skins or two shells, like a lobster or a crab —David R. Slavitt

(You are) vulnerable as the first buds of the maple —Marge Piercy

With all her stubbornness and punch, she could be sliced like scrapple —Sharon Sheehe Stark

SENTIMENT

Like most sentimentalists, his heart's as chilly as the Pole —Frank Swinnerton

Nostalgia ... like a lover's pain in the chest —John Hersey

Nostalgic ... like a letter from home —Mahalia Jackson
Jackson's frame of reference, gospel music, is particularly appropriate.

Sentimental as flowers pressed between the pages of a diary —Anon

(I've been) talking sentiment like a turtledove —Oliver Wendell Holmes, Sr.

SEPARATION
SEE: BEGINNINGS AND ENDINGS

SERIOUSNESS

Bearing his earnestness like an emblem —Donald MacKenzie

Every man will have his hours of seriousness; but like the hours of rest, they often are ill-chosen and unwholesome —Walter Savage Landor

Grave as a judge that's giving charge —Samuel Wesley

Grave as an old cat —Anon

Grave as an owl in a barn —George Farquhar

Sedate as a committeeman —William McIlvanney

Seriousness

Serious as a doctor —Eudora Welty

Serious as an overdue mortgage —Alexander King

Serious as a pig pissin' —C. J. Koch

(You are so) serious, as if a glacier spoke in your ear —Frank O'Hara

Serious as if at church —Émile Zola

Serious as the Ten Commandments —W. B. Yeats

Serious like a hyacinth ... which has had no sun —Virginia Woolf

Sober as a bone —Erich Maria Remarque

Sober as a coroner inspecting a corpse —Amelie Rives

Sober as a judge —Anon
> According to Stevenson's *Book of Proverbs, Maxims and Famous Sayings,* John Arbuthnot used the simile in *John Bull* in 1712, and 22 years later, Henry Fielding used it in *Don Quixote In England.* Since then, it has become common usage; its meaning more frequently tied to a serious manner than sobriety. In one of his *Tutt and Tutt* legal stories, Arthur Train added an interesting note of specificity with "Sober as a Kansas judge."

Solemn as a child in shock —C J. Koch

Solemn as a clergyman —Nina Bawden

Solemn as a lawyer at a will reading —J. B. Priestley

Solemn as a nun —R. Wright Campbell

Solemn as a soldier going to the front —Norman Mailer

Solemn as kewpie dolls —Diane Ackerman

Solemnly agreed, as though pledging allegiance to the flag —Robert Traver

Stern as a Tartar —Lorenz Hart
> The Tartar described is Queen Elizabeth. This is also the title of a song from Hart's lyrics for *The Garried Gaities of 1926.*

SERVILITY
SEE: MEEKNESS

348

SEE ALSO: MEN AND WOMEN

(To me they are) as as sexual as money; and, like money, unless
    they can engender passion, they are useless to me
    —W. P. Kinsella
        The frame of reference for Kinsella's double simile is the
        other woman.

Batten's [character in a novel] sex had wilted like a flag in the rain
    —George Garrett

Celibate, like the fly in the heart of an apple —Jeremy Taylor

A drop of semen seeped out, quivering on the head of my cock like
    a drop of hot wax —Scott Spencer

An erection like a steeple —Jilly Cooper

(Just the thought of what was going to happen in the next
    room ... gave me) an erection like a tire iron
    —T. Coraghessan Boyle

Erotic as an ape —Karl Shapiro

I felt an abrupt rush of my semen, racing through me like twin
    rivers —Scott Spencer

The fur between her legs like a possum —Jay Parini

Her climax came ... suddenly, like an accident —Scott Spencer

Her pubic hair looks like a robber's mask comically and frighteningly
    misplaced between her gorgeous young legs —R. V. Cassill

Her sex power ... hid in her eyes like a Sicilian bandit —Saul Bellow

His sex beat about like the cane of a furious blind man —Amos Oz

Horny as a tomcat —T. Coraghessan Boyle

In her passional life she was direct —like an axe falling
    —Lawrence Durrell

It's rather like a sneeze —Truman Capote, responding to television
    interviewer's question as to his feelings about sex

It [a first sexual encounter] was best when it was finished ... like
    having a cup of really good coffee and a Havana after an
    indifferently cooked but urgently needed meal —John Braine

Just whispering "teenage sex" is like yelling fire in a crowded theatre
    —Ellen Goodman

A lack of sexuality so total that her smart clothes and too heavy-
    make-up made her pathetic; like an unsuccessful geisha
    —John Fowles

Like flowers groping toward the sun, millions of Americans are
    groping towards sexual nirvana —Anon

Like hatred, sex must be articulated or, like hatred, it will produce a
    disturbing internal malaise —George Jean Nathan

Lowered steadily, like a flag at sunset, her panties were soon below
    her knees —Tom Robbins

(Her husband complained she) made love like an eager, clumsy cellist
    —J. D. McClatchy

My sex life ... it'd make Moll Flanders look like she needed hormone
    therapy —Sue Miller

The only sex we were exposed to was with dreadful old
    whores ... like diseased orchids —Tennesse Williams, *Playboy*,
    April, 1973

Orgasm is like a slight attack of apoplexy —Democritus

Orgasm is like the tickling feeling you get inside your nose before
    you sneeze —Children's 1972 sex education manual

Pornography is like peanut butter —a little goes a long way
    —Arthur Morowitz, *New York Times*, October 5, 1986

[Sexual] restraints fell from her like mere rags, or rather, like that
    dead skin which is scraped off in a steam bath
    —Marguerite Yourcenar

Sensual as a ripe, thick-veined scarlet fruit —John Logan

Sex becomes as routine as tying one's shoes —Deborah Phillips, *New
    York Times*/Personal Health, October 8, 1986

Sex is a subject like every other subject. Every bit as interesting as
    agriculture —Muriel Spark

Sex ... it's great stuff, like chocolate sundaes —Raymond Chandler

Sexless as a machine —Ellen Glasgow

Sexless as an anemic nun —Sinclair Lewis

(Some men have a) sexual disposition as vigorous, indiscriminate, and as demanding, as a digestive tract —John Cheever

Sexual pleasure, like rending pain, represents the stunning triumph of the immediate —Simone de Beauvoir

She seems to regard sex as a wholesome, slightly silly indulgence, like dancing and nice dinners —Alice Munro

Sometimes I feel like a public utility —Charles Johnson
    The character who makes this comparison about herself in Johnson's novel, *Oxherding Tale,* is a woman who has had "an army" of lovers.

There were people ... for whom love and sex came easy, without active solicitation, like a strong wind to which they had only to turn their faces —David Leavitt

Virility ... was like a gloss on him —Barbara Taylor Bradford

Wears her sex like an expensive perfume —Lawrence Durrell

(Lucille's aunt had) wrapped her own dank virginity round her like someone sharing a mackintosh —Elizabeth Bowen

SEXUAL INTERACTION
SEE: INSULTS

SHADOW

His shadow dragging like a photographer's cloth behind him
    —Elizabeth Bishop

Long shadows deep as oil —Philip Levine

My shadow spilled over the grass like great leaks of ink
    —Henry Van Dyke

Shadows black as parts of dreams —David Denby

Shadows deep as caves —Jerry Bumpus

Shadows [of elm trees] falling all over her head and shoulder like a web —Ellen Gilchrist

Shadows lay like broad hurdles across my path —Beryl Markham

The whole shadow of Man is only as big as his hat
    —Elizabeth Bishop

SHALLOWNESS
SEE: IMPORTANCE/UNIMPORTANCE

Shame

SHAME

As sheepish as a fowl —La Fontaine

Embarrassing, like showing up for a party on the wrong date and finding the host and hostess in the middle of a family squabble —Elyse Sommer

Embarrassment lay like a cloak over everyone's shoulders —Belva Plain

Embarrassment thickened in his throat like phlegm —Ross Macdonald

Embarrassing as a rich man without admirers —David Denby

Embarrassed as a nudist caught with his clothes on —Anon

He felt a drench of shame like a hot liquid over his neck and shoulders —Saul Bellow

In scandal, as in robbery, the receiver is always thought as bad as the thief —Lord Chesterfield

Looked embarrassed, as if he were a spy whose cover had been blown —Robert Barnard

Red-faced ... like a puppy caught in his own piss —R. Wright Campbell

Scandal will rub out like dirt when it is dry —John Ray's *Proverbs*

Shame came over me like a blanket of steam —Mary Gordon

Shame ... it came in twenty-eight delicious flavors, like Howard Johnson's ice cream —Harvey Swados

Uncomfortable as if she had tumbled out of a warm bed into a cold room and there was no time to dress before a crowd came to view her discomfort —Henrietta Weigel

Waves of shame ran through her, like savage internal blushes —Mary McCarthy

Shape
352

SHAPE

(Breasts) flat as paper —William Trevor

EMBARRASSED AS A NUDIST CAUGHT WITH HIS CLOTHES ON

Shape

As two-dimensional as a household weather vane —Saul Bellow

Flat and pale as an empty sheet of nonerasable bond —Lyn Lifshin

(The back of his head) flat as a book —T. Coraghessan Boyle

(Suit lapels as) flat as a cardboard —Derek Lambert

Flat as a carpet —Anon
>   To be more specific, there's "Flat as Oriental rugs."

Flat as a fashion model's breasts —Anon

Flat as a flounder —Anon
>   In his novel, *Death of the Fox*, George Garrett found a new
>   application for this commonly used simile: "I am panting
>   and my body twitches and heaves. Like a man with a
>   woman, flat as a flounder, beneath him."

[A cleft in a rock] flat as a fresco —John Farris

Flat as an empty wallet —Anon

Flat as a pancake
>   —American colloquialism, attributed to New England
>   >   The comparison which has been with us since the fifteenth
>   >   century applies most often to very flat persons and objects.

(A blue sea as) flat as a table top —Jean Stafford

Flat as a tracer bullet —Frank Conroy

Flat as a waiter's feet —Arthur Baer

Flat as melted iron —Joyce Cary

Flat as paper dolls —Elyse Sommer

Flat as the palm of one's hand
>   —American colloquialism, attributed to New England
>   >   A shorter version, "Flat as my hand," was used by Robert
>   >   Louis Stevenson in *Will O' the Will*.

(I lie on my single bed,) flat, like a piece of toast
>   —Margaret Atwood

(Her talk is) formless as a dream —Henry Miller

[A field of July corn] level as a mat —H. E. Bates

Long and slender like a cat's elbow —H. G. Bohn's *Handbook of Proverbs*

Pressed myself flat as a tick against the wood of the wall —Davis Grubb

(Pebbles ...) round and white as pearls —John Cheever

Round as a ball —Alexander Hamilton

Round as a melon —Anon

Round as a pillow —William Wordsworth

(The Jewish women were as ...) round as the earth —Thomas Wolfe

Round as the world —Dame Edith Sitwell

(Eyes as) shapeless as a kneecap —Charles Johnson

Shapeless as fear —Beryl Markham

(The neighbors lounged on each other's steps, big and) shapeless as worn cushions —Helen Hudson

Shapeless like a slug —Heinrich Böll

(Born) a shapeless lump, like anarchy —William Drummond

They [passing lovers] are flat as shadows —Sylvia Plath

SHARPNESS
SEE ALSO: PAIN

(A whippet head), barbed like a hunting arrow —Ted Hughes

Bite ... as deadly as a camel's —Wallace Stegner

Biting [language used in a book] as a chain saw —Bruce De Silva

(Her voice was) crisp as a freshly starched and ironed doily —Maya Angelou

Crisp as a handclap —Maxine Kumin
From a poem entitled *A New England Gardener Gets Personal*, the simile describes how kale comes to the salad bowl.

Crisp as frost —Babette Deutsch

Crisp as new bank notes —Charles Dickens

Sharpness

(A voice that) cut like a blade of ice —G. K. Chesterton

Cut like a knife —Rudyard Kipling Kipling's simile links the knife's sharpness to the wind.

[Cat's fangs ...] fine as a lady's needle —Ted Hughes

Incisively as an acid (a yell bit into the situation) —F. van Wyck Mason

Peppery as curry —Marge Piercy

Sharp as a bird's painted bill —Dame Edith Sitwell

Sharp as an assassin's dagger —Mike Sommer

(Face as) sharp as an ice pick —Graham Masterton

(The longing for lovely things ... became as) sharp as a pang —Ellen Glasgow

Sharp as a scorpion —Dame Edith Sitwell

Sharp as a two-edged sword —*The Holy Bible/Proverbs*

(The smell of smoke was) sharp as brimstone —John Gardner

(My ideas fade, yours come out) sharp as cameos —Joseph Conrad, letter to Stephen Crane

(Eyes) sharp as mica —R. Wright Campbell

(All these things fell on her) sharp as reproach —Lord Alfred Tennyson

Sharp as the teeth of a saw —Marge Piercy

Sharp as truth —John Greenleaf Whittier

Sharp as white paint in the January sun —Wallace Stevens

Sharper than birth —Madeleine L'Engle

Sharp like joy —Sharon Sheehe Stark

Sharp-tongued, like a sadistic dentist —Neil Gabler, a television movie commentator, thus described a colleague, Pauline Kael.

A tongue like a cat o' nine tails —Ben Hecht

Gleamed like dogs' eyes in a car's headlights —Frank Swinnerton

[A ballroom] polished like a skull —Lawrence Durrell

(Her face could) shine as a sack of apples —Wallace Whatley

Shine like a tear —Yocheved Bat-Miriam

[Hands] shine like old wood —Philip Levine

(A pool) shines, like a bracelet shaken in a dance —Wallace Stevens

Shines like a glowworm —Robert Penn Warren

Shines like a rhinestone in a trashcan —Nora Ephron reviewing a
     Jaqueline Susann novel within its context as a roman à clef

(Say to the court it glows and) shines like rotten wood
     —Sir Walter Raleigh

Shining and clear as white stones in a brook —George Garrett

[A table] shining like a pair of shoes —Shelby Hearon

[A room] shining like holiness —Jessamyn West

(Eyes) shining like the icing on a cake —Scott Spencer

Shone [the city in the light] as dazzling bright and pretty as money
     that you find in a dream of finding money
     —Edna St. Vincent Millay

Shone darkly, like water before a storm —Donald Seaman

Shone like a brand-new quarter —Karl Shapiro

Shone ... like a cloud of lightning bugs —Eudora Welty

Shone like a meteor streaming in the wind —John Milton

Shone like patent leather —Rita Mae Brown

(The rails) shone like quicksilver —John Yount

(Her black, oiled hair) shone like a river under the moon —Colette

(Porch-slats) shone like sculpture —Alan Williamson

Sparkle like wedding cakes —Graham Swift
          In Swift's novel, *The Sweet-Shop Owner*, the comparison
     refers the effects of the sun's rays on graves.

357

SHOCK

As dazed as a man who has just been told he hasn't long to live
   —Françoise Sagan

Felt amazed, as if the clouds had blown away, as if the bare bones
   were finally visible —Louise Erdrich
         In Erdrich's novel, *The Beet Queen,* the amazed feeling
         stems from a character's realization that he is homosexual

Felt as if I was being hit by a blast from a giant hair drier
   —Dominique Lapierre

The first shock [of English society] is like a cold plunge
   —Robert Louis Stevenson

He was white and shaken, like a dry martini —P. G. Wodehouse

(Then the familiarity of the name ...) hit him like a contract
   cancellation —William Beechcroft

[A brutal murder] shocked me and held onto me as if I'd shaken
   hands with a live wire —Jonathan Valin

The shock ... held everybody as in a still photo —Ray Bradbury

The shock hit me like a fist under the ribs —David Brierly

[Time awareness] shocking a douche of cold water
   —P. G. Wodehouse

Shocking as the realization that you're not invincible —Elyse Sommer

Shocking realization ... like a fist knocking the wind out of her
   —David Leavitt

Shock [went through room] like the twang of a bow string
   —Iris Murdoch

The shock numbed him out like a drug —George Garrett

(She can) shock you like a lightning bolt at high noon
   —Aharon Megged

Stunned ... as if a good boxer had just caught me with a startling
   left hook and a stultifying right —Norman Mailer

The sudden shock striking somewhere inside her chest like an electric
   bolt —William Styron

SHOULDERS
SEE ALSO: BODY

Bony shoulders ... like wings —Richard Ford

Protruding shoulder blades that pushed out the back of his shirt like hidden wings —Harvey Swados

Shoulder blades ... almost as soft and small as a bird's wings —Penelope Gilliatt

Shoulder blades jutted like a twin hump —Harvey Swados

[Protruding] shoulder blades ... like wedges —Jay Parini

Shoulders like a buffalo —Willa Cather

Shoulders like a five-barred gate —Donald Seaman

Shoulders like a pair of walking beams —H. C. Witwer

Shoulders like a wall —Paul J. Wellman

Shoulders like the ram of a battleship —P. G. Wodehouse

Shoulders like the Parthenon —H. L. Mencken

Shoulders protruding like a Swiss chalet —Rufus Shapley

Shoulders rounded like a question mark —T. Coraghessan Boyle

Sunburned shoulders like the knobs of well-polished furniture —Nadine Gordimer

SHREWDNESS
SEE: CLEVERNESS

SHYNESS
SEE: MEEKNESS, PERSONAL TRAITS

SICKNESS
SEE: ILLNESS

SIGNIFICANCE
SEE: IMPORTANCE/UNIMPORTANCE

SILENCE
SEE ALSO: SECRECY

Behaved a little like a stuffed frog with laryngitis —P. G. Wodehouse

A brief silence, like an indrawn breath —Sylvia Plath

Silence

A brittle silence stretched like iced cords through the kitchen —Anthony E. Stockanes

Dole out his words like federal grants —Shelby Hearon

Dumb as a drum with a hole in it —Charles Dickens

Dumb as a yearning brute —Martin Cruz Smith

The enfolding silence was like an echo —William Styron

Fall silently, like dew on roses —John Dryden

A great painful silence came down, as after the ringing of a church bell —Loren D. Estleman

Grew still, like a congregation in silent prayer —Edgar Lee Masters

Hears the silence ... like a heart that has ceased to beat —Joyce Carol Oates

(The room was suddenly full of ...) heavy silence, like a fallen cake —Raymond Chandler

Her silence bore down on him like a tombstone —Heinrich Böll

Her silence had a frequency all its own ... like one of those dog whistles that make a sound only dogs can hear—a sound that cracked eggs, or something —Larry McMurtry

He tried to say something but his tongue hung in his mouth like a dried fruit on a tree —Bernard Malamud

(The crowded courtroom grew as) hushed and still as a deserted church —Robert Traver

Hushed like a holy place —Lynn Sharon Schwartz

A hush prevailed like that in an art gallery —Jean Stafford

A hush rose like a noisy fog —Bernard Malamud

I'll be like an oyster —Ivan Turgenev
> The character making this statement in *A Month in the Country* underscores it with, "not another syllable."

Men fear silence as they fear solitude, because both give them a glimpse of the terror of life's nothingness —André Maurois

Moving as silently as fish under water —Ross Macdonald

Mute like a faded tapestry —Louis MacNeice

Mute as a fish —John Melton

Mute as a gargoyle —Sharon Sheehe Stark

My tongue lay like a stone in my mouth —Pat Conroy

Noiseless as fear in a wilderness —John Keats

Quiet as the visible murmur is their vaporizing breath
    —William Faulkner

Quiet and meaningless as wind in dry grass —T. S. Eliot

Quiet settled in the room like snow —Rumer Godden

Significant silences like fingers that point —William Bronk

The silence seemed to come drifting down like flakes of snow
    —Katherine Mansfield

Silence fell like a guillotine in the middle of raw, bleeding
    conversations —Susan Fromberg Schaeffer

The silence around them, like the silence inside a mouth, squirms
    with colors —James Dickey

Silence as absolute as death —Robert Penn Warren

Silence as deep as held breath —John Yount

(It was Sunday, and there was a feeling of quietness), a silence as
    though nature were at rest —W. Somerset Maugham

Silence beat about them like waves —Mavis Gallant

The silence between us ... it lay coiled like a sleeping cat, graceful in
    its way but liable to claw if stroked indelicately —Scott Spencer

Silence descending over the room like a blackwinged bird
    —John Rechy

Silence drifting in ... settling like dust —Helen Hudson

The silence [at the other end of telephone] ... felt absolute, as if he
    had been trying to telephone God —William McIlvanney

Silence filled the space [of empty room] like water in a lock
    —Julia Whedon

Silence filled the sunlit room like gas —Harvey Swados

Silent as the pictures on the wall —Henry Wadsworth Longfellow

Silence

Silent as the rays of the sun —Slogan, Silent Glow Oil Burner Corporation

Silent as thought —Sir William Davenant

Silent as your shadow —Colley Cibber

Silent ... like an empty room —Carlos Baker

Silent like a stockpiled bomb —C.D.B. Bryan

Silently as a dream —William Cowper
>"Silent as a dream" variations include: "Dumb as a dream" by Algernon Charles Swinburne and "Mute as any dream" by Elizabeth Barrett Browning.

(Made his way through the yard as) silently as a tom-cat on the prowl —Donald Seaman

Silently as a turtle —John Hersey

Silent men, like still waters, are deep and dangerous —H. G. Bohn's *Handbook of Proverbs*

(The crowd was) silent ... totally, in a hush like the air in the treetops —Paul Horgan

A small silence came between us, as precise as a picture hanging on a wall —Jean Stafford

So quiet ... it felt like Sunday without church —Elizabeth Spencer

(You were) so silent it was like playing with a snowman —Martin Cruz Smith

Soundless as a gong before it's struck —Donald Justice

Untalkative as native Vermonters —Max Lerner on commuters

Unheard like dog whistles pitched too high for human ears —George Garrett

Uses silence like a blackjack —Tim O'Brien

Vocal chords seem glued together like two uncut pages in a book —Elyse Sommer

Withdraw behind a wall of silence like children confronted with the disapproval of an authority figure —Margaret Millar

362

SILLINESS
SEE: ABSURDITY, IMPOSSIBILITY, STUPIDITY

SIMILARITY
SEE: DISSIMILARITIES

SIMPLICITY
SEE: EASE

SIN
SEE: EVIL

SINCERITY
SEE: CANDOR

SITTING
SEE: BEARING, IMMOBILITY

SKILLS
SEE: ABILITY

SKIN

The blue of her veins ... on her breasts, under the clear white skin, like some gorgeous secret —Joe Coomer

Each summer his skin becomes like brown velvet —John Rechy

Flesh ... as chill as that of a mermaid —Angela Carter

The flesh drooping like wattles beneath the jawbone —Nina Bawden

(Miss Quigg's) flesh looks as if it's been steeping in brine for years —Sharon Sheehe Stark

Flesh ... luminous as though coated with milk —Cynthia Ozick

Flesh ... soft and boneless as apple pulp —Margaret Millar

Flesh was as firm and clean as wood —Kay Boyle

Flesh, white as the moon —Charles Johnson

Freckles all over ... like a speckled egg —Phyllis Naylor

Grained like wood (where the sweat had trickled) —Willa Cather

Hairless as a statue —Harvey Swados

Hands and forehead were deeply spotted like a seagull's egg —Frank Tuohy

363

Skin

Her skin cracked like skim milk —Arthur Miller

Her skin felt like plaster of Paris —Nancy Huddleston Packer

Her skin had a startlingly fine texture, like flour when you dip your hand into it —John Updike

Her skin had the bad, stretched look of the white cotton hand towels they give you in poor hotels —Maeve Brennan

Her skin was as pink as sugar icing —Georges Simenon
> The simile underscores Simenon's characterization of a woman like a 'bonbon.'

Her skin was the color of smoked honey —R. V. Cassill

Her toadstool skin drapes her bones like cloth worn thin —William Hoffman
> The simile is taken from a scene in a short story describing a dying woman.

His skin hung on his bones like an old suit much too large for him —W. Somerset Maugham

His skin is pale and looks unwholesomely tender, like the skin under a scab —Margaret Atwood

His skin was tea-colored, like a farm boy's —Ella Leffland

My skin hangs about me like an old lady's loose gown —William Shakespeare

Pimpled like a brand-new basketball —M. Garrett Bauman
> The skin described in Bauman's short story *Out from Narragansett* belongs to a blowfish.

She had pale skin with the kind of texture that looked as if a pinch would crumble it —Jonathan Kellerman

Skin brown as a saddle —Linda West Eckhardt

(The waitress ... has) skin dark as garden earth —Leslie Garis, *New York Times Magazine*, February 8, 1987

Skin ... (slack, sallow and) draped like upholstery fabric over her short, boardlike bones —Louise Erdrich

Skin felt like a series of damp veils, like the wet paper you fold over the wires when you are making papier-mâché —Elizabeth Tallent

Skin felt like rawhide which hasn't been soaked —Niven Busch

Skin ... flushed as if by a fresh breeze —Franz Werfel

Skin freckled like a mango leaf —Derek Walcott

Skin, freckled like a lawn full of clover —Rosellen Brown

Skin glowed like a golden peach —Lillian de la Torre

Skin ... gray and rough like dirty milk —Heinrich Böll

Skin ... hard and leathery ... as though you could strike a kitchen match on it —Pat Conroy

Skin, hairless and white as bird droppings —Harvey Swados

Skin [when you're old and thin] hangs like trousers on a circus elephant —Penelope Gilliatt

The skin ... hung from her bones like a quilt on the line —Suzanne Brown

Skin like a baby's behind —François Camoin

(One of those lovely, ageless women, with) skin like an Oil of Olay ad —Tony Ardizzone

Skin like an overwashed towel —Jean Thompson

Skin like dark flames —Margaret Atwood

Skin like flan —Scott Spencer

Skin like ice cream, like toasted-almond ice cream —T. Coraghessan Boyle

Skin like polished stone —Richard Wilbur

(He was pale, his) skin like sausage casing —Paul Theroux

Skin like shells and peaches —M. J. Farrell

Skin ... like silk —*Arabian Nights*

Skin like the skin of fruit protected by shade —Paul Horgan

Skin like the underpetals of newly-opened June rosebuds
—Cornell Woolrich

Skin like wax paper —Frank Tuohy

Skin like wood —Elizabeth Harris

The skin merely hung at her neck like a patient animal waiting for the rest of her to join in the decline —Max Apple

The skin of her neck was like a piece of chamois leather that had been wrung out and left to dry in brownish, uncomfortable, awkward folds —H. E. Bates

Skin pale as a snowdrop —Jaroslav Seifert
This is both the first line and title of a poem.

Skin ... pale as glossy paper —Geoffrey Wolff

Skin [around neck] ... sagging like a turkey's —John Braine

Skin seemed as sheer as rubber, pulled over her hands like surgical gloves —Sue Grafton

Skin shines in dull gray translucence, like wax —Ira Wood

Skin shines like polished mahogany —R. Wright Campbell

Skin smelled like fresh cotton —John Updike

Skin ... smooth, as if dampened and then stretched on his skull
—Wright Morris

Skin smooth as Pratesi sheets ... eyes that shimmer like Baccarat at the bottom of a Bel Air hot tub ... earrings sparkling like all the chandeliers at Lincoln Center, in Malcolm Forbes yacht and maybe even in all of Donald Trump's Tower
—Stephanie Mansfield, *Washington Post*, June 21, 1986
Mansfield's string of similes sets the mood for a profile of Judith Krantz, renowned for her best sellers about glamorous people.

Skin ... soft and flabby as used elastic —Jean Rhys

Skin so unwholesomely deficient in the natural tinge, that he looked as though, if he were cut, he would bleed white
—Charles Dickens

Skin ... stretched over his bones like a piece of old shining oilcloth
—Dominique Lapierre

Skin stretched tight like a rubber ball —Margaret Atwood

Skin supple and moist like fine leather that had been expertly treated —Elizabeth Spencer

Skin, the color of creamed tea —W. P. Kinsella

Skin the color of ripe grapefruit —T. Coraghessan Boyle

Skin ... the texture like the pit of a peach —Stanley Elkin

Skin tight and rugged as a mountain climber's —Ward Just

The skin under the eyes was gray, as though she had stayed up every night since puberty —Ella Leffland

Skin [a baby's] was delicious to touch, fine-grained and blemishless, like silk without the worminess —John Updike

Skin was pale and drawn, her bones lay like shadows under it —William H. Gass

Skin was reddish brown like that of an overbaked apple —Jerzy Kozinski

Skin [of bald scalp] was sunburned, and ridged like dried leather —Cornell Woolrich

Skin ... weathering toward sunset like cracked glaze on porcelain —Dick Francis

The startling whiteness of her skin, lush and vulnerable, was like the petal of a gardenia —Kaatje Hurlbut

The texture of her skin was round and hard like the rind of winter fruit —Ellen Glasgow

The texture of his skin, like coffee grounds —Charles Johnson

White skin that looks like thin paper —John Cheever

SKY
SEE ALSO: CLOUD(S), MOON

Bleak [sky] ... as if the sun had just slipped off the edge of the world —Susan Welch

A blue, cloudless sky spread like a field of young violets —Hugh Walpole

The cloudless sky was like an inverted bowl that hemmed it in
—W. Somerset Maugham

The clouds formed like a beach and the stars were strewn among
them like shells and moraine —John Cheever

A cloudy grey sky through which the sun shone opaque like an Alka
Seltzer —Jilly Cooper

The evening sky, with its head dark and its scarves of color, looked
like an Italian woman with an orange in her hand
—Christina Stead

The expanse of the sky was like an infinite canvas on which human
beings were incapable of projecting images from their human life
because they would seem out of scale and absurd —Anaïs Nin

The gray (Seattle) sky lies around her, filmy and thick, like you
could eat it —Barry Hannah

The grey, soft, muffled sky moved like the sea on a silent day
—Nadine Gordimer

The horizon was like an open mouth —David Ignatow

Lifeless sky ... like the first day of creation —Edith Wharton

Light spread across the horizon like putty —T. Coraghessan Boyle

Skies like inverted cups —John Rechy

Sky ... as clear as a window —Beryl Markham

Sky as clear, as firm-looking, as blue marble —David Ignatow

Sky as drab as a cast-iron skillet —Jessamyn West

Sky ... as soft as clouds of blue and white hyacinths
—Ellen Glasgow

The sky bloomed like a dark rose —James Reiss

The sky covered with stars ... like dots in a child's puzzle
—Helen Hudson

Sky ... flat and unreal as a glimpse of distant ocean
—Sharon Sheehe Stark

The sky ... flung itself over the earth like a bolt of blue cloth
—Dianne Benedict

(Over the city) the sky hangs like a giant silken tent
—Erich Maria Remarque

The sky hangs like lead —Erich Maria Remarque

The sky hisses and bubbles like a cauldron —W. P. Kinsella

The sky hovering overhead like a soundless dirigible that was about to crash —Heinrich Böll

The sky hung over the valley ... like a slack white sheet —Elizabeth Bowen

The sky is darkening like a stain —W. H. Auden

The sky is like a heavy lid —Ridgely Torrence

The sky is like a human mind, with uncountable shifting pictures and caverns and heights and misty places, and lakes of blue, and big sheets of forgetting, and rainbows, illusions, thunderheads, mysteries —John Hersey

The sky is like a page from a book that hasn't been written —François Camoin

The sky is like a peach-colored sheet drawn taut at the horizon —Russell Banks

A sky like a dirty old slate —M. J. Farrell

A sky like a dustbin-lid —William McIlvanney

Sky like a forget-me-not —Joyce Cary

Sky like a great glass eye —George Garrett

Sky like an immense blue gentian —Henry Van Dyke

Sky like a pig's backside —Sylvia Plath

A sky like a tinted shell —Helen Hudson

The sky looked billowy, as if you could catch the corners of it and toss the stars around as in a net —Ada Jack Carver

Sky, pale and unreal as a photographer's background screen —Katherine Mansfield

The sky seemed to be spread like a bottomless lake above them —William Styron

The sky shone like enamel —John Cheever

Sky

The sky swayed like a blue balloon on a string —Ross Macdonald

A sky that looked like water, broad, blue, its clouds rolling like great, feathery waves —Charles Johnson

The sky was full of little puffs of white clouds, like the ships we saw sailing far out to sea —Wilbur Daniel Steele

The sky [on a windy day] was like an unmade bed —Helen Hudson

The sky was like glass —James Reiss

The sky was like muslin —John Ashbery

The sky was like new-cleaned window glass full of its own shine —Joyce Cary

The sky was ... like wet gray paper —Paul Horgan

The sky was overcast, monotone, as if it were made of pale gray rubber —Jean Thompson

The sky was pale and smudged like a dirty sheet —George Garrett

Smoke drifted across the sky looking like a gigantic horse's mane blowing in the wind —Boris Pasternak

A starless sky as dark and thick as ink —Émile Zola

The sun bubbled in the sky, giving off clouds like puffs of steam —Helen Hudson

Winter skies hover over Iowa like a gray dome —W. P. Kinsella

Slander

SLANDER

Slanderers are like flies; they leap over all a man's good parts to light upon his sores —John Tillotson

Slander is like a hornet; if you cannot kill it dead at the first blow, better not strike at it —Josh Billings

Slander, like coal, will either dirty your hand or burn it —Russian proverb

Sleep

SLEEP
SEE ALSO: DREAMS

Asleep and dreaming, like bees in cells of honey —Thomas McGuane
The simile completed McGuane's novel, *The Sporting Club.*

As near to sleep as a runner waiting for the starter's pistol
—J. B. Priestley

As sound asleep as a coon in a hollow log —Borden Deal

Awoke ... like some diver emerging from the depths of ocean
—Francis King

(Paul lay in his berth) between wakefulness and sleep, like a partially
anesthetized patient —John Cheever

(Mr. Samuel Pickwick) burst like another sun from his slumbers
—Charles Dickens

Came out of a deep sleep slowly, like a diver pausing at each
successive level —Norman Garbo

Come from sleep as if returning from a far country —Mary Hedin
The simile which begins the story, *Blue Transfer*, continues
with, "A stranger to myself, a stranger to my life."

Doze and dream like a lazy snake —George Garrett

Drowsy as an audience for a heavy speech after an even heavier
dinner —Anon

Emerges from slumber like some deep-sea creature hurled floundering
and gasping up into the light of day by a depth-charge
—Francis King

Fell into a sleep as blank as paving-stone —Patrick White

Felt himself falling asleep like gliding down a long slide, like slipping
from a float into deep water —Oakley Hall

Heavy with sleep, like faltering, lisping tongues —Boris Pasternak

I shall sleep like a top —Sir William Davenant
This simile has outlived the play from which it is taken,
The Rivals, as a colloquial expression. A somewhat
different version, "Slept like any top" appeared in the
German children's story, *Struwelpeter*, by Heinrich
Hoffman.

I want sleep to water me like begonias —Diane Wakoski

Kept falling in and out of it [sleep] like out of a boat or a tipping
hammock —Rose Tremain

371

Sleep

Lies asleep as softly as a girl dreaming of lovers she cannot keep
   —F. D. Reeve
         Reeves, a poet, is describing a river.

Lying awake like a worried parent —Robert Silverberg

Nodding, like a tramp on a park bench —Robert Traver

Not sleeping but dozing awake like a snake on stone
   —Malcolm Cowley

Sleep as smooth as banana skins —Diane Wakoski

Sleep came over my head like a gunny sack —Ross Macdonald

Sleep covered him like a breaker —Harris Downey

Sleep fell on her like a blow —Hortense Calisher

Sleeping like a lake —Theodore Roethke

Sleeping like a stone in an empty alcove of the cathedral
   —Clive Cussler

Sleep like a dark flood suspended in its course
   —Percy Bysshe Shelley

Sleep like a kitten, arrive fresh as a daisy
   —Slogan, Chesapeake & Ohio Railroad

Slept like a cocked pistol —Émile Zola

Slept a great deal, as if years of fatigue had overtaken him
   —Peter Matthiessen

Slept almost smiling, as if she had a secret —William McIlvanney

(He usually) slept like a corpse —Ring Lardner

(While the Weary Blues echoed through his head, he) slept like a
   rock or a man that's dead —Langston Hughes

Slept like he'd gone twelve rounds with a pro —Geoffrey Wolff

Slumber fell on their tired eyelids like the light rain of spring upon
   the fresh-turned earth —W. Somerset Maugham

Sunk into sleep like a stone dropped in a well —John Yount

Wake abruptly, with an alarm clock which breaks up their sleep like
   the blow of an ax —Milan Kundera

SLIGHTNESS
SEE: WEAKNESS

SLIMNESS
SEE: THINNESS

SLOPPINESS
SEE: ORDER/DISORDER

SMALLNESS

As tiny as the glint of a silver dime in a mountain of trash
—Elizabeth Spencer

Big as a broom closet —Anon
This modern colloquialism usually applies to a small living
or working space. A common variation often used with
"No bigger than" is "As big as a shoe box."

Big as your thumbnail —Julian Gloag

He [a very short man] with his chin up, gazing about as though
searching for his missing inches —Helen Hudson

Small and undistinguishable, like far-off mountains turned into clouds
—William Shakespeare

Small as a breadcrumb —Anon

Small as a fly in the fair enormity of a night sky
—Elizabeth Spencer

Small as a garden pea —Lawrence Durrell

Small as a snail —Babette Deutsch
The comparison describes the subject of a poem entitled
The Mermaid.

Small as grain of rice —Anon

Small as sesame seed —Anon

Small as snowflake —Anon

Tight as a gnat's cock —English expression used by engineers to
describe an extremely small space

(Paper ripped into pieces), tiny as confetti —Ann Beattie

(Jewelled chips) tiny as grass seed —Jayne Anne Phillips

SMELL
SEE ALSO: AIR

The air smelled like damp flannel —Jonathan Kellerman

The air smelled ... like the interior of the Bastille in 1760
    —Carlos Baker

As malodorous as a badly ventilated lion house in a zoo
    —John Cheever

A close antiseptic odor like an empty schoolroom —George Garrett

A dark wet smell like a cave —Pat Conroy

He smelled like something that spent the winter in a cave
    —Sue Grafton

It [a hotel lobby] smelled like fifty million dead cigars
    —J. D. Salinger

A kitchen odor hung about like a bad mood —Tom MacIntyre

The lingering odor of sweat like sour wheat —Louise Erdrich

(He gave off an) odor like a neglected gym locker —Wallace Stegner

The odor of her body, like salted flowers —Bernard Malamud

The odor (of newly turned earth) steamed up around him like
    incense —Dorothy Canfield Fisher

The office smelled like hot coffee —Richard Ford

An old man smells old ... like old clothes that need an airing
    —Saul Bellow

The place smells like a wrestler's armpit —Jilly Cooper

Pleasantly pungent, like the smell of one's own body —John Updike

Reek like last week's fish —Mike Sommer

The scent [from garden] rises like heat from a body
    —Margaret Atwood

Scent rising like incense (from the cleavage of her splendid bosom)
    —Jilly Cooper

The sea smelled like a sail whose billows had caught up water, salt,
    and a cold sun —Robert Goddard

Sexual smells, like the odor of an excellent cheese, are considered foul by those who experienced them without their appetites being involved —Judith Martin

A smell [of cheap cologne] like rotten bananas in a straw basket —Jonathan Valin

[Hallway of a hotel] smelled like hot bread and clean laundry —Richard Ford

Smelled like something the cat dragged in —American colloquialism

(Mrs. Lamb) smelled like spoiled lilacs —Richard Ford

[A boy] smelled like the bottom of a calf pen where the piss settled and burned the yellow straw red and when you turned the straw over with a fork the ammonia smell made your eyes water —Will Weaver

Smell fresh as apples —John Braine

(Soft-spoken women) smelling like washed babies —Philip Levine

Smell like an open drain —Louis MacNeice

Smell like a sick skunk —Elmer Kelton

The smell of moist earth and lilacs hung in the air like wisps of the past and hints of the future —Margaret Millar

Smells like the underneath of a car —Carolyn Chute

Smells badly like things that have been too long dead —Donald McCaig

Smells fresh as melting snow —W. P. Kinsella

Smell stronger than a ton of rotten mangoes —Hunter S. Thompson

Smell (of carnations) ... thick as smoke in the sun —Mary Stewart

[Honeysuckle smell] smothering, like an anesthetic —Lynne Sharon Schwartz

A stale smell like a bad embalming job —Jimmy Sangster

(The married man is grateful for) the stuffy room that smells of his wife like a bar smells of beer —David Denby

There was a foul reek of something fecund and feline, like the stench of old lion spore upon the veldt —Tama Janowitz

Wet fields reek like some long empty church —John Betjeman

SMILES

Adjusted her smile like a cardboard mask —Vicki Baum

An attempt at a smile creased Willie's face like old tissue
    —Paige Mitchell

Beamed like a child that stops crying the moment you return his
    favorite toy and promise never to confiscate it again
    —Natascha Wodin

Beamed like a lighthouse —Clive Cussler

Beamed like an August moon —F. van Wyck Mason

Beamed like a small boy uncrating his first bicycle —Robert Traver

Beamed like the sun —Mikhail Lermontov
        The sunshine-like smile in Lermontov's *A Hero of Our Time*
        is in response to a nod from a young woman at a dance.

Beams like a politician —Dilys Laing

The faint, slow smile clung like an edge of light to her lips
    —Ellen Glasgow

Flashed her smile [and] bit it off like a thread —John Cheever

A flashing smile, like a knife gleaming briefly from concealment
    —Ross Macdonald

Had a smile for every occasion, like Hallmark cards
    —Andrew Kaplan

Her vivid smile was like a light held up to dazzle me
    —Edith Wharton

His smile drops from his face like a mask with a broken cord
    —Erich Maria Remarque

His smile lit up the world like a strobe light —Herbert Gold

His smile spread across his bearded face in crooked jerks ... like a
    crack spreading across a dam —Rick Borsten

An indestructible smile cracked forever across the front of his face
    like the brim of a black ten-gallon hat —Joseph Heller

376

The comparison is particularly apt as it applies to a character who's a Texan.

Kept smiling, as if the corners of his mouth were strung up on invisible wires —Sylvia Plath

The lines of a smile split his jaw like a field furrow —Leigh Allison Wilson

Looked like a lizard regarding a fly —John Irving

A lovely smile, like a shining seal upon a contract —Graham Swift

On-and-off smile ... like a light-switch —Eleanor Clark

Pinched-lip smile that dug deep grooves like chisel strokes in her cheeks —Anthony E. Stockanes

A pure and radiant smile suddenly shone out under her beautiful wet eyelashes, like sunshine among branches after a summer shower —Anatole France

Quick smile like somebody with a fever —George Garrett

Quick smiles that were like small coins thrown without fuss to someone who has done a service —Graham Swift

She smiled like a belle —Jonathan Valin

(Smile more widely and) show his teeth like a politician visiting a high school —James Reiss

Simpering like a wolf —Dylan Thomas

A slight smile, like a knife mark in fresh dough —James Crumley

Sly, satisfied smile ... like a wink, a nudge in the ribs —Ann Petry

A small puckered-up smile like an old scar —Helen Hudson

Smile as spare as the décor along Death Row —Loren D. Estleman

Smile ... warm and steady as summer sun —Mary Hedin

Smile ... like a crack in old plaster —Rita Mae Brown

A smile, as artificial as the last touch of makeup —Marguerite Yourcenar

Smile as cold as a polar bear's feet —Eugene O'Neill

A smile as guileless as that of a serpent —R. Wright Campbell

The smile, as it went from her face, reminded me of a flame turned off by a tap —H. E. Bates

Smile as phony as that of a trained horse —James Crumley

Smile as sharp as a blade —Ellen Glasgow

Smile broke apart like a cheap tumbler shattering —Geoffrey Wolff

A smile broke over his face like the sunrise over Monadnock —Steven Vincent Benét

Smile ... cool as clean linen, friendly as beer —John Braine

Smiled as broad as a Halloween pumpkin —Charles Johnson

(Blinked and) smiled like a lizard on a rock —John D. MacDonald

Smiled like a submissive wife —Herbert Gold

Smiled like a wolf at the thought of the next meal —Mike Fredman

Smiled like a woman resigned to a fate worse than death —James Crumley

Smiled like La Gioconda —Gerald Kersh

Smiled [upon being introduced] like people who had been introduced years before and had flirted and were now hiding their acquaintance —Christina Stead

Smiled like she had just discovered a cure for the common cold —Arnold Sawislak

Smiled off and on, like a neon sign —Clancy Sigal

Smiled with all the charm and cunning of the dangerously insane —Miles Gibson

Smile, fixed like that of a ventriloquist's doll —Eric Ambler

A smile ... flashed like an inspired thought across her face —O. Henry

A smile had widened her lips, spreading like oil —Hortense Calisher

Smile ... it refreshes, like a shower from a watering pot —*A Broken-Hearted Gardener*, anonymous nineteenth century verse

Smile like a cocktail gone flat —Malcolm Cowley

Smile ... like a crack in an eggshell —Leslie Thomas

SMILED OFF AND ON LIKE A NEON SIGN

A smile like a cunning little flame came over his face, suddenly and involuntarily —D. H. Lawrence

Smile ... like a fresh saber scar —R. V. Cassill

A smile like a large plaster ornament —Marge Piercy

Smile ... like all the lights of a Christmas tree going on at once —George Garrett

Smile ... like an invitation —Flannery O'Connor

Smile like a plastic daisy —Marge Piercy

Smile like a razor-cut before the blood comes —John Dickson Carr

Smile ... like a white flower flung on an open wound —Adela Rogers St. Johns

A smile like Christmas morning —Harry Prince

Smile like heaven —Edith Wharton

Smile ... like holiday sunshine —John Le Carré

Smile ... like that of the boa constrictor about to swallow the rabbit —Arthur Train

Smile ... like the crêpe on a coffin —Lawrence Durrell

A smile like the first scratch on a new car —Tom Robbins

Smile ... like the smile of a chipmunk sucking on a toothpick —Don Robertson

Smile like transparent water stirred by a light breeze —Italo Svevo

(Flashes his eyes in) a smile like triumph —D. H. Lawrence

Smile of a man with a terminal headache —T. Coraghessan Boyle

A smile passed over his big face like a soundless storm —Erich Maria Remarque

A smile passed over her lined face like sunlight on a plowed field —Ross Macdonald

The smile she gave him was like a white flower flung on an open wound —Adela Rogers St. Johns

Smiles stolidly flickered like home movies —Stephen Sandy

Smiles tossed like fanciful flowers —Joan Chase

Smiles wanly ... like an actor with no conviction —Rosellen Brown

Smile sweet as cake —Lorrie Moore

A smile that came and went as quickly as a facial tic
   —John D. MacDonald

Smile that stretches like a rubber band —Daphne Merkin

Smile ... vacant and faint like the smile fading on an old photograph
   —V. S. Pritchett

A smile wide as a mousetrap —David Brierly

A smile with closed lips which was at once sorrowful and comic,
   very like a clown's —Storm Jameson

Smiling encouragingly but rather distantly, like friends saying good-
   bye in a hospital to a patient who is not expected, except by
   some miracle, to recover —John Mortimer

Smiling like a bailiff —Sumner Locke Elliott

Smiling like a birthday child —John Gardner

Smiling ... like a fat yellow cat —J. B. Priestley

Smiling like a winking shudder —Robert Campbell

Smiling secretly as cats do in the midst of mouse dreams
   —Sue Grafton

Smiling to himself like a mysterious Buddha —Margaret Landon

A soft silky smile [of mother] slipped over her [young daughter] like
   a new dress, making her feel beautiful —Helen Hudson

Stretching a smile across her face like a rubber band
   —Susan Ferraro, *New York Times*/Hers, March 12, 1987

Suddenly, like a crocus bursting out of winter earth, she [a child]
   looked up at Alison and smiled —John Fowles

The suggestion of an ironic smile rippled about her face like a breeze
   on a pond —James Crumley

(She smiled at me, and) the smile broke against my face like a cool
   wave —L. P. Hartley

Smiles

The way you smile, with your whole face, with your eyes, it's like a certificate of trust —T. Coraghessan Boyle

When Henry smiled, showing his newly crowned front teeth, he looked like a male lead in an old silent film —Kathleen Farrell

When she smiled her eyes and mouth lighted up as if a lamp shone within —Ellen Glasgow

A wide smile, glamorous and trembly, like a movie star's —Molly Giles

SMOKE
SEE: FIRE AND SMOKE

SNORES
SEE: SLEEP

SNOW
SEE: NATURE

SOAP OPERA
SEE: STAGE AND SCREEN

Softness

SOFTNESS

Feels like walking on velvet —Slogan, Clinton Carpet Co.

Flabby as an empty sack —Luigi Pirandello

Flabby as a sponge —Guy de Maupassant

(Arm ...) flabby as butter —Katherine Mansfield

Fluffy as thistledown —William Humphrey

(When I reached out to touch it, it) gave like a rubber duck —T. Coraghessan Boyle

Gentle as a pigeon's sound —Stephen Vincent Benét

(Squeezed the trigger as) gently as a bee touching down to drink from a cowslip —Donald Seaman

Gone limp as a bath towel —T. Coraghessan Boyle

Graceful as Venetian quill strokes —Clarence Major

Lank as a ghost —William Wordsworth

[A chocolate bar] limp as a slab of bacon —Margaret Atwood

382

Limp as calamari —Ira Wood

(Paper bags as) limp as cloth —Alice McDermott

(Arms) limp as old carrots —Anne Sexton

(The potted palms were) limp as old money —George Garrett

Looks soft as darkness folded on itself —Babette Deutsch

Soft and scented as a damask rose —Vita Sackville-West

Soft and silky as a kitten's purr —Slogan, Alfred Decker Society
     Brand clothes

(You are) soft as a bean curd —John Hersey

(The rock was as white and as) soft as a bed —Vladimir Nabokov

Soft as a bowl of jello —Anon

[A distant ridge] soft as a cloud —William Wordsworth

(Love's twilight hours) soft ... as a fairy's moan
     —John Greenleaf Whittier

Soft as a fat woman without a girdle —Anon

(Humble love in me would look for no return) soft as a guiding star
     that cheers, but cannot burn —William Wordsworth

(Cheeks) soft as a hound's ear —Theodore Roethke

Soft as a kitten's ear —Slogan used for both Hews & Potter belts
     and Spiegel Neckwear ties

Soft as a marshmallow —Anon
          Used primarily to imply a kind nature. "Soft as mush" is a
          common variation.

(His touch was) soft as an airbrush —Molly Giles

Soft as angel hair —Susan Richards Shreve

(Snow) soft as a young girl's skin —F. D. Reeve

(Waves looked) soft as carded wool —Henry Wadsworth Longfellow

Soft as fleece —Stephen Vincent Benét

Soft as linen —Hayden Carruth

The simile, which describes a stone, continues with another: "And flows like wax." A slight twist gave Scott tissues its "Soft as old linen" slogan.

Soft as lips that laugh —Algernon Charles Swinburne

Soft as love —Hallie Burnett

(Heartbeat) soft as snow on high snow falling —Daniel Berrigan

(Her cheeks were ...) soft as suet —Raymond Chandler

Soft as the thighs of women —W. D. Snodgrass

Soft as the west-wind's sigh —W. S. Gilbert
    This form of the west-wind comparison comes from *Ruddigore*. Using the qualitative comparison form, "Softer than it" dates back to the poet Shelley.

Soft as yesterday's ice cream —James Lee Burke

Soft as young down —William Shakespeare

Softening like pats of butter —John Updike
    In Updike's story *Made in Heaven,* the comparison refers to the softening light in windows he describes as golden.

(You are) soft like a shower of water —William H. Gass

Soft, like a strokable cat —Beryl Markham

Soft to the touch as a handful of yarn —Jessamyn West

[Bodies] wobbly as custard —Alice Munro

SOLIDITY
SEE: STRENGTH

SOLITUDE
SEE: ALONENESS

SORROW
SEE: GRIEF

SOUNDNESS
SEE: HEALTH

SOUNDS
SEE: NOISE

SPEAKING
SEE: CONVERSATION, TALKATIVENESS

SPEECHLESSNESS
SEE: SILENCE

SPIRIT
SEE: COURAGE

SPITE
SEE: MEANNESS

SPORTS
SEE ALSO: BASEBALL

Batted the [tennis] ball away like an irritating gnat —Rita Mae Brown

An American winning the French bicycle race is like a Frenchman winning most valuable baseball player —Chris Wallace commenting on Greg Le Mond's winning of Tour De France race, NBC-TV, July 26, 1986

Angling may be said to be so like the mathematics that it can never be fully learned —Izaak Walton

The [tennis] ball knifes right onto the face of the strings and stays there like a piece of cheese —Ron Carlson

Basketball is like poetry in motion
—Jim Valvano, North Carolina State coach, 1987

Bathers hop across the waves agilely, aimlessly, like fleas
—Malcolm Cowley

Coaching is like a monkey on a stick. You pass the same fellows on the way down as you pass on the way up
—Steve Owen, New York Giants football coach

[A swimmer] floated on her back [in water] like a pink air mattress
—Will Weaver

Having the America's Cup yacht race in San Diego instead of Newport is like going to Mardi Gras in Pittsburgh —Rhode Island Representative St. Germaine, *Wall Street Journal*, February 5, 1987

Hockey players are like mules. They have no fear of punishment and no hope of rewards —Emory Jones, general manager of the St. Louis Arena, *St. Louis Post-Dispatch*, December 26, 1963

Holds a siren yellow tennis ball up in front of her, like the torch on the Statue of Liberty, and hits it with a combination of force and grace —Daphne Merkin

If a tie is like kissing your sister, losing is like kissing your grandmother with her teeth out —George Brett, Kansas City Royals third baseman, *Sports Illustrated*, June 23, 1986

I saw more sails biting the wind than I've ever seen before; it was like sailing through the mouth of a shark —Jean Lamunière, September 15, 1986

Legs [bicycling] pumping like wheels —Murray Bail

Little Pat played [tennis] ... like a weekly wound up machine —John Updike

Records fell like ripe apples on a windy day —E. B. White

The reel was screaming ... humming like a telegraph wire in a sixty-mile gale —Arthur Train

The skaters [on the Ranger hockey team] ... perform like an electrocardiogram readout —Craig Wolff, *New York Times*, September 8, 1986
> Wolff's simile alluded to the team's impersonal performance.

Sports is like a war without killing
—Ted Turner, baseball team owner

Swim like a cannonball —Tony Ardizzone

(I can) swim like a duck —William Shakespeare

Swimming the English Channel, it was like swimming in dishwater —Sandra Blewett, long distance swimmer, *The Evening Standard*, August 21, 1979

Tearing through the water like a seal —Rosamond Lehmann

Tennis is like a lawsuit; you can always be surprised by what happens on the other side of the court —Anon

Their arms were so high on the follow-through it looked like a mass ascension of Mount Everest —Archie Oldham
> The simile, taken from a basketball story, *The Zealots of Cranston Tech*, describes a team of players all shooting for basket together.

The undulant fly line coiled out over the pond like a fleeing serpent
—Robert Traver

Violent exercise is like a cold bath. You think it does you good
because you feel better when you stop it —Robert Quillen

(Bicycling children) wheeled like swallows through luminous, lemon-
coloured air —Julia O'Faolain

Working out the [fishing] line at his feet, like a cowboy coiling a
rope —Robert Traver

You will find angling to be like the virtue of humility, which has a
calmness of spirit and a world of other blessings attending upon
it —Izaak Walton

SPREADING
SEE: PERVASIVENESS

SPRIGHTLINESS
SEE: ACTIVENESS

SPRING
SEE: SEASONS

STAGE AND SCREEN

An actor is a sculptor who carves in snow —Edwin Booth

An actor is like a cigar; the more you puff him, the smaller he gets
—Anon

Actors are like burglars: they always change their names for business
purposes —Frank Richardson

An actor's soul must be like a diamond. The more facets its got, the
more shining his name —Grace Paley

Every film is launched like a squid in an obscuring cloud of
spectacular publicity —Dudley Nichols

[Danny Kaye] feels about an audience the way most men feel about
a date. He woos them. He wants to make them happy —Sylvia
Fine, quoted in husband Kaye's obituary, *New York Times*, March
4, 1987

The movie actor, like the sacred king of primitive tribes, is a god in
captivity —Alexander Chase

A movie is like a person. Either you trust it or you don't
—Mike Nichols

Movie stars are like race horses. Everybody knows their name, but they have to obey the stable boys —MacDonald Harris

Not to go to the theater is like making one's toilet without a mirror —Arthur Schopenhauer

A play, like a bill, is of no value till it is accepted —Henry Fielding

Prologues, like compliments, are a loss of time —David Garrick

Sex percolates merrily through all of the daytime soaps like grounds in a coffee pot —Carin Rubenstein, *Channels Magazine*, March, 1986
See Also: SEX

Soap opera is like sex outside marriage: many have tried it, but most are ashamed of being caught —Peter Buckham

Television is like the little girl who had a little curl. When it is good, it is very, very good, and when it is bad, it is horrid —Melvin I. Cooperman, discussing quality of playwriting for stage, screen and television writers, *Word Wrap* (electronic bulletin board for writers), May 8, 1987

The theater is a communal event, like church —Marcia Norman, *New York Times Book Review* interview, May 24, 1987

Theater is like baseball; it depends on hits and runs —Anon

STANDING
SEE: BEARING, IMMOBILITY, PERSONAL PROFILES

STARES
SEE: FROWNS, LOOKS

STARTING AND STOPPING
SEE: BEGINNINGS/ENDINGS

STATELINESS
SEE: BEARING

STEALTH
SEE: SECRECY

STERILITY
SEE: EMPTINESS

STICKINESS
SEE: CLINGING

STIFFNESS
SEE: PAIN

STILLNESS
SEE: IMMOBILITY, SILENCE

STINGINESS
SEE: THRIFT

STOMACH
SEE: BODY, SHAPE, THINNESS

STRANGENESS

Alien and mysterious and uncanny, like sleeping out in the jungle
    alone —Christopher Isherwood

Eerie as a man carving his own epitaph —William McIlvanney

Miraculous as fire in the snow —Sam Shepard

Mysterious as an Agatha Christie story with the last page torn out
    —James Brooke

Mysterious as cells seen under a microscope —Ann Beattie
        In Beattie's story, *Janus*, the comparison refers to the bits of
        color in a ceramic bowl.

Mysterious as tea leaves —Vincent Canby

Mystery emanated from her like a fire alarm —Richard Ford

Peculiar as a middle-aged man undressed —David Denby

Queer as a green kielbasa —Petter Meinke
        A colloquialism on the same theme: "Queer as a three
        dollar bill."

Queer as a jaybird —Anon

The scenes and incidents had the strangeness of the transcendental,
    as if they were snatches torn from lives on other planets that
    had somehow drifted to the earth —Boris Pasternak

Strange as a wedding without a bridegroom —Anon

Strangeness

Strange, eerie: like something out of a fairy tale
—T. Coraghessan Boyle

Strength

STRENGTH
SEE ALSO: BODY, COURAGE

Air of impregnability that he carried with him like a briefcase full of secrets —Derek Lambert

As indestructible as a bride's first set of biscuits —Jim Murray, about football player Mike Garrett, *Los Angeles Herald*

Bones ... like bars of iron —*The Holy Bible/Job*

Built like a bouncer in a clip joint —Saul Bellow

Built like a brick shit-house —American colloquialism, popularized in American army.

> With slight alterations some of the more colorful army and country similes can be cleaned up with the original meaning still implicit. For example, in her novel, *Love Medicine*, Louise Erdrich describes a character as being "Built like a brick outhouse."

Built like a toolbox —Lee K. Abbott

A cobweb is as good as the mightiest cable when there is no strain upon it —Henry Ward Beecher

Gave off a sense of virility almost as positive as an odor —Samuel Yellen

Get the upper hand ... like a strong sun —Albert Camus

Grew strong, as if doubt never touched his heart —Wallace Stevens

(Our meaning together is) hardy as an onion (and layered) —Marge Piercy

I am as strong as a bull moose —Theodore Roosevelt

I am like a forest that has once been razed; the new shoots are stronger and brisker —Victor Hugo

Looked as durable and tough as a tree growing on a stony hillside —Mazo De La Roche

Solid and strong, like a little bull —Frank Tuohy

Solid as a temple —Louis MacNeice

EERIE AS A MAN CARVING HIS OWN EPITAPH

Strong and hard as a tree —Vicki Baum
> Some other strength/tree comparisons include: "Strong as an old apple tree" (Eudora Welty) and "Sturdy as an oak trunk" (Ignazio Silone).

Strong as a door —Reynolds Price

Strong as a giant —Erich Maria Remarque

(A soul) strong as a mountain river —William Wordsworth

(An alibi as) strong as a twenty-foot wall —Jimmy Sangster

(And the muscles of his brawny arms are) strong as iron bands —Henry Wadsworth Longfellow

Strong as jealousy —William Blake

Strong as money —Philip Levine
> What poet Levine is comparing to the strength of money is work.

(Somone wakens to a life as) strong as the smell of urine —Philip Levine

Strong as the summer sun —Anon

(Had grown) strong as the sun or the sea —Algernon Charles Swinburne

(This old woman is dangerous: she is as) strong as three men —George Bernard Shaw

Strong as the young, and as uncontrolled —Henry Wadsworth Longfellow

Stronger than mahogany —Anne Sexton

Strong, like a tower —Nina Bawden

(Vemish and his wife were) strong, like rocks, not like rivers. Their strength was more in remaining than in doing —Barry Targan

(Your blunderer is as) sturdy as a rock —William Cowper

Takes brute strength, like pushing a cow uphill —Anne Sexton

Using his fist the way a carpenter uses a hammer —Irwin Shaw

You're [Alais addressing King Henry in *The Lion in Winter*] like the rocks at Stonehenge; nothing knocks you down —James Goldman

STRUGGLE
SEE: LIFE

STUBBORNNESS
SEE: PERSISTENCE

STUDENTS
SEE: EDUCATION

STUPIDITY
SEE ALSO: ABSURDITY, INSULTS, MIND

Assholes are like weeds, a bitch to get rid of and when you do,
    another one grows back in the same place —Jonathan Kellerman

Brains like mashed potatoes —Anon

Dumb as a beetle —Anon
        The beetle has been linked to dullness and stupidity since
        the sixteenth century.

Dumb as a stick of wood —Anon

Dumb as pure white lead —John Updike

Had the brains of a Playboy bunny and fucked like one
    —Jonathan Valin

He'd be sharper than a serpent's tooth, if he wasn't as dull as ditch
    water —Charles Dickens
        A Dickensian twist on King Lear's lament about an
        ungrateful child.

He's like the man who thinks it's raining when you pee in his eyes
    —Anon

His head was as empty as a politician's speech —Anon

I'm as thick as a plank —Princess Diana excusing herself from
    playing a game with a patient during a hospital visit, quoted,
    Public Radio

(About as) intelligent as a bundle of shawls —Henry James

Isn't very intelligent ... he's like a hound that simply follows the
    scent. He crumples his nose up, looking for his fleas
    —Henri-Pierre Roche

Like dogs, that meeting with nobody else, bit one another
    —John Ray's *Proverbs*

Stupidity

(He) looked as if he'd stood in line twice when the brains were being handed out —Christopher Hale

Look stupid as a poet in search of a simile —Thomas Holcroft

A man with a small head is like a pin without any, very apt to get into things beyond his depth —Josh Billings

(A snail's about as) smart as mud —CBS-TV news story about snails being grown for escargot lovers, November 5, 1986

(That man is) so stupid it sits on him like a halo —Emlyn Williams

(The free press in Israel has belatedly awakened to the meaning of this act, which was as) stupid as cracking the safe of your own bank —William Safire, *New York Times*/Op-ed, March 9, 1987
    Safire's simile refers to Israel's recruitment of an American as a spy.

Stupid as jugs without handles —Honoré de Balzac

Stupid as oysters —August E. F. Von Kotzbue

To serve an unintelligent man is like crying in the wilderness, massaging the body of a dead man, planting water-lilies on dry land, whispering in the ear of the deaf —Panchatantra

While he was not dumber than an ox, he was not any smarter either —James Thurber

STURDINESS
SEE: STRENGTH

STYLE
SEE: CLOTHING

SUBSERVIENCE
SEE: MEEKNESS

Success/Failure

SUCCESS/FAILURE
SEE ALSO: BUSINESS

The anatomy of the first major success is like the young human body, a miracle only the owner can fully savor —John Fowles

As he rose like a rocket, he fell like a stick —Thomas Paine

A certain prosperity coats these people like scent or the layer of buttery light in a painting by Rubens —Jean Thompson

A conqueror, like a cannon ball, must go on; if he rebounds, his career is over —The Duke of Wellington

(The midlist author is) dogged by his past sales record, like a utility infielder with a .228 lifetime batting average —Phillip Lopate, *New York Times Book Review*, May 24, 1987

Failed ... like an old hanging bridge —Marge Piercy

Fail like a five-year plan —Derek Lambert

Failure grabs a man like an old and shabby suit —Derek Lambert

(A great beauty) flourishing like a rose —Isak Dinesen

Flourishing like a weed in a hot house —Susan Fromberg Schaeffer

Flourishing like trees —Hilma Wolitzer

Had risen to his great height like a man lifted to the ceiling by a sort of slow explosion —G. K. Chesterton

High office is like a pyramid; only two kinds of animals reach the summit, reptiles and eagles —Jean Le Rond d'Alembert

His life, day after day, was failing like an unreplenished stream —Percy Bysshe Shelley

Moving up hand over hand ... like a champion —Tom Wolfe

Pursued success as a knight the Holy Grail —Anon

Sailed through the world like a white yacht jubilant with flags —John Gardner

Selling like lemonade at a track meet —T. Coraghessan Boyle

Sell like hotcakes —Anon
> Different industries have coined many phrases for things which sell well. This American simile which came into use in the middle of the nineteenth century is still the most widely used. For a twist in meaning there's "Selling like cold hot cakes" from *The Last Good Kiss* by James Crumley.

Sold [books by nineteenth century author Karl May] like pancakes topped by wild blueberries and heavy cream —Vincent Canby, *New York Times*, June 25, 1986

Sold like picks and pans in a gold rush —Robert Guenther, *Wall Street Journal*, August 6, 1986

Success/Failure

Success is as ice cold and lonely as the North Pole —Vicki Baum

Success is feminine and like a woman, if you cringe before her, she will override you —William Faulkner
> Faulkner expanded on this simile still further: "So the way to treat her is to show her the back of your hand. Then maybe she will do the crawling."

Success on some men looks like a borrowed coat; it sits on you as though it had been made to order —Edith Wharton

Triumphs like a trumpet —Wallace Stevens

Wanted his success acknowledged ... like the high school loser who dreams of driving to the class reunion in a custom-made sports car —Jean Thompson

Winning an Oscar ... it's like getting thirty thousand red roses at one time —Louise Fletcher, from Rex Reed interview

Wore his success like his health —George Garrett

SUDDENNESS
SEE: SHOCK

SUMMER
SEE: SEASONS

Sun

SUN
SEE ALSO: MOON, SKY

The afternoon sunlight was like gold embroidery on the grass —Paul Horgan

Autumn sunlight poured out over the rock [of Quebec] like a heavy southern wine —Willa Cather

Bars of sunlight crossed the backyard like the bars of a bright strange cell —Carson McCullers

Bits of sunlight bright as butterflies —Eudora Welty

The citronade of the pale morning sun shimmered like a multitude of violins —Angela Carter

The daylight-saving sunshine lay like custard on the oaks and mistletoe —Wallace Stegner

The fast-setting sun lighted the tops of the trees like flames of candles —Z. Vance Wilson

The heat from the scorching [California] sun hit them like a knock-
out punch —Jilly Cooper

The high sun fell like balm on her body —Mary Hedin

The huge sun light flamed like a monstrous dahlia with petals of
yellow fire —Oscar Wilde

It [sunlight] licks thick as a tongue at my skin
—Sharon Sheehe Stark

The last of the sun [at dusk] like a great splash of blood on the sky
—George Garrett

The muffled sunlight gleamed like gold tissue through grey gauze
—Edith Wharton

The new morning sun shone like a pink rose in the heavens
—Kenneth Koch

A pale sun appeared over the clouds like an invalid sitting up in bed
—John Mortimer

A red sun as flat and still against the sky as moonlight on pond
water —Charles Johnson

The red sun was pasted on the sky like a wafer —Anon

The rising sun is like a ball of blood —Robert W. Service

A scarlet sun, round and brilliant as a blooded egg yolk
—Cynthia Ozick

A sharp-as-needle sun sat high over Virginia ... like a heathen god,
sure of itself —Thomas Keneally

The sinking sun hung like a red balloon over the Hudson River
—Belva Plain

The strong sun (of late April) pours down as though a gigantic
golden basin full of light and wind were being emptied on us
—Erich Maria Remarque

The sun advanced on the city and lit the topmost spines of the hill,
painting the olive drab slopes in crazy new colors, like the
drawing of a spangled veil —William Brammer

Sun ... as light and dry as old sherry —Raymond Chandler

Sun

The sun, as red as a furnace on the edge of the horizon
      —Émile Zola

The sun blazed like a flaming bronze mirror —Bernard Malamud

The sun breaks [over the land] like a cracked egg
      —T. Coraghessan Boyle

The sun breaks through the cloud like revelation —Delmore Schwartz

The sun burned feebly through the mist like a circle cut from
      Christmas paper —MacDonald Harris

The sun dazzled off the asphalt in fragments like breaking glass
      —George Garrett

The sun drew strength from them like a giant sponge
      —Caryl Phillips

The sun ... drops on our heads like a stone —Marge Piercy

The sun, dull, like the face of an old man —Maxim Gorky

The sun fades like the spreading of a peacock's tail —John Ashbery

The sun fell thick as a blanket —Lee Smith

The sun flared in the sky, fat and red as a tangerine
      —T. Coraghessan Boyle
            A variation by Marge Piercy: "The sun hangs like a
            tangerine."

The sun flashed like a torrent of warm white wine
      —Du Bose Heyward

The sun floats up above the horizon, like a shimmering white blimp
      —Margaret Atwood

The sun hangs overhead like a lantern —T. Coraghessan Boyle

The sun hits him like a slap in the face —T. Coraghessan Boyle

The sun ... shone like a polished brass knob —Helen Hudson

The sun hung in the cloudless sky like an unblinking yellow eye
      —Harvey Swados

(It was a misty autumn morning,) the sun just struggling through like
      a great chrysanthemum —Pamela Hansford Johnson

The sun lay like a friendly arm across her shoulder
   —Marjorie Kinnan Rawlings

The sun ... lay on the horizon like a dissolving orange suffused with
   blood —John Hawkes

The sunlight dripped over the house like golden paint over an art jar
   —F. Scott Fitzgerald

Sunlight dropped into it (the dark foliage) like a drizzle of gold
   —Isak Dinesen

Sunlight fell like a shower of gold through the leaves of the chestnut
   trees —Silvia Tennenbaum

The sunlight hit her like a boxing glove —Jilly Cooper

The sunlight ... plunged like tiny knives into my already bleary eyes
   —James Crumley

Sunlight splashed through the trees, the beams hazy like shafts of
   light filtered through stained glass —Robert J. Serling

Sunlight that was like a bright driving summer rain —Paule Marshall

Sun (is sitting atop the trees) like a big round cheddar
   —T. Coraghessan Boyle

The sun looks, through the mist, like a plum on the tree of heaven,
   or a bruise on the slope of your belly —William H. Gass

The sun lulled in the sky like a mule —Larry McMurtry

The sun overhead beat the surface of the pool like a drum
   —James B. Hall

The sun peeping above the trees, looked like a giant golf ball
   —P. G. Wodehouse
      Wodehouse was known for his golf stories so this is a
      particularly apt comparison for him.

The sun ... poised like a ball of fire on the very edge of the
   mountains —Henry Van Dyke

The sun popped over the edge of the prairie like a broad smiling
   face —Willa Cather

The sun poured down like fire —Isaac Bashevis Singer

Sun ... reflected back to me like a shiny bedspread whose design is
   hundreds of wind-driven roller coasters —Richard Brautigan

The sun rested like a warm palm on the back of her neck
    —Francis King

The sun rolled over the horizon like the red rim of a wagon wheel
    —Rita Mae Brown

The sun ... rose swiftly and flashed like a torch with dazzling rays
    —Felix Salten

The sunshine burned the pasture like fire —Rudyard Kipling

The sunshine [of January day] cut like icicles —Edith Wharton

The sunshine made spots before your eyes ... as though a thousand
    weddings were to be held that day —Boris Pasternak

Sunshine spread like butter over the fields
    —Lael Tucker Wertenbaker

Sunshine that stretched like cloth of gold all up and down Fifth
    Avenue —Helen Hudson

The sun shone as if there were no death —Saul Bellow

The sun shone like a million dollars —Larry McMurtry

The sun shone like Mr. Happy Face himself —Tom Robbins

The sun shone with such violence that in an illumination like a long-
    prolonged glare of lightning the heavens looked black and white
    —Eudora Welty

The sun shot upward and began to spin like a red cup on the point
    of a spear —Isaac Babel

Sun sizzling like a skillet in the sky —Helen Hudson

Sun slanting like a blade —Bin Ramke

The sun's rays like sheaves of wheat are gold and dry
    —Dame Edith Sitwell

The sun stood still like a great shining altar
    —Hans Christian Andersen

The sun swerves silently like a cyclist round the bend
    —Herbert Read

The sun throbbed like a fever —William Plomer

Sun ... huge as a mountain of diamonds —Dame Edith Sitwell

The sun up in the towering sky turns like a spinning ball
    —Edwin Muir

The sun was high enough to sit on the roofs of buildings like a
    great open fire warming everything —Mark Helprin

The sun was like a burning-glass —William Plomer
        This comparison from a poem entitled *In the Snake Park*
        refers to a lens used to focus the sun's rays to start a fire.

The sun was like a good cup of tea, strong and hot —Mike Fredman

The sun was like a hot iron on their backs —Paul Horgan

The sun was like a whip —T. Coraghessan Boyle

The sun was pouring in like maple syrup into a green bowl
    —Carlos Baker

The sun was shining like a congratulation —Margaret Millar

The sun was streaking the sky with strips of red and white, like a
    slab of bacon —Jean Thompson

[Sun] swung ... like a faded shabby orange —Hugh Walpole

(While they embraced,) the sun vanished as if it had been switched
    off —W. P. Kinsella

The white sun twinking like the dawn under a speckled cloud
    —Percy Bysshe Shelley

The yellow sun was ugly, like a raw egg on a plate
    —Elizabeth Bishop

SUPERFLUOUSNESS
SEE: NECESSITY

SURPRISE
SEE: SHOCK

SURVIVAL
SEE: IMPOSSIBILITY, SUCCESS/FAILURE

SUSPENSE
SEE: EXCITEMENT

SWEARING
SEE: WORD(S)

SWEAT
SEE: SMELL

SWEETNESS
SEE: TASTE

SWIMMING
SEE: SPORTS

SYMPATHY
SEE: KINDNESS

TACT
SEE: INSULTS

TALENT
SEE: ABILITY

Talkativeness

TALKATIVENESS
SEE ALSO: CONVERSATION

As full of words as a hen salmon of eggs —Ben Ames Williams

Babble as one mad with wine —Algernon Charles Swinburne

Chattered like a shipload of monkeys in a storm —Anon

Chattered like squirrels —Larry McMurtry

Chattered on like a lunatic chimpanzee —Truman Capote

Chattered on like a chickadee in a feed trough —Donald McCaig

Chattering ... like a flock of starlings —Jimmy Sangster

Chattering like magpies —Christina Rossetti

Chattering like one to whom speech was a new accomplishment
    —Calder Willingham

Chatter like a bluejay —Eleanor Clark

Chatter like a mob of sparrows —Jerome K. Jerome

Chatter like sick flies —Algernon Charles Swinburne

Gabbled on like machines set in motion —Charlotte Brontë

Gabbling at one another like so many turkeys —Harvey Swados

Great talkers are like leaky pitchers, everything runs out of them
  —H. G. Bohn's *Handbook of Proverbs*

Had a tongue that flapped like a banner in a fair wind
  —George Garrett

He was like a man who'd just emerged from six months in solitary,
  like the sole survivor of a shipwreck, Crusoe with a captive
  audience: he could not shut up —T. Coraghessan Boyle

Jabbered on like a drunk old uncle —Richard Ford

Like a book in breeches ... he [Macaulay] has occasional flashes of
  silence, that make his conversation perfectly delightful
  —Sydney Smith

Like a crane or a swallow, so did I chatter —*The Holy Bible/Isaiah*

Long-winded as a writer who gets paid by the word —Anon

Open [up, with information] like a wet envelope —Harold Adams

[Coleridge] speaks incessantly, not thinking or imagining or
  remembering, but combining all these processes into one; as a
  rich and lazy housewife might mingle her soup and fish, beef
  and custard into one unspeakable mass —Thomas Carlyle

Talkative persons are like barrels; the less there is in them, the more
  noise they make —John Gideon Mulligan

Talked and talked like a man in a high fever
  —Erich Maria Remarque

Talked on and on as if he was rehearsing for a speech
  —John Dos Passos

A tremendous talker and like a greedy eater at an ordinary dinner,
  keeping to himself an entire dish of which everyone present
  would like to have partaken —*Punch*, 1857

Went into detail ... like an obstetrician describing how he got two
  fingers in to turn the baby's head out of breech, or, yes, like an
  old fisherman taking you along step by step on how to bait a
  hook so that the wriggler stays alive —Norman Mailer

The words came out of his throat like a cataract —Carson McCullers

Words came tumbling out of me like coins from a change dispenser
  —Natascha Wodin

Talkativeness

Words flowed from him like oil from a gusher —O. Henry

Wordy like somebody with a fever —George Garrett

The world to him is a vast lecture-platform ... as one long after-dinner, with himself as the principal speaker of the evening —P. G. Wodehouse

Taste

TASTE

A mouth on me like a Turkish wrestler's jock-strap —M. C. Beaton

As pleasingly prickly as a kitten's tongue
    —Slogan for Gevrey-Chambertin wine

A fastidious taste is like a squeamish appetite; the one has its origin in some disease of the mind, as the other has in some ailment of the stomach —Robert Southey

Full of rich flavor as a piece torn off an old shirt
    —Raymond Chandler

His mouth felt as if it had been to a party without him
    —Peter DeVries

His mouth was tastelessly dry, as though he had been eating dust
    —Joseph Conrad

My mouth [from smoking a cigarette] tasted like a cross between charred sticks and spoiled eggs —Sue Grafton

My mouth was dry and tasty as a hen-coop floor —Harold Adams

My mouth tasted like an old penny —Robert B. Parker

My tongue felt like a slice of ham in my mouth, salty and pink
    —Jay Parini

Palates like shoe leather —Angela Carter

(Melons ... as) sweet to the tongue as gold is to the mind
    —Borden Deal

Tasted like a fart —Reynolds Price

Tasted like it had been fried in tar —Larry McMurtry

Taste is the luxury of abeyant claims and occurs, like Wordsworth's poetry, in a kind of tranquillity —Stanley Elkin

Taste like a cup of lukewarm consomme' at a spinsterish tearoom
—Raymond Chandler, on mystery writing

(The crap still in his mouth made everything) taste like feathers
—William McIlvanney

Taste like the Volga at low tide —Line from movie *Love At First Bite*.
The character making this comparison is Count Von Dracula.

Tastes like cool, wet sand under pearly seaside light —Slogan for
Château Guiraud's Château "G" wine

Tastes like the wrath to come —Irvin S. Cobb
Cobb used the comparison to describe the taste of corn
liquor.

Tastes rather like an old attic —J. B. Priestly

Tasty as summer's first peach —Elyse Sommer

Tasty, like an angel pissing on your tongue —Anon
This was used throughout the galleys of Great Lakes
steamships to describe good-tasting liquid or solid food.

TEACHERS/TEACHING
SEE: EDUCATION

TEDIUM
SEE: BOREDOM

TEETH

Beautiful teeth, like china plates —Rosellen Brown

Big teeth ... like chunks of solidified milk —Frank Swinnerton

Front teeth showed like those of a squirrel —George Ade

(When she opened her mouth) gaps like broken window panes could
be seen in her teeth —Sholem Asch

Her front teeth overlapped each other like dealt cards
—Alice McDermott

His teeth looked like a picket fence in a slum neighborhood
—Stephen King

His [false] teeth moved slightly, like the keyboards of a piano
—Pamela Hansford Johnson

Teeth

His teeth stood out like scored corks set in a jagged row
—Sterling Hayden

Lower teeth crooked, as if some giant had taken his face and squeezed them loose from his jaw —Larry McMurtry

My teeth felt like they had little sweaters on them —Anon

Sharp-worn teeth like slivers of rock —Ella Leffland

The shiny new false teeth gave him the peculiar look of someone who smiles for a living —Andrew Kaplan

Small pointed teeth, like a squirrel's —Willa Cather

Teeth all awry and at all angles like an old fence —George Garrett

Teeth, as yellow as old ivory —Frank Swinnerton

Teeth ... big and even as piano keys —Helen Hudson

Teeth ... channelled and stained like the teeth of an old horse
—R. Wright Campbell

Teeth ... chattering like castanets —Maurice Edelman

Teeth clatter like ice cubes in a blender —Ira Wood

Teeth clicking like dice —T. Coraghessan Boyle

Teeth like cream —Willa Cather

Teeth like a row of alabaster Britannicas —Joe Coomer

Teeth like pearls —Robert Browning

Teeth like piano keys —Elizabeth Spencer

Teeth like white mosaics shone —Herbert Read

Teeth ... tapping together like typewriter keys —Cornell Woolrich

White teeth, the kind that look like cheap dentures even when they are not —Eric Ambler

TEMPER
SEE: ANGER

TEMPERAMENT
SEE: PERSONAL TRAITS

TEETH CLICKING LIKE DICE

TEMPTATION
SEE: ATTRACTION

TENACITY
SEE: PERSISTENCE

TENDERNESS
SEE: KINDNESS

TENNIS
SEE: SPORTS

Tension

TENSION
SEE ALSO: ANXIETY, CANDOR

Back ... tense as a tiger's —D. H. Lawrence

Body rigid from shoulder to belly as though he had been stricken with elphantiasis —Kenzaburo Oë

(There continued to be) a certain strain, like dangerously stretched rubber bands —Thalia Selz

Feel tension rising off me like a fever —Anonymous

Felt his insides drawn together like the lips of a wound —Helen Hudson

Felt like a swimmer about to dive —Marguerite Yourcenar

His solar plexus knotted up like a sea anemone —Ursula Le Guin

In times of stress I enter into a semicomatose state like an instinct-driven opossum —Leigh Allison Wilson

My back became like a stick —Natsume Sōseki

My stomach drops as if I'm in a balky elevator —W. P. Kinsella

(Looked about as) relaxed as a safecracker —Joseph Wambaugh

Spines ... stiffened like pulled twine —Louise Erdrich

Stiffen like a cat that's been hit by something —Shirley Ann Grau

(When I approach you) stiffen like an egg white —Diane Ackerman

Stiffen like a stump —David Wagoner

Strung up like a piano wire —Elizabeth Spencer

(Body) taut like wire —Anaïs Nin

Tense and careful as a man handling a bomb
    —Dorothy Canfield Fisher

Tense and fluttering like a fish out of water —George Garrett

Tense and still like a figure in a frieze —Ross Macdonald

Tense as an animal in fear, ready to snap or go limp beneath its
    keeper's grasp —Louise Erdrich

(I lay) tense as a piano wire —W. P. Kinsella

Tense as a player on the bench —Maureen Howard, *New York Times
    Magazine*, May 25, 1986

Tense as a thoroughbred at the starting gate —Anon television
    feature on New York marathoners, November 1, 1986

Tense as a wound spring —Joseph Heller

(Voices) tense as barks —Edward Hoagland

(People were as) tense as fiddle strings —Dorothy Canfield Fisher

Tense as if my neck were tipped back, my mouth agape, and I was
    preparing for the dentist's needle —W. P. Kinsella

Tense as rectitude —Norman Mailer

Tension broke like heat after a thunderstorm in a nervous burst of
    laughter —Lael Tucker Wertenbaker

Tension ran like a red-hot wire through the men
    —Marjory Stoneman Douglas

Tension stretching like taut wires across the room —Ross Macdonald

Tension ... vibrates like a melancholy bell —David K. Shipler, *New
    York Times Book Review*, March 1, 1987

Tight as a duck —Graham Masterton
        The simile was found as part of a sex scene. In full context
        it reads: "With her own fingers, she slipped him inside her,
        and although she was as tight as a duck, she was also
        warm and wet and irresistible."

(His hand was) tight as a knot —Ann Beattie

Tension

Tight as a man going to the electric chair —Norman Mailer
> Mailer before being interviewed by Mike Wallace.

Tight as a quivering string —David Nevin

Tight as a sheet on a hospital bed —Anon

(Throats were) tight as tourniquets —Karl Shapiro

Tightly controlled ... as if he was tied down to his desk by leather straps —Anon White House colleague about Robert McFarlane during the Iran-Contra scandal, quoted in New York Times, March 2, 1987

(He always came back from the ballfield) turned tighter than the bolts on an automobile tire —Norman Keifetz
> The simile from a novel about a baseball player (*The Sensation*) continues as follows: "By that jack-handle known as 'being a pro'."

TENTATIVENESS
SEE: UNCERTAINTY

TERROR
SEE: FEAR

THEATER
SEE: STAGE AND SCREEN

THEORIES
SEE: IDEAS

Thickness

THICKNESS

Newspaper ... thick as a folded bath towel —W. P. Kinsella

Richly covered ... as a hen is with feathers —Anon

Thick ... as a brier patch with briers —Ellen Glasgow

Thick as a mist —Percy Bysshe Shelley

Thick as autumnal leaves —John Milton

Thick as blood —Anon
> This is used with many different reference points. To cite two examples from current fiction: "An aroma thick as blood" from Frank Conroy's *Stop-Time* and "Automobile traffic thick as blood" from the story, *White Gardens*, by Mark Helprin.

Thick as elephant trunks —Kay Boyle

Thick as foreign coffee —Sylvia Plath

(The atmosphere of sex is) thick as the dark —John Rechy

(Exudes self-disgust) thick as the smell of a slept-in undershirt
     —Rosellen Brown

(Fog) thick as night —Gertrude Atherton

THINNESS
SEE ALSO: BODY

Body ... as meager as a pole —Leslie Thomas

Lean and thin as a fallen leaf —George Garrett

Lean as a bird dying in the snow —Émile Zola

Lean as a herring —Irwin Shaw

Lean as a shadow or ghost —George Garrett

Lean as a snake —John Berryman

Lean as a whipcord —Norman Mailer

Lean as El Greco's Saint Andres —Harry Prince

Lean as the dead branch of a tree —Frank Swinnerton

Lean as Ugulino —Dylan Thomas
          The comparison refers to Count Ugolino of Pisa,
          imprisoned and starved to death in Dante's *Inferno*.

Leaner than wasps —Phyllis McGinley
          McGinley's comparison referred to the stone lions at the
          doors of the New York Hispanic Society building.

Looked beaky and thin, like a bird —Mavis Gallant

Looking as skinny and blue as a jailhouse tattoo —Tom Robbins

Looks as if he's been carved from a shadow —T. Coraghessan Boyle

[A red line in the sky at dawn] narrow as a needle
     —John D. MacDonald

Skinny as a fence post —George Garrett

Slender as a flower's stem —Arthur Sherburne Hardy

Thinness

Slim and evasive as a needle's eye —Paige Mitchell

Slim as a cat —Sue Grafton

Slim as a little serpent —Anton Chekhov

Slim as a mast —Geoffrey Chaucer

Slim ... like a twig stripped of bark —John Updike

So skinny he looked as though, if you shook him, his bones would sound like one of those Javanese musicians who play on coconut shells —Leslie Hanscomb, *Newsday*, September 11, 1986
> The thin man so described is Frank Sinatra in his early days.

So skinny he looked like he'd been pulled through a keyhole —Fred Allen

So skinny you clack like a floating crap game when you walk down the street —Russell Baker

So thin that he was like a clothed skeleton —Jean Rhys

So thin that if you touch her back you can feel the ribs, like ridges on a roll-top desk —Leslie Garis, *New York Times Magazine*, February 8, 1987
> The person thus described is author Joan Didion.

(She remained) thin as a baseball contract —Norman Keifetz

Thin and clear as green leaves in April —Elinor Wylie

Thin and quiet as shadows —George Garrett

Thin as a bean pole —Anon

Thin as a cobweb —Jean Garrigue

Thin as a dime —American colloquialism, attributed to New England

Thin as a file —Reynolds Price

Thin as a moonbeam —Max Apple

Thin as an empty dress —Marge Piercy

Thin as an exclamation mark —Anon

Thin as an onion shoot —Gloria Norris

Thin as a pauper's wallet —Anon

Thin as a pencil line —Mary Lee Settle

Thin as a rail —American colloquialism, attributed to New England

[A heron] thin as a safety pin —Susan Minot

Thin as a scythe —Donald Justice

Thin as a sheet (his mother came to him) —John Berryman

Thin as a sheeted ghost —Stevie Smith

Thin as a thread —William H. Hallhan

Thin as a switch —Mark Helprin

Thin as a thermometer —Albert L. Weeks

Thin as a walking stick —Doris Grumback

(The steering wheel is ...) thin as a whip —John Updike

Thin as a whisper —Anon

Thin as a wire —Raymond Chandler

Thin as breath —Sharon Sheehe Stark

Thin as chop-sticks —Rumer Godden

[Partitions] thin as crackers —Tom Robbins

Thin as linguini —Anon

[Children] thin as little white-haired ghosts —Carson McCullers

(The old man looked) thin as paper —Richard Ford
    An extension made popular in New England is: "Thin as
    the paper on the wall."

Thin as pared soap —Sharon Olds
    In the poem in which this appears, the simile is extended
    to include breasts "As opalescent as soap bubbles."

Thin as phantoms —Thomas Hardy

(Her face, without make-up, was an oval of white that looked as)
    thin as porcelain —Paul Theroux

[TV antennas] thin as skeletons —Italo Calvino

Thin as tapers —T. Coraghessan Boyle

Thin as the edge of the moon —Stephen Vincent Benét

Thin as the girl who didn't have enough to her to itch —Anon

Thin as the girl who swallowed the pit of an olive and was rushed to a maternity ward —Anon

Thin as the homeopathic soup that was made by boiling the shadow of a pigeon that had starved to death —Abraham Lincoln, October 13, 1852 speech

Thin as the line between self-confidence and conceit —Anon

Thin as the skin seaming a scar —Sylvia Plath

Thin as tissue —H. E. Bates

(Skin) thin as tracing paper —John Updike

Thin ... like a skeleton —Ann Petry

THOUGHTS
SEE ALSO: IDEAS, INTELLIGENCE

Common thoughts on common things, which time is shaking, day by day, like feathers from his wings —John Greenleaf Whittier

Each was in his own thoughts, like a sleeping-bag —William McIlvanney

Every thought is like dough; you have only to knead it well; you can make anything you like out of it —Ivan Turgenev

Exceptions [to theories] would crowd into her mind like a mob of unruly children —Peter Meinke

(He succeeded in starting) a familiar train of thought ... like a brackish taste in his mouth —Dorothy Canfield Fisher

Great thoughts, like great deeds, need no trumpet —P. J. Bailey

Heavy on my mind, like a lump of soggy yeast dough, expanding, suffocating, blotting out all other thoughts —Mignon F. Ballard

Her thought ran like a barge along a river —Marianne Wiggins

Her thoughts ran round and round like dogs trapped behind a fence —Marge Piercy

Her thoughts rose as a veil before her vision —Charles Johnson

Her thoughts seemed to lead backwards and forwards like a shuttle
weaving the moments, hours, days together in a pattern
—Rumer Godden

(Booksellers were like dope-pushers to him.) He was like a junkie on
thought —Saul Bellow
Bellow's simile describes an avid reader.

His thoughts like wild animals fed upon themselves
—Charles Johnson

His thoughts went round and round like rats in a cage
—Stephen Vincent Benét

Human thought is not a firework, ever shooting off fresh forms and
shapes as it burns; it is a tree growing very slowly
—Jerome K. Jerome

Human thought, like God, makes the world in its own image
—Adam Clayton Powell

I have thought about you until I feel like a bee —William Diehl

I will not go so far as to say that to construct a history of thought
without profound study of the mathematical ideas of successive
epochs is like omitting Hamlet from the play which (was) named
after him ... but it is certainly analogous to cutting out the part
of Ophelia —Alfred North Whitehead

Meditative ... like the chirping of a solitary little bird —Eudora Welty

Meditative, like a girl trying to decide which dress to wear to a party
—O. Henry

Men's thoughts are thin and flimsy like lace; they are themselves
pitiable like the lacemakers —Soren Kierkegaard

My mind paddles away like a wooden spoon in a bowl of dough
—Richard Maynard

My thoughts are like sprouts, like sprouts on the branch of your
brain —Edna O'Brien

My thoughts are whirled like a potter's wheel —William Shakespeare
A variation in common use: "My head is spinning like a
merry-go-round."

My thoughts turn over like a patchwork quilt —Diane Wakoski

Thoughts

Our thoughts are always happening ... like leaves floating down a
     stream or clouds crossing the sky, they just keep coming
          —Ram Dass and Paul Gorman

Preoccupied in following his own thought, like someone out to net a
     butterfly —William McIlvanney

Reasoning comes as naturally to man as flying to birds —Quintilian

Reflective as an old sextant —Richard Ford

Ripe in her thought like a fresh apple fallen from the limb
     —Karl Shapiro

Sudden a thought came like a full-blown rose —John Keats

Thinking is like loving and dying. Each of us must do it for himself
          —Josiah Royce

Thinking was like a fountain. Once it gets going at a certain
          pressure, well, it is almost impossible to turn it off
     —Walter de la Mare

Thought ascends, and buds from the brain, as the fruit from the root
     —Victor Hugo

A thought as neat and final as though a ticker tape had fed it into
     his brain and left off with a row of dots —Kaatje Hurlbut

The thought ... clanged like pipes in my mind —Scott Spencer

The thought kept beating in her like her heart —Wallace Stevens
          The World as Meditation, from which this is taken, follows
               the simile with this sentence: "The two kept beating
               together."

The thought [of women] ... once it came it usually tended to stay for
     several hours, filling his noggin like a cloud of gnats
     —Larry McMurtry

Thoughts buzzing in his head like crazy flies —H. E. Bates

(His) thoughts drove in like a night-cloud —Stevie Smith

Thoughts ... fall from him like chantering from an abundant poet
     —Wallace Stevens

Thoughts flickering like heat lightning —F. van Wyck Mason

Thoughts floating like light clouds through the upper air of his mind
     —George Santayana

Thoughts ... flowing in unison, like a mountain-stream and a lake-
     stream meeting, but not yet merging, in a single river
     —George Santayana

Thoughts ground each other as millstones grind when there is no
     corn in between —Rudyard Kipling

Thoughts like fleas jump from man to man, but they don't bite
     everybody —Anon

The thought ... slipped through his mind like a dot of quicksilver
     —Stanley Elkin

(Foolish) thoughts play in her mind like firelight and shadow in a
     dim room —George Garrett

Thoughts ran like squirrels in the boy's head —Conrad Richter

Thoughts rising like fish to the fluid surface of his mind
     —Ellen Glasgow

(Lying awake with her) thoughts running round and round inside her
     skull like trapped mice —Josephine Tey

Thoughts spinning and tumbling like a week's wash —Julia Whedon

Thoughts that peel off and fly away at breathless speeds like the last
     stubborn leaves ripped from wet branches —John Ashbery

Thoughts ... tied up in knots like snakes, squeezing and suffocating
     them —V. S. Pritchett

Thoughts ... twisting like snakes through his brain —Alice Walker

Thoughts ... untidily stacked like dishes slanting (in) a full sink
     —Lincoln Kirstein

Thoughts ... vague and pale, like ghosts —Jean Rhys

Thoughts veering through her like a flight of birds —Anon

Thoughts went on, coming and going like leaves blown in the wind
     —Ellen Glasgow

Thoughts wheeled like a flight of bats in her mind —Ellen Glasgow

Thoughts which moved, like the clouds, slowly, shedding dim yet
     vivid light —Iris Murdoch

Thoughts

Thoughts ... whirling around on themselves, like the apocryphal snake seizing its own tail and then devouring itself —Stanley Elkin

Unusable and contradictory thoughts filled Quinn's mind with almost physical duress as though his poor head were a golf ball which, slashed open, shows its severed rubber filaments snapping and racing about in confusion —Thomas McGuane

When thought grows old and worn with usage it should, like current coin, be called in, and from the mint of genius, reissued fresh and new —Alexander Smith

Thrift

THRIFT

Act like they are bargaining with some Arab street trader ... like they are buying lemons —John Wainwright

False economy is like stopping one hole in a sieve —Samuel Johnson, April 17, 1788

Frugal as a poor farmer's wife —George Garrett

Generous as someone who would give you the sleeves out of his vest —Anon

His money comes from him like drops of blood —John Ray's *Proverbs*

Kept his wallet shut tight as an accordion —Anon

Pinches a penny like money is going out of style —George Garrett

Soliciting a miser is like fishing in the desert —Solomon Ibn Gabirol

Thrifty as a French peasant —G. K. Chesterton

Tight as a miser's wallet —Anon

Tight as a scout knot —Geoffrey Wolff
    In his novel, *Providence*, Wolff expands upon the simile with "Wouldn't pay a nickel to watch an earthquake."

Tight as a tic —Anon

Tight as Dick's headband —American colloquialism
    This was coined by and is still used by Texas ranchers.

Tight as the bark to a tree —American colloquialism

This still popular simile originated in New Hampshire. A variation from Indiana, "Tight as a wad," has pretty much given way to the jargon word 'tightwad.' There's also Ulysses S. Grant's literal application to describe the pantaloons he had to wear as a West Point cadet as being, "Tight to my skin as the bark to a tree."

Tight as the paper on the wall —Mignon Eberhart

Watch pennies like a streetcar conductor —Irwin Shaw

THUNDER AND LIGHTNING
SEE ALSO: NATURE

(There was the low boom of) distant thunder echoing like cannon —Barbara Taylor Bradford

Heard the heat thunder roll ... like a hard apple rattling in the bottom of a barrel —James Lee Burke

Lightning plays over the horizon like the flicker of ideas —T. Coraghessan Boyle

Lightning and thunder spat and roared like a wounded tiger —Robert Traver

Lightning falls like silent saber blows —Erich Maria Remarque

Lightning flickers like a genie inside the bottle-shaped cloud —Walker Percy

Lightning flutters ... like a wing—like a broken bird —Katherine Mansfield

Lightning ... letting down thick drips of thunder like pig iron from the heart of a white-hot furnace —F. Scott Fitzgerald

Lightning snapped at the world like a whip —John Rechy

Lightning winked across the eastern sky like fitful fireflies —Fletcher Knebel

Thunder beating like tribal drums —T. Coraghessan Boyle

Thunder like great stones falling —Stephen Longstreet

Thunder rolled like a cannon —Anon

Thunder rustling like water down the sky's eaves —A. R. Ammons

Thunder and Lightning

Thunder sounded like a far-off cracking of the earth
　　—Martin Cruz Smith

Thunder steps down like a giant walking the earth
　　—T. Coraghessan Boyle

A thunderstorm came rushing down ... roaring like a brontosaur
　　—Carlos Baker

TIDINESS
SEE: ORDER/DISORDER

TIGHTNESS
SEE: TENSION, THRIFT

Time

TIME
SEE ALSO: DEATH, LIFE

About as much time left as an ice cube in a frying pan
　　—William Diehl

Any decent church service lasts forty-five minutes, like the sex act
　　—Heinrich Böll

As the waves make toward the pebbled shore, so do our minutes
　　hasten to their end —William Shakespeare

As the years go by me, my life keeps filling up with names like
　　abandoned cemeteries —Yehuda Amichai

The day runs through me as water through a sieve —Samuel Butler

The days chase one another like kittens chasing their tails
　　—H. L. Mencken

The days slipped by ... like apple-parings under a knife
　　—Stephen Vincent Benét

A decade falling like snow on top of another —Elizabeth Hardwick

Each class seemed endless to him, as if the hour were stuck to his
　　back like his damp shirt —Helen Hudson

Each year is like a snake that swallows its tail
　　—Robert Penn Warren
　　　　This line is the curtain raiser for Warren's poem, *Paradigm*.

Every day yawned like a week —Donald Seaman

Forty-five minutes passed, like a very slow cloud —Dylan Thomas

Here [at a country inn] time swings idly as a toy balloon
  —Phyllis McGinley

The hours weighed like centuries on his heart —Lawrence Durrell

If time seems to pass so quickly, this is because there are no
  landmarks. Like the moon when it is at its heights on the
  horizon —Albert Camus

The hours [with nothing to do] hunted him like a pack of
  bloodhounds —Edith Wharton

If you let slip time, like a neglected rose it withers on the stalk with
  languished head —John Milton

The lagging hours of the day went by like windless clouds over a
  tender sky —Percy Bysshe Shelley
       The word 'over' is spelled 'o'er' in the original.

Leisure is like a beautiful garment that will not do for constant wear
  —Anon

Life goes like the river —Clifford Odets

Like a run in a stocking. It [lost time] always got worse
  —Anne Morrow Lindbergh

Like January weather, the years will bite and smart —Dorothy Parker

Like sand poured in a careful measure from the hand, the weeks
  flowed down —Paule Marshall

Like the swell of some sweet tune, morning rises into noon, May
  glides onward into June —Henry Wadsworth Longfellow

Like the waves make towards the pebbled shore, so do our minutes
  hasten to their end —William Shakespeare

The minutes crawl like last year's flies —Ridgely Torrence

The minutes ticked off like separate eternities —Dan Wakefield

The moment hung in time like a miner's hat on an oaken peg in a
  saloon abandoned ninety years ago —Loren D. Estleman

The moment shimmered like a glass of full-bodied wine
  —Marge Piercy

The moments [between two people] were stretching longer and
  longer, like so many rubber bands —Elizabeth Spencer

My days are consumed like smoke —*The Holy Bible/Psalms*

The passing years are like a mist sweeping up from the sea of time
so that my memories acquire new aspects
—W. Somerset Maugham

Saw the days of the year stretching ahead like a series of bright,
white boxes, and separating one box from another was sleep, like
a black shade —Sylvia Plath

She was forever saving time, like bits of string —Helen Hudson

Slowly the generations pass, like sand through heaven's blue hour-
glass —Vachel Lindsay
Lindsay used this simile as a repeated refrain for his poem
Shantung.

The summer was melting away like the unfinished ice cream Sonny
left on his plate —Dan Wakefield

That night and the next day swept past like the waters of a rapids
—James Crumley

(Time seems thin, one-dimensional,) the hours long and slender,
stretched like a wire —Dan Wakefield

There is a rhythm inside a year of time, like a great mainspring that
keeps it ticking from spring to summer to fall to winter
—Borden Deal

Time ... a substance of some sort which existence burned up like a
fire —Susan Fromberg Schaeffer

Time can be nibbled away as completely as a tray of canapés in an
irresolute fat man's reach, or grandly lost in victory like the great
marlin in *The Old Man and the Sea* [by Hemingway]
—Charles Poore

Time crawled like ants —Marge Piercy

Time crouched, like a great cat, motionless but for tail's twitch
—Robert Penn Warren

Time dripped like drops of blood —Yukio Mishima

Time drops sail like a ketch in a lagoon —Diane Ackerman

Time fled past us like a startled bird —James Crumley

Time flies ... like an arrow —Amy Hempel

SHE WAS FOREVER SAVING TIME, LIKE BITS OF STRING

Time goes cooly through the funnel of his fingers ... like water over stones —William H. Gass

Time has moved on like a great flock of geese —Stephen Minot

Time is a storm in which we are all lost —William Carlos Williams

Time is like an enterprising manager always bent on staging some new and surprising production, without knowing very well what it will be —George Santayana

Time is like a river made up of the events which happen, and its current is strong. No sooner does anything appear than it is swept away and another comes in its place, and will be swept away too —Marcus Aurelius

Time is like money; the less we have of it to spare the further we make it go —Josh Billings

Time is like some balked monster, waiting outside the valley, to pounce on the slackers who have managed to evade him longer than they should —James Hilton

Time, like a flurry of wild rain, shall drift across the darkened pane —Charles G. D. Roberts

Time like an ever-rolling stream bears all its sons away —Isaac Watts

Time, like a pulse, shakes fierce through all the worlds —Dante Gabriel Rossetti

Time looked like snow dropping silently into a black room or ... like a silent film in an ancient theatre, one hundred billion faces falling like those New Year balloons, down and down into nothing —Ray Bradbury

Time moves ... like a treacle —Hortense Calisher

Time passes as on a fast day —Anon

Time pleated like a fan —Julia O'Faolain

Time pulses from the afternoon like blood from a serious wound —Hilma Wolitzer

Time roared in his ears like wind —John Barth
See Also: NOISE

Time roars in my ears like a river —Derek Walcott

Time rushes past us like the snowflake on the river —Gore Vidal

Time seemed to have slowed down, dividing itself into innumerable
   fractions, like Zeno's space or marijuana hours —Ross Macdonald

Time ... sounded like water running in a dark cave and voices crying
   and dirt dropping down upon hollow box lids, and rain
   —Ray Bradbury

Time sticking to her like cold grease —Marge Piercy

Time swells like a wave at a wall and bursts to eternity
   —George Barker

Time went on like an unchanging ribbon drawn across a turbulent
   background —Heinrich Böll

Upon his silver hairs, time, like a Panama hat, sits at a tilt and
   smiles —Karl Shapiro
         In his poem, *Boy-Man*, Shapiro expands on the simile as
         follows: " ... and smiles. To him the world has just begun.
         And every city waiting to be built."

The week is dealt out like a hand —Randall Jarrell

The week passed slowly ... like a prolonged Sunday —Edith Wharton

When a man sits with a pretty girl for an hour, it seems like a
   minute. When he sits on a hot stove for a minute, then it's
   longer than any hour —Albert Einstein

When you're deeply absorbed in what you're doing, time gives itself
   to you like a warm and willing lover —Brendan Francis

The years are crawling over him like wee red ants —Ogden Nash

The years come close around me like a crowd of the strangers I
   knew once —Randall Jarrell

The years dropped from Randstable [character in novel] like a heavy
   overcoat —James Morrow

The years like great black oxen tread the world, and God the
   herdsman goads them on behind —W. B. Yeats

The years peeled back like the skin of an onion, layer on top of
   layer —T. Coraghessan Boyle

The years rolled in against one another like a rush of water
   —Frieda Arkin

The years shall run like rabbits —W. H. Auden

The years ticked past like crabs —Randall Jarrell

Years which rushed over her like weathered leaves in a storm
    —Ellen Glasgow

A year that dragged like a terminal illness —Rosellen Brown

TIREDNESS
SEE: WEARINESS

TOBACCO
SEE: SMELLS

TONGUE
SEE: MOUTH, SHARPNESS

TRADING
SEE: SUCCESS/FAILURE

TRAFFIC
SEE: VEHICLES

TRANSIENCE
SEE: DEATH, LIFE

TRANSPORTATION
SEE: VEHICLES

TREES
SEE ALSO: NATURE

Apple-trees on which the apples looked like great shining soap
    bubbles —Hans Christian Andersen

The bark hung in ribbons from the trunks like the flayed skins of
    living creatures —R. Wright Campbell

Beeches ... their beautiful bare green trunks like limbs
    —Elizabeth Bowen

The big pine was like greenish bronze against the October sky
    —Ellen Glasgow

(In the moonlight) the big trees around us looked as bare as gallows
    —John Braine

The birches bend like women —Caroline Finkelstein

The birches stand out ... like gay banners on white poles
    —Erich Maria Remarque

The birch trees wavered their stark shadows across it [snow] like supplicating arms —Leo Tolstoy

Boughs ... as rough and hornily buckled as the hands of old farmers —Margaret Laurence

[Tree] branches ... looked like the powerful contorted fingers of a gigantic hand —Sholem Asch

The branches [of a weeping willow] were thin, like the bleached bones of a skeleton —Daphne du Maurier

Cedars ... black and pointed on the sky like a paper silhouette —William Faulkner

Chestnut trees ... their clusters of white blossoms like candelabras —Dorothea Straus

Copses of hazel and alder stood like a low, petrified forest —H. E. Bates

Cypresses rose like cathedral spires —Jilly Cooper

Elms rich like cucumbers —Joyce Cary

Evergreens as big as tents —Julia O'Faolain

Evergreens ... out of place [amid the other trees that change their foliage in Autumn] ... like poor relations at a rich man's feast —Jerome K. Jerome

Huge hardwood trees draped with clusters of Spanish moss guarded the house from the afternoon heat like overdressed sentinels —Paul Kuttner

Magnolia ... its chalices of flowers like superb classical emblems —H. E. Bates

Maples, burning like bonfires, pure yellow and pure red —Pamela Hansford Johnson

My poplars are ... like two old neighbors met to chat —Theodosia Garrison

The oaks stood silent and tired, like old, worn-out seekers after pleasure, unable to keep up in this grimy, mechanized world of ours —Anthony Powell

Palms ... like Spanish exclamation points —Sue Grafton

A pear tree glistened in bloom like a graceful drift of snow
—George Garrett

The pear tree lets its petals drop like dandruff on a tabletop
—W. D. Snodgrass

Pines ... moaning like the sea —John Greenleaf Whittier

Pines tossing their green manes like frightened horses
—George Garrett

The pines were packed like a quiver of arrows —John Farris

The pine-trees roared like waves in their topmost branches, their
stems creaked like the timber of ships —Katherine Mansfield

A poplar covered with snow looked, in the bluish mist, like a giant
in a winding sheet —Anton Chekhov

Poplars like dark feathers against the green and gold sunset
—Sharon Sheehe Stark

The poplars stood like tall guards, attentive, at attention
—Delmore Schwartz
A week after the poet entered this in his diary as a
fragment he incorporated it into a poem as follows: ''The
poplar stood like a rifle.''

Poplars that rose above the mist were like a beach stirred by the
wind —Gustave Flaubert

Red maples and orange oaks, shaped like hands —Jonathan Valin

The redwoods let sink their branches like arms that try to hold
buckets filling slowly with diamonds —James Dickey

Rows of bay trees like children's green lollipops —Graham Masterton

Saw the bare branches of a tree, like fine lace, against the blackness
[of garden] —Jean Rhys

The scarlet of the maples can shake me like a cry —Bliss Carman

The shadows hung from the oak trees to the road like curtains
—Eudora Welty

Tall trees like towers —Carlos Baker

A thick low-hanging branch sags like a wounded arm —John Rechy

The tops of pines moonlit, like floating Christmas trees
  —Frank Conroy

The tree, in full bloom, was like a huge mountain lit with candles
  —Alice Walker

Trees against walls, flattened like spies in old movies —Lisa Ress

The trees and the shrubbery seemed well-groomed and sociable, like
  pleasant people —Willa Cather

The tree sat like a party umbrella (trunk sturdy, branches gently
  arching) —W. P. Kinsella

Trees bent like arches —Graham Swift

The trees cast still shadows like intricate black laces —H. G. Wells

Trees darkening like clusters of frightened wrens —Philip Levine

The trees dimmed the whiteness [of snow] like a sparse coat of hair
  —John Cheever

The trees drooped like old men with back problems
  —T. Coraghessan Boyle

Trees grew close and spread out like bouquets —Stephen Crane

The trees have a look as if they bore sad names —Wallace Stevens

Trees ... hunched against the dawn sky like shaggy dark animals, like
  buffalo —Alice Munro

A tree slender as life, and as tall —Kenneth Patchen

Trees ... like burnt-out torches —Oscar Wilde

Trees ... like fresh-painted green —Danny Santiago

Trees ... like prophet's fingers —Dylan Thomas

Trees like tall ships —Sharon Sheehe Stark

Trees [planted 40 years ago] ... now stately, like patriarchs whose
  wisdom lives in their mere physical presence, after all sight and
  mind have been feebled —Paul Horgan

Trees spaced out in ordered formality ... like a ballet of spinsters
  —W. Somerset Maugham

Trees spread like green lather —F. Scott Fitzgerald

Trees ... spread their scant shade upon the ground like fine strands of hair —Yitzhak Shenhar

The trees stood motionless and white like figures in a marble frieze —Helen Keller

(In the park) the trees stood reticent as old men —Helen Hudson

Trees ... tall and straight as the masts of ships —Donald Hall

Trees tall as mythical giants —David Ignatow

Trees ... vibrating headily like coins shaken in a dark money-box —Robert Culff

The trees were beginning to put out buds like tiny wings —Helen Hudson

The trees were plucked like iron bars —Wallace Stevens

Trees whose branches spread like hugging, possessive arms —John Rechy

Trees with branches like the groping fingers of men long dead —Loren D. Estleman

Trunks like thick skirts hanging in folds —Paul Theroux

Twigs grasped for the sky like frayed electrical wires —Z. Vance Wilson

Willow trees ... their trailing leaves hung like waterfalls in the morning air —Eudora Welty

TREMBLING
SEE: ROCKING AND ROLLING

TRIUMPH
SEE: SUCCESS/FAILURE

TROUBLESOMENESS
SEE: DIFFICULTY

TRUST/MISTRUST
SEE: UNCERTAINTY

TRUTH
SEE ALSO: CANDOR

All the durable truths that have come into the world within historic times have been opposed as bitterly as if they were so many waves of smallpox —H. L. Mencken

As with the pursuit of happiness, the pursuit of truth is itself gratifying whereas the consummation often turns out to be elusive —Richard Hofstadter

Honest as the skin between his brows —William Shakespeare

Plain truths, like plain dishes, are commended by everybody, and everybody leaves them whole —Walter Savage Landor

Pure truth, like pure gold, has been found unfit for circulation, because men have discovered that it is far more convenient to adulterate the truth than to refine themselves
—Charles Caleb Colton

Random truths are all I find stuck like burrs about my mind
—Phyllis McGinley

Rich honesty dwells like a miser ... in a poor house; as your pearl in your foul oyster —William Shakespeare

Speaking the truth is like writing well, and only comes with practice
—John Ruskin

Truth ... drag it out and beat it like a carpet —Hortense Calisher

Truth is a cow which will yield such people no more milk, and so they are gone to milk the bull —Samuel Johnson

Truth is as difficult to lay hold on as air —Walter Savage Landor

Truth is as old as God —Emily Dickinson

The truth is cold, as a giant's knee will seem cold —John Ashbery

Truth is impossible to be soiled by any outward touch as the sunbeam —John Milton

Truth ... is not a thing to be thrown about loosely, like small change; it is something to be cherished and hoarded and disbursed only when absolutely necessary —H. L. Mencken

The truth is tough. It will not break, like a bubble, at a touch ... you may kick it about all day, like a football, and it will be round and full at evening —Oliver Wendell Holmes, Sr.

The truth kept wandering in and out of her mind like a lost child, never pausing long enough to be identified —Margaret Millar

Truth, like a bird, is ever poised for flight at man's approach —Jean Brown

Truth, like a gentle shower, soaks through the ears and moistens the intellect —Anon

Truth, like a point or line, requires an acuteness and intention to its discovery —Joseph Glanville

Truth, like a suit of armor, stubbornly resists all attempts to penetrate it —Robert Traver
> In his novel, *People Versus Kirk*, Traver continues the simile with " ... while the lie, under probing, almost invariably reveals some chinks and cracks."

Truth is like a torch, the more it is shook, the more it shines —Sir William Hamilton
> Modernized from "The more 'tis shook, it shines."

Truth, like gold, is not less so for being newly brought out of the mine —John Locke

Truth, like light, blinds —Albert Camus
> Camus prefaces his simile from *The Fall* as follows: "Sometimes it is easier to see clearly into the liar than into the man who tells the truth."

Truth, like the juice of the poppy, in small quantities, calms men; in larger, heats and irritates them, and is attended by fatal consequences in its excess —Walter Savage Landor

Truth's like a fire, and will burn through and be seen —Maxwell Anderson

A truth's prosperity is like a jest's; it lies in the ear of him that hears it —Samuel Butler

The way of truth is like a great highway. It is not hard to find —Mencius

TYRANNY
SEE: POWER

UNCERTAINTY

Accidental as life —Lord Shaftesbury

I am rather like a mosquito in a nudist camp; I know what I ought to do but I don't know where to begin —Stephen Bayne
> Mr. Bayne's comment was made in 1986 upon assuming a newly created job.

Indecision is like the stepchild: if he doesn't wash his hands, he is called dirty; if he does, he is wasting the water —Madagascan proverb
> Modern day psychologists have adopted this as a neurosis and labeled it a "double bind."

Indecision sent me forward and back, as if I were propelled by a piston in my back —Joan Hess

Indecisive as a fellow who pulls back one leg as he moves forward with the other —Anon
> Probably inspired by this Arabic proverb: "He advances one leg and draws back the other."

Like children with a piece of ice ... neither able to hold it nor willing to let it go —Plutarch

Not quite sure of herself, like a new kitten in a house where they don't care much about kittens —Raymond Chandler

An obscure doubt brushed her, like a dove that wavers to a perch and is gone again without lighting —Marjorie Kinnan Rawlings

(He'd become about as) predictable as a Chinese earthquake —Joseph Wambaugh

Predictable as a Tijuana dog race —Joseph Wambaugh

Swing [uncertainly] like a hammock in the breeze —Anon

Tentative as first taste of hot soup —Anon

Tentative as a schoolgirl —Richard Ford

Uncertain as the glory of an April day —William Shakespeare

Uncertain ... like a golf ball hit by a new golfer, continually getting close to the hole-in-one, but only getting into it by a fluke —Anon

Uncertainty ... as vertiginous as a lift descending down a bottomless shaft —Graham Masterton

Up in the air, like jugglers in a freeze-frame —John Updike

UNDEMONSTRATIVENESS
SEE: COLDNESS, REMOTENESS

UNEMPLOYMENT
SEE: WORK

UNFAIRNESS
SEE: INTOLERANCE

UNGRACIOUSNESS
SEE: MANNERS

UNHAPPINESS
SEE: DEJECTION

UNHELPFULNESS
SEE: USEFULNESS/USELESSNESS

UNLIKELIHOOD
SEE: IMPOSSIBILITY

UNPREDICTABILITY
SEE: UNCERTAINTY

UNRELIABILITY
SEE: RELIABILITY/UNRELIABILITY

UNRESPONSIVENESS
SEE: COLDNESS, REMOTENESS

UNTIDINESS
SEE: ORDER/DISORDER

UNTRUSTWORTHINESS
SEE: TRUST/MISTRUST

URGENCY
SEE: IMPORTANCE/UNIMPORTANCE

Usefulness/ Uselessness

USEFULNESS/USELESSNESS
SEE ALSO: NECESSITY

As much use as a life preserver to a duck —Anon

Effective as a bullet —Edgar Saltus

Effective as an umbrella in a hurricane —Anon

Effective as bailing out a boat with a sieve —Anon

434

Effective as chicken soup. It can't hurt —Anon

Effective as dousing a fire with a dixie cup full of water —Anon

Effective as fixing a broken leg with a bandaid —Anon

Feel like an old clerk on a high stool —Wilfrid Sheed

Handy as a pocket in a shirt —Bartlett's Dictionary of Americanisms

Helpful as a bathing suit in a blizzard —Ed McBain

(The information was probably as) helpful as a wooden compass
    —William McIlvanney

Helpful as throwing a drowning man both ends of a rope
    —Arthur Baer

Ineffective as breaking into a bank vault and taking a bag of pennies
    —Anon

Ineffective like putting the steak on the fire and the skillet on top of
    the steak —Norman Mailer

Ineffective, like sending flies in pursuit of fly paper —Elliot Janeway,
    Barron's, January 20, 1986

(Lonely and) ineffectual as two left-handed gloves —Helen Rowland

Ineffectually as a firefly in Hell —Stephen Vincent Benét

It [Medicare's health-care coverage] is like walking around in a
    bulletproof vest with a hole over the heart —Senator John Heinz,
    Wall Street Journal, October 15, 1986

It's [everything valued by others] like so much fluff
    —Anton Chekhov

A lot of useless barging around, like a man with his sleeve in a
    thresher —Richard Ford

Making lists is like taking too many notes at school; you feel you've
    achieved something when you haven't —Dodie Smith

Pointless ... like you'd give caviar to an elephant —William Faulkner

(Educating you would be about as) redundant as teaching a lion to
    like red meat —line from movie *Victor-Victoria*, spoken by Julie
    Andrews

Usefulness / Uselessness

Sending a teacher into a classroom with no cane is like sending a boxer into the ring with one hand tied behind his back
—Philip Squire

Some men are like a clock on a roof ... useful only to the neighbors
—Austin O'Malley

Some people are like wheelbarrows, only useful when pushed, and very easily upset —Jack Hebert

Unhelpful ... like someone running round with black-currant lozenges to the victims of an earthquake —Josephine Tey

Unnecessary as another designer label —Anon

Useful as a bale of hay in a garage —Anon

Useful as a bicycle without tires —Anon

Useful as a buttonhole without buttons —Anon

Useful as a comb to a bald man —Anon

Useful as a defective parachute —Anon

Useful as an annuity —Anon

Useful as an umbrella to a fish —Anon

Useful as a pocket with a big hole in it —Anon

Useful as a sixth finger —Anon

Useful as a Swiss army knife —Anon

Useful as a thermometer or a scale without markings —Anon

Useful as a third nostril —Peter Benchley

Useful as hayfever when the pollen count is high —Mike Fredman

Useful as information trying to convey the locality and intentions of a cloud —Joseph Conrad

Useful as teats on a boar hog —American colloquialism

Useful as the marketable skill mom told you to acquire —Anon

Useless as a bell that doesn't ring —Anon

Useless as putting a bandaid on a gunshot wound —Anon

Useless as a broken feather —Anon

USELESS AS A HALF-BUILT BRIDGE

Usefulness/Uselessness

Useless as a bump on a log —Anon
> A variation on this familiar simile from *The Last Good Kiss* by James Crumley: "Stood around like a knot on a log."

Useless as a car without gasoline —Anon

Useless as a glass eye at a keyhole —Louis Monta Bell

Useless ... as a half-built bridge —William H. Hallhan

Useless as an expectant lover —Ellen Glasgow

Useless as a single glove —Anon

Useless as a torn sock —Marianne Hauser

Useless as a twisted arm —Desmond O'Grady

Useless as Ronald Reagan's right ear —Joseph Wambaugh

Useless ... like buying an air conditioner for a building without electricity —Anon

Useless ... like the cow that gives a good pail of milk, and then kicks it over —H. G. Bohn's *Handbook of Proverbs*

VALOR
SEE: COURAGE

VALUE
SEE: IMPORTANCE/UNIMPORTANCE

Vanity

VANITY
SEE ALSO: PRIDE

An aura of self-love clung to him like a cloak —Robert Traver

Arrogance ... was escaping from him like steam —Cornell Woolrich

Arrogant as a hummingbird with a full feeder —A. E. Maxwell

As careful about his looks as a young girl getting ready for her first dance —Carlos Fuentes

Conceit grows as natural as hair on one's head; but it is longer in coming out —Bartlett's Dictionary of Americanisms

Conceit like a high gloss varnish smeared over him —Rosa Guy

Conceit that plays itself in an elevated nose ... that is only playing at being conceited; like children play at being kings and queens and go strutting around with feathers and trains
—Jerome K. Jerome

The ego blows up like a big balloon —Delmore Schwartz

Flaunt my knowledges, like a woman will flaunt her pretty body
—Borden Deal

He was like a cock who thought the sun had risen to hear him crow
—George Eliot

He [a man without vanity] would be a very admirable man, a man to be put under a glass case, and shown round as a specimen, a man to be stuck upon a pedestal, and copied like a school exercise —Jerome K. Jerome
> Jerome concluded his comparison as follows: "A man to be reverenced, but not a man to be loved, not a human brother whose hand we should care to grip."

(Ed Koch) is like the rooster who takes credit for the sunrise
—Jack Newfield, *Village Voice*, October 7, 1986

Looks at herself in the mirror like she was the first woman in the world —George Garrett

A man is inseparable from his congenital vanities and stupidities, as a dog is inseparable from its fleas —H. L. Mencken

A man who shows me his wealth is like the beggar who shows me his poverty; they are both looking for alms ... the rich for the alms of envy, the poor man for the alms of my pity
—Ben Hecht

My vanity [after hurtful remark] like a newly-felled tree, lies prone and bleeding —Carolyn Kizer

Preening himself like a courting rooster —Robert Traver

Preening like a politician after a landslide victory —Elyse Sommer

Puffed himself up like a ship in full sail —Hans Christian Andersen

Self-love is a cup without any bottom; you might pour all the great lakes into it, and never fill it up —Oliver Wendell Holmes, Sr.

Sleek and smug as a full-bellied shark —T. Coraghessan Boyle

Strutting ... like a pouter pigeon —Jerome K. Jerome

Vanity

The pigeon named for its propensity for puffing out its distensible crops provides a novel alternative of the more commonly used "Strutting like a peacock."

Vanity is as ill at ease under indifference as tenderness is under a love which it cannot return —George Eliot

Vanity, like murder, will out —Hannah Parkhouse Cowley

Vanity, like sexual impulse, gives rise to needless self-reproach —Charles Horton Cooley

Cooley followed up on his simile with "Why be ashamed of anything so human? What, indeed should we be without it."

Vanity may be likened to the smooth-skinned and velvet-footed mouse, nibbling about forever in expectation of a crumb —William Gilmore Simms

Vehicles

VEHICLES

Beechcraft Twin [airplane] ... its wings flapping hectically like a fat squawking goose unable to get itself aloft —Herbert Lieberman

Brakes squawk like Donald Duck —Joyce Cary

The bus rode on the highway, like a ship upon the sea, rising and falling on hills that were like waves —Nathan Asch

Buzz of traffic ... like the hum of bees working a field of newly blossomed clover —James Crumley

Car accelerated silently like a lioness which has sighted the prey —Elizabeth Spencer

A car is just like a gun. In the wrong hands it is nothing less than an instrument of death —Charles Portis

Car ... ran as if lubricated with peanut butter —Peter De Vries

Cars shot by like large bees —Cynthia Ozick

Cars ... their taillights like cigarette embers —Daphne Merkin

The cloud of exhaust [from car] rose like a sail behind them —Alice Mc Dermott

The engines [of a Mercedes] ticking like wizard-made toy millipedes —Saul Bellow

The exhaust [of car] bloomed in the air like a bizarre, blue-white
flower —William Dieter

Felt about cars the way Casanova felt about women —Mike Fredman

Guzzles gas the way computers gobble up bytes —Anon

Headlights [of cars on highway] flash by like a procession of candles
—Stuart Dybek

Like a wasp rising from a rose, a helicopter chut-chut-chutted toward
them —Will Weaver

The limousine slid to the curb and nestled there, sleek as a wet otter
stretched out in the noonday sun —Paige Mitchell

The ... limousine slid up to the curb, like a great, rolling onyx
—Hortense Calisher

The motor [of car engine] sounded like a polishing drum with a
dozen new agates turning inside —Will Weaver

Parked cars ... stretched like a file of shiny beetles
—Donald MacKenzie

Planes humming across the sky like bees —H. E. Bates

[A car] polished until light glanced off it like a knife
—Jayne Anne Phillips

The power of the big tractor drew the plow through the damp earth
like a potter's knife through wet clay —Will Weaver

A Rolls Royce glittering like a silver tureen —Saul Bellow

The rumbles of the big diesel engine were like ocean surf
—Will Weaver

A ship ... its masts jabbing the sky like upended toothpicks
—Francis King

(The bus) spews out fumes black and substantial as octopus oil
—W. P. Kinsella

Square black automobiles ... like glossy black beetles
—Robert Silverberg

Taillights [of car] gleaming like malevolent eyes —Stanley Elkin

Taillights red as smudged roses —Richard Ford

Vehicles

Tires humming like inflated snakes —John Hawkes

Tractors [at night] ... like neon tetras drifting in the dark tank of the fields —Will Weaver

Train ... wriggling like some long snake —Natsume Sōseki

The windshield wipers [of the car] kicked like a weary dance team —Elizabeth Spencer

VERBOSENESS
SEE: TALKATIVENES

VEXATION
SEE: ANGER, IRRITABLENESS

VICE
SEE: EVIL

VICTORY
SEE: SUCCESS/FAILURE

VIGOR
SEE: ENTHUSIASM, STRENGTH

VIOLENCE
SEE: ADVANCING

Virtue

VIRTUE

Admirable as the rabbit that lets a tortoise win the race —Mike Sommer

Chaste as ice —William Shakespeare

Chastity consists, like an onion, of a series of coats —Nathaniel Hawthorne

Good as a mother —Vicki Baum

Hanging on to his virtue like a thief to his loot —Paige Mitchell

Like gentle streams beneath our feet innocence and virtue meet —William Blake

Many individuals have, like uncut diamonds, shining qualities beneath a rough exterior —Juvenal

Piety is like garlic. A little goes a long way —Rita Mae Brown

Rare virtues are like rare plants or animals, things that have not
    been able to hold their own in the world —Samuel Butler
        Butler's comparison continues as follows: "A virtue to be
        serviceable must, like gold, be alloyed with some
        commoner but more durable metal."

Rich in virtue, like an infant —Lao Tzu

True merit, like a river, the deeper it is, the less noise it makes
    —Lord Halifax

Virginal as Eve before she knew Adam —Anon

Virgins are bores ... like people with overpriced houses
    —Thomas McGuane

Virtue and learning, like gold, have their intrinsic value; but if they
    are not polished, they certainly lose a great deal of their luster;
    and even polished brass will pass upon more people than rough
    gold —Lord Chesterfield

Virtue is a kind of health, beauty and good habit of the soul —Plato

A virtue is like a city set upon a hill, it cannot be hid
    —Robert Hichens

Virtue is like an enemy avoided —Dante Alighieri

Virtue is like a polar star, which keeps its place, and all stars turn
    towards it —Confucius

Virtue is like a rich stone, best plain set —Francis Bacon

Virtue is like health: the harmony of the whole man
    —Thomas Carlyle

Virtue is like precious odors—most fragrant when they are incensed
    or crushed —Francis Bacon

Virtue lies like the gold in quartz; there is not very much of it and
    much pain has to be spent on the extracting of it
    —Jerome K. Jerome

Virtue, like a strong and hardy plant, takes root in any place, if she
    finds there a generous nature and a spirit that shuns no labor
    —Plutarch

Virtues, like essences, lose their fragrance when exposed
    —William Shenstone

Virtue

Virtuous as convict in the death house —H. L. Mencken

Voice(s)

VOICE(S)

(Voice ...) artificial, like paper flowers or the cheapest kind of greasepaint —Heinrich Böll

Bitterness had come through into her voice, buzzing like a wasp —Ross Macdonald

A cold voice ... like a big freezer that whines slowly and precisely —Ariel Dorfman

A deep quiet voice like wrapped thunder —Loren D. Estleman

A disagreeable voice like the grating of broken glass —Aharon Megged

A frank, vaguely rural voice more or less like a used car salesman —Richard Ford

A frosty sparkle in his voice that presupposed opposition—like the feint of a boxer getting ready —Willa Cather

A grand rolling voice, like the sound of an underground train in the distance —Frank Swinnerton

Her tone clicked like pennies —Ross Macdonald

Her voice bristled like a black cat's fur —John Updike

Her voice burst from her like a bubble of blood from her mouth —Marge Piercy

Her voice was like the mirrored wind chimes in a lost lake house of long ago —John MacDonald

Her voice was rich and dark like good brandy, yet somehow lively too, like the very best champagne —George Garrett

High chirpy voice like a cricket —Marge Piercy

His voice was somehow familiar, yet ... it had a quality that made it unrecognizable, like one's own dress worn by someone else —L. P. Hartley

(Skinner was ready to melt with sweetness;) his tone sounded like Romeo in the balcony scene —Rex Stout

His voice rumbled like a bumblebee in a dry gourd —Nelson Algren

In old age her voice had become thin as a bird's —Pauline Smith

His voice tremored defiantly, like that of a man presenting doubtful credentials at a bank —Hortense Calisher

It [her voice] sprang from her mouth like water from a spring —Guy de Maupassant

Loud enthusiastic voices like the Amens said in country churches —Flannery O'Connor

A loud, hurrying voice, like the bell of a steamboat —Henry James

Muffled voices sobbed like foghorns —Kay Boyle

Official-sounding, something like a radio announcer —Bobbie Ann Mason

Raised his voice like an auctioneer's —Truman Capote

Talked like she had a Jew's harp struck in her throat —Will Weaver

A terrible edge to her voice like a line of force holding back a flood —R. Wright Campbell

Urgent tone, like a buzzer —Daphne Merkin

Voice ... like a ship lost at sea —Mike Fredman

Voice ... whining and self-pitying, like some teenage-tragedy song —Bobbie Ann Mason

Voice and lecturing style ... like a chilled aperitif: enticing you to the main course —Robert Goddard

Voice as confidential as that of a family doctor —Donald MacKenzie

Voice as freshly perked as morning coffee —Patricia Leigh Brown, *New York Times*, June 12, 1986

Voice as intimate as the rustle of sheets —Dorothy Parker

Voice as lonely as the stars —Justin Scott

A voice as warm and tender as a wound —Julian Symons

Voice ... blunt as a blow —Ben Ames Williams

Voice ... both jarring and vulnerable: like a bloodshot eye —Tom Robbins

Voice burst up and broke like boiling water —Cynthia Ozick

Voice(s)

Voice clear as a bell, yet slithery with innuendo, it leaped like a deer, slipped like a snake —Norman Mailer

Voice ... clear-pitched like an actor's —Christopher Isherwood

Voice ... clenched like a fist —Borden Deal

Voice ... controlled, chilly, beautiful, like a hillside spring on an August afternoon —F. van Wyck Mason

Voice ... flavored with a stout sweetness as though her words were sopped in rich, old wine —Jean Stafford

Voice ... high and clear as running water over a settled stream bed —Sherley Anne Williams

Voice ... jaggedly precise ... as if every word emitted a quick white thread of great purity, like hard silk, which she was then obliged to bite clearly off —Cynthia Ozick

A voice light and soaring, like a lark's —Joseph Conrad

A voice like a bird —Marge Piercy

Voice ... like a dull whip —Ayn Rand

Voice like a gurgling water pipe —Hugh Walpole

Voice like an iron bell —Peter Meinke

Voice like a parrot's scream —Robert Campbell

Voice ... like a wind chime rattling —Louise Erdrich

A voice like blowing down an empty straw —Helen Hudson

Voice like butter when he wanted something from you and poison if you got in the way (of story character's 15% commission) —Victor Canning

Voice ... like gravel spread with honey —Jay McInerney

Voice like ice —Raymond Chandler

Voice ... like saw grass when the edges duel in the wind blowing over swampland —Lael Tucker Wertenbaker

(Ask weakly. His) voice like that of a child being squeezed in wrestling and asking for mercy —John Updike

Voice ... like that of a helpless orphan —Ignazio Silone

Voice ... like the tolling of a funeral bell —Paule Marshall

A voice like the stuff they use to line summer clouds with
    —Raymond Chandler

Voice ... like the uncanny, unhuman gibber of new wine fermenting
    in a vat —W. Somerset Maugham

Voice ... like thin ice breaking —James Thurber

Voice ... opulent and vast like an actor's —Arthur A. Cohen

A voice queerly pitched, like a parrot's —Mary McCarthy

A voice rich as chocolate
    —David Tuller, *New York Times*, August 24, 1986

Voice roaring like the inside of a shell —Susan Neville

Voice ... rough-smooth, like velvet dragged over fine sandpaper
    —Loren D. Estleman

(Our dried) voices (when we whisper together) are quiet and
    meaningless as wind in dry grass —T. S. Eliot

Voices [of ball field vendors] like crows crowing —W. P. Kinsella

Voices like gongs reverberate in the mind —C. S. Lewis

Voices [of children] ... like the fluttering of wings —Anon

Voices like uniforms, tinny, meaningless ... voices that they brandish
    like weapons —Jean Rhys

Voice ... smooth as cheesecake, sweet and proper —Patricia Henley

Voice smooth as whipping cream —Harvey Swados

Voice ... so low it sounded like a roll of thunder —Maya Angelou

(He had spoken with taut control, and his) voice sounding like the
    steady firmness of a cello muted in the minor mode
    —Arthur A. Cohen

Voices ... went mad, like a chorus of frogs on a spring evening
    —D. H. Lawrence

A voice that boomed and echoed, like a man standing under a
    bridge, ankle-deep in rushing water —Paige Mitchell

Voice thin and distinct as a distant owl's call —John Updike

Voice(s)

Voice ... very sweetly piercing, like the sight of the moon in winter
—Angela Carter

A warm voice ... quivering like corn in a light summer wind
—Aharon Megged

Worry remained suspended in her voice like a fly in amber
—Jonathan Kellerman

VOTERS
SEE: POLITICS

VULGARITY
SEE: TASTE

VULNERABILITY
SEE: SENSITIVENESS

WARMTH
SEE: COMFORT, HEAT

WATCHFULNESS
SEE: ATTENTION, SCRUTINY

WATER
SEE: SEASCAPES

Weakness

WEAKNESS
SEE ALSO: INSULTS, PERSONALITY TRAITS, SOFTNESS

Arms felt like spaghetti —Dan Wakefield

As much strength as a seaweed —Ann Beattie

(A poor weak rag of a man with a) backbone like a piece of string
—Dorothy Canfield Fisher

Boneless as poured water —George Garrett

Diminished and flat, as after radical surgery —Sylvia Plath

(The great white sails of the ships were) drooping like weary wings
—Mazo De La Roche

Feeble as a babe —Ted Hughes

Feel as if I'm strung together by threads that pop and snap
—Rosellen Brown

Feel diluted, like watered-down stew —Susan Minot

Felt a faintness stunning her senses as though someone had cut open the arteries of her wrists and all the blood rushed out of her body —Anzia Yezierska

Felt as if my legs had turned to warm lead —Stephen King

Forceful as a wet noodle —Anon

Forceless as a child —Aeschylus

The program has been like an elderly turtle on its back: it twitches feebly every now and then, but gets nowhere
—Jack D. Kirwan, *Wall Street Journal*, March 19, 1987
The turtle comparison referred to the tragedy-weakened Challenger space program.

Knees like liquid —Elizabeth Spencer

(The man sprawls ... spent, empty) limp as a drowned man tossed on the sand —George Garrett

(He was) limp as laundry —W. P. Kinsella

(I must have been worked up even more than I'd thought those past weeks, for now that it was all over I was) limp as a rag
—Wilbur Daniel Steele

Looking like an advertisement for jelly —Mike Fredman

My legs felt as if ... made of two lengths of rope —George Garrett

No more backbone than a chocolate eclair —Theodore Roosevelt
Roosevelt coined this simile about President McKinley when he was Secretary of the Navy.

She was like an overstretched bow, almost breaking
—Stephen French Whitman

Softened and weakened, like a wax doll left too near the flame
—George Garrett

Strength running out of him like sawdust —Vicki Baum

Was washed out like a disemboweled sack —Aharon Megged

Weak as a broken arm —Raymond Chandler

Weak as air —Ann Bradstreet
By contrast, you could also say "Strong as air," especially if you've ever seen a ship in dry dock.

Weakness

Weak as an nonagenarian —T. Coraghessan Boyle

(He's as) weak as a stick —Mary Lee Settle
> In Settle's novel, *Celebration*, the simile relates to emotional weakness.

Weak as water —*The Holy Bible/Ezkiel*

Weak ... like a cream puff with the cream squeezed out —Tom Robbins

Weak, like a moth newly broken out from its chrysalis —E. F. Benson

WEALTH
SEE: RICHES

Weariness

WEARINESS

Adrenalin ... seeps out of us like sawdust seeping from a stuffed toy —W. P. Kinsella

An atmosphere of luxurious exhaustion, like a ripened shedding rose —Truman Capote

Eyelids feel as if they are being held open by taxidermy needles —Jay McInerney

Fatiguing as the eternal hanging on of an uncompleted task —William James

Feel ... as is if my machine has temporarily run down —Janet Flanner

Feel like a sneaker that's been through a ringer —Nicholas S. Daniloff, television interview, September 14, 1986
> Daniloff's simile expressed his feelings after two weeks in Russian captivity.

Felt like an old soldier exhausted by a long retreat from battle —Kenzaburo Oë

Felt like Sisyphus taking a five-minute break, like Muhammad Ali at the end of the fourteenth round in Manila —T. Coraghessan Boyle

Felt perpetually tired, as though she were bleeding —Francis King

Felt tired as though she had spent the day on a hot beach —Mary Hedin

A flurry of fatigue swept over us like a tropical rainstorm, dropping us like sodden flies —James Crumley

Growing drowsier ... as if he had been counting a flock of pedigree Southdowns —Sylvia Townsend Warner

Had the look of an overworked nag —Sholom Aleichem

His state [from working all day] was like a flabby orange whose crushed skin is thin with pulling, and all dented in
—Amy Lowell

I could lie down like a tired child, and weep away the life of care
—Percy Bysshe Shelley

Looked haggard ... like a child after too much carnival
—John D. MacDonald

(My time is past), my blood is dry as my bones —Grace Paley

My fingers and back feel like I'm Quasimodo —Ray Schmidt
  Schmidt's weariness was caused by a long session of entering data into his computer, September 24, 1986

Squeezed out like an old paint-tube —Lawrence Durrell

Tired as an old coal miner —Reynolds Price

Tired as a preacher in a border town —Thomas Zigal

Tired-eyed as a diplomat —Frank Swinnerton

A wave of sleepiness knocked me over like an ocean breaker
—Gloria Norris

Weariness ... like a crushing weight —Kaatje Hurlbut

(Shrugs) weary and eloquent as an ox under a yoke —George Garrett

Weary and exhausted as though I had travelled along an unending road —Stefan Zweig

Wearying as a holiday to a workaholic —Elyse Sommer

Wore me out like a fever —Sholom Aleichem

WEATHER
SEE: CLOUD(S), COLDNESS, HEAT, MIST, SUN, THUNDER AND LIGHTNING, WIND

WEIGHT
SEE: LIGHTNESS

WELL-BEING
SEE: HEALTH

WHITE
SEE: COLORS

WICKEDNESS
SEE: EVIL

WIND

Wind

Breeze [after a very hot day] ... as torrid as the air from an oven
—Ellen Glasgow

The breeze flowed down on me, passing like a light hand
—Louise Erdrich

The breeze ... sent little waves curling like lazy whips along the
shingle [of a house] —John Fowles

A breeze which came like a breath —Paul Horgan

A draft ... struck through his drenched clothes like ice cold needles
—Cornell Woolrich

A gathering wind sent the willows tossing like a jungle of buggy
whips —William Styron

High wind ... like invisible icicles —Rebecca West

Level winds as flat as ribbons —M. J. Farrell

A northeaster roared down on us like a herd of drunken whales
—T. Coraghessan Boyle

A northeast wind which cut like a thousand razors
—Frank Swinnerton

A sandy wind blowing rough as an elephant —Truman Capote

The sound of wind is like a flame —Yvor Winters

The sunless evening wind slid down the mountain like an invisible
river —Dorothy Canfield Fisher

The night wind rushed like a thief along the streets —Brian Moore

There came a wind like a bugle —Emily Dickinson

■ This is both title and first line of a poem.

The warm spring wind fluttered against his face like an old kiss
—Michael Malone

Wind ... beat like a fist against his face —Vicki Baum

The wind blew gusts of wind into his face that were much like a
shower-bath —Honoré de Balzac

The wind blew him like a sail up against a lifeboat
—F. Scott Fitzgerald

Wind ... blowing down from a flat black sky like painted cardboard
—Marge Piercy

Wind ... driving the dry snow along with it like a mist of powdered
diamonds —Henry Van Dyke

The wind drove against him like a granite cliff —Edith Wharton

Wind ... dry and faint, like the breath of some old woman
—Joe Coomer

Wind ... dry and fresh as ice —Frank Ross

The wind filled his shirt like a white sail —Yitzhak Shenhar

The wind flicked about a little like the tail of a horse that's trying to
decide what sort of mood it's in tonight —Douglas Adams

The wind howls like a chained beast in pain —Delmore Schwartz

The wind howls like air inside a shell —Tracy Daugherty

The wind is like a dog that runs away —Wallace Stevens

The wind is like a hand on my forehead, in caress
—John Hall Wheelock

Wind like a hungry coyote's cry —Patricia Henley

Wind like a perfumed woman in heat —Clive Irving

The wind like a razor —Miles Gibson

The wind like a saw-edged knife —Paul J. Wellman

The wind [in autumn] moves like a cripple among the leaves
—Wallace Stevens

453

Wind

The wind plunged like a hawk from the swollen clouds
  —Ellen Glasgow

(The gray winter) wind prowling like a hungry wolf just beyond the windows —George Garrett

The wind ran in the street like a thin dog —Katherine Mansfield

Wind ringing in their ears like well-known old songs
  —Hans Christian Andersen

The wind rose out of the depth below them, sounding as if it were pushing boulders uphill —Martin Cruz Smith

Wind ... rustling the ... child's hair like grass —Marguerite Duras

The wind screamed like a huge, injured thing —Scott Spencer

Wind ... surges into your ear like breath coming and going
  —Philip Levine

The wind swept the snow aside, ever faster and thicker, as if it were trying to catch up with something —Boris Pasternak

The wind whistled ... like a pack of coyotes —Paige Mitchell

A wind will ... knock like a rifle-butt against the door
  —Wallace Stevens
    The comparison appears in Stevens' poem, *The Auroras of Autumn*. The full line from which the rifle-butt comparison is taken includes "A wind will spread its windy grandeurs round and ... "

WINNING
SEE: SPORTS, SUCCESS/FAILURE

WINTER
SEE: SEASONS

WISDOM
SEE: EDUCATION

WISH
SEE: DESIRE

WIT
SEE: CLEVERNESS, HUMOR

WOMEN
SEE: HEART(S), MEN AND WOMEN

SEE ALSO: WORDS OF PRAISE

Applying words like bandages —William McIlvanney

Words should be scattered like seed; no matter how small the seed may be, if it has once found favorable ground, it unfolds its strength —Seneca

Words, like Nature, half reveal and half conceal the Soul within —Alfred, Lord Tennyson

Her words still hung in the air between us like a whisp of tobacco smoke —Evelyn Waugh

It is with words as with sunbeams, the more they are condensed, the deeper they burn —Robert Southey

Words, like men, grow an individuality; their character changes with years and with use —Anon

Words, like fine flowers, have their color too —Ernest Rhys

Words, like clothes, get old-fashioned, or mean and ridiculous, when they have been for some time laid aside —William Hazlitt

Words, like fashions, disappear and recur throughout English history —Virginia Graham

The word seemed to linger in the air, to throb in the air like the note of a violin —Katherine Mansfield

Her words at first seemed fitful like the talking of the trees —Dante Gabriel Rossetti

(She spoke to them slowly), dropping the words like ping pong balls —Helen Hudson

Every word hanging like the sack of cement on a murdered body at the bottom of the river —Diane Wakoski

Her words fell like rain on a waterproof umbrella; they made a noise, but they could not reach the head which they seemed destined to deluge —Frances Trollope

His words were smoother than oil (and yet be they swords) —*The Book of Common Prayer*

It is as easy to draw back a stone thrown from the hand, as to recall a word once spoken —Menander

Like blood from a cut vein, words flowed —James Morrow

Word(s)

My words slipped from me like broken weapons —Edith Wharton

An old sentence ... ran through her mind like a frightened mouse in a maze —Babs H. Deal

The rest [words meant to remain unspoken] rolled out like string from a hidden ball of twine —Lynne Sharon Schwartz

The sentence rang over and over again in his mind like a dirge —Margaret Millar

Stiff as frozen rope words poke out —Marge Piercy

They [a group at a party] flung them [words] like weapons, handled them like jewels, tossed them on air with reckless abandon as though they scattered confetti —Mary Hedin

The word hissed like steam escaping from an overloaded pressure system —Ross Macdonald

A word once spoken, like an arrow shot, can never be retracted —Anon
 This simile was first used by Talmudic rabbis

Words as meaningless and wonderful as wind chimes —Sharon Sheehe Stark

The words came out like bullets —H. E. Bates

Words came out ... tumbling like a litter of puppies from a kennel —F. van Wyck Mason

The words crumbled in his mouth like ashes —William Diehl

Words ... danced in my mind like wild ponies that moved only to my command —Hortense Calisher

Words falling softly as rose petals —Mary Hedin

Words, frothy and toneless like a chain of bursting bubbles —L. P. Hartley

Words gushing and tumbling as if a hose had been turned on —Rose Tremain

Words gush like toothpaste —Margaret Atwood

The words [just spoken] hung like smoke in the air —Doris Grumbach

Words ... like bits of cold wind —Mary Hedin

(She dealt her) words like blades —Emily Dickinson

Words, like butterflies, stagger from his lips —John Updike

Words, like glass, obscure when they do not aid vision
    —Joseph Joubet

Words ... limp and clear like a jellyfish ... hard and mean and
    secretive like a horned snail ... austere and comical as top hats,
    or smooth and lively and flattering as ribbons —Alice Munro
        The narrator of Munro's story, *Spelling,* contemplates the
        meaning of words while visiting an old woman.

The word spiralled through the silence like a worm in wood
    —Harris Downey

The words (out) of his mouth were smoother than butter, but war
    was in his heart; his words were softer than oil, yet they were
    drawn swords —*The Holy Bible/Psalms*

Words ... plunked down with a click like chessmen
    —Yehuda Amichai

Words ... poured wetly from her red lips as from a pitcher
    —Lynne Sharon Schwartz

The words rang in the silence like the sound of a great cash register
    —Kingsley Amis

Words ran together too quickly, like rapid water
    —Joanna Wojewski Higgins

Words roll around in Benna's mouth [heroine of novel, *Anagrams,* by
    Lorrie Moore] like Life Savers on a tongue —Carol Hills, *New
    York Times Book Review,* November 2, 1986

Words that string and creep like insects —Conrad Aiken

Words ... tumbling out and tripping over each other like mice
    —Susan Fromberg Schaeffer

The words went by like flights of moths under the star-soaked sky
    —Adrienne Rich

Words ... white and anonymous as a snowball —Donald McCaig

(If he once ... let loose ... the) words would come like a great flood,
    like vomiting —George Garrett

Word(s)

Your words to the end, hard as a pair of new cowboy boots
  —A. D. Winans

WORDINESS
SEE: TALKATIVENESS

Words of Praise

WORDS OF PRAISE

For you, words are like birds. They sing. They fly —Helen Hudson
  The character who thus praises a friend's gift with words describes himself as someone for whom ''Words are worms.''

(My wife ... always) looks like a barrel full of stardust —Moss Hart

My doll is as dainty as a sparrow
  —Oscar Hammerstein II, from lyric for *South Pacific*
    The lyric heaps simile upon simile with ''Where she's narrow, she's as narrow as an arrow.''

My sister, my spouse, is a secret spring —John Hall Wheelock
  This is the first line and leitmotif of a poem entitled *An Old Song.*

She seemed like a yellow sunrise on mountain tops —O. Henry

She shines against the backdrop of this provincial place like a jewel on a beggar's coat. She is like the moon forgotten by the pale sky of the day. She is like a butterfly over a plain of snow
  —Milan Kundera

When I walk with you I feel as if I had a flower in my buttonhole
  —William Makepeace Thackeray

When she passed it seemed like the ceasing of exquisite music
  —Henry Wadsworth Longfellow

When you came, you were like red wine and honey ... now you are like morning bread, smooth and pleasant —Amy Lowell

When you get up, it's like the flag being raised. I want to pledge allegiance —John Updike

You're a girl like candy —Clifford Odets

You're beautiful, like a May fly —Ernest Hemingway to Mary Welsh before she became Mrs. Hemingway

You're perfect as a textbook example —Sharon Olds

Poet Olds uses the simile in a poem dedicated to her father and aptly entitled *The Ideal Father*.

Your lips taste like paradise —Isaac Bashevis Singer

WORK
SEE ALSO: ATTENTION, BOREDOM

All the romance had been scuffed off it [playing professional baseball against small-town teams] like the gloss on a brand-new baseball after nine innings of hard use —Howard Frank Mosher

All work is as seed sown; it grows and spreads, and sows itself anew —Thomas Carlyle

The back-breaking sixteen-hour day, like a heavy hand slapping —Bernard Malamud

Being a president is like riding a tiger. A man has to keep on riding or be swallowed —Harry S. Truman

(Reagan's nostalgic wit was contributing to the feeling that he) dropped in and out of his job, like a cameo star on "The Love Boat" —Gerald Gardner

(My mom) getting paid for giving advice is like the Cookie Monster getting paid for eating cookies —Glenn Sapadin, upon hearing that his mother, Linda Sapadin, was finalist in contest to select a replacement for advice columnist Ann Landers, *New York Times*/About New York, April 11, 1987

This job [being a prize fighter] needs gorgeous concentration ... it's like being a priest; our work comes first —Clifford Odets

The job [dean at a university] is like being pecked to death by ducks —John Roche, lecture at Ohio State University, 1962

Jobs are like lobster pots, harder to get out of them than into —Hugh Leonard

Labor like Hercules —William H. Gass

The only time some people work like a horse is when the boss rides them —Gabriel Heatter

Toiled like movers trying to get a refrigerator into a fifth-floor walk-up —Russell Baker

Work

Toiling like a bee in a hive
—Noël Coward, lyrics for "World Weary"

(Fifty-two Sundays a year ... for three hours my mother was) unemployed in her own house. Like a queen —Philip Roth
Roth's comparison of a mother to an unemployed queen comes from his novel, *The Ghost Writer.*

Unemployed people (i.e. actors between plays) like ghosts looking for bodies to inhabit —Gail Godwin

Work drives you like a motor —Janet Flanner

Working the rivet line [at auto factory] is like being paid to flunk high school the rest of your life —Ben Hamper in article on changes at General Motors, *Mother Jones,* September 1986

Work is as much a necessity to man as eating and sleeping
—Karl Wilhelm Humboldt

Work like a beaver —American colloquialism
This expression was popularized by the fur trappers who roamed the Rockies during the nineteenth century. Like many such terms it has gained much wider currency and seeded off-shoots like "Eager as a beaver" and "Busy as a beaver."

Work like a Trojan —Anon
A still popular simile that had its origins in the Greek classics which portrayed the Trojans as hard workers.

The work was getting to be like licking stamps eight hours a day
—Loren D. Estleman

WORLD
SEE: LIFE

WORRY
SEE: ANXIETY

WORTHINESS
SEE: VIRTUE

WORTHLESSNESS
SEE: IMPORTANCE/UNIMPORTANCE

WOUND
SEE: PAIN

THE WORK WAS GETTING TO BE LIKE LICKING STAMPS
EIGHT HOURS A DAY

WRATH
SEE: ANGER

WRINKLES
SEE: SKIN

WRISTS
SEE: ARMS

YAWN
SEE: MOUTH(S), OPEN/SHUT

YEARNING
SEE: DESIRE

YELLOW
SEE: COLORS, HAIR

YOUTH
SEE ALSO: AGE

Youth

As young as truth —Dante Gabriel Rossetti

At sixty-eight, he is as pink and fat as a baby, ingenuous as a
    teenager —T. Coraghessan Boyle

Between eighteen and twenty, life is like an exchange where one
    buys stocks, not with money, but with actions —André Malraux

Childish, like believing in Beauty and the Beast —Janet Flanner

Each youth is like a child born in the night who sees the sun rise
    and thinks that yesterday never existed —W. Somerset Maugham

He is like one of those young-old engineers at Boeing, who at
    seventy wear bow ties and tinker in their workshops
    —Walker Percy

It is like a long hopeless homesickness ... missing those young days
    —Grace Paley

Like the tongue that seeks the missing tooth I yearned for my
    extracted youth —Ogden Nash

Looked about sixteen and as defenseless as a babe at a Mafia
    convention —Jimmy Sangster

Midway between youth and age like a man who has missed his
    train: too late for the last and too early for the next
    —George Bernard Shaw

Seemed as perpetually youthful as movie stars —Donald Justice

She was just eighteen, rich and warm as one eagerly waiting for the play to begin —Arthur Schopenhauer

Their [young people's] impulses are keen but not deep-rooted ... like sick people's attacks of hunger —Aristotle

The young leading the young is like the blind leading the blind —Lord Chesterfield

Youth ... flashing like a star out of the twilight —Willa Cather
    The simile is from an introductory poem to Cather's novel, *O Pioneer.*

Youthful rashness skips like a hare over the meshes of good counsel —William Shakespeare

Youth is like spring, an overpraised season: delightful if it happen to be a favored one, but in practice very rarely favored and more remarkable, as a general rule, for biting east winds than genial breezes —Samuel Butler

Youth ... it did not go by me like a flitting dream. Tuesdays and Wednesdays were as gay as Saturday nights —Grace Paley

Youth like summer morn ... youth like summer brave —William Shakespeare
    Shakespeare used these similes in his poem, *The Passionate Pilgrim,* to describe the pleasures of youth, alternating them with comparisons about age and the weather.

(My) youth passed like a sleep —Dame Edith Sitwell

ZEAL
SEE: AMBITION, ENTHUSIASM

Author Index

All references are to page numbers in the listed categories.

Abbott, Lyman
Patience
Abbott, Lee K.
Strength
Ackerman, Diane
Bending/Bent, Colors, Destruction, Fighting, Ideas, Moon, Seriousness, Tension, Time
Acton, Harold
Desire
Adamic, Louis
Eating and Drinking, Jewelry
Adams, Alice
Bearing
Adams, Franklin P.
Cleverness
Adams, Douglas
Bearing, Hand(s), Moon, Wind
Adams, Harold
Animals, Bearing, Calmness, Clothing, Excitement, Humor, Insects, Insults, Looks, Mouth, Persistence, Reliability, Scrutiny, Secrecy, Talkativeness, Taste
Adams, Henry
Education
Adams, Joey
Clothing, Face(s)
Addison, Joseph
Cleverness
Ade, George
Health, Insults, Kindness, Teeth
Adler, Felix
Belief
Aeschylus
Weakness
Agee, James
Bending/Bent
Ai, Sin
Destruction, Places
Aiken, Conrad
Word(s)
Aiken, Joan
Flowers

Alain
Manners
Albo, Josepiz
Evil
Alcott, Louisa May
Attention, Bearing, Cause/Effect Coldness, Comfort, Eating and Drinking, Happiness
Aldiss, Brian W.
Air
Aldrich, James
Immobility
Aldridge, John W.
Permanence
Aldrich, Thomas Bailey
Bending/Bent, Sensitiveness
Aleichem, Sholom
Difficulty, Excitement, Fire and Smoke, Heart(s), Houses, Pain, Remoteness, Weariness
Alexander, Shana
Closeness, Scrutiny
Alfred, William
Change, Destruction, Dishonesty, Gossip, Heat, Pride
Algren, Nelson
Hair, Places, Voice(s)
Alighieri, Dante
Eye(s), Virtue
Allen, Fred
Impossibility, Insults, Thinness
Allen, Roberta
Facial Expressions, Miscellaneous
Allen, Walter
Guilt
Allende, Isabel
Anger
Alvarez, A.
Certainty; Clinging; Criticism, Dramatic and Literary; Money; Physical Appearance
Ambler, Eric
Eye(s), Smiles, Teeth

Amichai, Yehuda
Destruction, Heart(s), Life, Men and Women, Time, Word(s)

Amis, Kingsley
Bearing, Impossibility, Pain, Personality Traits, Word(s)

Amis, Martin
Pain

Ammons, A. R.
Belief, Flowers, Importance/Unimportance, Thunder and Lightning

Anarchis
Laws

Andersen, Hans Christian
Coldness, Seascapes, Sun, Trees, Vanity, Wind

Anderson, Maxwell
Body, Coldness, Impossibility, Truth

Anderson, Robert
People, Interaction

Anderson, Sherwood
Hand(s),Illness, Love, Defined

Anderson, Susan Heller
Power

Angelou, Maya
Air, Burst, Conversation, Physical Appearance, Sharpness, Voice(s)

Anouilh, Jean
Ability, Aloneness

Anthony, Piers
Fear

Appelfeld, Aharon
Attraction, Courage, Fear

Apperley, Charles James
Heart(s)

Apple, Max
Attraction; Criticism, Dramatic and Literary; Disappearance; People, Interaction; Skin; Thinness

Aquinas, St. Thomas
Sense

Arabian Nights
Body, Hand(s), Joy, Skin

Arbuthnot, John
Law, Seriousness

Ardizzone, Tony
Clinging, Clothing, Dejection, Furniture and Furnishings, Hand(s), Irritableness, Politics/Politicians, Skin

Aretino, Pietro
Friendship

Aristippus
Ability

Aristophanes
Destruction

Aristotle
Laws, Patience, Youth

Arkin, Frieda
Time

Asch, Nathan
Vehicles

Asch, Sholem
Illness, Jumping, Teeth, Trees

Ascher, Barbara Lazear
Destruction, Manners, Pain, Power

Ascher, Carol
Hair

Ashe, Thomas
Pain

Ashbery, John
Calmness, Darkness, Dreams, Emptiness, Memory, Questions/Answers, Sky, Sun, Thoughts, Truth

Atherton, Gertrude
Thickness

Atwood, Margaret
Advancing, Animals, Brevity, Eye(s), Hair, Heat, Shape, Skin, Smell, Softness, Sun, Word(s)

Auchincloss, Louis
Excitement, Flowers, Frowns, Looks, Mind, Nature

Auden, W. H.
Anxiety, Evil, Freedom, Life, Noise, Permanence, Physical Appearance, Power, Rarity, Readers/Reading, Sky, Time

Auerbach, Berthold
Character, Kindness

Aurelius, Marcus
Anger, Life, Time

Austin, Mary
Hair

Axelrod, George
Gossip

Babel, Isaac
Clothing; Criticism, Dramatic and Literary; Humor; Hunger; Moon; Pain; Sun

Bacon, Francis
Ability, Death, Fortune/Misfortune, Money, Revenge, Virtue

Baer, Arthur
Hand(s), Impossibility, Inappropriateness, Shape, Usefulness/Uselessness

Bagnold, Enid
Burst

Bail, Murray
Sports

Bailey, Nathan
Comfort

Bailey, P. J.
Joy, Thoughts

Baille, Joanna
 Grief
Bakeland, Brooks
 Clinging
Baker, Carlos
 Character, Enthusiasm, Fire and
 Smoke, Happiness, Hunger, Memory,
 Persistence, Smell, Sun, Thunder and
 Lightning, Trees
Baker, Russell
 Certainty,
 Completeness/Incompleteness, Fame,
 Politics/Politicians, Thinness, Work
Baldwin, James
 Money
Ballard, Mignon F.
 Thoughts
Balzac, Honoré de
 Advancing; Body; Candor; Courage;
 Excitement; Fear; Gossip; Looks; Love,
 Defined; Meekness; Mind; Mouth;
 Personality Profiles; Physical
 Appearance; Rarity; Self-Confidence;
 Stupidity; Wind
Bankhead, Tallulah
 Absurdity
Banks, Russell
 Sky
Barca, Pedro Calderon de la
 Power
Barker, Clive
 Anxiety
Barker, George
 Death,Time
Barker, Paul
 Death
Barnard, Robert
 Shame
Barnes, Linda
 Calmness
Barnum, P. T.
 Money
Barr, Pat
 Rarity
Barrie, J. M.
 Clinging
Barron, Susan
 Anxiety
Barth, John
 Time
Bartlett's Dictionary of Americanisms
 Evil, Happiness, Impossibility, Money,
 Secrecy, Usefulness/Uselessness, Vanity
Baryshnikov, Mikhail
 Fame
Bate, Julius
 Enthusiasm
Bates, H. E.
 Anger, Eating and Drinking, Hair,

Hand(s), Houses, Impossibility,
Kindness, Legs, Nature, Pain, Self-
Confidence, Shape, Smiles, Thinness,
Thoughts, Trees, Vehicles, Word(s)
Bates, Lewis J.
 Coldness, Intelligence, Skin
Bat-Miriam, Yocheved
 Shining
Baum, Vicki
 Anxiety, Life, Pain, Physical
 Appearance, Smiles, Strength,
 Success/Failure, Virtue, Weakness,
 Wind
Bauman, M. Garrett
 Advancing, Skin
Bawden, Nina
 Bending/Bent, Closeness, Conversation,
 Frowns, Seriousness, Skin, Strength
Bayne, Stephen
 Uncertainty
Beach, Rex
 Personality Traits
Beaton, M. C.
 Taste
Beattie, Ann
 Absurdity, Arm(s), Guilt, Hair,
 Smallness, Strangeness, Tension,
 Weakness
Beaumont, Francis
 Ambition, Calmness, Destruction, Envy,
 Intensity
Beauvoir, Simone de
 Sex
Beck, Warren
 Animals
Beckett, Samuel
 Mind
Beecher, Henry Ward
 Body; Character; Kindness; Laws; Love,
 Defined; Politics/Politicians; Strength
Beecham, Sir Thomas
Beechcroft, William
 Certainty, Face(s), Shock
Beerbohm, Max
 Moon
Behan, Brendan
 Criticism, Dramatic and Literary
Behn, Aphra
 Busyness
Bell, Jack
 Self-Confidence
Bell, Louis Monta
 Enthusiasm, Usefulness/Uselessness
Bell, Madison Smartt
 Difficulty
Bellah, James Warner
 Fear
Bellamann, Henry
 Memory

467

Belloc, Hilaire
Animals, Books
Bellow, Saul
Air; Anger; Beginnings/Endings;
Change; Cloud(s); Fire and Smoke;
Hair; Heat; Houses; Immobility; Insults;
Jumping; Landscapes; Looks; Mind;
People, Interaction; Physical
Appearance; Questions/Answers;
Rarity; Sex; Shame; Shape; Smell; Sun;
Thoughts; Vehicles
Bemelmans, Ludwig
Landscapes, Strength
Benchley, Nathaniel
Pain
Benchley, Peter
Anxiety; Fear, Impossibility; People,
Interaction; Usefulness/Uselessness
Benedict, Dianne
Furniture and Furnishings, Sky
Benét, Stephen Vincent
Animals, Beauty, Calmness, Darkness,
Fear, Fighting, Hand(s), Kindness,
Pride, Rarity, Secrecy, Self-Confidence,
Smiles, Softness, Thinness, Thoughts,
Time, Usefulness/Uselessness
Benham, W.G.
Enthusiasm
Benjamin, Park
Beginnings/Endings
Bennett, Arnold
Rocking and Rolling
Bennetts, Leslie
Inappropriateness
Benson, E. F.
Weakness
Benson, Stella
Cloud(s)
Bergman, Ingrid
Age
Berkman, Sylvia
Body, Coldness, Fear, Sensitiveness
Berkow, Ira
Baseball, Intensity
Berlin, Isaiah
Questions/Answers
Berriault, Gina
Flowers
Berrigan, Daniel
Emptiness, Kindness, Softness
Berryman, John
Pain, Thinness
Betjeman, John
Pride, Smell
Bhartrihari
Death
Bialik, Hayyim Naham
Mouth

Bible, The Holy
Anger, Bareness, Courage, Death,
Dejection, Destruction, Dishonesty,
Education, Envy, Grief, Heat, Idleness,
Justice, Life, Manners, Physical
Appearance, Sharpness, Strength,
Talkativeness, Time, Word(s)
Bierce, Ambrose
Beauty, Belief, Pain
Billings, Josh (Henry Wheeler Shaw)
Ambition; Coldness; Destruction;
Dishonesty; Fame; Humor; Ignorance;
Joy; Laws; Love, Defined; Money;
Slander; Stupidity; Time
Bird, Sarah
Bearing, Houses, Looks
Bishop, Elizabeth
Grief, Insects, Landscapes, Lightness,
Physical Appearance, Power, Shadow,
Sun
Bisson, Terry
Clinging, Coldness
Blackie, John Stuart
Beauty
Blackman, M. C.
Looks
Blake, William
Emptiness, Moon, Strength, Virtue
Blanchard, Edwin L.
Love, Defined
Blasco-Ibâñez, Vincente
Persistence
Blassingame, Wyatt
People, Interaction
Blessington, Marguerite, Countess
Ability, Dishonesty
Blewett, Sandra
Sports
Blixen, Baroness Karen
See, Dinesen, Isak
Boccaccio
Hair
Boerne, Ludwig
Cleverness, Education,
Politics/Politicians
Bohn, Henry G.'s Handbook of Proverbs
Absurdity, Dishonesty, Idleness,
Impossibility, Insults, Kindness, Mind,
Pride, Selfishness, Shape,
Talkativeness, Usefulness/Uselessness
Böll, Heinrich
Colors, Fear, Furniture and
Furnishings, Illness, Memory, Shape,
Skin, Sky, Time, Voice(s)
Bombeck, Erma
Education
Bonacich, Peter J.
Reliability/Unreliability

Book of Common Prayer
Word(s)

Booth, Edwin
Stage and Screen

Boretz, Alvin (-)
Change

Borsten, Rick
Smiles

Bossuet, Jaques Benigne
Kindness

Bottome, Phyllis
Air, Anger, Beauty, Moon, Mountains, Pain

Boucicault, Dion
Pride

Bowen, Elizabeth
Attention, Dejection, Desire, Eating and Drinking, Furniture and Furnishings, Inappropriateness, Manners, Mind, Nature, Sex, Sky, Trees

Bowles, Jane
Clinging

Boyd, William
Darkness, Mountains, Self-Confidence

Boyesen, Hjalmar Hjorth
Love, Defined

Boylan, Clare
Hand(s), Looks

Boyle, T. Coraghessan
Advancing, Air, Anger, Baseball, Beards, Bearing, Blue, Certainty, Clothing, Darkness, Dejection, Destruction, Eating and Drinking, Enthusiasm, Fear, Fortune/Misfortune, Frowns, Guilt, Hair, Hand(s), Heat, Immobility, Impossibility, Jumping, Lightness, Mountains, Nature, Pain, Persistence, Physical Appearance, Sex, Shape, Shoulders, Silence, Skin, Sky, Smiles, Softness, Strangeness, Success/Failure, Sun, Talkativeness, Teeth, Thinness, Thunder and Lightning, Time, Trees, Vanity, Weakness, Weariness, Wind, Youth

Boyle, Kay
Arm(s), Coldness, Skin, Smiles, Thickness, Voice(s)

Boyle, Robert
Character

Bracken, Peg
Order/Disorder

Bradbury, Ray
Shock, Time, Time

Bradford, Barbara Taylor
Landscapes, Thunder and Lightning

Bradley, George
Dreams

Bradstreet, Anne
Power, Weakness

Braine, John
Air, Comfort, Ease, Fortune/Misfortune, Hair, Happiness, Impartiality, Money, Moon, Necessity, Power, Sex, Skin, Smell, Smiles, Trees

Brammer, William
Beginnings/Endings, Importance/Unimportance, Intensity, Sun

Brautigan, Richard
Sun

Brecht, Bertold
Coldness; Completeness/Incompleteness; Desire; Immobility; Legs; Love, Defined

Brennan, Maeve
Air, Places, Skin

Breslin, Jimmy
Belief

Brett, George
Sports

Brierley, David
Difficulty, Fire and Smoke, Heat, Physical Appearance, Shock, Smiles

Brinkley, David
Gossip

Broadhurst, George
Impossibility

Brodkey, Harold
Personality Traits

Brombeck, Erma
Guilt

Bromfield, Louis
Completeness/Incompleteness, Dejection, Emptiness, Hand(s), Houses, Physical Appearance, Pride

Bronk, William
Death

Brontë, Charlotte
Busyness, Calmness, Cause/Effect, Evil, Permanence, Talkativeness

Brontë, Emily
Importance/Unimportance; Love, Defined; Meekness; Nature

Brook, Mel
Criticism, Dramatic and Literary

Brooke, James
Strangeness

Brookes, Warren T.
Destruction

Brookhiser, Richard
Completeness/Incompleteness

Brookner, Anita
Beauty

Brooks, Van Wyck
Aloneness

Broun, Heywood
Baseball

Brown, Jean
  Truth
Brown, John Mason
  Criticism, Dramatic and Literary;
  Readers/Reading
Brown, John
  Certainty
Brown, Patricia Leigh
  Voice(s)
Brown, Rita Mae
  Advancing; Ambition; Attention; Burst;
  Business; Change; Clinging; Clothing;
  Death; Destruction; Flowers;
  Immobility; Innocence; Kindness; Love,
  Defined; Nature; Order/Disorder; Pain;
  Personality Traits; Pride; Rocking and
  Rolling; Shining; Smiles; Sports; Sun;
  Virtue
Brown, Rosellen
  Conversation, Ideas, Immobility, Looks,
  Skin, Smiles, Teeth, Thickness, Time,
  Weakness
Brown, Suzanne
  Skin
Browne, Sir Thomas
  Meekness
Browning, Elizabeth Barrett
  Silence
Browning, Robert
  Advancing, Calmness, Innocence,
  Meekness, Teeth
Bryan, C. D. B.
  Advancing
Bryant, William Cullen
  Dejection
Buckahm, Peter
  Stage and Screen
Buckley, Christopher
  Difficulty, Sensitiveness
Bukowski, Charles
  Arm(s)
Bulwer-Lytton, Edward
  Age, Fame, Patience
Bumpus, Jerry
  Mouth, Shadow
Bunin, Ivan
  Eye(s)
Burgess, Gelett
  Calmness, Ideas
Burke, Edmund
  Beauty, Laws
Burke, James Lee
  Arm(s), Eye(s), Freedom, Pain, Thunder
  and Lightning
Burke, William Talbot
  Ambition
Burkitt, William
  Kindness

Burnand, Sir Francis C.
  Heat
Burnett, Hallie
  Enthusiasm, Hair, Softness
Burns, Robert
  Love, Defined
Burton, Robert
  Clinging, Illness
Busch, Niven
  Darkness, Dejection, Legs, Pain, Skin
Bush, Katherine
  Jumping
Butler, Samuel
  Art and Literature, Certainty, Life,
  Money, Time, Truth, Virtue, Youth
Byrd, Senator Robert
  Gossip
Byron, Lord
  Age, Anger, Attention, Beauty, Blue,
  Clinging, Darkness
Cain, James
  Busyness
Calisher, Hortense
  Advancing, Face(s), Hand(s), Money,
  Remoteness, Scrutiny, Sleep, Smiles,
  Time, Truth, Vehicles, Voice(s),
  Word(s)
Calvino, Italo
  Birds, Dreams, Thinness
Camoin, François
  Fear, Readers/Reading, Skin, Sky
Campbell, Joseph
  Age
Campbell, Robert
  Belief; Calmness; Clothing; Darkness;
  Friendship; Houses; Irritableness;
  Looks; Money; People, Interaction;
  Smiles; Voice(s)
Campbell, R. Wright
  Arm(s), Calmness, Excitement, Fear,
  Immobility, Looks, Noise, Seriousness,
  Shame, Sharpness, Skin, Smiles, Teeth,
  Trees, Voice(s)
Campion, Nardi Reeder
  Destruction
Camus, Albert
  Pain, Strength, Time, Truth
Canby, Vincent
  Candor; Criticism, Dramatic and
  Literary; Excitement; Rarity; Risk;
  Strangeness; Success/Failure
Canin, Ethan
  Air
Canning, Victor
  Voice(s)
Capote, Truman
  Activeness, Aloneness, Beauty, Change,
  Cloud(s), Gossip, Heat, Insults, Legs,
  Pain, Physical Appearance, Places, Sex,

Talkativeness, Voice(s), Weariness,
Wind
Cardozo, Benjamin
Riches
Carleton, Will
Heat
Carlisle, Kitty
Age
Carlson, Ron
Sports
Carlyle, Thomas
Beauty, Grief,
Importance/Unimportance,
Talkativeness, Virtue, Work
Carman, Bliss
Trees
Carr, John Dickson
Smiles
Carroll, Lewis
Attention, Eating and Drinking,
Questions/Answers
Carruth, Hayden
Moon, Softness
Carter, Angela
Bareness, Beauty, Colors, Heat, Houses,
Mouth, Noise, Skin, Sun, Taste,
Voice(s)
Carver, Raymond
Bearing
Cary, Joyce
Clothing, Cloud(s), Coldness, Darkness,
Fame, Frowns, Immobility, Landscapes,
Legs, Moon, Pain, Permanence,
Persistence, Physical Appearance,
Shape, Sky, Trees, Vehicles
Casper, John
Personality Traits
Casper, Leonard
Love, Defined
Cassill, R. V.
Clothing, Remoteness, Secrecy, Sex,
Skin, Smiles
Cather, Willa
Aloneness, Bearing, Emptiness, Face(s),
Fear, Happiness, Immobility, Mouth,
Scrutiny, Seasons, Shoulders, Skin,
Sun, Teeth, Trees, Voice(s), Youth
Cavell, Mary Ladd
Personality Profiles
Celine, Louis-Ferdinand
Legs
Cervantes, Miguel de
Completeness/Incompleteness,
Darkness, Hair, Secrecy
Chandler, Raymond
Aloneness, Clothing, Coldness,
Difficulty, Ease, Emptiness, Fear, Guilt,
Hair, Hand(s), Heat, Hunger,
Importance/Unimportance,

Inappropriateness, Memory, Moon,
Rarity, Rocking and Rolling, Sex, Sun,
Taste, Thinness, Uncertainty, Voice(s),
Weakness
Chapin, E. H.
Kindness
Chapman, George
Envy
Charron, Pierre
Dejection
Chase, Alexander
People, Interaction; Stage and Screen
Chase, Joan
Change, Colors, Happiness,
Importance/Unimportance, Smiles
Chase, Mary Ellen
Clinging, Legs
Chatterton, Ruth
Pain
Chaucer, Geoffrey
Activeness, Beauty, Busyness, Freedom,
Thinness
Cheever, Dr. David W.
Enthusiasm
Cheever, John
Baseball, Beginnings/Endings, Clinging,
Cloud(s), Desire, Destruction,
Excitement, Fear, Joy, Nature, Sex,
Shape, Skin, Sky, Sleep, Smell, Smiles,
Trees
Chekhov, Anton
Aloneness, Clinging, Ease, Hair,
Happiness, Idleness, Moon, Thinness,
Trees, Usefulness/Uselessness
Chesterfield, Lord
Art and Literature, Beauty, Character,
Shame, Virtue, Youth
Chesterton, G. K.
Art and Literature, Destruction,
Emptiness, Fear, Immobility, Moon,
Persistence, Rocking and Rolling,
Sharpness, Success/Failure, Thrift
Chrysostam, Saint John
Envy
Christie, Agatha
Business, Mind
Churchill, Charles
Fortune/Misfortune
Churchill, Winston
Politics/Politicians
Chute, Carolyn
Arm(s), Clothing, Noise, Smell
Ciardi, John
Certainty
Cibber, Colley
Irritableness, Silence
Cicero
Books

Ciment, Jill
Impartiality, Permanence, Scrutiny

Clark, Eleanor
Arm(s), Attention, Permanence, Emptiness, Smiles, Talkativeness

Clarke, John
Cleverness, Pride

Clemens, Samuel Langhorne
See, Twain, Mark

Clement, Saint
Riches

Clift, Eleanor
Politics/Politicians

Cobb, Irvin S.
Ability, Brevity, Fortune/Misfortune, Freedom, Mouth, Taste

Cocteau, Jean
Art and Literature, Mouth

Coffin, Harold
Art and Literature

Cohen, Arthur A.
Business, Clinging, Completeness/Incompleteness, Face(s), Hand(s), Looks, Pain, Voice(s)

Cohen, Eddie
Noise

Cohen, Senator William S.
Remoteness

Coleridge, Hartley
Death, Smallness

Coleridge, Mary
Aloneness

Coleridge, Samuel Taylor
Calmness, Friendship, Idleness, Joy, Laws

Colette (Sidonie Gabrielle Colette)
Bending/Bent, Immobility, Lightness, Mountains, Nature, Shining

Collins, John Churton
Memory

Colloquialisms
Anger, Beauty, Blue, Busyness, Certainty, Change, Cleverness, Clinging, Clothing, Coldness, Comfort, Courage, Darkness, Dishonesty, Ease, Eye(s), Happiness, Head(s), Humor, Hunger, Impossibility, Intelligence, Irritableness, Necessity, Order/Disorder, Shape, Smell, Strength, Thinness, Thrift, Usefulness/Uselessness, Work

Colton, Charles Caleb
Bending/Bent, Body, Death, Dishonesty, Evil, Laws, Politics/Politicians, Power, Pride, Truth

Colwin, Laurie
Ability; Clothing; Difficulty; Eye(s); Frowns; Heat; Houses; Irritableness; Landscapes; Love, Defined; Memory; Physical; Appearance;

Questions/Answers; Remoteness; Sensitiveness

Combe, George
Places

Confucious
Education, Heart(s), Virtue

Congreve, William
Beauty; Certainty; Gossip; Love, Defined

Conklin, Hilda
Age

Connell, Richard
Irritableness

Conrad, Joseph
Aloneness, Clinging, Ease, Fear, Fire and Smoke, Irritableness, Lightness, Moon, Mouth, Seascapes, Sensitiveness, Sharpness, Taste, Usefulness/Uselessness

Conroy, Frank
Fear, Heat, Importance/Unimportance, Thickness, Trees

Conroy, Pat
Activeness, Arm(s), Art and Literature, Attraction, Bearing, Busyness, Insects, Jumping, Legs, Moon, Shape, Skin, Smell

Cooke, Alistair
Innocence, Jumping

Cooley, Charles Horton
Vanity

Coolidge, Susan
Disappearance

Coomer, Joe
Bareness, Skin, Teeth, Wind

Cooper, Jilly
Hunger, Legs, Mist, Moon, Sensitiveness, Sex, Sky, Smell, Sun, Trees

Cooperman, Melvin I.
Dreams, Stage and Screen

Cortázar, Julio
Men and Women

Coughlin, T. Glen
Baseball, Clinging

Cousins, Norman
Freedom

Coward, Noël
Beginnings/Endings, Coldness, Fear, Work

Cowley, Abraham
Fame

Cowley, Hanna Parkhouse
Vanity

Cowley, Malcolm
Life, Sleep, Smiles

Cowper, William
Courage, Idleness, Kindness, Life, Sports, Strength

Denker, Henry
Bearing
Descartes, Rene
Books
De Silva, Bruce
Ability, Beauty, Sharpness
Deutsch, Babette
Birds, Colors, Conversation, Furniture
and Furnishings, Heat, Life,
Remoteness, Secrecy, Sharpness,
Smallness, Softness
De Vries, Peter
Books, Eating and Drinking, Frowns,
Gossip, Legs, Mouth, Taste, Vehicles
Dewey, John
Politics/Politicians
Diana, Princess of Wales
Stupidity
Diaphenia
Beauty
Dickens, Charles
Age; Aloneness; Anger; Anxiety; Birds;
Cleverness; Clinging; Destruction;
Disappearance; Eating and Drinking;
Ideas; Kindness; Landscapes; Lightness;
People, Interaction; Sharpness; Skin;
Sleep; Stupidity
Dickey, James
Silence, Trees
Dickinson, Emily
Books, Fighting, Truth, Wind, Word(s)
Diehl, William
Absurdity, Bearing, Burst, Coldness,
Courage, Education, Guilt,
Order/Disorder
Dieter, William
Darkness, Moon, Vehicles
Dietz, Howard
Insults
Dimnet, Ernest
Books
Dinesen, Isak (Baroness Karen Blixen)
Advancing, Air, Attention, Attraction,
Bearing, Calmness, Clinging, Ideas,
Innocence, Jewelry, Mind, Seascapes,
Secrecy, Success/Failure, Sun
Disraeli, Benjamin
Air; Aloneness; Bearing; Books;
Criticism, Dramatic and Literary
Dixon, W. Macneile
Nature
Dobell, Sidney
Grief
Doddridge, Sir John
Laws
Dominick, Peter
Politics/Politicians
Donleavy, Brian
Closeness, Destruction

Donne, John
Age
Dorfman, Ariel
Hand(s), Legs, Voice(s)
Dorris, Michael
Looks
Dos Passos, John
Anger, Bending/Bent, Cloud(s),
Dishonesty, Excitement, Insults, Pain,
Self-Confidence, Talkativeness
Dostoevski, Fyodor
Meekness
Douglas, Marjory Stoneman
Ability, Tension
Dowd, Maureen
Places
Downey, Harris
Fear, Sleep, Word(s)
Doyle, Arthur Conan
Burst, Disappearance
Drabble, Margaret
Bearing, Dejection, Meekness
Drummond, William
Shape
Drury, John
Pain
Dryden, John
Beauty, Business, Certainty, Death,
Envy, Freedom, Heat, Persistence
Dubus, Andre
Body, Comfort, Fear, Life
Dudar, Helen
Bareness; Criticism, Dramatic and
Literary
Dumas, Alexandre, Père
Calmness
du Maurier, Daphne
Ability, Books, Emptiness, Seascapes,
Trees
Du Maurier, George
Happiness
Dunn, Robert
Places
Dunne, Finley Peter
Freedom
Dunsany, Lord
Sense
Duranty, Walter
Jumping
Duras, Marguerite
Body, Change, Wind
Durrell, Lawrence
Air; Anger; Anxiety; Art and
Literature; Beginnings/Endings;
Bending/Bent; Birds; Blue; Change;
Clinging; Clinging; Cloud(s); Dejection;
Destruction; Disappearance; Ideas;
Irritableness; Looks; Pain; People,
Interaction; Personality Traits;

Ferraro, Susan
    Education, Smiles
Fessendon, Thomas G.
    Emptiness
Fiedler, Leslie A.
    Meekness
Field, Eugene
    Ideas
Fielding, Henry
    Hunger, Seriousness, Stage and Screen,
    Writer/Writing
Fierstein, Harvey
    Candor; People, Interaction
Fine, Sylvia
    Stage and Screen
Finkelstein, Caroline
    Trees
Fisher, Dorothy Canfield
    Burst, Clinging, Face(s), Fear, Flowers,
    Humor, Smell, Tension, Thoughts,
    Weakness, Wind
Fitzgerald, F. Scott
    Age, Beauty, Books, Clothing,
    Dejection, Destruction, Emptiness,
    Frowns, Jewelry, Looks, Necessity,
    Pervasiveness, Remoteness, Sun, Trees,
    Wind
Fitzsimmons, Paul M.
    Air
Flanagan, Robert
    Colors
Flanner, Janet
    Cleverness, Clinging, Compatibility,
    Desire, Destruction, Enthusiasm,
    Flowers, Illness, Mind, Money,
    Order/Disorder, Politics/Politicians,
    Power, Seasons, Sensitiveness,
    Weariness, Work, Youth
Flaubert, Gustave
    Dejection, Desire, Destruction, Flowers,
    Hair, Ideas, Immobility,
    Order/Disorder, Trees
Flecknoe, Richard
    Power
Fletcher, John
    Calmness, Intensity
Fletcher, Louise
    Success/Failure
Fletcher, Phineas
    Love, Defined
Flexner, Abraham
    Education
Forbes, Bryan
    Politics/Politicians
Forbes, Colin
    Conversation
Ford, James L.
    Attention

Ford, Henry
    Money
Ford, Richard
    Aloneness; Anxiety; Blue;
    Boredom/Boring; Coldness; Comfort;
    Fear; Furniture and Furnishings;
    Hand(s); Happiness; Health; Heat;
    Ideas; Inappropriateness; Innocence;
    Irritableness; Jewelry; Legs; Life;
    Manners; Mouth; Necessity; People,
    Interaction; Physical Appearance;
    Remoteness; Rocking and Rolling;
    Shoulders; Smell; Strangeness;
    Talkativeness; Thinness; Thoughts;
    Uncertainty; Usefulness/Uselessness;
    Vehicles; Voice(s)
Fort, Joseph
    Reliability/Unreliability
Fosdick, Harry Emerson
    Death
Fowles, John
    Clinging, Fear, Landscapes, Men and
    Women, Mountains, Necessity,
    Remoteness, Sex, Smiles,
    Success/Failure, Wind
Frady, Marshal
    Excitement
France, Anatole
    Art and Literature; Belief, Insects;
    Insults; Love, Defined; Mouth; Nature;
    Smiles
Francis, Brendan
    Time
Francis, Dick
    Questions/Answers, Skin
Francis, Dorothy B.
    Anxiety, Fear, Nature
Frankfurter, Justice Felix
    Ability
Franklin, Benjamin
    Comfort, Eating and Drinking, Pride,
    Riches
Fraser, Antonia
    Silence
Fraser, George Macdonald
    Calmness, Looks
Frayn, Michael
    Dejection
Fredman, Mike
    Advancing, Body,Enthusiasm, Self-
    Confidence, Smiles, Sun,
    Usefulness/Uselessness, Vehicles,
    Voice(s), Weakness
Freemantle, Anne
    Art and Literature
Freud, Sigmund
    Art and Literature, Life
Fromm, Erich
    Dreams

Frost, Robert
    Cause/Effect
Fuentes, Carlos
    Mountains, Vanity
Fuller, Roy
    Cloud(s)
Fuller, Thomas
    Books, Death, Dishonesty, Evil,
    Friendship, Gossip, Humor, Idleness,
    Insults, Intelligence, Meekness, Money,
    Riches
Gabler, Neil
    Sharpness
Gablik, Suzi
    Anger
Gale, Zona
    Love, Defined
Gallant, Mavis
    Education, Mind
Galsworthy, John
    Thinness
Garbo, Norman
    Darkness, Grief, Sleep
Gardner, John
    Beauty, Busyness, Ideas, Sharpness,
    Smiles, Success/Failure
Gardner, Tonita S.
    Anger, Eating and Drinking
Garis, Leslie
    Skin, Thinness
Garland, Hamlin
    Heat
Garrett, George
    Air; Animals; Attention; Bareness;
    Bearing; Beauty; Beginnings/Endings;
    Blue; Calmness; Certainty; Clinging;
    Cloud(s); Coldness; Compatibility;
    Courage; Destruction; Dishonesy;
    Dreams; Ease; Eating and Drinking;
    Emptiness; Enthusiasm; Face(s); Fear;
    Flowers; Formality; Fragility, Furniture
    and Furnishings; Hair; Hand(s);
    Happiness; Health; Heart(s);
    Inappropriateness; Intensity; Joy; Laws;
    Legs; Lightness; Looks; Mountains;
    Noise; Order/Disorder; Pain; Patience;
    People, Interaction; Permanence;
    Personality Traits; Physical Appearance;
    Pride; Rarity; Riches; Seasons; Sex;
    Shape; Shock; Sky; Sleep; Smell;
    Smiles; Softness; Success/Failure; Sun;
    Talkativeness; Teeth; Tension;
    Thinness; Thoughts; Thrift; Trees;
    Vanity; Voice(s); Weakness; Weariness;
    Wind; Word(s)
Garrigue, Jean
    Kindness, Looks, Thinness
Garrison, Theodosia
    Trees

Gary, Romain
    Burst, Cloud(s), Looks
Gash, Jonathan
    Hand(s); People, Interaction
Gass, William H.
    Air, Aloneness, Anger, Arm(s), Bearing,
    Bending/Bent, Coldness, Darkness,
    Eating and Drinking,) Envy, Hand(s),
    Heat, Inappropriateness, Pain,
    Pervasiveness, Skin, Softness, Sun,
    Time, Work
Gassett, José Ortega
    Kindness
Gates, W. I. E.
    Courage
Gautier, Théophile
    Hand(s)
Gay, John
    Envy, Pride
Gaylin, Willard
    Selfishness
Gertler, T.
    Physical Appearance
Getty, J. Paul
    Money
Getz, William
    Power
Gibbs, Woolcot
    Face(s)
Gibran, Kahlil
    Ambition; Enthusiasm; Love, Defined
Gibson, Miles
    Cleverness, Eye(s), Mouth, Physical
    Appearance, Seascapes, Smiles, Wind
Gide, André
    Happiness, Joy
Gifford, Fannie Stearns
    Immobility
Gilbert, Michael
    Inappropriateness
Gilbert, W. S.
    Power, Sense, Softness
Gilchrist, Ellen
    Ideas, Inappropriateness, Innocence,
    Insults, Shadow
Gildner, Gary
    Calmness, Hair
Giles, Molly
    Pain, Smiles, Softness
Gill, Brendan
    Anxiety
Gillers, Stephen
    Risk
Gillespie, Alfred
    Hair
Gilliatt, Penelope
    Animals, Attention, Coldness,
    Completeness/Incompleteness,
    Conversation, Fear, Physical

Appearance, Shoulders, Skin

Gioseffi, Daniela
Certainty,
Completeness/Incompleteness,
Darkness, Desire

Giraudoux, Jean
Happiness

Gissing, George
Secrecy

Gladstone, William E.
Politics/Politicians

Glanville, Joseph
Body, Truth

Glasgow, Ellen
Air, Blue, Death, Dejection, Dreams,
Fire and Smoke, Fortune/Misfortune,
Hand(s), Heart(s), Immobility, Legs,
Meekness, Permanence, Remoteness,
Seasons, Sex, Sharpness, Skin, Sky,
Smiles, Thickness, Thoughts, Trees,
Usefulness/Uselessness, Wind

Gloag, Julian
Clinging, Smallness

Goddard, Robert
Smell, Voice(s)

Godden, Rumer
Irritableness, Thinness, Thoughts

Godwin, Gail
Change, Work

Goethe, Johann Wolfgang von
Books, Ease, Fortune/Misfortune, Laws,
Life, Nature, Questions/Answers

Gogol, Nikolai V.
Blue

Gold, Herbert
Attention, Conversation, Smiles

Goldberg, Aaron
Enthusiasm

Goldman, James
Strength

Goldsmith, Oliver
Busyness, Fighting, Kindness

Goldwin, Francis
Sensitiveness

Goodman, Ellen
Sex

Gordimer, Nadine
Attention, Burst, Conversation, Guilt,
Impartiality, Jewelry, Joy, Legs,
Remoteness, Sky

Gordon, Mary
Cause/Effect Certainty, Desire,
Excitement, Inappropriateness, Looks,
Shame

Gorky, Maxim
Attention, Clinging, Evil, Sun

Gorman, Paul
Hand(s), Thoughts

Gornick, Vivian
Absorbabiity

Gosse, Edmond
Courage

Goyen, William
Jumping

Gracian, Valtasar
Age

Grafton, Sue
Body; Cause/Effect Cloud(s); Eating
and Drinking, Eye(s); Fear; Furniture
and Furnishings; Grief; Hair; Head(s);
Houses; People, Interaction;
Persistence; Scrutiny; Skin; Smell;
Smiles; Taste; Thinness; Trees

Graham, Virginia
Word(s)

Grahame, J.
Business

Grant, Ulysses S.
Thrift

Grau, Shirley Ann
Nature, Tension

Graves, Robert
Jumping

Gray, Francine Du Plessix
Aloneness, Seascapes

Greenaway, Kate
Seascapes

Greene, A. C.
Sensitiveness

Greene, Barbara
Clinging

Greene, Graham
Books, Secrecy

Greer, Germaine
Bareness

Greer, Peter
Difficulty

Gregor, Arthur
Lightness

Grenville, Kate
Hand(s), Mountains

Grey, Zane
Physical Appearance

Gross, Jane
Persistence

Gross, John
Permanence

Grubb, Davis
Beauty, Coldness, Destruction, Grief,
Shape

Grumbach, Doris
Thinness, Word(s)

Guenther, Robert
Success/Failure

Guerney, A.R. Jr.
Closeness

Heine, Heinrich
    Books, Nature, Politics/Politicians
Heinz, Senator John
    Usefulness/Uselessness
Heller, Joseph
    Anger, Face(s), Physical Appearance,
    Self-Confidence, Smiles, Tension
Heller, Steve
    Eating and Drinking
Hellman, Sam
    Riches
Helps, Sir Arthur
    Belief
Helprin, Mark
    Envy; Furniture and Furnishings;
    People, Interaction; Rocking and
    Rolling; Sun; Thickness; Thinness
Hemingway, Ernest
    Insects, Lightness, Words of Praise
Hempel, Amy
    Time
Henley, Patricia
    Moon, Necessity, Voice(s), Wind
Henry, Matthew
    Anger
Henry, Patrick
    Freedom
Hentoff, Nat
    Attraction
Hergesheimer, Joseph
    Sensitiveness
Herman, Tom
    Criticism, Dramatic and Literary
Herod, Dan P.
    Love, Defined
Herriot, Edouard
    Politics/Politicians
Hersey, John
    Grief, Pride, Sentiment, Silence, Sky,
    Softness
Hess, Joan
    Advancing, Bearing, Hair, Uncertainty
Hesse, Hermann
    Pride
Hewlett, Maurice
    Clinging, Hair
Heyward, du Bose
    Sun
Heywood, John, Proverbs
    Clothing, Coldness
Hichens, Robert
    Virtue
Higgins, George V.
    Coldness, Physical Appearance,
    Reliability/Unreliability
Higgins, Joanna Wojewski
    Word(s)
Hills, Carol
    Word(s)

Hilton, James
    Houses, Memory, Time
Hinds, Michael de Courcy
    Difficulty
Hitchcock, Alfred
    Men and Women
Hoagland, Edward
    Animals, Books, Moon, Tension
Hoelterhoff, Manuela
    Reliability/Unreliability
Hoffman, Heinrich
    Sleep
Hoffman, William
    Skin
Hofstadter, Richard
    Truth
Hogan, Linda
    Clothing
Hogg, James
    Love, Defined
Holcroft, Thomas
    Stupidity
Holland, Josiah Gilbert
    Irritableness
Holmes, John Andrew
    Age, Secrecy
Holmes, Oliver Wendell, Sr.
    Beauty, Colors, Death, Hair, Ignorance,
    Insults, Intolerance, Laws, Permanence,
    Persistence, Sentiment, Truth, Vanity
Hood, Mary
    Heart(s), Irritableness, Order/Disorder,
    Pride
Hood, Thomas
    Irritableness
Horace
    Anger, Change, Fame
Horgan, Paul
    Cloud(s), Eating and Drinking,
    Mountains, Mouth, Silence, Skin, Sky,
    Sun, Trees, Wind
House, Karen Elliott
    Power
Howard, Maureen
    Hair, Tension
Howard, Richard
    Destruction
Howe, Ed
    Belief
Howe, Edgar Watson
    Secrecy
Howe, Tina
    Emptiness
Howell, James
    Busyness
Howell, Margery Eldredge
    Grief
Howells, William Dean
    Happiness

Howland, Bette
Legs
Hoyt, Charles H.
Men and Women
Hubbard, Elbert
Business, Impossibility, Riches,
Sensitiveness
Huddle, David
Darkness
Hudson, Helen
Animals; Books; Clothing; Cloud(s);
Dishonesty; Emptiness; Eye(s); Flowers;
Furniture and Furnishings; Hair;
Hand(s); Houses; Immobility;
Irritableness; Moon; Nature; People,
Interaction; Places;
Reliability/Unreliability; Scrutiny;
Shape; Sky; Smallness; Smiles; Sun;
Teeth; Tension; Time; Time; Trees;
Voice(s); Word(s); Words of Praise
Hudson, H. W.
Fear, Innocence
Hughes, Langston
Love, Defined; Sleep
Hughes, Ted
Bearing, Fire and Smoke, Heat,
Sharpness, Weakness
Hugo, Victor
Aloneness, Anxiety, Bending/Bent,
Calmness, Dejection, Immobility,
Insects, Irritableness, Persistence,
Remoteness, Strength, Thoughts
Hulme, T. E.
Moon
Humboldt, Karl Wilhelm
Work
Humphrey, George
Impossibility
Humphrey, William
Cleverness, Furniture and Furnishings,
Softness
Huneker, James
Ambition, Permanence
Hunt, Leigh
Flowers
Hurlbut, Kaatje
Skin, Thoughts, Weariness
Hurst, Fannie
Bending/Bent
Huxley, Aldous
Death, Meekness
Ibn Ezra, Moses
Education
Ibn Gabirol, Solomon
Education, Thrift
Ibn Vega, Solomon
Guilt
Ibsen, Henrik
Comfort, Insults

Ignatow, David
Arm(s), Legs, Looks, Nature, Sky,
Trees
Ingalls, Rachel
Beauty, Clinging
Ingersoll, Robert, G.
Kindness
Ionesco, Eugene
Happiness
Irving, Clive
Mist, Wind
Irving, John
Smiles
Irving, Washington
Houses, Landscapes, Personality Traits
Irwin, Inez Haynes
Mouth
Isherwood, Christopher
Absurdity, Anger, Bearing, Clothing,
Mouth, Physical Appearance,
Questions/Answers, Strangeness,
Voice(s)
Jackson, Mahalia
Sentiment
Jackson, Robert H.
Freedom
Jacobson, Dan
Air, Heat
Jacoby, Henry D.
Difficulty
James, Henry
Art and Literature, Belief, Calmness,
Cleverness, Clothing, Health,
Immobility, Innocence, Jewelry,
Lightness, Power, Stupidity, Voice(s)
James, William
Activeness; Burst; Criticism, Dramatic
and Literary; Education; Eye(s); Mind;
Weariness
Jameson, Storm
Mind, Smiles
Janeway, Elliot
Usefulness/Uselessness
Janowitztama
Smell
Jarrell, Randall
Age, Eye(s), Life, Time
Jasperson, Ann
Memory
Jefferson, Thomas
Politics/Politicians
Jeffrey, Lord Francis
Humor, Illness, Intolerance
Jeffries, Roderic
Mind
Jennings, Peter,
Impossibility
Jerrold, Douglas
Art and Literature; Fortune/Misfortune;

Love, Defined

Jerome, Jerome K.
Fighting; Furniture and Furnishings; Idleness; Life; Love, Defined; Seasons; Talkativeness; Thoughts; Trees; Vanity; Virtue; Weariness

Jhabvala, Ruth Prawer
Houses, Manners, Moon

Jonson, Ben
Ambition, Permanence, Courage, Enthusiasm, Gossip

Johnson, Charles
Certainty, Closeness, Emptiness, Fear, Heart(s), Immobility, Nature, Permanence, Sex, Shape, Skin, Sky, Smiles, Sun, Thoughts

Johnson, Denis
Advancing

Johnson, Nora
Gossip, Permanence

Johnson, Pamela Hansford
Pride, Sun, Teeth, Trees

Johnson, Samuel
Books, Education, Friendship, Grief, Happiness, Idleness, Importance/Unimportance, Insults, Life, Manners, Sense, Thrift, Truth

Jones, Emory
Sports

Jong, Erica
Fighting

Joubert, Joseph
Attention, Word(s)

Judah
Life

Just, Ward
Mind, Skin

Justice, Donald
Animals, Comfort, Landscapes, Seascapes, Thinness, Youth

Juvenal
Rarity, Virtue

Kantor, Mackinlay
Ease,

Kaplan, Andrew
Body; People, Interaction; Physical Appearance; Questions/Answers; Smiles; Teeth

Karmel-Wolfe, Henia
Necessity

Kates, Joanne
Men and Women

Kaufmann, George
Bending/Bent

Kawabata, Yasunari
Memory

Kaye-Smith, Sheila
Animals

Kazantzakis, Nikos
Landscapes

Keats, John
Beauty, Fame, Permanence, Thoughts

Keifetz, Norman
Baseball, Health, Tension, Thinness

Keller, Helen
Books, Trees

Kellerman, Jonathan
Arm(s), Frowns, Impossibility, Pain, Physical Appearance, Skin, Smell, Voice(s)

Kelly, Eleanor Mercein
Beauty

Kelton, Elmer
Smell

Kemp, Peter
Personality Profiles

Kempton, Murray
Ability

Ken Kesey
Kindness

Keneally, Thomas
Burst, Sun

Kennan, George
Secrecy

Kennedy, John F.
Difficulty

Kennedy, William
Bending/Bent, Pain

Kersh, Gerald
Age, Blue, Body, Darkness, Destruction, Emptiness, Hand(s), Irritableness, Jewelry, Rocking and Rolling, Smiles

Kesey, Ken
Noise

Kierkegaard, Soren
Thoughts

King, Alexander
Insults, Seriousness

King, Francis
Manners, Noise, Sleep, Sun, Vehicles, Weariness

King, Martin Luther
Justice

King, Stephen
Physical Appearance, Teeth, Weakness

Kinnell, Galway
Air, Happiness

Kinsella, W. P.
Anxiety, Baseball, Clothing, Cloud(s), Dejection, Desire, Difficulty, Envy, Gossip, Houses, Impossibility, Insects, Joy, Jumping, Lightness, Manners, Mind, Moon, Pain, Questions/Answers, Scrutiny, Seasons, Sex, Skin, Sky, Smell, Sun, Tension, Thickness, Trees, Vehicles

MacDonald, George
Dejection, Intensity
MacDonald, John D.
Aloneness, Freedom, Furniture and
Furnishings, Legs, Lightness, Moon,
Patience, Permanence, Remoteness,
Smiles, Thinness, Voice(s), Weariness
Macdonald, Ross
Arm(s); Bearing; Body; Change;
Clinging; Clothing; Danger;
Enthusiasm; Evil; Hair; Jumping; Legs;
Looks; Mouth; Pain; People,
Interaction; Personality; Profiles;
Physical Appearance; Rarity; Shame;
Sky; Sleep; Smiles; Tension; Time;
Voice(s); Word(s)
MacInnes, Helen
Emptiness
MacIntyre, Tom
Smell
MacKenzie, Donald
Looks, Questions/Answers, Seriousness,
Voice(s)
Macklin, Charles
Laws
MacLean, Norman
Looks
Macmillan, Harold
Power
MacMillan, Ian
Legs
Macneice, Louis
Guilt, Riches, Seasons, Silence, Smell,
Strength
Macy, John
Change
Mailer, Norman
Anxiety, Bearing, Coldness, Fear,
Houses, Impossibility, Insults, Joy,
Kindness, Memory, Mind, Persistence,
Seriousness, Shock, Talkativeness,
Tension, Thinness,
Usefulness/Uselessness, Voice(s)
Major, Clarence
Innocence, Softness
Malamud, Bernard
Anxiety, Baseball, Dejection, Emptiness,
Fear, Frowns, Moon, Pain, Silence,
Smell, Sun, Work
Mallock, W. H.
Impossibility
Malone, Michael
Clothing, Wind
Malraux, André
Joy, Moon, Youth
Maltz, Albert
Bearing
Mandelstamm, Benjamin
Heart(s)

Manley, Dexter
Dejection
Mann, Thomas
Darkness
Manning, Olivia
Freedom, Sensitiveness
Mansfield, Katherine
Aloneness, Beauty, Cloud(s), Courage,
Excitement, Eye(s), Face(s), Flowers,
Innocence, Joy, Jumping, Landscapes,
Men and Women, Pain, Silence, Sky,
Softness, Thunder and Lightning,
Trees, Wind, Word(s)
Mansfield, Stephanie
Skin
Markham, Beryl
Advancing, Anger, Boredom/Boring,
Burst, Coldness, Courage,
Disappearance, Fear, Friendship,
Gossip, Heat, Immobility, Impossibility,
Landscapes, Legs, Looks, Patience,
Physical Appearance, Pride,
Reliability/Unreliability, Rocking and
Rolling, Shadow, Shape, Sky, Softness
Marlow, Christopher
Aloneness
Marmion, Shackerley
Joy
Marquand, John P.
Darkness
Marquis, Don
Idleness
Marryatt, Captain Frederick
Fortune/Misfortune
Marsh, Edward
Compatibility, Face(s), Health
Marsh, Ngaio
Compatibility
Marshall, Paule
Anxiety, Bearing, Eating and Drinking,
Legs, Sun, Time, Voice(s)
Martial
Kindness
Martin, Ian Kennedy
Aloneness
Martin, Judith
Remoteness, Smell
Martineau, Harriet
Insults
Marvell, Andrew
Colors
Mascagni, Pietro
Danger
Mason, Bobbie Ann
Bearing, Houses, Mountains,
Remoteness, Scrutiny, Voice(s)
Mason, John M.
Meekness, Revenge

Mason, F. Van Wyck
Bareness, Coldness, Difficulty, Disappearance, Eye(s), Hair, Hand(s), Legs, Looks, Manners, Rocking and Rolling, Sharpness, Smiles, Thoughts, Voice(s), Word(s)

Maspero, Francois
Comfort, Mouth

Massey, Gerald
Heart(s)

Masters, Edgar Lee
Ability, Ideas, Silence

Masters, Hilary
Animals, Busyness, Pride

Masterton, Graham
Bending/Bent, Dejection, Sharpness, Tension, Trees, Uncertainty

Matthews, William
Face(s)

Matthiessen, Peter
Emptiness, Fear, Sleep

Maucaulay, Thomas Babington
Silence

Maugham; W. Somerset
Art and Literature; Attention; Bearing; Beauty; Beginnings/Endings; Body; Cloud(s); Dejection; Fame; Money; Moon; Mouth; People, Interaction; Physical Appearance; Readers/Reading; Seascapes; Skin; Sky; Sleep; Time; Trees; Voice(s); Youth

Maupassant, Guy de
Flowers; Hand(s); Life; Love; Defined; Softness; Taste; Voice(s)

Maurois, André
Art and Literature, Courage, Silence

Maxwell, A. E.
Air, Colors, Desire, Emptiness, Pain, Vanity

Mayakovsk, Vladimir
Criticism, Dramatic and Literary

Maynard, Richard
Animals, Arm(s), Danger, Dejection, Seascapes, Thoughts

McBain, Ed
Clinging, Completeness/Incompleteness, Looks, Permanence, Usefulness/Uselessness

McCaig; Donald
Calmness; Closeness; Colors; Comfort; Enthusiasm; Frowns; Lightness; Love, Defined; Pain; Smell; Talkativeness; Word(s)

McCarthy, Eugene
Conversation, Politics/Politicians

McCarthy, Mary
Activeness, Aloneness, Attention, Attraction, Danger, Inappropriateness, Intensity, Looks, Scrutiny, Shame, Voice(s)

McClatchy, J. D.
Sex

McCorquodale, Robin
Desire

McCoy, Larry
Change

McCullers, Carson
Heart(s), Physical Appearance, Riches, Rocking and Rolling, Sun, Talkativeness

McDermott, Alice
Aloneness, Availability, Bending/Bent, Boredom/Boring, Colors, Danger, Furniture and, Furnishings, Mist, Moon, Physical Appearance, Self-Confidence, Softness, Teeth, Vehicles

McDonald, Gregory
Fear, Scrutiny

McFee, William
Business

McGahern, John
Ease, Scrutiny

McGinley, Phyllis
Dreams, Fame, Opinions, Thinness, Time, Truth

McGivern, William
Attraction

McGuane, Thomas
Danger, Friendship, Sleep, Thoughts, Virtue

Mcilvanney, William
Availability, Bending/Bent, Body, Calmness, Clothing, Conversation, Difficulty, Embraces, Envy, Formality, Fortune/Misfortune, Humor, Impossibility, Inappropriateness, Innocence, Jewelry, Scrutiny, Seriousness, Sky, Sleep, Strangeness, Taste, Thoughts, Usefulness/Uselessness, Word(s)

McInerney, Jay
Advancing, Memory, Physical Appearance, Voice(s), Weariness

McKinney, Frank
Baseball

McMahon, Thomas
Hair

McMurtry, Larry
Beginnings/Endings, Conversation, Dejection, Desire, Frowns, Heat, Houses, Life, Looks, Personality Profiles, Physical Appearance, Silence, Sun, Talkativeness, Taste, Teeth, Thoughts

McNally, Leonard
Closeness

McNamara, Eugene
Body

McNutt, William Slavens
Happiness
Megged, Aharon
Advancing, Arm(s), Bending/Bent,
Emptiness, Excitement, Fear,
Happiness, Heat, Legs,
Questions/Answers, Shock, Voice(s),
Weakness
Meinke, Peter
Air, Birds, Fear, Houses, Physical
Appearance, Thoughts, Voice(s)
Melton, John
Silence
Melville, Herman
Bearing, Destruction, Noise,
Permanence
Menander
Word(s)
Mencius
Truth
Mencken, H. L.
Absurdity, Art and Literature, Candor,
Intelligence, Money, Shock, Time,
Truth, Vanity, Virtue
Mengers, Sue
Inappropriateness
Mercer, Johnny
Cloud(s)
Merkin, Daphne
Bending/Bent, Coldness, Criticism,
Dramatic and Literary, Eating and
Drinking, Immobility, Memory, Men
and Women, Smiles, Sports, Vehicles,
Voice(s)
Meyer, Philip K.
Difficulty
Michael, David
Destruction
Michaels, Leonard
Bending/Bent, Hand(s)
Michelangelo
Aloneness
Millar, Margaret
Animals, Arm(s), Birds, Change,
Clinging, Connections, Dejection,
Dreams, Face(s), Fire and Smoke,
Furniture and Furnishings, Hair,
Health, Heat, Immobility, Pride,
Seascapes, Silence, Skin, Smell, Sun,
Truth, Word(s)
Millay, Edna St. Vincent
Life; Memory; People, Interaction;
Shining
Miller, Allan
Attraction
Miller, Arthur
Arm(s), Attention, Eye(s), Fear, Skin
Miller, Bryan
Colors

Miller, Henry
Intensity, Shape
Miller, Nolan
Legs
Miller, Sue
Physical Appearance, Sex
Miller, Warren
Order/Disorder
Millhauser, Steven
Art andLiterature
Mills, Clifford
Rocking and Rolling
Mills, C. Wright
Power
Mills, James
Ability, Clothing
Milton, John
Destruction, Grief, Shining, Time,
Truth
Minot, Susan
Bending/Bent, Clothing, Hair,
Thinness, Weakness
Minot, Stephen
Time
Mishima, Yukio
Body, Boredom/Boring, Time
Mitchell, James
Fear
Mitchell, Margaret
Clinging, Fighting
Mitchell, Paige
Anger, Arm(s), Bearing, Clothing,
Connections, Courage, Darkness,
Desire, Dreams, Excitement, Fear, Hair,
Houses, Jewelry, Men and Women,
Moon, Questions/Answers, Scrutiny,
Smiles, Tension, Thinness, Vehicles,
Virtue, Voice(s), Wind
Molière
Closeness
Montaigne, Michel de
Desire, Education, Opinions, Riches
Montesquieu, Charles de Secondat
Laws
Moore, Brian
Aloneness, Fear, Wind
Moore, George
Art and Literature
Moore, Lorrie
Attraction, Certainty, Dreams,
Emptiness, Hair, Silence, Smiles
Moore, Marianne
Baseball, Personality Profiles
Moore, Thomas
Friendship
Moravia, Albert
Ideas
Morgan, Speer
Difficulty, Immobility, Secrecy

Morowitz, Arthur
Sex
Morris, Chuck
Criticism, Dramatic and Literary
Morris, Governeur
Pain
Morris, Mary
Necessity, Order/Disorder
Morris, Wright
Hair, Skin
Morrow, George
Business
Morrow, James
Emptiness, Hair, Time, Word(s)
Mortimer, John
Availability, Joy, Smiles, Sun
Moser, Penny Ward
Pain
Mosher, Howard Frank
Baseball, Jumping, Work
Motherwell, Robert
Fame
Mourand, Paul
Compatibility
Muggeridge, Malcolm
Compatibility, Politics/Politicians
Muir, Edwin
Sun
Mullen, Harryette
Memory; People, Interaction; Physical
Appearance
Mulligan, John Gideon
Talkativeness
Mulock, D. M.
Secrecy
Munro, Alice
Remoteness, Sex, Softness, Trees,
Word(s)
Murchison, Clint
Money
Murdoch, Iris
Beauty, Eating and Drinking, Frowns,
Joy, Meekness, Memory, Mouth, Pain,
Shock, Thoughts
Murrow, Edward R.
Remoteness
Murray, Jim
Strength
Nabokov, Vladimir
Houses, Softness
Naham, Bratzlav
Desire
Naj, Amal Kumar
Enthusiasm
Najarian, Peter
Disappearance
Napoleon Bonaparte
Courage, Freedom

Nappaha, Johann B.
Dishonesty
Nash, Ogden
Bending/Bent, Burst, Calmness,
Cleverness, Clinging, Courage,
Kindness, Money, Mouth, Time, Youth
Nathan, George Jean
Art and Literature, Permanence, Sex
Naylor, Phyllis
Dejection, Embraces, Legs, Skin
Ndebele, Njabulo
Embraces
Nemy, Enid
Rarity
Neruda, Pablo
Death
Neuberger, Maurine
Impossibility
Neville, Susan
Air, Voice(s)
Nevin, David
Tension
Newcastle, Duchess of
Riches
Newfield, Jack
Vanity
Newman, Barnett
Art and Literature
Newman, Paul
Difficulty
Newton, John
Ambition, Enthusiasm
Nichols, Dudley
Stage and Screen
Nichols, Mike
Stage and Screen
Nietzsche, Friedrich
Nature
Nin, Anaïs
Aloneness, Conversation, Eye(s),
Jewelry, Money, Order/Disorder,
Selfishness, Sky, Tension
Niven, David
Mouth
Noble, Marty
Baseball
Norman, Marcia
Stage and Screen
Norris, Gloria
Anger, Bearing, Cleverness, Excitement,
Illness, Looks, Thinness, Weariness
Norris, John
Joy
North, Richard
Darkness
Nowell, Clare
Pervasiveness
Noyes, Alfred
Dreams

Sleep, Strangeness, Sun, Wind

Patchen, Kenneth
Idleness, Importance/Unimportance, Trees

Paterson, William
Beauty

Patmore, Coventry
Love, Defined

Paulsen, Pat
Absurdity

Payne, Les
Questions/Answers

Peden, William
Joy

Penn, William
Envy, Patience

Percy, Walker
Activeness, Face(s), Hand(s), Houses, Landscapes, Thunder andLightning, Youth

Perot, Ross
Impossibility

Petronius
Courage

Petry, Ann
Hair, Importance/Unimportance, Smiles, Thinness

Phelps, William Lyon
Mind

Phillips, Caryl
Bending/Bent, Sun

Phillips, Deborah
Sex

Phillips, H. I.
Closeness

Phillips, Jayne Anne
Air, Bending/Bent, Disappearance, Hair, Hand(s), Looks, Smallness, Vehicles

Phillips, John
Moon, Secrecy

Phillips, Wendell
Politics/Politicians

Phocylides
Kindness

Picasso, Pablo
Art and Literature

Piercy; Marge
Advancing; Anger; Arm(s); Bending/Bent; Boredom/Boring; Busyness; Certainty; Clinging; Coldness; Darkness; Death; Dejection; Desire; Difficulty; Ease; Emptiness; Excitement; Hair; Happiness; Heat; Houses; Hunger; Immobility; Inappropriateness; Joy; Kindness; Life; Mind; Moon; Nature; Order/Disorder; Pain; People, Interaction; Persistence; Physical Appearance; Power; Seasons;

Secrecy; Sensitiveness; Sharpness; Smiles; Strength; Success/Failure; Sun; Thinness; Thoughts; Time; Voice(s); Wind; Word(s)

Pierson, Lewis E.
Business, Moon

Pike, James A.
Change

Pilcher, Rosamund
Clothing

Piper, Anne
Legs

Pirandello, Luigi
Softness

Plain, Belva
Grief, Shame, Sun

Planche, J.R.
Looks

Plath, Sylvia
Boredom/Boring, Darkness, Disappearance, Idleness, Landscapes, Shape, Silence, Sky, Smiles, Thickness, Thinness, Time, Weakness

Plato
Body, Virtue

Plautus
Kindness, Manners

Plomer, William
Sun

Plutarch
Uncertainty, Virtue

Poe, Edgar Allen
Aloneness, Dejection, Disappearance, Grief, Rocking and Rolling

Poniatowska, Elena
Pain

Poore, Charles
Time

Pope, Alexander
Dishonesty, Freedom, Laws, Life, Riches, Sense

Porte, J. Hampden
Busyness

Porter, Katherine Anne
Aloneness; Noise; People, Interaction; Physical Appearance

Porter, William Sydney
See O. Henry

Portis, Charles
Vehicles

Portillo, Lopez
Fighting

Pound, Ezra
Permanence

Powell, Adam Clayton
Thoughts

Powell, Anthony
Friendship, Legs, Power, Trees

Powers, J. F.
　Pride
Prather, Richard S.
　Legs
Prentice, Archibald
　Courage
Price, Nancy
　Remoteness
Price, Reynolds
　Bearing, Calmness, Coldness,
　Emptiness, Heat, Immobility, Insults,
　Power, Remoteness, Strength, Thinness,
　Weariness
Priestly, J. B.
　Advancing, Seriousness, Sleep, Smiles
Prince, Harry
　Attraction, Busyness, Certainty,
　Coldness, Comfort, Courage, Darkness,
　Ease, Face(s), Hunger, Impossibility,
　Pain, Reliability/Unreliability,
　Sensitiveness, Smiles, Thinness
Pritchett, V. S.
　Eye(s), Furniture and Furnishings,
　Physical Appearance, Smiles, Thoughts
Probst, Bethamy
　Criticism, Dramatic and Literary
Proffitt, Nicholas
　Aloneness, Arm(s), Excitement
Pronzini, Bill
　Difficulty, Fire and Smoke
Proust, Marcel
　Aloneness, Clothing, Gossip, Moon
Proverbs, Misc.
　Absurdity; Anger; Art and Literature;
　Bearing; Beauty; Closeness; Coldness;
　Courage; Difficulty; Ease; Education;
　Evil; Fame; Fighting;
　Fortune/Misfortune; Friendship;
　Happiness; Hunger; Ignorance;
　Impossibility; Joy; Justice; Laws; Life;
　Love, Defined; Men and Women; Pain;
　People, Interaction; Pride; Riches;
　Slander; Uncertainty
Puffendorf, Baron Samuel von
　Difficulty
Pushkin, Alexander
　Fame, Fear
Pym, Barbara
　Hair, Jumping, Legs,
　Reliability/Unreliability
Pynchon, Thomas
　Emptiness
Queen, Ellery
　Enthusiasm, Physical Appearance
Quillen, Robert
　Sports
Quindlen, Anna
　Body

Quintilian
　Thoughts
Racine, Jean
　Evil, Happiness
Radford, Dollie
　Beauty
Radley, Sheila
　Comfort, Physical Appearance
Raison, Milton
　Mountains
Ralph, Julian
　Rarity
Ramke, Bin
　Clothing, Destruction, Flowers,
　Furniture and Furnishings, People,
　Interaction, Sun
Rand, Ayn
　Intelligence, Voice(s)
Randolph, John
　Evil
Rascoe, Judith
　Attraction; Difficulty; People,
　Interaction
Rawlings, Marjorie Kinnan
　Grief, Sun, Uncertainty
Ray, John, Proverbs
　Art and Literature, Bareness, Busyness,
　Cleverness, Clinging, Danger,
　Dejection, Dishonesty, Enthusiasm,
　Hunger, Lightness, Men and Women,
　Necessity, Personality Profiles,
　Personality Traits, Riches, Stupidity,
　Thrift
Read, T. Buchanan
　Clinging
Read, Herbert
　Death, Life, Sun, Teeth
Reade, Charles
　Enthusiasm
Rechy, John
　Birds, Dejection, Flowers, Furniture and
　Furnishings, Mountains, Silence, Skin,
　Sky, Thickness, Thunder and
　Lightning, Trees
Reed, Ishmael
　Pervasiveness
Reed, Rex
　Mouth, Personality Profiles, Physical
　Appearance
Reed, Thomas B.
　Politics/Politicians
Reeve, F. D.
　Age, Coldness, Mouth, Sleep, Softness
Reeve, James
　Persistence
Reid, Alastair
　Age, Rocking and Rolling
Reid, Barbara
　Life

Sciller
  Clinging
Scott, Justin
  Voice(s)
Scott; Sir Walter
  Advancing; Age; Bareness; Busyness;
  Darkness; Irritableness; People,
  Interaction; Physical Appearance;
  Reliability/Unreliability; Silence
Scully, Vin
  Baseball
Seale, Jan Epton
  Calmness
Seaman, Barbara
  Fame
Seaman, Donald
  Advancing, Cleverness, Coldness, Ease,
  Landscapes, Power, Softness, Time,
  Vehicles
Searls, Hank
  Rocking and Rolling
Sedley, Sir Charles
  Closeness
Segal, Erich
  Looks
Seifert, Jaroslav
  Furniture and Furnishings, Life,
  Memory, Skin
Selden, John
  Pride, L
Selz, Thalia
  Tension
Selzer, Richard
  Age, Death
Seneca
  Word(s)
Serling, Robert J.
  Sun
Service, Robert W.
  Sun
Settle, Elkanah
  Courage
Settle, Mary Lee
  Beauty, Comfort, Health, Physical
  Appearance, Weakness
Sexton, Anne
  Arm(s), Burst, Conversation, Guilt,
  Immobility, Innocence, Persistence,
  Softness, Strength, Thinness
Shaftesbury, Lord
  Manners, Uncertainty
Shagan, Steve
  Body
Shakespeare, William
  Aloneness, Anger, Beauty,
  Boredom/Boring, Calmness, Certainty,
  Coldness, Permanence, Courage, Death,
  Desire, Destruction, Dishonesty, Ease,
  Eating and Drinking, Education,

Emptiness, Enthusiasm, Evil, Fame,
  Fighting, Fortune/Misfortune, Freedom,
  Health, Heat, Ignorance, Immobility,
  Patience, Permanence, Skin, Sleep,
  Smallness, Softness, Sports, Thoughts,
  Time, Truth, Uncertainty, Virtue, Youth
Shamfort, Sebastian
  Gossip
Shapiro, Karl
  Cleverness, Disappearance, Dreams,
  Fame, Ignorance, Memory, Mountains,
  Persistence, Tension, Thoughts, Time
Sharp, Marilyn
  Kindness, Looks
Shaw, Arty
  Impossibility
Shaw, George Bernard
  Art and Literature, Death, Manners,
  Meekness, Youth
Shaw, Henry Wheeler
  See, Billings, Josh
Shaw, Irwin
  Busyness, Kindness, Legs, Rocking and
  Rolling, Strength, Thinness, Thrift
Sheed, Wilfrid
  Humor, Ideas, Intensity,
  Order/Disorder, Persistence,
  Usefulness/Uselessness
Sheiner, Robin R
  Cleverness
Shelley, Percy Bysshe
  Beauty, Calmness, Change, Clinging,
  Coldness, Courage, Death, Destruction,
  Emptiness, Heart(s), Power, Sleep,
  Success/Failure, Sun, Thickness, Time,
  Weariness
Shenhar, Yitzhak
  Mountains, Trees, Wind
Shenstone, William
  Education, Virtue
Shepard, Sam
  Strangeness
Sheridan, Richard Brinsley
  Gossip, Persistence
Sherwood, Robert E.
  Fear
Shields, Mark
  Pervasiveness
Shipler, David K.
  Politics/Politicians, Tension
Shreve, Susan Richards
  Softness
Shulman, Alix Kates
  Fire and Smoke
Shulman, Max
  Frowns
Sigal, Clancy
  Calmness, Excitement, Irritableness,
  Smiles

Silk, Leonard
Fighting
Silko, Leslie
Looks
Sillery, Charles Doyne
Death
Silone, Ignazio
Bearing, Dejection, Strength, Voice(s)
Silverberg, Robert
Fear, Houses, Immobility, Mind, Pain,
Rocking and Rolling, Sleep, Vehicles
Simenon, Georges
Excitement, Skin
Simic, Charles
Beauty, Birds, Furniture and
Furnishings, Nature
Simmons, G.
Ambition
Simms, William Gilmore
Vanity
Simon, Neil
Conversation
Simon, Scott
Excitement
Simpson, E. L.
Ideas
Singer, Isaac Bashevis
Beginnings/Endings, Fear, Fire and
Smoke, Mouth, Sun, Words of Praise
Sira, Ben
Friendship
Sitwell, Dame Edith
Colors, Eye(s), Fear, Flowers, Nature,
Questions/Answers, Sun, Youth
Slavitt, David R.
Enthusiasm, Ideas, Persistence
Slesar, Henry
Guilt
Slesinger, Tess
Aloneness, Inappropriateness
Slogans
Calmness, Comfort, Ease, Friendship,
Lightness, Silence, Sleep, Softness
Smith, Alexander
Thoughts
Smith, Dodie
Usefulness/Uselessness
Smith, Henry
Laws
Smith, Lee
Air, Availability, Certainty, Cloud(s),
Embraces, Mountains, Sun
Smith, Lillian
Freedom
Smith, Martin Cruz
Money, Silence, Thunder and
Lightning, Wind
Smith, Pauline
Voice(s)

Smith, Stevie
Art and Literature, Calmness, Thinness,
Thoughts
Smith, Sydney
Humor, Opinions, Talkativeness
Smollett, Tobias
Manners
Snodgrass, W. D.
Darkness, Fear, Rocking and Rolling,
Softness, Trees
Solovyou, Vladmir and Elena
Power
Solzhenitsyn, Alexander
Cloud(s)
Somer, W.
Men and Women
Sommer, Elyse
Activeness, Anxiety, Attraction,
Clinging, Comfort, Compatibility,
Completeness/Incompleteness,
Immobility, Impossibility,
Inappropriateness, Irritableness, Looks,
Opinions, Order/Disorder, Pain,
Permanence, Rarity, Silence, Taste,
Vanity, Weariness
Sommer, Mike
Absurdity, Anxiety, Availability,
Candor, Courage, Inappropriateness,
Smell, Virtue
Sōseki, Natsume
Ignorance, Tension, Vehicles
South, Robert
Absurdity, Necessity
Southern, Terry
Clinging
Southey, Robert
Bending/Bent, Friendship, Taste,
Word(s)
Spencer, Elizabeth
Difficulty, Emptiness, Heat, Immobility,
Moon, Patience, Power, Skin,
Smallness, Teeth, Tension, Time,
Vehicles, Weakness
Spencer, Herbert
Certainty
Spencer, Scott
Absurdity, Beginnings/Endings,
Difficulty, Fear,
Importance/Unimportance, Insults,
Silence, Skin, Thoughts, Wind
Spring, Howard
Flowers, Health, Hunger, Mist
Spurgeon, C. H.
Insults
Squire, Philip
Usefulness/Uselessness
Staël, Madame de
Life

495

Stafford, Jean
Air, Anger, Attention, Permanence, Grief, Hair, Innocence, Looks, Permanence, Silence, Voice(s)

Stallings, Laurence
Impossibility

Stargel, Willie
Baseball

Stark, Sharon Sheehe
Activeness, Age, Air, Arm(s), Bareness, Bending/Bent, Body, Burst, Calmness, Certainty, Cleverness, Colors, Comfort, Permanence, Death, Hand(s), Landscapes, Legs, Lightness, Looks, Moon, Nature, Pain, Personality Profiles, Skin, Sky, Sun, Thinness, Trees, Word(s)

Stead, Christina
Dejection, Joy, Riches, Sky, Smiles

Steele, Sir Richard
Readers/Reading

Steele, Wilbur Daniel
Arm(s), Immobility, Impossibility, Landscapes, Rocking and Rolling, Sky, Weakness

Steffens, Lincoln
Art and Literature

Stegner, Wallace
Activeness, Advancing, Anger, Hair, Heat, Looks, Moon, Persistence, Reliability/Unreliability, Smell, Sun

Steinbeck, John
Flowers, Places

Stern, James
Hand(s)

Sterne, Laurence
Fame, Pain

Stevens, Wallace
Activeness, Bareness, Cloud(s), Coldness, Frowns, Hunger, Men and Women, Moon, Nature, Opinions, Strength, Success/Failure, Thoughts, Trees, Wind

Stevenson, Adlai
Politics/Politicians

Stevenson, Robert Louis
Activeness; Destruction; Eye(s); Face(s); Fear; Health; Health; Life; Love, Defined; Questions/Answers

Stewart, Mary
Flowers, Immobility, Kindness, Looks, Moon, Smell

Stockanes, Anthony E.
Business, Cloud(s), Physical Appearance, Silence, Smiles

Stockton, Frank R.
Reliability/Unreliability

Stone, Irving
Aloneness

Stone, Robert
Embraces

Storrs, Emory
Politics/Politicians

Stout, Rex
Fear, Voice(s)

Straus, Dorothea
Permanence, Excitement, Houses, Reliability/Unreliability, Trees

Stryker, Lloyd Paul
Laws

Styron, William
Hand(s), Insects, Irritableness, Moon, Silence, Sky, Wind

Suckling, Sir John
Evil, Face(s)

Suckow, Ruth
Face(s)

Suskind, Patrick
Kindness

Sutherland, Margaret
Availability, Cloud(s), Life, Nature

Svevo, Italo
Smiles

Swados, Harvey
Aloneness, Attention, Certainty, Clothing, Connections, Desire, Hair, Hand(s), Houses, Impossibility, Joy, Landscapes, Lightness, Looks, Meekness, Persistence, Silence, Skin, Sun, Talkativeness, Voice(s)

Swetchine, Madame
Happiness

Swift, Graham
Bearing, Pain, Smiles, Trees

Swift, Jonathan
Bareness, Beauty, Beginnings/Endings, Cleverness, Friendship, Innocence

Swinburne, Algernon Charles
Activeness, Age, Beauty, Bending/Bent, Coldness, Connections, Courage, Embraces, Emptiness, Silence, Talkativeness

Swinnerton, Frank
Advancing, Anxiety, Bearing, Calmness, Clinging, Comfort, Connections, Darkness, Excitement, Face(s), Gossip, Hand(s), Happiness, Immobility, Jumping, Kindness, Looks, Mind, Mouth, Patience, Persistence, Rocking and Rolling, Softness, Strength, Teeth, Thinness, Voice(s), Weariness, Wind

Symons, Julian
Voice(s)

Syrus, Publilius
Fortune/Misfortune

Tagore, Rabindranath
Life, Mist

Tallent, Elizabeth
  Skin
Talleyrand, Alexandre de
  Character
Talmud
  Education
Talmud, Babylonian
  Difficulty, Dreams, Evil
Talmud, Palestinian
  Life
Targan, Barry
  Strength
Tate, Narun
  Meekness
Taylor, Bayard
  Aloneness, Ignorance
Taylor, Ellen du Pois
  Permanence
Taylor, Elizabeth
  Calmness, Danger, Embraces, Frowns,
  Furniture and Furnishings, Hand(s),
  Jewelry, Questions/Answers
Taylor, Fred
  Danger
Teasdale, Sara
  Happiness
Temple, Sir William
  Ability
Tennenbaum, Silvia
  Sun
Tennyson, Alfred, Lord
  Ambition, Beauty, Burst, Dreams,
  Emptiness, Grief, Intensity, Kindness,
  Word(s)
Tey, Josephine
  Bearing, Thoughts,
  Usefulness/Uselessness
Theroux, Paul
  Ability, Animals, Bearing, Birds,
  Cloud(s), Excitement, Hair, Heat,
  Landscapes, Life, Mist, Nature,
  Physical Appearance, Skin, Thinness,
  Trees
Thomas, Dylan
  Ability, Cloud(s), Dejection, Fear, Joy,
  Meekness, Physical Appearance,
  Smiles, Thinness, Time, Trees
Thomas, Leslie
  Arm(s), Hand(s), Smiles, Thinness
Thomas, Ross
  Attention
Thompson, H. W.
  Busyness
Thompson, Hunter S.
  Smell
Thompson, James
  Freedom
Thompson, Jean
  Activeness, Cloud(s), Embraces, Face(s),

Fire and Smoke, Grief, Guilt, Hand(s),
Heat, Houses, Hunger, Life, Mind,
Noise, Skin, Sky, Success/Failure, Sun
Thoreau, Henry David
  Age, Life
Thurber, James
  Attraction, Stupidity, Voice(s)
Thurm, Marian
  Pride
Tillotson, John
  Candor, Slander
Tolstoy, Leo
  Anxiety; Coldness; Criticism, Dramatic
  and Literary; Grief; Guilt; Irritableness;
  Landscapes; Looks; Meekness; Mist;
  Moon; Trees
Toohey, John Peter
  Burst
Torre, Lillian de la
  Skin
Torrence, Ridgely
  Sky, Time
Toulet, Paul Jean
  Love, Defined
Towne, Charles Hanson
  Formality
Train, Arthur
  Head(s), Pain, Smiles, Sports
Traver, Robert
  Bareness, Bearing, Clinging, Cloud(s),
  Emptiness, Evil, Frowns, Furniture and
  Furnishings, Landscapes, Laws, Looks,
  Smiles, Politics/Politicians, Sleep,
  Sports, Thunder and Lightning, Truth,
  Vanity
Tremain, Rose
  Age, Air, Darkness, Life, Sleep
Trevor, William
  Beauty
Trollope, Frances
  Word(s)
Truman, Harry S
  Opinions, Work
Tuckwell, Barry
  Difficulty
Tuohy, Frank
  Eating and Drinking, Excitement,
  Innocence, Mouth, Skin, Strength
Tuke, Sir Samuel
  Fame
Tuller, David
  Voice(s)
Turgenev, Ivan
  Comfort, Gossip, Hand(s), Ideas,
  Immobility, Joy, Pride, Silence,
  Thoughts
Turner, Ted
  Sports

Turner, Wallace
Impossibility
Turnley, Joseph
Intensity
Twain, Mark (Samuel Langhorne Clemens)
Aloneness, Calmness, Darkness, Ease, Education, Freedom, Inappropriateness, Personality Traits
Tyler, Ann
Persistence
Tzu, Lao
Virtue
Updike, John
Advancing, Air, Arm(s), Art and Literature, Attention, Bearing, Calmness, Clinging, Death, Fear, Freedom, Frowns, Hair, Houses, Innocence, Mind, Mouth, Remoteness, Rocking and Rolling, Skin, Smell, Softness, Sports, Stupidity, Thinness, Uncertainty, Voice(s), Word(s)
Valin, Jonathan
Absurdity, Arm(s), Bearing, Candor, Conversation, Evil, Eye(s), Face(s), Frowns, Furniture and Furnishings, Guilt, Hand(s), Head(s), Houses, Justice, Jewelry, Legs, Men and Women, Mouth, Noise, Physical Appearance, Smell, Smiles, Speech Patterns, Stupidity, Trees
Valois, Marguerite de
Attraction
Valvano, Jim
Sports
Vanderbilt, William K.
Riches
Van Dyke, Henry
Humor, Jewelry, Remoteness, Sky, Sun, Wind
Van Vechten, Carl
Activeness
Vaughan, Henry
Permanence
Vecsey, George
Baseball
Venning, Ralph
Riches
Veuillot, Louis
Fear
Victoria, Queen
Remoteness
Vidal, Gore
Ambition, Time
Viertel, Jack
Enthusiasm
Villiers, George
Fame
Vinez, Robert
Difficulty

Virgo, Seán
Looks
Voltaire
Calmness, Certainty, Cloud(s), Ideas, Power
Wagner, Jane
Ability, Life, Mind, Mouth
Wagoner, David
Tension
Wainwright, John
Absurdity, Bending/Bent, Eye(s), Happiness, Thrift
Wakefield, Dan
Art and Literature, Attraction, Boredom/Boring, Calmness, Clothing, Education, Fear, Jumping, Memory, Time, Time
Wakoski, Diane
Aloneness, Anger, Dejection, Difficulty, Dreams, Emptiness, Heart(s), Mind, Sleep, Thoughts
Walcott, Derek
Mind, Moon, Mountains, Skin, Time
Walker, Alice
Cleverness, Thoughts, Trees
Wallace, Chris
Sports
Walling, R.A. J.
Calmness
Walpole, Hugh
Beginnings/Endings, Birds, Cloud(s), Fear, Fire and Smoke, Head(s), Landscapes, Mountains, Physical Appearance, Sky, Sun, Voice(s)
Walters, Barbara
Fame
Walton, Izaak
Sports
Walton, Susan
Fear
Wambaugh, Joseph
Busyness, Candor, Gossip, Looks, Persistence, Reliability/Unreliability, Tension, Uncertainty, Usefulness/Uselessness
Ward, Edward
Bareness
Wardle, Jane
Art and Literature
Warner, Charles Dudley
Conversation
Warner, Sylvia Townsend
Coldness, Weariness
Warren, Robert Penn
Cleverness, Lightness, Silence, Time
Washburn, Leonard
Eye(s)
Washington, George
Certainty

Watts, Alan
Difficulty
Watts, Isaac
Activeness, Time
Waugh, Evelyn
Anxiety, Boredom/Boring, Fear,
Word(s)
Weatherley, F. E.
Heart(s)
Weaver, Gordon
Memory
Weaver, Raymond M.
Importance/Unimportance
Weaver, Will
Air, Arm(s), Clinging, Heat,
Landscapes, Legs, Men and Women,
Nature, Smell, Sports, Vehicles,
Voice(s)
Weber, Dee
Formality
Weeks, Albert L.
Thinness
Weil, Simone
Friendship
Weisbrod, Rosine
Air
Welch, Susan
Sky
Wellington, Duke of
Success/Failure
Wellman, Paul J.
Face(s), Wind
Wells, H. G.
Connections, Difficulty, Trees
Welty, Eudora
Activeness, Animals, Calmness,
Cloud(s), Colors, Danger, Darkness,
Emptiness, Flowers, Hair, Hand(s),
Happiness, Landscapes, Lightness,
Moon, Mouth, Nature, Strength, Sun,
Trees
Werfel, Franz
Frowns, Skin, Thoughts
Wertenbaker, Lael Tucker
Bearing, Desire, Education, Face(s),
Grief, Immobility, Jewelry, Mouth,
Questions/Answers, Sun, Tension,
Voice(s)
Wertime, Richard
Moon
West, Jessamyn
Meekness, Sky, Softness
West, Rebecca
Art and Literature, Coldness, Looks,
Places, Wind
Westcott, Edward Noyes
Clinging
Westlake, Donald E.
Beauty, Physical Appearance

Wharton, Edith
Age, Art and Literature, Attraction,
Bearing, Calmness, Change, Character,
Connections, Dejection, Eye(s), Flowers,
Furniture and Furnishings, Grief, Hair,
Landscapes, Meekness, Mind, Mouth,
Nature, Pain, Physical Appearance,
Remoteness, Sky, Smiles,
Success/Failure, Sun, Time, Word(s)
Whateley, Richard
Dishonesty
Whedon, Julia
Permanence, Remoteness, Silence,
Wind
Wheelock, John Hall
Cloud(s), Permanence, Mist, Moon,
Thoughts, Wind, Words of Praise
Wheeler, Kate
Remoteness, Silence
White, Antonia
Joy
White, Curtis
Necessity
White, E. B.
Houses, Lightness, Sports
White, Lynn, Jr.
Freedom
White, Patrick
Clinging, Physical Appearance, Sleep
Whitehead, Alfred North
Ideas, Intelligence, Thoughts
Whitehill, Joseph
Excitement
Whitman, Stephen French
Hair, Weakness
Whittier, John Greenleaf
Beauty, Bending/Bent, Calmness,
Dejection, Fear, Gossip, Heart(s),
Immobility, Lightness, Pain,
Permanence, Softness, Thoughts, Trees
Wiggins, Marianne
Thoughts
Wilbur, Richard
Birds, Calmness, Darkness, Jumping,
Mind, Noise, Skin
Wilde, Oscar
Beauty; Criticism, Dramatic and
Literary; Eye(s); Flowers; Ignorance;
Jewelry; Men; and Women; Nature;
Order/Disorder; Pain; Sun; Trees
Wilde, Richard Henry
Life
Wilhelm, Kate
Physical Appearance
Wilkinson, Alec
Landscapes
Will, George F.
Anger; Baseball; Criticism, Dramatic
and Literary; Destruction; Fighting;

Young, Andrew
    Power
Young, Francis Brett
    Eye(s)
Young, Marguerite
    Activeness, Hair
Yount, John
    Age, Attraction, Hair, Immobility,
    Lightness, Physical Appearance,
    Silence, Sleep
Yourcenar, Marguerite
    Cleverness, Clinging, Furniture and
    Furnishings, Ideas, Irritableness,
    Opinions, Physical Appearance, Smiles,

Tension
Zangwill, Israel
    Aloneness, Health, Pride
Zigal, Thomas
    Busyness, Health, Weariness
Zola, Émile
    Ability, Anger, Comfort, Eye(s),
    Fortune/Misfortune, Immobility,
    Mouth, Physical Appearance, Sky,
    Sleep, Sun, Thinness
Zweig, Stefan
    Aloneness, Arm(s), Calmness,
    Difficulty, Ideas, Immobility, Memory,
    Moon, Remoteness, Weariness